ECONOMICS, ECOLOGY, ETHICS

CONTRIBUTORS

Kenneth E. Boulding, *Department of Economics, University of Colorado*
John Cobb, *School of Theology at Claremont, California*
Earl Cook, *Dean of Geosciences, Texas A & M University*
Herman E. Daly, *Department of Economics, Louisiana State University*
Anne H. Ehrlich, *Department of Biological Sciences, Stanford University*
Paul R. Ehrlich, *Department of Biological Sciences, Stanford University*
Nicholas Georgescu-Roegen, *Department of Economics, Vanderbilt University*
Bruce Hannon, *Center for Advanced Computation, University of Illinois*
Garrett Hardin, *Department of Biology, University of California, Santa Barbara*
John P. Holdren, *Energy and Resources Group, University of California, Berkeley*
C. S. Lewis (1898–1963), *former Professor of Medieval and Renaissance Literature at Cambridge University*
E. J. Mishan, *Economist, London School of Economics*
Talbot Page, *Environmental Quality Laboratory, California Institute of Technology*
E. F. Schumacher (1911–1977), *former Economist, Surrey, England*
Robert L. Sinsheimer, *Chancellor, University of California, Santa Cruz*
Gerald Alonzo Smith, *Department of Economics, Mankato State University, Mankato, Minnesota*
Peter A. Victor, *Faculty of Environmental Studies, York University, Ontario, Canada*

ECONOMICS, ECOLOGY, ETHICS

ESSAYS TOWARD A STEADY-STATE ECONOMY

Edited by

Herman E. Daly
Louisiana State University

 *W. H. Freeman and Company*
New York   San Francisco

Sponsoring Editor: *Richard J. Lamb*
Project Editor: *Larry Olsen*
Copyeditor: *Susan Weisberg*
Designer: *Sharon H. Smith*
Production Coordinator: *William Murdock*
Illustration Coordinator: *Cheryl Nufer*
Compositor: *Graphic Typesetting Service*
Printer and Binder: *The Maple-Vail Book Manufacturing Group*

Library of Congress Cataloging in Publication Data
Main entry under title:

Economics, ecology, ethics.

In part a revision of Toward a steady state economy,
1973, edited by H. E. Daly.
Includes bibliographies and index.
1. Economic development—Addresses, essays, lectures.
2. Wealth, Ethics of—Addresses, essays, lectures.
3. Economic development—Environmental aspects—
Addresses, essays, lectures. 4. Equilibrium (Econom-
ics)—Addresses, essays, lectures. I. Daly,
Herman E. II. Title: Toward a steady-state economy.
HD82.E36   338.9   79–29712
ISBN   0-7167-1178-8
ISBN   0-7167-1179-6 pbk.

3 4 5 6 7 8 9   MP   4 3 2 1 0 8 9 8 7 6

CONTENTS

PREFACE

As students often realize more quickly than their professors, we absolutely must revise our economic thinking so that it will be more in conformity with the finite energy and resource limits of the earth, and with the finite limits of man's stomach. This book seeks to present a single, coherent point of view —that of a steady-state economy—which is based on both physical and ethical first principles. This particular theoretical viewpoint seems to me (and to many other people) to be the one that is fundamentally correct and therefore most likely to yield useful insights and policies.

The development of a steady-state economy will be the product of an unpredictable but conscious social evolution in which many ideas will be tried out. However, just as an auctioneer must begin by calling out some specific price, so it seems we must begin by calling out some specific notions about a steady-state economy, even though we know that they are no more likely to be the final solution than the auctioneer's initial price is likely to be equilibrium price. Yet both initial actions provide starting points for a feedback process of approximation, by trial and error, to something better.

This book began as a second edition of *Toward a Steady-State Economy* but ended up somewhere between a revised edition and a new book. Roughly sixty percent of the material is new, and much of the retained forty percent has been revised. Although most of the book is different, the basic core and structure are the same. Therefore, "truth in labeling" would seem to forbid calling it either a revised edition or a new book. This dilemma was resolved by giving the book a new title indicating its coverage of subjects while using the old title as a subtitle to indicate both the thrust and the connection with the earlier book.

The dominant perspective of this book is that of economics, but a much expanded economics. Standard economics confines its attention to the study of how best to allocate given means among given ends. It does not inquire very deeply into the nature of means or the nature of ends. Yet, without a clear conception of the basic means at our disposal—of what in the physical world is the ultimately useful stuff that we must use up and cannot ourselves create—our narrow economics is likely to commit the error of wishful thinking (assuming that just because something is desirable it must also be possible). Likewise, unless we inquire into the nature of ends and face the questions of ultimate value, ethics, and the ranking of our ends, we are likely to commit the opposite error, that of technical determinism (assuming that just because something is possible it must also be desirable). Scarcity will still force hard choices among desirable possibilities, so there remains ample scope for standard economics.

The extension of economics into the biophysical world (Part I, on ecology) is a corrective to wishful thinking, while Part II, ethics, is a corrective to technical determinism. Part III, on economics, offers some materials from which we might begin to construct an improved economics free of both wishful thinking and technical determinism.

Each of the articles deals to some extent with all three areas—ecology, ethics, and economics. The grouping of the articles into three parts is according to emphasis rather than total content and is sometimes rather arbitrary. The interrelationships among ecology, ethics, and economics are far from arbitrary, however, and are discussed in the Introduction. Readers will not be surprised to find occasional disagreements among so diverse a group of thinkers. The minimum consensus among them is that economic growth can easily end up costing more than it is worth. Beyond that, especially regarding the alternative to the growth economy, there is a complex mixture of varying degrees of agreement, disagreement, and silence.

As editor, I have provided a relatively long introduction to the general subject, short introductions to each of the three parts, and a postscript for clearing up some misconceptions and replying to several critics of the steady-state position.

November 1979   *Herman E. Daly*
                                                         Baton Rouge, Louisiana

ECONOMICS, ECOLOGY, ETHICS

INTRODUCTION TO THE STEADY-STATE ECONOMY

Herman E. Daly

PARADIGMS IN POLITICAL ECONOMY

This book is a part of an emerging paradigm shift in political economy. The terms *paradigm* and *paradigm shift* come from Thomas Kuhn's insightful book *The Structure of Scientific Revolutions,*[1] in which Kuhn explores the ways that entire patterns of thought—a kind of gestalt for which he uses the word *paradigm*—are established and changed. Kuhn contends that paradigm shifts—occasional discontinuous, revolutionary changes in tacitly shared points of view and preconceptions of science—are an integral part of scientific thought. They form the necessary complement to *normal science,* which is what Kuhn calls the day-to-day cumulative building on the past, the puzzle solving, and the refining of models that fit within the paradigm shared by all the scientists of a particular discipline. Indeed, science students are taught to accept the prevailing paradigm so their work will adhere to the same designs, rules, and standards, thus assuring the *cumulative* building of knowledge.

Part of the introduction was originally published in *The Patient Earth,* John Harte and Robert H. Socolow, eds. Copyright © 1971 by Holt, Rinehart and Winston, Inc. Adapted and reprinted by permission of the editors.

Just as we are unconscious of the lenses in our own eyeglasses until we have trouble seeing clearly, so we are unconscious of paradigms until the clarity of scientific thought becomes blurred by anomaly. Even under the stress of facts that do not seem to fit, paradigms are not easily abandoned. If they were, the cohesion and coherence necessary to form a scientific *community* would be lacking. Most anomalies, after all, do become resolved within the paradigm; they must, if the paradigm is to command the loyalty of scientists. To abandon one paradigm in favor of another is to change the entire basis of intellectual community among the scientists within a discipline, which is why Kuhn calls such changes scientific revolutions. Discontinuous with the preceding paradigm, a new paradigm must at first rely on its own criteria for justification, for many of the questions that can be asked and many of the answers that can be found are likely to be absent from the previous paradigm. Indeed, even logical debate between adherents of different paradigms is often very limited, for proponents of two paradigms may not agree on what is a problem and what is a solution.

The history of science contains numerous examples of anomalies that brought crisis to old paradigms and were answered with new ones. Shall we take the earth or the sun as the center of our cosmos? Does a stone swinging on a string represent constrained fall or pendulum motion? Are species fixed or slowly evolving? And problems arise in political economy that may require more than normal puzzle solving. Shall we conceive of economic growth as a permanent normal process of a healthy economy or as a temporary passage from one steady state to another? Shall we take the flow of income or the stock of wealth as the magnitude most directly responsible for the satisfaction of human wants? Shall we conceive of land, labor, and capital as each being productive, and think in terms of three sources of value, or shall we conceive of labor as the only productive factor, the only source of value, and find that land and capital enhance the productivity of labor?

In a way, it all depends on how we want to look at it. And yet, there is far more to it than that. Which point of view is simpler or more appealing aesthetically? Which removes the intellectually or socially most vexing anomalies? Which is likely to suggest the most interesting and fruitful problems for future research? These kinds of criteria are not reducible to logical or factual differences. They involve a gestalt, an element of faith, personal commitment, and values.

That revolutionary paradigm shifts, both large ones and small ones, are historically and logically descriptive of the physical sciences has been admirably shown by Kuhn in his book and by Arthur Koestler in *The Sleepwalkers*.[2] Michael Polanyi takes a related viewpoint in his admirable book *Personal Knowledge*.[3] The focus of all three writers is physical science, and Koestler focuses especially on astronomy. But scientific revolutions characterize all of science, including political economy. Since values are a larger part of social science and also influence the acceptance or rejection of paradigms, such shifts may be even more characteristic of the social sciences.

The history of economic thought brings several such shifts to mind.

In the mercantilist paradigm of the Renaissance period, wealth meant precious metal, treasure easily convertible into armies and national power. The way to attain wealth was from mines or from a favorable balance of international trade. The implication of this paradigm was that the way to riches was to devote a nation's labor power to digging up metal that had no other use than as coinage, or to making goods to be given to foreigners in exchange for such minimally useful metal. Moreover, maintaining a surplus balance of trade required low prices on goods exported for sale in competitive markets, which meant low wages to home workers inasmuch as labor was the major cost of production. Making sure that the supply of laborers was large was one means of keeping wages low. The anomalous outcome was that, for a mercantilist nation to be "wealthy," it needed a large number of poor laborers.

The physiocrats of mid-eighteenth-century France—the first economic theorists—tried to explain economics in accordance with natural law and saw agriculture and Mother Earth as the source of all net value. Reproduction of plants and animals provided the paradigm by which all other increase in wealth was understood. Money was sterile. The concept that it "reproduced" through interest was rejected, because it did not fit the paradigm. But the anomaly of interest did not disappear, and the process of tracing all net value back to land became very complex.

The classical economists, witnesses to the problems of mercantilism as well as the beginnings of the Industrial Revolution, saw labor as the source of wealth and division of labor and improvement in the "state of the arts" as the source of productivity. Their main concern was how the product of labor got distributed among the social classes that cooperated to produce it. Adam Smith believed that an "invisible hand"—competition—would control the economy and that a certain natural order would keep atomistic individuals from exploiting each other, thereby harnessing individual self-interest to the social good. Classical economists thought that, over the long run, population growth and diminishing returns would unavoidably channel the entire economic surplus into rent, thus reducing profit to zero and terminating economic growth. What was anomalous about classical economics was not iits long-run implications, however, but the then-existing misery of the working class, misery which gave the lie to the belief that the invisible hand could effectively prevent exploitation.

Karl Marx was largely a classical economist, to the extent that he saw labor as the source of net economic product. But in place of atomistic individuals acting in natural harmony and short-run cooperation among three classes —landlords, laborers, and capitalists—Marx saw two classes in direct day-to-day conflict: the owners of the means of production and the nonowners. The owners kept the net product of labor, paying the workers only what their replacement would cost. Atomistic competition would continue to exist *within* each class; but the essential idea of Marxist economics is the exploitative relation *between* classes, which Marx believed would lead to revolution. The earlier classical economists recognized the likelihood of long-run class conflicts, but Marx emphasized this as a central economic factor. This emphasis constituted a paradigm shift.

The neoclassical economists shifted the paradigm back to atomism, though adding an analysis of imperfect competition as they did so. Their big change, however, was to conceive of net value as the result of psychic want satisfaction rather than the product of labor. The origin of value was subjective, not objective. The focus was not on distribution among classes but on efficiency of allocation—how could a society get the maximum amount of want satisfaction from scarce resources, *given* a certain distribution of wealth and income among individuals and social classes? Pure competition provided the optimal allocation.

John Maynard Keynes, observing the economic problems of the 1930s, could not accept the anomaly presented by the wide disuse of resources that were supposed to be optimally allocated. He was less concerned that resources be "optimally" allocated in some refined sense than that they should not lie unused. Classical and neoclassical economics, with Say's Law among their premises, required that unemployment be viewed as an aberration. Social reality, however, insisted that unemployment was central. Keynes changed the theoretical viewpoint accordingly.

The present-day Keynesian-neoclassical synthesis seeks full macroeconomic employment and optimal microeconomic allocation of resources. The *summum bonum* to be maximized is no longer psychic want satisfaction, which is unmeasurable, but annual aggregate real output, GNP—Gross National Product—a value index of the quantity flow of annual production. Distribution recedes into the background; the goal becomes to make the total pie bigger, thereby enabling everyone to get absolutely more without changing the relative size of parts. Both full employment and efficient allocation serve to increase the growth of real GNP. Conversely, and perhaps more importantly, growth of GNP is necessary to maintain full employment. In one of the first important contributions to growth theory, Evesy Domar stated the issue very well:

> The economy finds itself in a serious dilemma: if sufficient investment is not forthcoming today, unemployment will be here today. But if enough is invested today, still more will be needed tomorrow.
>
> It is a remarkable characteristic of a capitalistic economy that while, on the whole, unemployment is a function of the difference between its actual income and its productive capacity, most of the measures (i.e., investment) directed toward raising national income also enlarge productive capacity. It is very likely that the increase in national income will be greater than that of capacity, but the

whole problem is that the increase in income is temporary and presently peters out (the usual multiplier effect), while capacity has been increased for good. So far as unemployment is concerned, investment is at the same time a cure for the disease and the cause of even greater ills in the future.[4]

Thus, continual growth in both capacity (stock) and income (flow) is a central part of the neoclassical growth paradigm. But in a finite world continual growth is impossible.[5] Given finite stomachs, finite lifetimes, and the kind of man who does not live by bread alone, growth becomes undesirable long before it becomes impossible. But the tacit, and sometimes explicit, assumption of the Keynesian-neoclassical growthmania synthesis is that aggregate wants are infinite and should be served by trying to make aggregate production infinite, and that technology is an omnipotent *deus ex machina* who will get us out of any growth-induced problems.

To call the ideas and resultant changes hastily sketched above *paradigm shifts* is to use Kuhn's term with a bit of poetic license. In the physical sciences, to which Kuhn applied the term, reality does not change except on an evolutionary time scale. The *same* things are perceived in different ways. But social reality changes more rapidly. This, however, can be viewed as an additional reason for the periodic necessity, in the social sciences, of regrinding our lenses to a new prescription.

Ideology, ethical apology, and ethical criticism are also sources of paradigm shifts in the social sciences. As Marx said, the goal is not just to interpret the world but to change it. And he was right. Even if we wish to be neutral or "value-free," we cannot, because the paradigm by which people try to understand their society is itself one of the key determining features of the social system. No one denies that the distinction between *is* and *ought* is an elementary rule of clear thinking. To say *is* when we should say *ought* is wishful thinking. To say *ought* when we should say *is* (or never to say *ought* at all) is apology for the status quo. But these distinctions belong in the mind of the individual thinker. They are not proper lines for division of labor between individuals, much less between professions. Attempts to divide thought in this way contribute heavily to the schizophrenia of the modern age.

Kuhn notes that paradigm shifts are usually brought about by the young or by people new to a discipline, those relatively free of the established preconceptions. Accordingly, we find that thought on a steady-state economy has been more eagerly received by physical scientists and biologists than economists and by the relatively young among economists. The interests of the physical and life sciences in the issue of growth versus steady state is evident from the program of the American Association for the Advancement of Science (AAAS) 1971 meetings. Consider the following report:

Another way of interpreting the content of the AAAS meeting is to describe major themes that keep recurring. . . . Three topics appear this year in a variety of forms and contexts. They seek answers to:

How to live on a *finite* earth?
How to live a *good life* on a finite earth?
How to live a good life on a finite earth *at peace and without destructive mismatches?*[6]

The many sessions in which these themes appear are then listed, including the presidential address.

Simultaneously with the AAAS meetings in Philadelphia, the American Economic Association (AEA) held meetings in New Orleans, where, judging from the detailed program, not one of these questions was even on the agenda. Yet the question "How to live a *good* life on a *finite* earth?" would seem to be of more direct concern to economists than to physicists and biologists. Why this striking discrepancy? Do economists have more important questions on their minds? I think not. It is simply that economists must undergo a revolutionary paradigm shift and sacrifice large intellectual (and material?) vested interests in the perpetual growth theories and policies of the last thirty years before they can really come to grips with these questions. The advantage of the physical scientists is that, unlike economists, they are viscerally convinced that the world is a finite, open system at balance in a near steady state, and they have not all invested time and energy in economic growth models. As Kuhn points out,

Scientific revolutions . . . need seem revolutionary only to those whose paradigms are affected by them . . . astronomers, for example, could accept X-rays as a mere addition to knowledge, for their paradigms were unaffected by the existence of the new radiation. But for men like Kelvin, Crookes, and Roentgen, whose research dealt with radiation theory or with cathode ray tubes, the emergence of X-rays necessarily violated one paradigm as it created another. That is why these rays could be discovered only by something's first going wrong with normal research.[7]

A steady-state economy fits easily into the paradigm of physical science and biology—the earth approximates a steady-state open system, as do organisms. Why not our economy also, at least in its physical dimensions of bodies and artifacts? Economists forgot about physical dimensions long ago and centered their attention on value. But the fact that wealth is measured in value units does not annihilate its physical dimensions. Economists may continue to maximize value, and value could conceivably grow forever, but the physical mass in which value inheres must conform to a steady state, and the constraints of physical constancy on value growth will be severe and must be respected.

Perhaps this explains why many of the essays in this volume on political economy were written by physicists and biologists. But lest I be unfair to my own profession, I must observe that some leading economists, particularly Kenneth Boulding and Nicholas Georgescu-Roegen, have made enormous contributions toward reorienting economic thought along lines more congruent with a finite physical world. It is time for the profession to follow their lead.[8]

ENDS, MEANS, AND ECONOMICS

Chemistry has outgrown alchemy, and astronomy has emerged from the chrysalis of astrology, but the moral science of political economy has degenerated into the amoral game of politic economics. Political economy was concerned with scarcity and the resolution of the social conflicts engendered by scarcity. Politic economics tries to buy off social conflict by abolishing scarcity—by promising more things for more people, with less for no one, for ever and ever—all vouchsafed by the amazing grace of compound interest. It is not politic to remember, with John Ruskin,

> the great, palpable, inevitable fact—the root and rule of all economy—that what one person has, another cannot have; and that every atom of substance, of whatever kind, used or consumed, is so much human life spent; which if it issue in the saving present life or the gaining more, is well spent, but if not is either so much life prevented, or so much slain.[9]

Or, as Ruskin more succinctly put it in the same discussion, "there is no wealth but life."

Nor is it considered politic economics to take seriously the much more compelling demonstration of the same insight by Georgescu-Roegen, who has made us aware that

> the maximum of life quantity requires the minimum rate of natural resources depletion. By using these resources too quickly, man throws away that part of solar energy that will still be reaching the earth for a long time after he has departed. And everything that man has done in the last two hundred years or so puts him in the position of a fantastic spendthrift. There can be no doubt about it: any use of natural resources for the satisfaction of nonvital needs means a smaller quantity of life in the future. If we understand well the problem, the best use of our iron resources is to produce plows or harrows as they are needed, not Rolls Royces, not even agricultural tractors.[10]

Significantly, the masterful contribution of Georgescu-Roegen is not so much as mentioned in the *Journal of Economic Literature*'s 1976 survey of the literature on environmental economics. The first sentence of that survey beautifully illustrates the environmental hubris of growth economics: "Man has probably always worried about his environment because he *was once* totally dependent on it" (emphasis added).[11] Contrary to the implication, our dependence on the environment is still total, and it is overwhelmingly likely to remain so. Nevertheless, Robert Solow suggests that, thanks to the substitutability of other factors for natural resources, it is not only conceivable but likely that "the world can, in effect, get along without natural resources."[12] In view of such statements, it is evidently impossible to insist too strongly that, in Frederick Soddy's words,

> life derives the whole of its physical energy or power, not from anything self-contained in living matter, and still less from an external diety, but solely

from the inanimate world. It is dependent for all the necessities of its physical continuance primarily upon the principles of the steam-engine. The principles and ethics of human convention must not run counter to those of thermo-dynamics.[13]

Lack of respect for the principles of the steam engine also underlies the basic message of the very influential book *Scarcity and Growth,* by Harold Barnett and Chandler Morse. We are told that "nature imposes particular scarcities, not an inescapable general scarcity," and we are asked to believe that

advances in fundamental science have made it possible to take advantage of the uniformity of matter/energy—a uniformity that makes it feasible, without preas-signable limit, to escape the quantitative constraints imposed by the character of the earth's crust. . . . Science, by making the resource base more homogeneous, erases the restrictions once thought to reside in the lack of homogeneity. In a neo-Ricardian world, it seems, the particular resources with which one starts increasingly become a matter of indifference. The reservation of particular resources for later use, therefore, may contribute little to the welfare of future generations.[14]

Unfortunately for the politic economics of growth, it is not the uniformity of matter-energy that makes for usefulness but precisely the opposite. If all materials and all energy were uniformly distributed in thermodynamic equilibrium, the resulting "homogeneous resource base" would be no resource at all. It is nonuniformity—differences in concentration and temperature—that make for usefulness. The mere fact that all matter-energy may ultimately consist of the same basic building blocks is of little significance if it is the *potential for ordering those blocks* that is ultimately scarce, as the entropy law tells us is the case. Only at Maxwell's Sorting Demon[15] could turn a luke-warm soup of electrons, protons, neutrons, quarks, and whatnot into a re-source. And the entropy law tells us that Maxwell's demon does not exist. In other words, nature really *does* impose "an inescapable general scarcity," and it is a serious delusion to believe otherwise.

The differences in viewpoint cited above could hardly be more fundamen-tal. It seems necessary, therefore, to start at the very beginning if we are to root out the faddish politic economics of growth and replant the traditional political economy of scarcity. Standard textbooks have long defined econom-ics as the study of the allocation of scarce means among competing ends; thus a reconsideration of ends and means will provide our starting point. Modern economics' excessive devotion to growth will be explained in terms of an incomplete view of the total ends-means spectrum. The arguments of the two main traditions—the "scarce means arguments" and the "competing high-er ends arguments"—provide the basic organizing principle for this volume.

In the largest sense, humanity's ultimate economic problem is to use ulti-mate means wisely in the service of the Ultimate End. It is thus not hard to understand our tendency to divide up the single, overwhelming problem into a number of smaller subproblems, as illustrated in Figure I.1. This is a good

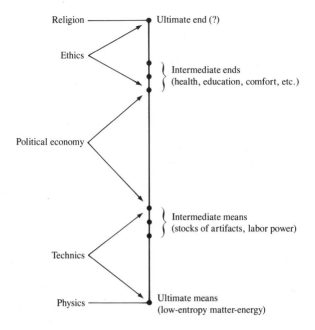

FIGURE I.1

Ends-means spectrum.

procedure as long as we do not forget about other parts of the spectrum in our zeal to solve the problem of one segment.

At the top of the spectrum is the Ultimate End—that which is intrinsically good and does not derive its goodness from any instrumental relation to some higher good. At the bottom is ultimate means, the useful stuff of the world, low-entropy matter-energy, which we can only use up and cannot create or replenish, and whose net production, therefore, cannot possibly be the end of any human activity. Each intermediate category on the spectrum is an end with respect to lower categories and a means with respect to higher categories. Below the Ultimate End we have a hierarchy of intermediate ends, which are in a sense means in the service of the Ultimate End. Intermediate ends are ranked with reference to the Ultimate End. The mere fact that we speak of priorities among our goals presumes a first place, an ordering principle, an Ultimate End. We may not be able to define it very well, but logically we are forced to recognize its existence. Above ultimate means are intermediate means (physical stocks), which can be viewed as ends directly served by the use of ultimate means (the entropic flow of matter-energy, the *throughput*).

On the left of the spectrum line are listed the traditional disciplines of study that correspond to each segment of the spectrum. The central, intermediate position of economics is highly significant. In looking only at the middle range, economics has naturally not dealt with ultimates or absolutes, which are found only at the extremes, and has falsely assumed that the middle-range pluralities, relativities, and substitutabilities among competing ends and scarce means were representative of the whole spectrum. Absolute limits are absent from the economists' paradigm because absolutes are encountered only in confrontation with the ultimate poles of the spectrum, which have been excluded from the focus of our attention. Even ethics and technics exist for the economist only at the very periphery of professional awareness.

In terms of this diagram, economic growth implies the creation of ever more intermediate means (stocks) for the purpose of satisfying ever more intermediate ends. Orthodox growth economics, as we have seen, recognizes that particular resources are limited but does not recognize any general scarcity of all resources together. The orthodox dogma is that technology can always substitute new resources for old, without limit. Ultimate means are not considered scarce. Intermediate means are scarce, it is argued, only because our capacity to transform ultimate means has not yet evolved very far toward its unlimited potential. Growth economists also recognize that any single intermediate end or want can be satisfied for any given individual. But new wants keep emerging (and new people as well), so the aggregate of all intermediate ends is held to be insatiable, or infinite in number if not in intensity. The growth economists' vision is one of continuous growth in intermediate means (unconstrained by any scarcity of ultimate means) in order to satisfy ever more intermediate ends (unconstrained by any impositions from the Ultimate End). Infinite means plus infinite ends equals growth forever.

A consideration of the ultimate poles of the spectrum, however, gives us a very different perspective, forcing us to ask two questions: (1) What, precisely, are our ultimate means, and are they limited in ways that cannot be overcome by technology? (2) What is the nature of the Ultimate End, and is it such that, beyond a certain point, further accumulation of intermediate means (bodies and artifacts) not only fails to serve the Ultimate End but actually renders a disservice? It will be argued in this volume that the answer to both sets of questions is *yes*. The absolute scarcity of ultimate means limits the *possibility* of growth (Part I). The competition from other ends, which contribute more heavily at the margin toward the Ultimate End, limits the *desirability* of growth (Part II). Moreover, the interaction of desirability and possibility provides the *economic* limit to growth, which is the most stringent, and should be the governing, limit (Part III).

Paradoxically, growth economics has been both too materialistic and not materialistic enough. In ignoring the ultimate means and the laws of thermodynamics, it has been insufficiently materialistic. In ignoring the Ultimate End and ethics, it has been too materialistic.

Critics of growth can be classified into ends-based (moral) and means-based (biophysical). Many writers are, to some extent, in both traditions. This is to be expected, because the two traditions are not as logically independent as may at first appear. For example, many moral issues regarding distributive justice and intergenerational equity hardly arise if one believes that continual economic growth is biophysically possible. Likewise, if one's arena of moral concern excludes the poor, future generations, and subhuman life, then many biophysical constraints are no longer of interest. To crack the nut of growth mania, it is not enough to hammer from above with moral arguments, because there is sufficient "give" underneath for optimistic biophysical assumptions to cushion the blow (space colonies, green revolutions, breeder reactors, etc.) Hammering only from below with biophysical arguments leaves too much room for elastic morality to absorb the blow. (The interest rate automatically looks after the future; growth itself is the Ultimate End, or as close as we can come to it; our manifest destiny is to colonize space as the earth is a mere dandelion gone to seed; etc.) Growth chestnuts have to be placed on the unyielding anvil of biophysical realities and then crushed with the hammer of moral argument. The entropy law and ecology provide the biophysical anvil. Concern for future generations and subhuman life and inequities in current wealth distribution provide the moral hammer.

Human beings are both material creatures in absolute dependence upon their physical environment and rational beings who have purposes and strive to become better. These two aspects must be consistent with each other. Improvement presupposes survival, and survival in an entropic and evolving world is impossible without continual striving for improvement. Biophysically based conclusions about economic growth, or any other subject, should be in accord with morally based conclusions. A discrepancy indicates a flawed understanding of the natural world or a warped set of values. That ends-based and means-based arguments should converge in their rejection of growthmania is both comforting and not unexpected.

The overall problem is how to use ultimate means to serve best the Ultimate End. We might call this ultimate political economy, or *stewardship*. To state the problem in this way is to emphasize at once both its wholeness and the necessity of breaking it into more manageable subproblems, for the overall problem must be tackled one step at a time. Yet one step is valueless without the others, and one correct step is worse than valueless if the steps it takes for granted were false steps. If our concept of the Ultimate End is evil rather than good, then an inverted ethics is better for us than a consistent ethics. If our ethical priorities are upside down, then an inverted or incorrect imputation of value to intermediate means is better than a correct imputation. If our intermediate means are incorrectly valued, then a technology that efficiently and powerfully converts ultimate means into the most valuable intermediate means is worse than a weak technology. And an erroneous physics that will cause technology to stumble rather than advance an evil end efficiently is better than a correct physics.

The parts of the total economic problem are related not only from the top down but also from the bottom up. Our customary ethical ordering of intermediate ends conditions our perception of the Ultimate End. We tend to take our conventional priorities as given and then deduce the nature of the Ultimate End as that which legitimates the conventional priorities. We tend also to order our intermediate ends in such a way that we can effectively serve them with the existing evaluation of intermediate means. Further, there is a tendency to value the intermediate means according to the technical and physical possibilities for producing them. If it is possible, we must do it.

I do not mean to say that working only in one direction is always proper and in the other always improper. The point is that the parts of the problem are highly interrelated and cannot be dealt with in isolation, and, even though ideally our starting point should be the Ultimate End, we can only see that end dimly and may find clues to its nature in our experience with ethical, economic, and even technical problems encountered on the way.

The total problem of relating the five subproblems—theology, ethics, political economy, technology, physics—is more delicate than any of the subproblems themselves, but not for that reason any less imperative. Surely we must have a vision of the total problem, otherwise we do not understand what our specialties are. It is hoped that the collection of articles in this book will help to fill out such a total vision. Clearly, each stage can be dealt with only in a partial and incomplete manner. But the premise on which this volume rests is that it is better to deal incompletely with the whole than to deal wholly with the incomplete.

Let us now turn to an overview of the particular paradigm this collection seeks to develop, one that will lead to a steady-state economy. The terms *steady state* and *stationary state* are used synonymously. The former is common in physical sciences, the latter common in economics and demography.

THE STEADY-STATE ECONOMY

Any discussion of the relative merits of the steady, stationary, or no-growth economy, and its opposite, the economy in which wealth and population are growing, must recognize some important quantitative and qualitative differences between rich and poor countries and between rich and poor classes within countries. To see why this is so, consider the familiar ratio of Gross National Product (GNP) to total population (P). This ratio, per capita annual product (GNP/P), is the measure usually employed to distinguish rich from poor countries, and, in spite of its many shortcomings, it does have the virtue of reflecting in one ratio the two fundamental life processes of production and reproduction. Let us ask two questions of both numerator and denominator for both rich and poor countries—namely, what is the quantitative rate of growth; and, qualitatively, exactly what is it that is growing?

1. The rate of growth in the denominator, P, is much higher in poor countries than in rich countries. Although mortality is tending to equality at low levels throughout the world, fertility[16] in poor nations remains roughly *twice* that of rich nations. The average Gross Reproduction Rate (GRR)[17] for rich countries is around 1.5, and that for poor countries is around 3.0 (that is, on the assumption that all survive to the end of reproductive life, each mother would be replaced by 1.5 daughters in rich countries and 3 in poor countries). Moreover, all poor countries have a GRR greater than 2.0, and all rich countries have a GRR less than 2.0, with practically no countries falling in the area of the 2.0 dividing point. No other social or economic index divides the world so clearly and consistently into "developed" and "underdeveloped" as does fertility.[18]

2. Qualitatively, the incremental population in poor countries consists largely of hungry illiterates; in rich countries it consists largely of well-fed members of the middle class. The incremental person in poor countries contributes negligibly to production but makes few demands on world resources —although from the point of view of his poor country, these few demands of many new people can easily dissipate any surplus that might otherwise be used to raise productivity.[19] The incremental person in the rich country contributes to his country's GNP, and to feed his high standard of living contributes greatly to depletion of the world's resources and pollution of its spaces.

3. The numerator, GNP, has grown at roughly the same rate in rich and poor countries, around 4 or 5 percent annually, with the poor countries probably growing slightly faster. Nevertheless, because of the poor countries' more rapid population growth, their per capita income has grown more slowly than that of rich countries. Consequently, the gap between rich and poor has widened.[20]

4. The incremental GNP of rich and poor nations has an altogether different qualitative significance. This follows from the two most basic laws of economics: (a) the law of diminishing marginal utility, which really says nothing more than that people satisfy their most pressing wants *first*—thus each additional dollar of income or unit of resource is used to satisfy a less pressing want than the previous dollar or unit; and (b) the law of increasing marginal cost, which says that producers *first* use the best qualities of factors (most fertile land, most experienced worker, and so on) and the best combination of factors known to them. They use the less efficient (more costly) qualities and combinations only when they run out of the better ones, or when one factor, such as land, becomes fixed (nonaugmentable). Also, in a world of scarcity, as more resources are devoted to one use, fewer are available for other uses. The least important alternative uses are sacrificed first, so that as more of any good is produced, progressively more important alternatives must be sacrificed; that is, a progressively higher price (opportunity cost) must be paid. Applied to GNP, the first law means that the marginal (incremental) benefits from equal increments of output are decreasing, and the second law means that the marginal cost of equal increments in output is increasing.

At some point, perhaps already passed in the United States, an extra unit of GNP costs more than it is worth. Technological advances can put off this point, but not forever. Indeed, they may bring it to pass sooner because more powerful technologies tend to provoke more powerful ecological backlashes and to be more disruptive of habits and emotions. To put things more concretely, growth in GNP in a poor country means more food, clothing, shelter, basic education, and security, whereas for the rich country it means more electric toothbrushes, yet another brand of cigarettes, more tension and insecurity, and more force-feeding through more advertising. In sum, extra GNP in a poor country, assuming it does not go mainly to the richest class of that country, represents satisfaction of relatively basic wants, whereas extra GNP in a rich country, assuming it does not go mainly to the poorest class of that country, represents satisfaction of relatively trivial wants.

For our purposes, the upshot of these differences is that, for the poor, growth in GNP is still a good thing, but for the rich it is probably a bad thing. Growth in population, however, is a bad thing for both: For the rich, population growth is bad because it makes growth in GNP (a bad thing) less avoidable. For the poor, population growth is bad because it makes growth in GNP, and especially in per capita GNP (a good thing), more difficult to attain. We shall be concerned in this book mainly with a rich, affluent-effluent economy such as that of the United States. Our purposes will be to define more clearly the concept of steady state, to see why it is necessary, to consider its economic and social implications, and finally to comment on an emerging political economy of finite wants and nongrowth.

THE NATURE AND NECESSITY OF THE STATIONARY STATE

The term *stationary state* (steady state) is used here in its classical sense.[21] Over a century ago, John Stuart Mill, the great synthesizer of classical economics, spoke of the stationary state in words that could hardly be more relevant today, and they will serve as the starting point in our discussion.

> But in contemplating any progressive movement, not in its nature unlimited, the mind is not satisfied with merely tracing the laws of its movement; it cannot but ask the further question, to what goal? . . .
> It must always have been seen, more or less distinctly, by political economists, that the increase in wealth is not boundless: that at the end of what they term the progressive state lies the stationary state, that all progress in wealth is but a postponement of this, and that each step in advance is an approach to it . . . if we have not reached it long ago, it is because the goal itself flies before us [as a result of technical progress].
> I cannot . . . regard the stationary state of capital and wealth with the unaffected aversion so generally manifested towards it by political economists of

the old school. I am inclined to believe that it would be, on the whole, a very considerable improvement on our present condition. I confess I am not charmed with the ideal of life held out by those who think that the normal state of human beings is that of struggling to get on; that the trampling, crushing, elbowing, and treading on each other's heels which form the existing type of social life, are the most desirable lot of human kind, or anything but the disagreeable symptoms of one of the phases of industrial progress. The northern and middle states of America are a specimen of this stage of civilization in very favorable circumstances; . . . and all that these advantages seem to have yet done for them (notwithstanding some incipient signs of a better tendency) is that the life of the whole of one sex is devoted to dollar-hunting, and of the other to breeding dollar-hunters.

. . . Those who do not accept the present very early stage of human improvement as its ultimate type may be excused for being comparatively indifferent to the kind of economical progress which excites the congratulations of ordinary politicians; the mere increase of production and accumulation. . . . I know not why it should be a matter of congratulation that persons who are already richer than anyone needs to be, should have doubled their means of consuming things which give little or no pleasure except as representative of wealth. . . . It is only in the backward countries of the world that increased production is still an important object: in those most advanced, what is economically needed is better distribution, of which one indispensable means is a stricter restraint on population.

There is room in the world, no doubt, and even in old countries, for a great increase in population, supposing the arts of life to go on improving, and capital to increase. But even if innocuous, I confess I see very little reason for desiring it. The density of population necessary to enable mankind to obtain, in the greatest degree, all the advantages both of cooperation and of social intercourse, has, in all the most populous countries, been attained. A population may be too crowded, though all be amply supplied with food and raiment. It is not good for a man to be kept perforce at all times in the presence of his species. . . . Nor is there much satisfaction in contemplating the world with nothing left to the spontaneous activity of nature; with every rood of land brought into cultivation, which is capable of growing food for human beings; every flowery waste or natural pasture plowed up, all quadrupeds or birds which are not domesticated for man's use exterminated as his rivals for food, every hedgerow or superfluous tree rooted out, and scarcely a place left where a wild shrub or flower could grow without being eradicated as a weed in the name of improved agriculture. If the earth must lose that great portion of its pleasantness which it owes to things that the unlimited increase of wealth and population would extirpate from it, for the mere purpose of enabling it to support a larger, but not a happier or a better population. I sincerely hope, for the sake of posterity, that they will be content to be stationary, long before necessity compels them to it.

It is scarcely necessary to remark that a stationary condition of capital and population implies no stationary state of human improvement. There would be as much scope as ever for all kinds of mental culture, and moral and social progress; as much room for improving the Art of Living and much more likelihood of its being improved, when minds cease to be engrossed by the art of getting on. Even the industrial arts might be as earnestly and as successfully cultivated, with this sole difference, that instead of serving no purpose but the increase of wealth, industrial improvements would produce their legitimate effect, that of abridging labor.[22]

The direction in which political economy has evolved in the last hundred years is not along the path suggested by Mill. In fact, most economists are hostile to the classical notion of stationary state and dismiss Mill's discussion as "strongly colored by his social views"[23] (as if the neoclassical theories were not so colored!), and "nothing so much as a prolegomenon to Galbraith's *Affluent Society*" (which also received a hostile reception from the economics profession). While giving full credit to Mill for his many other contributions to economics, most economists consider his discussion of the stationary state as something of a personal aberration. Also his "relentless insistence that every conceivable policy measure must be judged in terms of its effects on the birth rate" is dismissed as "hopelessly dated." The truth is, however, that Mill is even more relevant today than in his own time.

With this historical background, let us now analyze the steady state with a view toward clarifying what Mill somewhat mistakenly thought "must have always been seen more or less distinctly by political economists," namely, "that wealth and population are not boundless."

By *steady state* is meant a constant stock of physical wealth (capital), and a constant stock of people (population).[24] Naturally, these stocks do not remain constant by themselves. People die, and wealth is physically consumed, that is, worn out, depreciated. Therefore, the stocks must be maintained by a rate of inflow (birth, production) equal to the rate of outflow (death, consumption). But this equality may obtain, and stocks remain constant, with a high rate of throughput (equal to both the rate of inflow and the rate of outflow) or with a low rate. Our definition of steady state is not complete until we specify the rates of throughput by which the constant stocks are maintained. For a number of reasons we specify that the rate of throughput should be as low as possible. For an equilibrium stock, the average age at "death" of its members is the reciprocal of the rate of throughput. The faster the water flows through the tank, the less time an average drop spends in the tank. For the population, a low rate of throughput (a low birth rate and an equally low death rate) means a high life expectancy, and it is desirable for that reason alone—at least within limits. For the stock of wealth, a low rate of throughput (low production and equally low consumption) means greater life expectancy or durability of goods and less time sacrificed to production. This means more "leisure" or nonjob time to be divided into consumption time, personal and household maintenance time, culture time, and idleness.[25] This, too, seems socially desirable, at least within limits.

To these reasons for the desirability of a low rate of throughput we must add some reasons for the impracticability of high rates. Since matter and energy cannot be created, production inputs must be taken from the environment, which leads to depletion. Since matter and energy cannot be destroyed, an equal amount of matter and energy in the form of waste must be returned to the environment, leading to pollution. Hence lower rates of throughput lead to less depletion and pollution, higher rates to more. The limits regarding what rates of depletion and pollution are tolerable must be supplied by ecology. A definite limit to the size of maintenance flows of matter and energy is set by ecological thresholds which, if exceeded, cause a breakdown of the system. To keep flows below these limits, we can operate on two variables: the *size* of the stocks and the *durability* of the stocks. As long as we are well below these thresholds, economic cost-benefit calculations of depletion and pollution can be relied on as a guide. But as these thresholds are approached, marginal cost and marginal benefit become meaningless, and Alfred Marshall's erroneous motto that "nature does not make jumps" and most of neoclassical marginalists economics become inapplicable. The "marginal" cost of one more step may be to fall over the precipice.

Of the two variables—size of stocks and durability of stocks—only the second requires further clarification. *Durability* means more than just how long a particular commodity lasts. It also includes the efficiency with which the after-use "corpse" of a commodity can be recycled as an input to be born again as the same or a different commodity. Within certain limits, to be discussed below, durability of stocks ought to be maximized in order that depletion of resources might be minimized.

We might suppose that the best use of resources would imitate the model that nature has furnished: a closed-loop system of material cycles powered by the sun (what A. J. Lotka called the "mill wheel of life" or the "world engine").[26] In such an "economy," durability is maximized, and the resources on earth could presumably last as long as the sun continues to radiate the energy to turn the closed material cycles.

We can set up an economy in imitation of nature in which all waste products are recycled. Instead of the sun, however, we use other sources of energy because of the scale of our industrial activity. Even modern agriculture depends as much on geologic capital (to make fertilizers, machines, and pesticides) as on solar income. This capital (fossil fuels and fission materials), from which we now borrow, may not last more than a couple of centuries, but there is another possible energy source, controlled thermonuclear fusion, which may someday provide a practically inexhaustible supply of energy with little radioactive waste, thereby alleviating problems of resource depletion and radioactive contamination. At least that is the claim of fusion enthusiasts.

Nevertheless, the serious problem of waste heat remains. The second law of thermodynamics tells us that it is impossible to recycle energy and that eventually all energy will be converted into waste heat. Also, it is impossible to recycle materials with one hundred percent completeness. Some material is irrecoverably lost in each cycle. Eventually, all life will cease as entropy or chaos approaches its maximum. But, the second law of thermodynamics implies that, even before this very long-run universal thermodynamic heat-death occurs, we will be plagued by thermal pollution, for whenever we use energy, we must produce unusable waste heat. When a localized energy process causes a part of the environment to heat up, thermal pollution can have serious effects on ecosystems, since life processes and climatic phenomena are regulated by temperature.

We have already argued that, given the size of stocks, the throughput should be minimized, since it is really a cost. But the throughput is in two forms, matter and energy, and the ecological cost will vary, depending on how the throughput is apportioned between them. The amount of energy throughput will depend on the rate of material recycling. If we recycle none of our used material goods, then we must expend energy to replace those goods from raw materials, and this energy expenditure is in many instances greater than the energy needed to recycle the product. For example, the estimated energy needed to produce a ton of steel plate from iron ore is 2700 kilowatt-hours, whereas merely 700 kilwatt-hours is needed to produce the same ton by recycling scrap steel.[27] However, this is not the whole story. The mere expenditure of energy is not sufficient to close material cycles, since energy must work through the agency of material implements. To recycle aluminum cans requires more trucks to collect the cans as well as more energy to run the trucks. More trucks require more steel, glass, rubber, and so forth, which require more iron ore and coal, which require still more trucks. This is the familiar web of interindustry interdependence reflected in an input-output table.[28] All of these extra intermediate activities required to recycle the aluminum cans involve some inevitable pollution as well. If we think of each industry as adding recycling to its production process, then this will generate a whole chain of direct and indirect demands on matter and energy resources which must be taken away from final demand uses and devoted to the intermediate activities of recycling. It will take more intermediate products and activities to support the same level of final output.

As we attempt to recycle more and more of our produced goods, we will reach the point of diminishing returns; the energy expenditure alone will give rise to a ruinous amount of waste heat or thermal pollution. On the other hand, if we recycle too small a fraction of our produced goods, then nonthermal pollution and resource depletion become a severe problem.

The introduction of material recycling permits a trade-off; that is, it allows us to choose that combination of material and energy depletion and pollution which is least costly in the light of specific local conditions. *Cost* here means total ecological cost, not just pecuniary costs, and it is extremely difficult to measure.

In addition to the trade-offs involved in minimizing the ecological cost of the throughput for a given stock, we must recognize that the total stock (consisting of wealth and people) is variable both in total size and in composition. Since there is a direct relationship between the size of the stock and the size of the throughput necessary to maintain the stock, we have a trade-off between size of total stock (viewed as benefit) and size of the flow of throughput (viewed as a cost); in other words, an increase in benefit implies an increase in cost. Furthermore, a given throughput can maintain a constant total stock consisting of a large substock of wealth and a small substock of people or a large substock of people and a small substock of wealth. Here we have a trade-off in the form of an inverse relationship between two benefits. This latter trade-off between people and wealth is imposed by the constancy of the total stock and is limited by minimal subsistence per capita wealth at one extreme and by minimal technological requirements for labor to maintain the stock of wealth at the other extreme. Within these limits this trade-off essentially represents the choice of a standard of living. Economics and ecology can at best specify the terms of this trade-off; the actual choice depends on ethical judgments.

In sum, the steady state of wealth and population is maintained by an inflow of low-entropy matter-energy (depletion) and an outflow of an equal quantity of high-entropy matter-energy (pollution). Stocks of wealth and people, like individual organisms, are open systems that feed on low entropy.[29] Many of these relationships are summarized in Figure I.2.

The classical economists thought that the steady state would be made necessary by limits on the depletion side (the law of increasing cost or diminishing returns), but in fact the main limits seem to be occurring on the pollution side. In effect, pollution provides another foundation for the law of increasing costs, but it has received little attention in this regard, since pollution costs are social, whereas depletion costs are usually private. On the input side, the environment is partitioned into spheres of private ownership. Depletion of the environment coincides, to some degree, with depletion of the owner's wealth and inspires at least a minimum of stewardship. On the output side, however, the waste absorption capacity of the environment is not subject to partitioning and private ownership. Air and water are used freely by all, and the result is a competitive, profligate exploitation—what biologist Garrett Hardin calls the "commons effect," what welfare economists call "external diseconomies," and what I like to call the "invisible foot." Adam Smith's invisible hand leads private self-interest unwittingly to serve the common good. The invisible foot leads private self-interest to kick the common good to prices. Private ownership and private use under a competitive market give rise to the invisible hand. Public ownership with unrestrained private use gives rise to the invisible foot. Public ownership with public restraints on use gives rise to the visible hand (and foot) on the planner. Depletion has been partially restrained by the invisible hand, while pollution has been encouraged by the invisible foot. It is therefore not surprising to find limits occurring mainly on the pollution side —which, of course, is not to deny depletion limits.

It is interesting that the first school of economists, the physiocrats, emphasized human beings' dependence on nature. For them only the "natural" activity of agriculture was capable of producing a net product of value. Indeed, the word *physiocracy* meant rule of nature. Something of the physiocrats' basic vision, if not their specific theories, is badly needed in economics today.

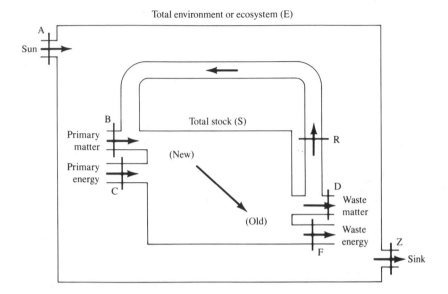

FIGURE I.2

Rectangle (E) is the total ecosystem, which contains the total stock (S) of wealth and people as one of its mutually dependent components. The ecosystem imports energy from outer space (sun, A) and exports waste heat to outer space (sink, Z). The stock contains matter in which a considerable amount of available energy is stored (mined coal, oil in oil tanks, water on high ground, living things, wood products, and the like), as well as matter in which virtually no available energy is stored. Matter and energy in the stock must be separately maintained. The stock is maintained in a steady state when B is equal to D and C is equal to F. In the steady state throughput equals either input (B plus C) or output (D plus F), since input and output are equal to each other. When input and output are not equal, then the throughput is measured by the smaller of the two.

From the second law of thermodynamics, we know that energy cannot be recycled. Matter may be recycled (R), but only by using more energy (and matter) to do it. In the diagram, energy moves only from left to right, whereas matter moves in both directions.

For a constant S, the lower the rate of throughput the more durable or longer-lived is the total stock. For a given throughput, the lower the rate of recycling (R), the more durable are the individual commodities. The optimum durability of an individual commodity is attained when the marginal production cost of increased durability equals the marginal recycling cost of not having increased durability further. *Cost* is total ecological cost and is extremely difficult to measure.

Both the size of the stock and the rate of throughput must not be so large relative to the total environment that they obstruct the natural ecological processes which form the biophysical foundations of wealth. Otherwise, the total stock and its associated throughput become a cancer which kills the total organism.

ECONOMIC AND SOCIAL IMPLICATIONS
OF THE STEADY STATE

The economic and social implications of the steady state are enormous and revolutionary. The physical flows of production and consumption must be *minimized, not maximized* subject to some desirable population and standard of living.[30] The central concept must be the stock of wealth, not, as presently, the flow of income and consumption. Furthermore, the stock must not grow. For several reasons, the important issue of the steady state will be distribution, not production. The problem of relative shares can no longer be avoided by appeals to growth. The argument that everyone should be happy as long as his absolute share of the wealth increases, regardless of his relative share, will no longer be available. Absolute and relative shares will move together, and the division of physical wealth will be a zero-sum game. In addition, the arguments justifying inequality in wealth as necessary for savings, investment, and growth will lose their force. With production flows (which are really *costs* of maintaining the stock) kept low, the focus will be on the distribution of the stock of wealth, not on the distribution of the flow of income. Marginal productivity theories and "justifications" pertain only to flow and therefore are not available to explain or "justify" the distribution of stock ownership. Also, even though physical stocks remain constant, increased income in the form of leisure will result from continued technological improvements. How will it be distributed, if not according to some ethical norm of equality? The steady state would make fewer demands on our environmental resources but much greater demands on our moral resources. In the past, a good case could be made that leaning too heavily on scarce moral resources, rather than relying on abundant self-interest, was the road to serfdom. But in an age of rockets, hydrogen bombs, cybernetics, and genetic control, there is simply no substitute for moral resources and no alternative to relying on them, whether they prove sufficient or not.

On the question of maximizing versus minimizing the flow of production, there is an interesting analogy with ecological succession. Young ecosystems (early stages of succession) are characterized by a high production efficiency, and mature ecosystems (late stages of succession) are characterized by a high maintenance efficiency. For a given B (biomass stock), young ecosystems tend to maximize P (production flow), giving a high production efficiency P/B; mature ecosystems, on the other hand, tend to minimize P for a given B, thus attaining a high maintenance efficiency, B/P. According to ecologist Eugene P. Odum, young ecosystems seem to emphasize production, growth, and quantity, whereas mature ecosystems emphasize protection, stability, and quality.[31] For the young system, the flow of production is the quantitative source of growth and is maximized. For the mature, the flow of production is the maintenance cost of protecting the stability and quality of the stock and is minimized. If we conceive of the human economy as an ecosystem moving from an earlier to a later stage of succession (from the "cowboy economy" to the "spaceman economy," as Boulding puts it), then we would expect, by analogy, that production, growth, and quantity would be replaced by protective maintenance, stability, and quality as the major social goals. The cardinal virtues of the past become the cardinal sins of the present.

With constant physical stocks, economic growth must be in nonphysical goods: service and leisure.[32] Taking the benefits of technological progress in the form of increased leisure is a reversal of the historical practice of taking the benefits mainly in the form of goods and has extensive social implications. In the past, economic development has increased the physical output of a day's work while the number of hours in a day has, of course, remained constant, with the result that the opportunity cost of a unit of time in terms of goods has risen. Time is worth more goods, a good is worth less time. As time becomes more expensive in terms of goods, fewer activities are "worth the time." We become goods-rich and time-poor. Consequently, we crowd more activities and more consumption into the same period of time in order to raise the return on nonwork time so as to bring it into equality with the higher returns on work time, thereby maximizing the total returns to total time. This gives rise to what Staffan Linder has called the "harried leisure class."[33] We use not only work time but also personal consumption time more efficiently, and we even try to be efficient in our sleep by attempting subconscious learning. Time-intensive activities (friendships, care of the aged and children, meditation, and reflection) are sacrificed in favor of commodity-intensive activities (consumption). At some point, people will feel rich enough to afford more time-intensive activities, even at the higher price. But advertising, by constantly extolling the value of material-intensive commodities, postpones this point. From an ecological view, of course, this is exactly the reverse of what is called for. What is needed is a low relative price of time in terms of material commodities. Then time-intensive activities will be substituted for material-intensive activities. To become less materialistic in our habits, we must raise the relative price of matter. Keeping physical stocks constant and using technology to increase leisure time will do just that. Thus a policy of nonmaterial growth, or leisure-only growth, in addition to being necessary for keeping physical stocks constant, has the further beneficial effect of encouraging a more generous expenditure of time and a more careful use of physical goods. A higher relative price of material-intensive goods may at first glance be thought to encourage their production. But material goods require material inputs, so costs as well as revenues would increase, thus eliminating profit incentives to expand.

In the 1930s Bertrand Russell proposed a policy of leisure growth rather than commodity growth and viewed the unemployment question in terms of the distribution of leisure. The following words are from his delightful essay "In Praise of Idleness."

> Suppose that, at a given moment, a certain number of people are engaged in the manufacture of pins. They make as many pins as the world needs, working (say)

eight hours a day. Someone makes an invention by which the same number of men can make twice as many pins as before. But the world does not need twice as many pins. Pins are already so cheap that hardly any more will be bought at a lower price. In a sensible world, everybody concerned in the manufacture of pins would take to working four hours instead of eight, and everything else would go on as before. But in the actual world this would be thought demoralizing. The men still work eight hours, there are too many pins, some employers go bankrupt, and half the men previously concerned in making pins are thrown out of work. There is, in the end, just as much leisure as on the other plan, but half the men are totally idle while half are still overworked. In this way it is insured that the unavoidable leisure shall cause misery all round instead of being a universal source of happiness. Can anything more insane be imagined?[34]

In addition to this strategy of leisure-only growth, and the resulting reinforcement of an increased price of material-intensity relative to time-intensity, we can internalize some pollution costs by charging pollution taxes. Economic efficiency requires only that a price be placed on environmental amenities; it does not tell us who should pay the price. The producer may claim that the use of the environment to absorb waste products is a right that all organisms and firms must of necessity enjoy, and whoever wants air and water to be cleaner than it is at any given time should pay for it. Consumers may argue that the use of the environment as a source of clean inputs of air and water takes precedence over its use as a sink, and that whoever makes the environment dirtier than it otherwise would be should be the one to pay. Again the issue becomes basically one of distribution—not what the price should be, but who should pay it. The fact that the price takes the form of a tax automatically decides who will receive it—the government. But this raises more distribution issues; and the "solutions" to these problems are ethical, not technical.

Another possibility of nonmaterial growth is to redistribute wealth from the low utility uses of the rich to the high utility uses of the poor, thereby increasing total "social utility." Joan Robinson has noted that this egalitarian implication of the law of diminishing marginal utility was "sterilized . . . mainly by slipping from utility to physical output as the object to be maximized."[35] As we move back from physical output to nonphysical utility, the egalitarian implications become "unsterilized."

Economic growth has kept at bay two closely related problems. First, growth is necessary to maintain full employment. Only if it is possible for nearly everyone to have a job can the income-through-jobs ethic of distribution remain workable. Second, growth takes the edge off of distributional conflicts. If everyone's absolute share of income is increasing, there is a tendency not to fight over relative shares, especially since such fights may interfere with growth and even lead to a lower absolute share for all. But these problems cannot be kept at bay forever, because growth cannot continue indefinitely.

Growth, by allowing full employment, permits the old principles of distribution (income-through-jobs link) to continue in effect. But with no growth in physical stocks, and a policy of using technological progress to increase leisure, full employment and income-through-jobs are no longer workable mechanisms for distribution. Furthermore, we add a new dimension to the distribution problem—how to distribute leisure. The point is that distribution issues must be squarely faced and not left to work themselves out as the by-product of full-employment policies aimed at promoting growth.

A stationary population, with low birth and death rates, would imply a greater percentage of old people than in the present growing population, though hardly a geriatric society as some youth worshippers claim. The average age, assuming that current U.S. mortality holds, would change from twenty-seven to thirty-seven. One hears much nonsense about the conservatism and reactionary character of older populations and the progressive dynamism of younger populations, but a simple comparison of Sweden (old but hardly reactionary) with Brazil (young but hardly progressive) should make us cautious about such facile relationships. It is also noted that the age pyramid of a stationary U.S. population would be essentially rectangular up to about age fifty and then would rapidly taper off, and that the age "pyramid" would no longer be roughly congruent with the pyramid of authority in hierarchical organizations, with the result that the general correlation between increasing age and increasing authority would not hold for very many people. Quite true, but a salutary result could well be that more people will seek their personal fulfillment outside the structure of hierarchical organizations and that fewer people would rise to levels of their incompetence within bureaucracies. Since old people do not work, this further accentuates the distribution problem. However, the percentage of children will diminish, so in effect there will be mainly a change in the direction that payments are transferred. More of the earnings of working adults will be transferred to the old, and less to children.

What institutions will provide the control necessary to keep the stocks of wealth and people constant, with the minimum sacrifice of individual freedom? This, I submit, is the question we should be struggling with. It would be far too simpleminded to blurt out "socialism" as the answer, since socialist states are as badly afflicted with growthmania as capitalist states. The Marxist eschatology of the classless society is based on the premise of complete abundance; consequently, economic growth is exceedingly important in socialist theory and practice. Also, population growth, for the orthodox Marxist, cannot present problems under socialist institutions. This latter tenet has weakened a bit in recent years, but the first continues in full force. However, it is equally simpleminded to believe that the present big capital, big labor, big government, big military type of private profit capitalism is capable of the required foresight and restraint and that the addition of a few pollution and severance taxes here and there will solve the problem. The issues are much deeper and inevitably impinge on the distribution of income and wealth.

All economic systems are subsystems within the big biophysical system of ecological interdependence. The ecosystem provides a set of physical constraints to which all economic systems must conform. The facility with which an economic system can adapt to these constraints is a major, if neglected, criterion for comparing economic systems. This neglect is understandable, because in the past ecological constraints showed no likelihood of becoming effective. But population growth, growth in the physical stock of wealth, and growth in the power of technology all combine to make ecological constraints effective. Perhaps this common set of constraints will be one more factor favoring convergence of economic systems.

Why do people produce junk and cajole other people into buying it? Not out of any innate love for junk or hatred of the environment, but simply in order to earn an income. If, with the prevailing distribution of wealth, income, and power, production governed by the profit motive results in the output of great amounts of noxious junk, then something is wrong with the distribution of wealth and power, the profit motive, or both. We need some principle of income distribution independent of and supplementary to the income-through-jobs link.[36] Perhaps a start in this direction was made by Oskar Lange in his *On the Economic Theory of Socialism*,[37] in which he attempted to combine some socialist principles of distribution with the allocative efficiency advantages of the market system. However, at least as much remains to be done here as remains to be done in designing institutions for stabilizing population. But before much progress can be made on these issues, we must recognize their necessity and blow the whistle on growthmania.

AN EMERGING POLITICAL ECONOMY OF FINITE WANTS AND NONGROWTH

Although the ideas expressed by Mill have been totally dominated by growthmania, a growing number of economists have frankly expressed their disenchantment with the growth ideology. Arguments stressing ecologically sound limits to wealth and population have been made by Boulding and by Spengler (both past presidents of the American Economic Association).[38] Recently E. J. Mishan, Tibor Scitovsky, and Staffan Linder have made penetrating antigrowth arguments.[39] There is also much in Galbraith that is antigrowth —at least against growth of commodities for which the want must be manufactured along with the product.[40]

In spite of these beginnings, most economists are still hung up on the assumption of infinite wants, or the postulate of nonsatiety, as the mathematical economists call it. Any single want can be satisfied, but all wants in the aggregate cannot be. Wants are infinite in number if not in intensity, and the satisfaction of some wants stimulates other wants. If wants are infinite, growth is always justified—or so it would seem.

Even while accepting the foregoing hypothesis, we could still object to growthmania on the grounds that, given the completely inadequate definition of GNP, "growth" simply means the satisfaction of ever more trivial wants while simultaneously creating ever more powerful externalities which destroy ever more important environmental amenities. To defend ourselves against these externalities, we produce even more, and instead of subtracting the purely defensive expenditures, we add them! For example, the medical bills paid for treatment of cigarette-induced cancer and pollution-induced emphysema are added to GNP when, in a welfare sense, they should clearly be subtracted. This should be labeled *swelling*, not growth. The satisfaction of wants created by brainwashing and "hogwashing" the public over the mass media also represents mostly swelling. A policy of maximizing GNP is practically equivalent to a policy of maximizing depletion and pollution.

We may hesitate to say "maximizing" pollution on the grounds that the production inflow into the stock can be greater than the consumption outflow as long as the stock increases, as it does in our growing economy. To the extent that wealth becomes more durable, the production of waste can be kept low by expanding the stock. But is this in fact what happens? In the present system, if we want to maximize production, we must have a market for it. Increasing the durability of goods reduces the replacement demand. The faster things wear out, the greater can be the flow of production and income. To the extent that consumer apathy and weakening competition permit, there is every incentive to minimize durability. Planned obsolescence and programmed self-destruction and other waste-making practices, so well discussed by Vance Packard, are the logical result of maximizing a marketed physical flow.[41] If we must maximize something, it should be the stock of wealth, not the flow—but with full awareness of the ecological limits that constrain this maximization.

But why this perverse emphasis on flows, this "flow fetishism" of standard economic theory? Again, I believe the underlying issue is distribution. There is no theoretical explanation, much less justification, for the distribution of the stock of wealth. It is a historical datum. But the distribution of the flow of income is at least partly explained by marginal productivity theory, which at times is even misinterpreted as a justification. Everyone gets a part of the flow—call it wages, interest, rent, or profit—and it all looks rather fair. But not everyone owns a piece of the stock, and that does not seem quite so fair. Looking only at the flow helps to avoid disturbing thoughts.

Even the common-sense arguments for infinite wants—that the rich seem to enjoy their high consumption—cannot be generalized without committing the fallacy of composition. If all earned the same high income, a consumption limit occurs sooner than if only a minority had high incomes. The reason is that a large part of the consumption by plutocrats is consumption of personal services rendered by the poor, which would not be available if all were rich. Plutocrats can easily spend large sums on consumption, since all the maintenance work of the household can be done by others. By hiring the poor to maintain and even purchase commodities for them, the rich devote their limited consumption time only to the most pleasurable aspects of consumption. The rich only ride their horses; they do not clean, comb, saddle, and feed them, nor do they clean out the stable. If all did their own maintenance work, consumption would perforce be less. Time sets a limit to consumption.

The big difficulty with the infinite wants assumption, however, is that pointed out by Keynes, who, in spite of the use made of his theories in support of growth, was certainly no advocate of unlimited growth, as can be seen in the following quotation:

> Now it is true that the needs of human beings may seem to be insatiable. But they fall into two classes—those needs which are absolute in the sense that we feel them whatever the situation of our fellow human beings may be, and those which are relative in the sense that we feel them only if their satisfaction lifts us above, makes us feel superior to, our fellows. Needs of the second class, those which satisfy the desire for superiority, may indeed be insatiable; for the higher the general level, the higher still are they. But this is not so true of the absolute needs—a point may soon be reached, much sooner perhaps than we are all of us aware of, when those needs are satisfied in the sense that we prefer to devote our further energies to noneconomic purposes.[42]

For Keynes, real absolute needs are those that can be satisfied and do not require inequality and invidious comparison for their very existence; relative wants are the wants of vanity and are insatiable. Lumping the two categories together and speaking of infinite wants in general can only muddy the waters. The same distinction is implicit in the quotation from Mill, who spoke disparagingly of "consuming things which give little or no pleasure except as representative of wealth."

Some two and a half millennia before Keynes, the prophet Isaiah, in a discourse on idolatry, developed the theme more fully.

> [Man] cuts down cedars; or he chooses a holm tree or an oak and lets it grow strong among the trees of the forest; he plants a cedar and the rain nourishes it. Then it becomes fuel for a man; and he takes a part of it and warms himself, he kindles a fire and bakes bread; also he makes a god and worships it, he makes a graven image and falls down before it. Half of it he burns in the fire; over the half he eats flesh, he roasts meat and is satisfied; also he warms himself and says, "Aha, I am warm, I have seen the fire!" And the rest of it he makes into a god, his idol; and he falls down to it and worships it; he prays to it and says; "Deliver me, for thou art my god!"
>
> They know not, nor do they discern; for he has shut their eyes so that they cannot see, and their minds so that they cannot understand. No one considers, nor is there knowledge or discernment to say, "Half of it I burned in the fire, I also baked bread on its coals, I roasted flesh and have eaten; and shall I make the residue of it an abomination? Shall I fall down before a block of wood?" He feeds on ashes, a deluded mind has led him astray, and he cannot deliver himself or say, "Is there not a lie in my right hand?" [Isa. 44:14–20]

The first half of the tree burned for warmth and food, the finite absolute wants of Keynes, the bottom portion of GNP devoted to basic wants—these are all approximately synonymous. The second or surplus half of the tree used to make an idol, Keynes's infinite relative wants or wants of vanity, the top or surplus (growing) portion of GNP used to satisfy marginal wants—these are also synonymous. Furthermore, the surplus half of the tree used to make an idol, an abomination, is symbolic of the use made of the economic surplus throughout history of enslaving and coercing others by gaining control over the economic surplus and obliging people to "fall down before a block of wood." The controllers of the surplus may be a priesthood that controls physical idols made from the surplus and used to extract more surplus in the form of offerings and tribute. Or they may be feudal lords who, through the power given by possession of the land, extract a surplus in the form of rent and the *corvée;* or capitalists (state or private) who use the surplus in the form of capital to gain more surplus in the form of interest and quasi-rents. If growth must cease, the surplus becomes less important, and so do those who control it. If the surplus is not to lead to growth, then it must be consumed, and ethical demands for equal participation in the consumption of the surplus could not be countered by arguments that inequality is necessary for accumulation. Accumulation in excess of depreciation, and the privileges attached thereto, would not exist.

We no longer speak of worshiping idols. Instead of idols we have an abomination called GNP, large parts of which, however, bear such revealing names as Apollo, Poseidon, and Zeus. Instead of worshiping the idol, we maximize it. The idol has become rather more abstract and conceptual and rather less concrete and material, while the mode of adoration has become technical rather than personal. But fundamentally, idolatry remains idolatry, and we cry out to the growing surplus, "Deliver me, for thou art my god!" Instead we should pause and ask with Isaiah, "Is there not a lie in my right hand?"

NOTES

1. Thomas S. Kuhn, *The Structure of Scientific Revolutions,* 2nd ed., Chicago: University of Chicago Press, 1969.

2. Arthur Koestler, *The Sleepwalkers,* New York: Macmillan, 1968.

3. Michael Polanyi, *Personal Knowledge,* New York: Harper & Row, 1964.

4. Evesy Domar, "Expansion and Employment," *American Economic Review,* March 1947, pp. 34–55.

5. This, of course, is a *physical* axiom. If a "quantity" has no physical dimensions, it is not limited by physical finitude. Thus "psychic income" or welfare may increase forever. But the physical stock that yields want-satisfying services, and the physical flows which maintain that stock, are limited. What about GNP? If we choose to measure GNP in such a way that it reflects total want satisfaction, then presumably it could increase forever. However, this is emphatically *not* the way we measure GNP at present. Prices (exchange values) and quantities are the basis of GNP. Prices bear no relation whatsoever to total utility or want satisfaction.

Quantity probably has borne a direct relation to welfare in the past. Whether it still does today in affluent countries is very debatable. But, in any event, quantities are limited by physical considerations. Even quantities of "services rendered" have some irreducible physical dimension. It is always some *thing* that yields a service —for example, a machine or a skilled person.

6. *Science,* November 19, 1971, pp. 847–848.

7. Kuhn, *Structure of Scientific Revolutions,* p. 92.

8. The high professional reputations of Boulding and Georgescu-Roegen are based on their many contributions within the orthodox paradigm. Their work outside that paradigm has probably diminished rather than enhanced their academic prestige.

9. J. Ruskin, *Unto This Last: Four Essays on the First Principles of Political Economy,* ed. Lloyd J. Hubenka, Lincoln: University of Nebraska Press, 1967, p. 86 (originally published 1860).

10. Nicholas Georgescu-Roegen, *The Entropy Law and the Economic Process,* Cambridge, Mass.: Harvard University Press, 1971, p. 21.

11. A. C. Fisher and F. M. Peterson, ''The Environment in Economics: A Survey,'' *Journal of Economic Literature,* March 1976, p. 1.

12. Robert Solow, ''The Economics of Resources or the Resources of Economics,'' *American Economic Review,* May 1974, p. 11.

13. Frederick Soddy, *Cartesian Economics: The Bearing of Physical Science upon State Stewardship,* London: Hendersons, 1922, p. 9.

14. Harold Barnett and Chandler Morse, *Scarcity and Growth: The Economics of Natural Resource Availability,* Resources for the Future. Baltimore: Johns Hopkins University Press, 1963, p. 11.

15. Imagine a demon who opens and shuts a window in a partition separating two volumes of gas so as to let the fast-moving molecules go from right to left and the slow-moving molecules go from left to right, thereby sorting the two. If the two compartments were originally at equilibrium (equal temperature), then the sorting action of the demon would cause a "spontaneous" increase in temperature of the left compartment and a decrease in the right compartment. This would contradict the entropy law, which forbids spontaneous movement away from equilibrium. The natural or "downhill" direction is toward more mixing of entities; sorting of entities would be like going uphill, which should use energy rather than liberate energy. The temperature differential created by the demon would provide a source of continuous energy, a kind of perpetual motion machine, which is contrary to the laws of physics.

16. *Fertility* refers to actual reproduction, as opposed to *fecundity,* which refers to reproductive potential or capacity. One measure of fertility is the Gross Reproduction Rate, defined in note 17.

17. GRR is roughly the ratio of one generation to the preceding generation, assuming that all children born survive to the end of their reproductive life. It is usually defined in terms of females only. The length of a generation is the mean age of mothers at childbirth.

18. United Nations, *Population Bulletin of the United Nations,* No. 7, 1963, New York: United Nations, 1965.

19. Goran Ohlin, *Population Control and Economic Development*, Paris: Development Centre of the Organisation for Economic Co-operation and Development, 1967.

20. According to Robert E. Baldwin: "In the 1957–58 to 1963–64 period, the less developed nations maintained a 4.7 percent annual growth rate in gross national product compared to a 4.4 percent rate in the developed economies. The gap in per capita income widened because population increased at only 1.3 percent annually in the developed countries compared to a 2.4 percent annual rate in the less developed economies." (*Economic Development and Growth*, New York: Wiley, 1966, p. 8).

21. The term *stationary state* has been burdened with two distinct meanings in economics. The classical meaning is that of an actual state of affairs toward which the real world is supposed to be evolving; that is, a teleological or eschatological concept. The neoclassical sense of the terms is entirely mechanistic—an epistemologically useful fiction like an ideal gas or frictionless machine—and describes an economy in which tastes and techniques are constant. The latter sense is more current in economics today, but the former meaning is the relevant one in this discussion.

22. J. S. Mill, *Principles of Political Economy*, Vol. II, London: John W. Parker, 1857, pp. 320–326, with omissions.

23. All quotes in this paragraph are from Mark Blaug, *Economy Theory in Retrospect*, Homewood, Ill.: Irwin, 1968, pp. 214–221. Blaug's views are, I think representative of orthodox economists.

24. By *stock* is meant a quantity measured at a point in time; for example, a population census or a balance sheet of assets and liabilities as of a certain date. By *flow* is meant a quantity measured across some actual or conceptual boundary over a period of time; for example, births and deaths per year or an income and loss statement for a given year.

   The boundary lines separating the stock of wealth from the rest of the physical world may sometimes be fuzzy. But the main criterion is that physical wealth must in some way have been transformed by human beings to increase its usefulness over its previous state as primary matter or energy. For example, coal in the ground is primary matter and energy; coal in the inventory of firms and households is physical wealth; coal after use in the form of carbon dioxide and soot is waste matter. The heat produced by the coal is partly usable and partly unusable. Eventually, all the heat becomes unusable or waste heat, but, while it is usable, it is a part of the physical stock of wealth. For some purposes, we may wish to define proven reserves in mines as part of wealth, but that presents no problems.

25. Staffan B. Linder, *The Harried Leisure Class*, New York: Columbia University Press, 1970.

26. A. J. Lotka, *Elements of Mathematical Biology*, New York: Dover, 1957. Republication. See especially Chapter 24.

27. Report of the Committee for Environmental Information before Joint Congressional Committee on Atomic Energy, January 29, 1970. Quoted in "The Space Available Report of the Committee for Environmental Information," *Environment*, March 1970, p. 7.

28. Herman E. Daly, "On Economics as a Life Science," *Journal of Political Economy*, July, 1968, pp. 392–406. Reprinted in this volume.

29. Erwin Schrödinger, *What Is Life?* New York: Macmillan, 1945.

30. Kenneth E. Boulding, "The Economics of the Coming Spaceship Earth," in Henry Jarrett, ed., *Environmental Quality in a Growing Economy*, Baltimore: Johns Hopkins Press, 1966. Reprinted in this volume.

31. Eugene P. Odum, "The Strategy of Ecosystem Development," *Science*, April 18, 1969.

32. Services are included in GNP and are not in themselves physical outputs. However, increasing service outputs often require increases in physical inputs to the service sector, so that there is an indirect physical component. Leisure is not counted in GNP, and more physical inputs are not necessarily required as the amount to leisure is increased.

33. Linder, *Harried Leisure Class*.

34. Bertrand Russell, *In Praise of Idleness and Other Essays*, London: Allen and Unwin, 1935, pp. 16–17.

35. Joan Robinson, *Economic Philosophy*, London: Watts, 1962, p. 55.

36. Robert Theobald, *Free Men and Free Markets*, Garden City, N.Y.: Doubleday, 1965.

37. Oskar Lange, *On the Economic Theory of Socialism*, ed. Benjamin E. Lippincott, New York: McGraw-Hill, 1964.

38. Boulding, "Economics of Coming Spaceship Earth"; J. J. Spengler, Public Address, Yale Forestry School, Summer 1969.

39. E. J. Mishan, *The Costs of Economic Growth*, New York: Praeger, 1967; Tibor Scitovsky, "What Price Economic Growth," *Papers on Welfare and Growth*, Stanford, Calif.: Stanford University Press, 1964; Linder, *Harried Leisure Class*.

40. J. K. Galbraith, *The Affluent Society*, Boston: Houghton Mifflin, 1958.

41. Vance Packard, *The Waste Makers*, New York: Pocket Books, 1963.

42. J. M. Keynes, "Economic Possibilities for Our Grandchildren," in *Essays in Persuasion*, New York: Norton, 1963 (originally published 1931).

I

ECOLOGY: ULTIMATE MEANS AND BIOPHYSICAL CONSTRAINTS

Any physical object which by its influence
deteriorates its environment commits suicide.

ALFRED NORTH WHITEHEAD, *Sciences and the Modern World*, 1925

INTRODUCTION

Herman E. Daly

"All flesh is grass," said the prophet Isaiah. That is probably the most concise statement ever made of the ecological constraints on human life. But such visions of unity and wholeness have been fragmented by the specialization of modern thought. The economist's abstract world of commodities, with its laws of motion and equilibrium, has very few points of contact left with "grass," and is even in danger of losing touch with "flesh." Seemingly, economics has become detached from its own biophysical foundations. Standard textbooks do little to counteract this trend, representing the economic process—according to economist Nicholas Georgescu-Roegen—with a mechanistic diagram of a circular flow, "a pendulum movement between production and consumption within a completely closed system." In modern economic growth theory, aggregate production functions generally ignore nature and natural resources completely. Physical scientists, such as M. King Hubbert, find this neglect rather perplexing:

> One speaks of the rate of growth of GNP. I haven't the faintest idea what this means when I try to translate it into coal, and oil, and iron, and the other physical quantities which are required to run an industry. So far as I have been able to find out, the quantity GNP is a monetary bookkeeping entity. It obeys

the laws of money. It can be expanded or diminished, created or destroyed, but it does not obey the laws of physics.[1]

Even though GNP is an abstract entity, it is a value *index* of an aggregate of *physical* quantities. Value is the product of prices times those quantities. In calculating real GNP and its growth rate, we hold constant both absolute and relative prices for the purpose of isolating and measuring *quantitative* change. Although GNP cannot be expressed in simple physical units, it remains an index of physical quantities and therefore should be very much subject to laws of physics. Economic models that ignore this dependence are grossly deficient and are in large part responsible for our present ecological crisis.

Earlier thinkers have called attention to this deficiency, and some of their words bear repeating. J. A. Hobson, a British economic heretic of the late nineteenth and early twentieth century (familiar to economics students for his theory of underconsumption, which influenced Keynes, and his theory of imperialism, which influenced Lenin), noted that

> all serviceable organic activities consume tissue and expend energy, the biological costs of the services they render. Though this economy may not correspond in close quantitative fashion to a pleasure and pain economy or to any conscious valuation, it must be taken as the groundwork for that conscious valuation. For most economic purposes we are well-advised to prefer the organic test to any other test of welfare, bearing in mind that many organic costs do not register themselves easily or adequately in terms of conscious pain or disutility, while organic gains are not always interpretable in conscious enjoyment.[2]

The mathematical biologist A. J. Lotka, noted for his contributions to demography in the early years of the twentieth century, expressed a similar insight:

> Underlying our economic manifestations are biological phenomena which we share in common with other species; and . . . .the laying bare and clearly formulating of the relations thus involved—in other words the analysis of biophysical foundations of economics—is one of the problems coming within the program of physical biology.[3]

Clearly, Hobson and Lotka saw the importance of natural bases for economic thinking.

And so do the authors in Part I. The articles here deal with the biophysical foundations of economics and the groundwork for conscious valuation. In "Humanity at the Crossroads," biologists Paul and Anne Ehrlich provide an overview of the issue in terms of a historical choice point between the "growth-manic" path of the orthodox economist and the "sustainable society" path of the ecologists and bioeconomists. Perhaps the major blind spots of growth economists are their lack of appreciation of the second law of thermodynamics and its manifold implications and their failure to recognize the magnitude and fragility of the life-support services provided by the very natural systems whose proper functioning is being disrupted by the ever-larger entropic flow of materials and energy required by economic growth. As R. L. Sinsheimer has noted, not only economic growth but the very process of scientific en-deavor "rests upon the faith that our technological ventures will not displace some key element of our protective environment and thereby collapse our ecological niche." Sinsheimer's article is included in Part II, but, like most of the articles in this volume, it cuts across the categories of ecology, ethics, and economics.

An introduction to "Availability, Entropy, and the Laws of Thermodyna-mics" is provided by Ehrlich, Ehrlich, and Holdren, setting the stage for Nicholas Georgescu-Roegen's discussion of "The Entropy Law and the Eco-nomic Problem" which is essentially the introduction to his magistral work *The Entropy Law and the Economic Process,* a book that made a major contribution toward reuniting economics with its biophysical foundations. The implications of this analysis are extended in the excerpts from his "Energy and Economic Myths," and some general policy implications, which he calls a "minimal bioeconomic program," are spelled out. Georgescu-Roegen's reser-vations about the concept of a steady-state economy are also included (and replied to in my Postscript).

Geologist Earl Cook's discussion of the "Limits to Exploitation of Non-renewable Resources" gives a factual, concrete discussion of one source of low entropy, the concentrated deposits of minerals in the earth's crust, provid-ing an empirical counterpart to Georgescu-Roegen's more theoretical discus-sion. As Cook points out, "mineral and energy deposits have low entropy relative to average rock." Resource depletion plus waste accumulation there-fore comes to the same thing as entropy increase.

Renewable resources provide a means of tapping the other source of low entropy, the relatively permanent flow of solar energy, which, if managed on a sustainable-yield basis, can provide a quasi-permanent source of useful low entropy. But renewable resources can easily be rendered nonrenewable by overexploitation. The institutional conditions leading to overexploitation are analyzed by biologist Garrett Hardin in his classic "Tragedy of the Com-mons," now supplemented by a new section of "Second Thoughts" on the subject, which Dr. Hardin kindly wrote at the editor's invitation.

NOTES

1. M. K. Hubbert *in* F. F. Darling and J. P. Milton, eds., *Future Environments of North America,* Garden City, N.Y.: The Natural History Press, 1966, p. 291.

2. J. A. Hobson, *Economics and Ethics,* Boston: Heath, 1929, p. xxi.

3. A. J. Lotka, *Elements of Mathematical Biology,* New York: Dover, 1957.

1

HUMANITY AT
THE CROSSROADS

Paul R. Ehrlich and Anne H. Ehrlich

A favorite pastime of biologists and historians is identifying past "revolutions," such as the evolution of the genetic code and of multicellularity, the adoption of an arboreal life-style by the primates, the cultural revolution, the agricultural revolution, the industrial revolution, and so on. These revolutions can be viewed as historical "choice points." Would our ancestors remain bumbling coacervate droplets, unable accurately to replicate themselves, or would they have a simple but elegant genetic code that permitted highly accurate copying? Would human beings be highly dispersed, nomadic organisms with considerable leisure time and a few simple artifacts, or would they become highly "clumped" in their distribution, relatively sedentary, hard working, and possessed of numerous massive artifacts?

With the benefit of hindsight, the "choices" made seem obvious, natural, and even inevitable, but they might not have seemed so natural to a sophisti-

Reprinted with permission of authors and publisher from *The Stanford Magazine*, Spring/Summer 1978, published by the Stanford Alumni Association.

cated observer at the time. One can imagine that many systems of controlling replication were tried and proved failures. A brilliant coacervate droplet might even have concluded that self-copying was an impossible dream. Similarly, we can be sure that many of the early attempts at farming were disastrous flops under the impact of inclement weather, pests, or aggressive nomads. Many concerned citizens of ten millennia ago might have questioned the wisdom of abandoning the tried and true life-style of gathering and hunting. Why increase both the work and the risks?

Today, *Homo sapiens* is at another historical choice point. This one is unique in the history of Earth because it involves a global culture and the choices are being openly debated. To oversimplify, they may be described as the choice between a business-as-usual "growthmanic" scenario and an ecologically oriented "sustainable society" scenario.

The growthmanic scenario is the one found in most newspapers, magazines, and between the ears of most businessmen, politicians, and economists. It is grounded in the dominant social paradigm. Fundamentally, that paradigm assumed that the course taken by Western civilization in the past century or so, and particularly in the years since World War II, is the road to Utopia. Continuing economic growth will lead to an earthly paradise. The poor will get rich and the rich will get richer. Problems of resource depletion and pollution will be solved by applications of higher and higher technology, paid for by an ever larger Gross National Product. Problems of hunger will be solved by spreading Western agricultural technology over the entire Earth and improving its already high performance. Problems of population growth (if they are perceived as problems) will be solved by improved contraceptive technology promoted by satellite educational systems. Indeed, under this scenario all humans problems are basically seen as being solved by a combination of economic growth and technological cleverness. Even the threat of nuclear war can be removed by ending poverty, by balancing terrors, and/or by electronic surveillance of terrorists. The major constraints on the system are viewed not to be limits imposed by nature but a lack of political and social will and the opposition of Luddites.

The sustainable society scenario—which we, most other ecologists, and some economists favor—is based on a diametrically opposed view of the human situation. Continuing economic growth in overdeveloped countries and population growth everywhere are viewed as harbingers of catastrophe. According to this view, experience indicates that more economic growth in overdeveloped countries is unlikely to improve the condition of the world's poor—indeed, it is more likely to worsen it. Under the sustainable society scenario, the Gross National Product is viewed as a profoundly limited indicator that measures very little of significance to the human condition—an indicator that tends to confuse waste with product. Growth is seen not as a cure, but as a disease. Emphasis is placed on ending population growth and making a rapid transition to a society with a steady-state economy (SSE).

An SSE is one in which material throughput is minimized by limiting resource depletion (and thus automatically limiting pollution), the quality of capital stocks is maximized, and the distribution of wealth is made relatively equitable. It is not necessarily a static economy—progress in efficiency and trade-offs among different competing firms and activities can go on within the constraint of minimal throughput.

Another feature of a sustainable society is dependence primarily on renewable forms of energy such as solar, wind, and hydroelectric (that is, a soft energy path) rather than on depletable fossil fuels or nuclear power, which are both overcentralized and too hazardous. We feel, as do many other advocates of a sustainable society, that both decentralization and a reduction of the *scale* of human activities would be highly desirable.

Why do we favor the sustainable society rather than continued growth? The best reason is that, contrary to what many think, the growthmanic scenario is a recipe for disaster. The persistence of the notion that long-continued growth is both possible and desirable can largely be traced to the nearly complete ignorance of the public in general, and many economists in particular, of basic natural laws. Examples of this ignorance abound. Harvard economist Richard Zeckhauser has stated, in effect, that oil could be recycled. Two economists for Resources for the Future, Harold Barnett and Chandler Morse, have written that "advances in fundamental science have made it possible to take advantage of the uniformity of energy/matter—a uniformity that makes it feasible without preassignable limit to escape the quantitative constraints imposed by the character of the earth's crust."

Of course, that most indestructible of physical laws, the second law of thermodynamics, makes both of those statements the rough equivalent of saying, "Fear not, we'll run the world with perpetual-motion machines." Indeed, one of a group of economists busily planning perpetual-motion-machine solutions to the problem of having infinite growth on a finite planet once asked us, "Who knows what the second law will be like in a hundred years?" The answer is that the law is not based on any complex theory—it is supported by billions of observations made daily by all of us. If it did not hold, the world would truly be interesting—ice cubes would be as likely to appear spontaneously in a martini as to melt in it, it would be as easy to sort salt out of a salt-sugar mixture as to mix the two, and squashed cats could reassemble themselves on the highway and trot off.

But even if most economists and businessmen choose to ignore the laws of nature, there is still little excuse for their continuing love affair with the concept of perpetual growth. They presumably all are able to work compound-interest problems and so are quite capable of evaluating one of the most fundamental tenets of the business-as-usual scenario—that growth always will be a central feature of a healthy economic system. A few simplified calculations immediately expose how preposterous this notion is. Suppose that we began living in an economic paradise where a steady 5 percent annual growth in per capita real Gross National Product were occurring. After about a century of such growth, the United States would hit the so-called "millionaire barrier" and the average per capita income would be one million 1978 dollars per person. If equity in distribution had been achieved by then, everybody would be a millionaire, and each family would have several million dollars available to it annually. This presumably would represent the earthly paradise visualized by the average economist. Would everybody own a Cadillac or a Porsche? If so, who would build them? Who would service them? Who would pump the gas into them? Few millionaires, I suspect, would be anxious to do the routine chores necessary to keep society functioning. Furthermore, although everyone's absolute needs would be satisfied by some miracle, relative needs (under standard economic thinking) would remain in a nation of millionaires, presumably requiring further growth.

Of course, humanity is not going to have to worry about reaching the millionaire barrier. Material growth on Earth will be stopped in the not-too-distant future—quite likely within the next 50 years—because the ecological costs of growth will become greater than society can pay. In the United States, these costs are likely to put the brakes on growth even sooner.

The primary constraints on growth will be the impact of human activities on the absolutely essential public-service functions of ecological systems. These systems maintain the quality of the atmosphere, dispose of our wastes, recycle essential nutrients, control the vast majority of potential pests and disease vectors, supply us with food from the sea, generate soils, and run the hydrological cycle, among other vital services. From the point of view of long-term human welfare, the assaults that society mounts on these systems are far more important than the direct effects on human health of various pollutants.

Living in a polluted environment presents the personal threat of early death from cancer, heart attack, emphysema, and other nasty diseases. Statistically, this results in lowered life expectancies and, to the degree that society wishes to try to ameliorate the effects, in increased costs of health care. But our species got along with life expectancies in the vicinity of 30 years for more than a million years and some groups of human beings still do not have much higher life expectancies today. Civilization could persist even if there were a 10- or 20-year reduction in life expectancy. But civilization could not persist without those free life-support services rendered by ecological systems.

The ignorant will claim that, with application of more energy and technology, substitutes could be found to replace those ecological services. But in most cases either no one knows how to replace them or substitution on the required scale is impossible.

Furthermore, the amount of energy used by a society is the best index available of the level of assault that it makes on ecological systems. Energy is used to plow under and pave over ecosystems and to generate the pollutants that poison them and otherwise disrupt their functioning. Further increasing the use of energy will thus tend to exacerbate, not solve, environmental problems. Environmental deterioration is very clearly a function (albeit a complex function) of the number of people in a society and their per capita energy use. With both of those figures climbing globally at rapid rates, the prospects for maintaining the public-service functions of ecosystems seem dim indeed. Yet such growth is precisely what seems promised under the business-as-usual scenario. One must note also that the ultimate breakdown of the ecological systems might not come gradually. One potential abrupt cause is thermonuclear war, which itself could be triggered by increasing competition for increasingly scarce resources.

The above comments should help explain why ecologists have a totally different view of the "energy crisis" from that held by most people. We see the crisis as one of *too much energy use* rather than too little energy supply. It also explains in part why we do not view continued economic growth in countries like the United States as a way to cure poverty. The ecological systems of the planet cannot stand much more pressure from the rich countries. These countries should be striving to reduce their economic throughput and relax the pressures they are placing on life-support systems. What economic growth there is to be in the future should be concentrated in poor countries and carefully controlled and directed there.

Another reason for being unenthusiastic about growth as a cure for poverty is the historical record—this notion and the related "trickle-down" theory of development simply do not stand up under scrutiny. Growth has *not* reduced the gap between the rich and the poor, and simple economic analysis shows that growth alone will not. Growth comes from the reinvestment of economic surpluses and naturally the owners of those surpluses make investments intended to benefit themselves.

But there are some rays of hope. The traditional economic paradigm is under attack from economists as well as ecologists. Increasingly, people within the profession are looking for the causes of the failure of economics to solve the basic problem of allocation of scarce goods within a democratic framework, to deal with the questions of absolute scarcity (or even recognize its existence), and to face up to the constraints under which any economic system must operate. In the United States, economists in the Marxian tradition like Stanford's John Gurley, rebels like John Kenneth Galbraith (who believes that absolute wants should be segregated from relative wants), and champions of steady-state, spaceship, and bioeconomics like Herman Daly, Kenneth Boulding, Nicholas Georgescu-Roegen, and Emile Benoit are making it increasingly difficult for the old guard to pretend that all is well. The change in economic thinking reflected in Daly's brief and brilliant new book, *Steady-State Economics* (W. H. Freeman and Company, 1977), is likely to be more profound than the Keynesian revolution of the 1930s and '40s. In the course of outlining an ecologically and ethically sensible economic system, Daly exposes the intellectual bankruptcy of growthmanic economics with the precision of a fine surgeon dissecting out a brain tumor.

Like other diagnosticians before him, Daly recognizes that his profession is suffering from an advanced case of "physics envy." Erroneously believing that the natural sciences are value free, economists eschew the judgments that should be the essence of political economy. Absurdly, the "scientific" economist is unable to decide whether a gallon of fuel from society's stock would be more efficiently used to help keep a poor man's family from freezing than to drive a rich man's yacht an additional tenth of a mile. Interpersonal comparisons of utility are thought unscientific because they cannot be quantified and are thus defined out of economics!

Having no goals (since goals too are "unscientific"), value-free economics gallops on like the headless horseman; the ride itself apparently is sufficient end. Along the way, the horseman frequently uses arcane mathematical techniques for what Kenneth Boulding has called "suboptimization"—doing efficiently that which should never be done at all.

Humanity is rushing toward the crossroads. One fork is the path of the headless horseman and his lethal conventional wisdom. He gestures us to follow, to ride ever faster down a foggy road to an unspecified destination. The horseman admits there is a fallen bridge ahead but assures us that the chasm is so far down the road that we need not concern ourselves with it. Ecologists and the new breed of economists recommend the other turn. That road is also blanketed with a fog of uncertainty, and there is an unbridged gulf on that route, too. But the advocates of a soft energy path and a steady-state economy recommend not acceleration but deceleration. They want to stop safely and establish a sustainable society on this side of the abyss.

2

AVAILABILITY, ENTROPY, AND THE LAWS OF THERMODYNAMICS

Paul R. Ehrlich, Anne H. Ehrlich, and John P. Holdren

Many processes in nature and in technology involve the transformation of energy from one form into others. For example, light from the sun is transformed, upon striking a meadow, into thermal energy in the warmed soil, rocks, and plants; into latent heat of vaporization as water evaporates from the soil and through the surface of the plants; and into chemical energy captured in the plants by phothosynthesis. Some of the thermal energy, in turn, is transformed into infrared electromagnetic radiation heading skyward. The imposing science of thermodynamics is just the set of principles governing the bookkeeping by which one keeps track of energy as it moves through such transformations. A grasp of these principles of bookkeeping is essential to an understanding of many problems in environmental sciences and energy technology.

From *Ecoscience* by Paul R. Ehrlich, Anne H. Ehrlich, and John P. Holdren. W. H. Freeman and Company. Copyright © 1977.

The essence of the accounting is embodied in two concepts known as the first and second laws of thermodynamics. No exception to either one has ever been observed. The first law, also known as the law of conservation of energy, says that energy can neither be created nor destroyed. If energy in one form or one place disappears, the same amount must show up in another form or another place. In other words, although transformations can alter the *distribution* of amounts of energy among its different forms, the *total* amount of energy, when all forms are taken into account, remains the same. The term *energy consumption,* therefore, is a misnomer; energy is used, but it is not really consumed. One can speak of fuel consumption, because fuel, as such, does get used up. But when we burn gasoline, the amounts of energy that appear as mechanical energy, thermal energy, electromagnetic radiation, and other forms are exactly equal all together to the amount of chemical potential energy that disappears. The accounts must always balance; apparent exceptions have invariably turned out to stem from measurement errors or from overlooking categories. The immediate relevance of the first law for human affairs is often stated succinctly as, "You can't get something for nothing."

Yet, if energy is stored work it might seem that the first law is also saying, "You can't lose!" (by saying that the total amount of stored work in all forms never changes). If the amount of stored work never diminishes, how can we become worse off? One obvious answer is that we can become worse off if energy flows to places where we can no longer get at it—for example, infrared radiation escaping from Earth into space. Then the stored work is no longer accessible to us, although it still exists. A far more fundamental point, however, is that *different kinds of stored work are not equally convertible into useful, applied work.* We can therefore become worse off if energy is transformed from a more convertible form to a less convertible one, even though no energy is destroyed and even if the energy has not moved to an inaccessible place. The degree of convertibility of energy—stored workinto applied work is often called *availability.*

Energy in forms having high availability (that is, in which a relatively large fraction of the stored work can be converted into applied work) is often called high-grade energy. Correspondingly, energy of which only a small fraction can be converted to applied work is called low-grade energy, and energy that moves from the former category to the latter is said to have been degraded. Electricity and the chemical energy stored in gasoline are examples of high-grade energy; the infrared radiation from a light bulb and the thermal energy in an automobile exhaust are corresponding examples of lower-grade energy. The quantitative measure of the availability of thermal energy is temperature. More specifically, the larger the *temperature difference* between a substance and its environment, the more convertible into applied work is the thermal energy the substance contains; in other words, the greater the temperature difference, the greater the availability. A small pan of water boiling at 100° C in surroundings that are at 20° C represents considerable available energy because of the temperature difference; the water in a swimming pool at the same 20° C temperature as the surroundings contains far more total thermal energy than the water in the pan, but the availability of the thermal energy in the swimming pool is zero, because there is no temperature difference between it and its surroundings.

With this background, one can state succinctly the subtle and overwhelmingly important message of the second law of thermodynamics: *all physical processes, natural and technological, proceed in such a way that the availability of the energy involved decreases.* (Idealized processes can be constructed theoretically in which the availability of the energy involved stays constant, rather than decreasing, but in all real processes there is *some* decrease. The second law says that an *increase* is not possible, even in an ideal process.) As with the first law, apparent violations of the second law often stem from leaving something out of the accounting. In many processes, for example, the availability of energy in some *part* of the affected system increases, but the decrease of availability elsewhere in the system is always large enough to result in a net decrease in availability of energy overall. What is consumed when we use energy, then, is not energy itself but its availability for doing useful work.

The statement of the second law given above is deceptively simple; whole books have been written about equivalent formulations of the law and about its implications. Among the most important of these formulations and implications are the following:

1. In any transformation of energy, some of the energy is degraded.

2. No process is possible whose sole result is the conversion of a given quantity of heat (thermal energy) into an equal amount of useful work.

3. No process is possible whose sole result is the flow of heat from a colder body to a hotter one.

4. The availability of a given quantity of energy can only be used once; that is, the property of convertibility into useful work cannot be "recycled."

5. In spontaneous processes, concentrations (of anything) tend to disperse, structure tends to disappear, order becomes disorder.

That Statements 1 through 4 are equivalent to or follow from our original formulation is readily verified. To see that statement 5 is related to the other statements, however, requires establishing a formal connection between order and availability of energy. This connection has been established in thermodynamics through the concept of *entropy,* a well defined measure of disorder that can be shown to be a measure of unavailability of energy, as well. A statement of the second law that contains or is equivalent to all the others is: *all physical processes proceed in such a way that the entropy of the universe increases.* (Not only can't we win—we can't break even, and we can't get out of the game!)

Consider some everyday examples of various aspects of the second law. If a partitioned container is filled with hot water on one side and cold water on the other and is left to itself, the hot water cools and the cold water warms—heat flows from hotter to colder. Note that the opposite process (the hot water getting hotter and the cold getting colder) does not violate the first law, conservation of energy. That it does not occur illustrates the second law. Indeed, many processes can be imagined that satisfy the first law but violate the second and therefore are not expected to occur. As another example, consider adding a drop of dye to a glass of water. Intuition and the second law dictate that the dye will spread, eventually coloring all the water—concentrations disperse, order (the dye/no dye arrangement) disappears. The opposite process, the spontaneous concentration of dispersed dye, is consistent with conservation of energy but not with the second law.

A more complicated situation is that of the refrigerator, a device that certainly causes heat to flow from cold objects (the contents of the refrigerator —say, beer—which are made colder) to a hot one (the room, which the refrigerator makes warmer). But this heat flow is not the *sole* result of the operation of the refrigerator: energy must be supplied to the refrigeration cycle from an external source, and this energy is converted to heat and discharged to the room, along with the heat removed from the interior of the refrigerator. Overall, availability of energy has decreased, and entropy has increased.

One illustration of the power of the laws of thermodynamics is that in many situations they can be used to predict the maximum efficiency that could be achieved by a perfect machine, without specifying any details of the machine! (Efficiency may be defined, in this situation, as the ratio of useful work to total energy flow.) Thus, one can specify, for example, what *minimum* amount of energy is necessary to separate salt from seawater, to separate metals from their ores, and to separate pollutants from auto exhaust without knowing any details about future inventions that might be devised for these purposes. Similarly, if one is told the temperature of a source of thermal energy—say, the hot rock deep in Earth's crust—one can calculate rather easily the maximum efficiency with which this thermal energy can be converted to applied work, regardless of the cleverness of future inventors. In other words, *there are some fixed limits to technological innovation, placed there by fundamental laws of nature. . . .*

More generally, the laws of thermodynamics explain why we need a continual input of energy to maintain ourselves, why we must eat much more than a pound of food in order to gain a pound of weight, and why the total energy flow through plants will always be much greater than that through plant-eaters, which in turn will always be much greater than that through flesh-eaters. They also make it clear that *all* the energy used on the face of the Earth, whether of solar or nuclear origin, will ultimately be degraded to heat. Here the laws catch us both coming and going, for they put limits on the efficiency with which we can manipulate this heat. Hence, they pose the danger . . . that human society may make this planet uncomfortably warm with degraded energy long before it runs out of high-grade energy to consume.

Occasionally it is suggested erroneously that the process of biological evolution represents a violation of the second law of thermodynamics. After all, the development of complicated living organisms from primordial chemical precursors, and the growing structure and complexity of the biosphere over the eons, do appear to be the sort of spontaneous increases in order excluded by the second law. The catch is that Earth is not an isolated system; the process of evolution has been powered by the sun, and the decrease in entropy on Earth represented by the growing structure of the biosphere is more than counterbalanced by the increase in the entropy of the sun. . . .

It is often asked whether a revolutionary development in physics, such as Einstein's theory of relativity, might not open the way to circumvention of the laws of thermodynamics. Perhaps it would be imprudent to declare that in no distant corner of the universe or hitherto-unexplored compartment of subatomic matter will any exception ever turn up, even though our intrepid astrophysicists and particle physicists have not yet found a single one. But to wait for the laws of thermodynamics to be overturned as descriptions of everyday experiences on this planet is, literally, to wait for the day when beer refrigerates itself in hot weather and squashed cats on the freeway spontaneously reassemble themselves and trot away.

3

THE ENTROPY LAW AND
THE ECONOMIC PROBLEM

Nicholas Georgescu-Roegen

I

A curious event in the history of economic thought is that, years after the mechanistic dogma has lost its supremacy in physics and its grip on the philosophical world, the founders of the neoclassical school set out to erect an economic science after the pattern of mechanics—in the words of Jevons, as *"the mechanics of utility and self-interest."*[1] And while economics has made great strides since, nothing has happened to deviate economic thought from the mechanistic epistemology of the forefathers of standard economics. A glaring proof is the standard textbok representation of the economic process by a circular diagram, a pendulum movement between production and consumption within a completely closed system.[2] The situation is not different

"The Entropy Law and the Economic Problem" appeared previously in The University of Alabama *Distinguished Lecture Series,* No. 1, 1971. Reprinted by permission of the author and The University of Alabama.

with the analytical pieces that adorn the standard economic literature; they, too, reduce the economic process to a self-sustained mechanical analogue. The patent fact that between the economic process and the material environment there exists a continuous mutual influence which is history-making carries no weight with the standard economist. And the same is true of Marxist economists, who swear by Marx's dogma that everything nature offers man is a spontaneous gift.[3] In Marx's famous diagram of reproduction, too, the economic process is represented as a completely circular and self-sustaining affair.[4]

Earlier writers, however, pointed in another direction, as did Sir William Petty in arguing that labor is the father and nature is the mother of wealth.[5] The entire economic history of mankind proves beyond question that nature, too, plays an important role in the economic process as well as in the formation of economic value. It is high time, I believe, that we should accept this fact and consider its consequences for the economic problem of mankind. For, as I shall endeavor to show in this paper, some of these consequences have an exceptional importance for the understanding of the nature and the evolution of man's economy.

II

Some economists have alluded to the fact that man can neither create nor destroy matter or energy[6]—a truth which follows from the principle of conservation of matter-energy, alias the first law of thermodynamics. Yet no one seems to have been struck by the question—so puzzling in the light of this law—"what then does the economic process do?" All that we find in the cardinal literature is an occasional remark that man can produce only utilities, a remark which actually accentuates the puzzle. How is it possible for man to produce something material, given the fact that he cannot produce either matter or energy?

To answer this question, let us consider the economic process as a whole and view it only from the purely physical viewpoint. What we must note first of all is that this process is a partial process which, like all partial processes, is circumscribed by a boundary across which matter and energy are exchanged with the rest of the material universe.[7] The answer to the question of what this *material* process does is simple: it neither produces nor consumes matter-energy; it only absorbs matter-energy and throws it out continuously. This is what pure physics teaches us. However, economics—let us say it high and loud—is not pure physics, not even physics in some other form. We may trust that even the fiercest partisan of the position that natural resources have nothing to do with value will admit in the end that there is a difference between what goes into the economic process and what comes out of it. To be sure, this difference can be only qualitative.

An unorthodox economist—such as myself—would say that what goes into the economic process represents *valuable natural resources* and what is thrown out of it is *valueless waste*. But this qualitative difference is confirmed, albeit in different terms, by a particular (and peculiar) branch of physics known as thermodynamics. From the viewpoint of thermodynamics, matter-energy enters the economic process in a state of *low entropy* and comes out of it in a state of *high entropy*.[8]

To explain in detail what entropy means is not a simple task. The notion is so involved that, to trust an authority on thermodynamics, it is "not easily understood even by physicists."[9] To make matters worse not only for the layman, but for everyone else as well, the term now circulates with several meanings, not all associated with a physical coordinate.[10] The 1965 edition of *Webster's Collegiate Dictionary* has three entires under "entropy." Moreover, the definition pertaining to the meaning relevant for the economic process is likely to confuse rather than enlighten the reader: "a measure of unavailable energy in a closed thermodynamic system so related to the state of the system that a change in the measure varies with change in the ratio of the increment of heat taken in the absolute temperature at which it is absorbed." But (as if intended to prove that not all progress is for the better) some older editions supply a more intelligible definition. "A measure of the unavailable energy in a thermodynamic system"—as we read in the 1948 edition—cannot satisfy the specialist but would do for general purposes. To explain (again in broad lines) what unavailable energy means is now a relatively simple task.

Energy exists in two qualitative states—*available* or *free* energy, over which man has almost complete command, and *unavailable* or *bound* energy, which man cannot possibly use. The chemical energy contained in a piece of coal is free energy because man can transform it into heat or, if he wants, into mechanical work. But the fantastic amount of heat-energy contained in the waters of the seas, for example, is bound energy. Ships sail on top of this energy, but to do so they need the free energy of some fuel or of the wind.

When a piece of coal is burned, its chemical energy is neither decreased nor increased. But the initial free energy has become so dissipated in the form of heat, smoke and ashes that man can no longer use it. It has been degraded into bound energy. Free energy means energy that displays a differential level, as exemplified most simply by the difference of temperatures between the inside and the outside of a boiler. Bound energy is, on the contrary, chaotically dissipated energy. This difference may be expressed in yet another way. Free energy implies some ordered structure, comparable with that of a store in which all meat is on one counter, vegetables on another, and so on. Bound energy is energy dissipated in disorder, like the same store after being struck by a tornado. This is why entropy is also defined as a measure of disorder. It fits the fact that a copper sheet represents a lower entropy than the copper ore from which it was produced.

The distinction between free and bound energy is certainly an anthropomorphic one. But this fact need not trouble a student of man, nay, even a student of matter in its simple form. Every element by which man seeks to get in mental contact with actuality can be but anthropomorphic. Only, the case of thermodynamics happens to be more striking. The point is that it was the economic distinction between things having an economic value and waste which prompted the thermodynamic distinction, not conversely. Indeed, the discipline of thermodynamics grew out of a memoir in which the French engineer Sadi Carnot (1824) studied for the first time the *economy* of heat engines. Thermodynamics thus began as a physics of economic value and has remained so in spite of the numerous subsequent contributions of a more abstract nature.

III

Thanks to Carnot's memoir, the elementary fact that heat moves by itself only from the hotter to the colder body acquired a place among the truths recognized by physics. Still more important was the consequent recognition of the additional truth that once the heat of a closed system has diffused itself so that the temperature has become uniform throughout the system, the movement of the heat cannot be reversed without external intervention. The ice cubes in a glass of water, once melted, will not form again by themselves. In general, the free heat-energy of a closed system continuously and irrevocably degrades itself into bound energy. The extension of this property from heat-energy to all other kinds of energy led to the second law of thermodynamics, alias the entropy law. This law states that the entropy (i.e., the amount of bound energy) of a closed system continuously increases or that the order of such a system steadily turns into disorder.

The reference to a closed system is crucial. Let us visualize a closed system, a room with an electric stove and a pain of water that has just been boiled. What the entropy law tells us is, first, that the heat of the boiled water will continuously dissipate into the system. Ultimately, the system will attain thermodynamic equilibrium—a state in which the temperature is uniform throughout (and all energy is bound). This applies to every kind of energy in a closed system. The free chemical energy of a piece of coal, for instance, will ultimately become degraded into bound energy even if the coal is left in the ground. Free energy will do so in any case.

The law also tells us that once thermodynamic equilibrium is reached, the water will not start boiling by itself.[11] But, as everyone knows, we can make it boil again by turning on the stove. This does not mean, however, that we have defeated the entropy law. If the entropy of the room has been decreased as the result of the temperature differential created by boiling the water, it is only because some low entropy (free energy) was brought into the system from the outside. And if we include the electric plant in the system, the entropy of this new system must have decreased, as the entropy law states. This means that the decrease in the entropy of the room has been obtained only at the cost of a greater increase in entropy elsewhere.

Some writers, impressed by the fact that living organisms remain almost unchanged over short periods of time, have set forth the idea that life eludes the entropy law. Now, life may have properties that cannot be accounted for by the natural laws, but the mere thought that it may violate some law of matter (which is an entirely different thing) is sheer nonsense. The truth is that every living organism strives only to maintain its own entropy constant. To the extent to which it achieves this, it does so by sucking low entropy from the environment to compensate for the increase in entropy to which, like every material structure, the organism is continuously subject. But the entropy of the entire system—consisting of the organism and its environment—must increase. Actually, the entropy of a system must increase faster if life is present than if it is absent. The fact that any living organism fights the entropic degradation of its own material structure may be a characteristic property of life, not accountable by material laws, but it does not constitute a violation of these laws.

Practically all organisms live on low entropy in the form found immediately in the environment. Man is the most striking exception: he cooks most of his food and also transforms natural resources into mechanical work or into various objects of utility. Here again, we should not let ourselves be misled. The entropy of copper metal is lower than the entropy of the ore from which it was refined, but this does not mean that man's *economic* activity eludes the entropy law. The refining of the ore causes a more than compensating increase in the entropy of the surroundings. Economists are fond of saying that we cannot get something for nothing. The entropy law teaches us that the rule of biological life and, in man's case, of its economic continuation is far harsher. In entropy terms, the cost of any biological or economic enterprise is always greater than the product. In entropy terms, any such activity necessarily results in a deficit.

IV

The statement made earlier—that, from a purely physical viewpoint, the economic process only transforms valuable natural resources (low entropy) into waste (high entropy)—is thus completely vindicated. But the puzzle of why such a process should go on is still with us. And it will remain a puzzle as long as we do not see that the true economic output of the economic process is not a material flow of waste, but an immaterial flux: the enjoyment of life. If we do not recognize the existence of this flux, we are not in the economic world. Nor do we have a complete picture of the economic process if we ignore the fact that this flux—which, as an entropic feeling, must characterize life at all levels—exists only as long as it can continuously feed itself on environmental low entropy. And if we go one step further, we discover that every object of economic value—be it a fruit just picked from a tree, or a piece of clothing, or furniture, etc.—has a highly ordered structure, hence, a low entropy.[12]

There are several lessons to be derived from this analysis. The first lesson is that man's economic struggle centers on environmental low entropy. Second, environmental low entropy is scarce in a different sense than Ricardian land. Both Ricardian land and the coal deposits are available in limited amounts. The difference is that a piece of coal can be used only once. And, in fact, the entropy law is the reason why an engine (even a biological organism) ultimately wears out and must be replaced by a *new* one, which means an additional tapping of environmental low entropy.

Man's continuous tapping of natural resources is not an activity that makes no history. On the contrary, it is the most important long-run element of mankind's fate. It is because of the irrevocability of the entropic degradation of matter-energy that, for instance, the peoples from the Asian steppes, whose economy was based on sheep-raising, began their Great Migration over the entire European continent at the beginning of the first millennium. The same element—the pressure on natural resources—had, no doubt, a role in other migrations, including that from Europe to the New World. The fantastic efforts made for reaching the moon may also reflect some vaguely felt hope of obtaining access to additional sources of low entropy. It is also because of the particular scarcity of environmental low entropy that ever since the dawn of history man has continuously sought to invent means for sifting low entropy better. In most (though not in all) of man's inventions one can definitely see a progressively better economy of low entropy.

Nothing could, therefore, be further from the truth than the notion that the economic process is an isolated, circular affair—as Marxist and standard analysis represent it. The economic process is solidly anchored to a material base which is subject to definite constraints. It is because of these constraints that the economic process has a unidirectional irrevocable evolution. In the economic world only money circulates back and forth between one economic sector and another (although, in truth, even the bullion slowly wears out and its stock must be continuously replenished from the mineral deposits). In retrospect it appears that the economists of both persuasions have succumbed to the worst economic fetishism—money fetishim.

V

Economic thought has always been influenced by the economic issues of the day. It also has reflected—with some lag—the trend of ideas in the natural sciences. A salient illustration of this correlation is the very fact that, when economists began ignoring the natural environment in representing the economic process, the event reflected a turning point in the temper of the entire scholarly world. The unprecedented achievements of the Industrial Revolution so amazed everyone with what man might do with the aid of machines that the general attention became confined to the factory. The landslide of spectacular scientific discoveries triggered by the new technical facilities strengthened this general awe for the power of technology. It also induced the literati to overestimate and, ultimately, to oversell to their audiences the powers of science. Naturally, from such a pedestal one could not even conceive that there is any real obstacle inherent in the human condition.

The sober truth is different. Even the lifespan of the human species represents just a blink when compared with that of a galaxy. So, even with progress in space travel, mankind will remain confined to a speck of space. Man's biological nature sets other limitations as to what he can do. Too high or too low a temperature is incompatible with his existence. And so are many radiations. It is not only that he cannot reach up to the stars, but he cannot even reach down to an individual elementary particle, nay, to an individual atom.

Precisely because man has felt, however unsophisticatedly, that his life depends on scarce, irretrievable low entropy, man has all along nourished the hope that he may eventually discover a self-perpetuating force. The discovery of electricity enticed many to believe that the hope was actually fulfilled. Following the strange marriage of thermodynamics with mechanics, some began seriously thinking about schemes to unbind bound energy.[13] The discovery of atomic energy spread another wave of sanguine hopes that, this time, we have truly gotten hold of a self-perpetuating power. The shortage of electricity which plagues New York and is gradually extending to other cities should suffice to sober us up. Both the nuclear theorists and the operators of atomic plants vouch that it all boils down to a problem of cost, which in the perspective of this paper means a problem of a balance sheet in entropy terms.

With natural sciences preaching that science can do away with all limitations felt by man and with the economists following suit in not relating the analysis of the economic process to the limitations of man's material environment, no wonder that no one realized that we cannot produce "better and bigger" refrigerators, automobiles, or jet planes, without producing also "better and bigger" waste. So, when everyone (in the countries with "better and bigger" industrial production) was, literally, hit in the face by pollution, scientists as well as economists were taken by surprise. But even now no one seems to see that the cause of all this is that we have failed to acknowledge the entropic nature of the economic process. A convincing proof is that the various authorities on pollution now to try to sell us, on the one hand, the idea of machines and chemical reactions that produce no waste, and, on the other, salvation through a perpetual recycling of waste. There is no denial that, in principle at least, we can recycle even the gold dispersed in the sand of the seas just as we can recycle the boiling water in my earlier example. But in both cases we must use an additional amount of low entropy much greater than the decrease in the entropy of what is recycled. There is no free recycling just as there is no wasteless industry.

VI

The globe to which the human species is bound floats, as it were, within the cosmic store of free energy, which may be even infinite. But for the reasons mentioned in the preceding section, man cannot have access to all this fantastic amount, nor to all possible forms of free energy. Man cannot, for example, tap directly the immense thermonuclear energy of the sun. The most important impediment (valid also for the industrial use of the "hydrogen bomb") is that no material container can resist the temperature of massive thermonuclear reactions. Such reactions can occur only in free space.

The free energy to which man can have access comes from two distinct sources. The first source is a *stock,* the stock of free energy of the mineral deposits in the bowels of the earth. The second source is a *flow,* the flow of solar radiation intercepted by the earth. Several differences between these two sources should be well marked. Man has almost complete command over the terrestrial dowry; conceivably, we may use it all within a single year. But, for all practical purposes, man has no control over the flow of solar radiation. Neither can he use the flow of the future *now.* Another asymmetry between the two sources pertains to their specific roles. Only the terrestrial source provides us with the low entropy materials from which we manufacture our most important implements. On the other hand, solar radiation is the primary source of all life on earth, which begins with chlorophyll photosynthesis. Finally, the terrestrial stock is a paltry source in comparison with that of the sun. In all probability, the active life of the sun—during which the earth will receive a flow of solar energy of significant intensity—will last another five billion years.[14] But hard to believe though it may be, the entire terrestrial stock could only yield a few days of sunlight.[15]

All this casts a new light on the population proboem, which is so topical today. Some students are alarmed at the possibility that the world population will reach seven billion by 2000A.D.—the level predicted by United Nations demographers. On the other side of the fence, there are those who, like Colin Clark, claim that with a proper administration of resources the earth may feed as many as forty-five billion people.[16] Yet no population expert seems to have raised the far more vital question for mankind's future: How long can a given world population—be it of one billion or of forty-five billion—be maintained? Only if we raise this question can we see how complicated the population problem is. Even the analytical concept of optimum population, on which many population studies have been erected, emerges as an inept fiction.

What has happened to man's entropic struggle over the last two hundred years is a telling story in this respect. On the one hand, thanks to the spectacular progress of science man has achieved an almost miraculous level of economic development. On the other hand, this development has forced man to push his tapping of terrestrial sources to a staggering degree (witness offshore oil-drilling). It has also sustained a population growth which has accentuated the struggle for food and, in some areas, brought this pressure to critical levels. The solution, advocated unanimously, is an increased mechanization of agriculture. But let us see what this solution means in terms of entropy.

In the first place, by eliminating the traditional partner of the farmer—the draft animal—the mechanization of agriculture allows the entire land area to be allocated to the production of food (and to fodder only to the extent of the need for meat). But the ultimate and the most important result is a shift of the low entropy input from the solar to the terrestrial source. The ox or the water buffalo—which derive their mechanical power from the solar radiation caught by chlorophyll photosynthesis—is replaced by the tractor—which is produced and operated with the aid of terrestrial low entropy. And the same goes for the shift from manure to artificial fertilizers. The upshot is that the mechanization of agriculture is a solution which, though inevitable in the present impasse, is antieconomical in the long run. Man's biological existence is made to depend in the future more and more upon the scarcer of the two sources of low entropy. There is also the risk that mechanized agriculture may trap the human species in a cul-de-sac because of the possibility that some of the biological species involved in the other method of farming will be forced into extinction.

Actually, the problem of the economic use of the terrestrial stock of low entropy is not limited to the mechanization of agriculture only: it is the main problem for the fate of the human species. To see this, let S denote the present stock of terrestrial low entropy and let r be some average annual amount of depletion. If we abstract (as we can safely do here) from the slow degradation of S, the *theoretical* maximum number of years until the complete exhaustion of that stock is S/r. This is also the number of years until the *industrial* phase in the evolution of mankind will forcibly come to its end. Give the fantastic disproportion between S and the flow of solar energy that reaches the globe annually, it is beyond question that, even with a very parsimonious use of S, the industrial phase of man's evolution will end long before the sun will cease to shine. What will happen then (if the extinction of the human species is not brought about earlier by some totally resistant bug or some insidious chemical) is hard to say. Man could continue to live by reverting to the stage of a berry-picking species—as he once was. But, in the light of what we know about evolution, such an evolutionary reversal does not seem probable. Be that as it may, the fact remains that the higher the degree of economic development, the greater must be the annual depletion r and, hence, the shorter becomes the expected life of the human species.

VII

The upshot is clear. Every time we produce a Cadillac, we irrevocably destroy an amount of low entropy that could otherwise be used for producing a plow or a spade. In other words, every time we produce a Cadillac, we do it at the cost of decreasing the number of human lives in the future. Economic development through industrial abundance may be a blessing for us now and for those who will be able to enjoy it in the near future, but it is definitely against the interest of the human species as a whole, if its interest is to have a lifespan as long as is compatible with its dowry of low entropy. In this paradox of economic development we can see the price man has to pay for the unique privilege of being able to go beyond the biological limits in his struggle for life.

Biologists are fond of repeating that natural selection is a series of fantastic blunders since future conditions are not taken into account. The remark, which implies that man is wiser than nature and should take over her job, proves that man's vanity and the scholar's self-confidence will never know their limits. For the race of economic development that is the hallmark of modern civilization leaves no doubt about man's lack of foresight. It is only because of his biological nature (his inherited instincts) that man cares for the fate of only some of his immediate descendants, generally not beyond his great-grandchildren. And there is neither cynicism nor pessimism in believing that, even if made aware of the entropic problem of the human species, mankind would not be willing to give up its present luxuries in order to ease the life of those humans who will live ten thousand or even one thousand years from now. Once man expanded his biological powers by means of industrial artifacts, he became *ipso facto* not only dependent on a very scarce source of life support but also addicted to industrial luxuries. It is as if the human species were determined to have a short but exciting life. Let the less ambitious species have a long but uneventful existence.

Issues such as those discussed in these pages pertain to long-run forces. Because these forces act extremely slowly we are apt to ignore their existence or, if we recognize them, to belittle their importance. Man's nature is such that he is always interested in what will happen until tomorrow, not in thousands of years from now. Yet it is the slow-acting forces that are the more fateful in general. Most people die not because of some quickly acting force —such as pneumonia or an automobile accident—but because of the slow-acting forces that cause aging. As a Jain philosopher remarked, man begins to die at birth. The point is that it would not be hazardous to venture some thoughts about the distant future of man's economy any more than it would be to predict in broad lines the life of a newly born child. One such thought is that the increased pressure on the stock of mineral resources created by the modern fever of industrial development, together with the mounting problem of making pollution less noxious (which places additional demands on the same stock), will necessarily concentrate man's attention on ways to make greater use of solar radiation, the more abundant source of free energy.

Some scientists now proudly claim that the food problem is on the verge of being completely solved by the imminent conversion on an industrial scale of mineral oil into food protein—an inept thought in view of what we know about the entropic problem. The logic of this problem justifies instead the prediction that, under the pressure of necessity, man will ultimately turn to the contrary conversion, of vegetable products into gasoline (if he will still have any use for it).[17] We may also be quasi-certain that, under the same pressure, man will discover means by which to transform solar radiation into motor power directly. Certainly, such a discovery will represent the greatest possible breakthrough for man's entropic problem, for it will bring under his command also the more abundant source of life support. Recycling and pollution purification would still consume low entropy, but not from the rapidly exhaustible stock of our globe.

NOTES

1. W. Stanley Jevons, *The Theory of Political Economy* (4th ed., London, 1924), p. 21.

2. For examples, R. T. Bye, *Principles of Economics* (5th ed., New York, 1956), p. 253; G. L. Bach, *Economics* (2nd ed., Englewood Cliffs, N.J., 1957), p. 60; J. H. Dodd, C. W. Hasek, T. J. Hailstones, *Economics*. (Cincinnati, 1957), p. 125; R. M. Havens, J. S. Henderson, D. L. Cramer, *Economics* (New York, 1966), p. 49; Paul A. Samuelson, *Economics* (8th ed., New York, 1970), p. 42.

3. Karl Marx, *Capital* (3 vols., Chicago, 1906–1933), I, 94, 199, 230, and passim.

4. *Ibid.*, II, ch. XX.

5. *The Economic Writings of Sir William Petty,* ed, C. H. Hull (2 vols., Cambridge, Eng., 1899), II, 377. Curiously, Marx went along with Petty's idea; but he claimed that nature only "helps to create use-value without contributing to the formation of exchange value." Karl Marx, *Capital*, I, 227. See also ibid., p. 94.

6. For example, Alfred Marshall, *Principles of Economics* (8th ed., New York, 1924), p. 63.

7. On the problem of the analytical representation of a process, see N. Georgescu-Roegen, *The Entropy Law and the Economic Process* (Cambridge, Mass., 1971), pp. 211–231.

8. This distinction together with the fact that no one would exchange some natural resources for waste disposes of Marx's assertion that "no chemist has ever discovered exchange value in a pearl or a diamond." Karl Marx, *Capital*, **1**, 95.

9. D. ter Harr, "The Quantum Nature of Matter and Radiation," in *Turning Points in Physics*, ed. R. J. Blin-Stoyle et al. (Amsterdam, 1959), p. 37.

10. One meaning that has recently made the term extremely popular is "the amount of information." For an argument that this term is misleading and for a critique of the alleged connection between information and physical entropy, see N. Georgescu-Roegen, *The Entropy Law and the Economic Process*, Appendix B.

11. This position calls for some technical elaboration. The opposition between the entropy law—with its unidirectional qualitative change—and mechanics—where everything can move either forward or backward while remaining self-identical—is accepted without reservation by every physicist and philosopher of science. However, the mechanistic dogma retained (as it still does) its grip on scientific activity even after physics recanted it. The result was that mechanics was soon brought into thermodynamics in the company of randomness. This is the strangest possible company, for randomness is the very antithesis of the deterministic nature of the laws of mechanics. To be sure, the new edifice (known as statistical mechanics) could not include mechanics under its roof and, at the same time, exclude reversibility. So, statistical mechanics must teach that a pail of water may start boiling by itself, a thought which is slipped under the rug by the argument that the miracle has not been observed because of its extremely small probability. This position has fostered the belief in the possibility of converting bound into free energy or, as P. W. Bridgman wittily put it, of bootlegging entropy. For a critique of the logical fallcies of statistical mechanics and of the various attempts to patch them, see N. Georgescu-Roegen, *The Entropy Law and the Economic Process*, ch. VI.

12. This does not mean that everything of low entropy necessarily has economic value. Poisonous mushrooms, too, have a low entropy. The relation between low entropy and economic value is similar to that between economic value and price. An object can have a price only if it has economic value, and it can have economic value only if its entropy is low. But the converse is not true.

13. See note 11, above.

14. George Gamow, *Matter, Earth, and Sky* (Englewood Cliffs, N. J., 1958), pp. 493f.

15. Four days, according to Eugene Ayres, "Power from the Sun," *Scientific American*, August 1950, p. 16. The situation is not changed even if we admit that the calculations might be in error by as much as one thousand times.

16. Cohn Clark, "Agricultural Productivity in Relation to Population," in *Man and His Future*, ed. G. Wolstenholme (Boston, 1963), p. 35.

17. That the idea is not far-fetched is proved by the fact that in Sweden, during World War II, automobiles were driven by the poor gas obtained by heating wood with wood.

4

SELECTIONS FROM "ENERGY AND ECONOMIC MYTHS"

Nicholas Georgescu-Roegen

• • •

MYTHS ABOUT MANKIND'S
ENTROPIC PROBLEM

Hardly anyone would nowadays openly profess a belief in the immortality of mankind. Yet many of us prefer not to exclude this possibility; to this end, we endeavor to impugn any factor that could limit mankind's life. The most natural rallying idea is that mankind's entropic dowry is virtually inexhaustible, primarily because of man's inherent power to defeat the Entropy Law in some way or another.

To begin with, there is the simple argument that, just as has happened with many natural laws, the laws on which the finiteness of accessible resources rests will be refuted in turn. The difficulty of this historical argument is that history proves with even greater force, first, that in a finite space there can be only a finite amount of low entropy and, second, that low entropy continuously and irrevocably dwindles away. The impossibility of perpetual motion (of both kinds) is as firmly anchored in history as the law of gravitation.

More sophisticated weapons have been forged by the statistical interpretation of thermodynamic phenomena—an endeavor to reestablish the supremacy of mechanics propped up this time by a *sui generis* notion of probability.

Reprinted by permission of the author and *Southern Economic Journal*, 41, 3, January 1975. Notes are renumbered from the original version.

According to this interpretation, the reversibility of high into low entropy is only a highly improbable, not a totally impossible event. And since the event is *possible,* we should be able by an ingenious device to cause the event to happen as often as we please, just as an adroit sharper may throw a "six" almost at will. The argument only brings to the surface the irreducible contradictions and fallacies packed into the foundations of the statistical interpretation by the worshipers of mechanics [32, ch. vi]. The hopes raised by this interpretation were so sanguine at one time that P. W. Bridgman, an authority on thermodynamics, felt it necessary to write an article just to expose the fallacy of the idea that one may fill one's pockets with money by "bootlegging entropy" [11].

Occasionally and *sotto voce* some express the hope, once fostered by a scientific authority such as John von Neumann, that man will eventually discover how to make energy a free good, "just like the unmetered air" [3, 32]. Some envision a "catalyst" by which to decompose, for example, the sea water into oxygen and hydrogen, the combustion of which will yield as much available energy as we would want. But the analogy with the small ember which sets a whole log on fire is unavailing. The entropy of the log and the oxygen used in the combustion is lower than that of the resulting ashes and smoke, whereas the entropy of water is higher than that of the oxygen and hydrogen after decomposition. Therefore, the miraculous catalyst also implies entropy bottlegging.[1]

With the notion, now propagated from one syndicated column to another, that the breeder reactor produces more energy than it consumes, the fallacy of entropy bootlegging seems to have reached its greatest currency even among the large circles of literati, including economists. Unfortunately, the illusion feeds on misconceived sales talk by some nuclear experts who extol the reactors which transform fertile but nonfissionable material into fissionable fuel as the breeders that "produce more fuel than they consume" [81, 82]. The stark truth is that the breeder is in no way different from a plant which produces hammers with the aid of some hammers. According to the deficit principle of the Entropy Law . . . , even in breeding chickens a greater amount of low entropy is consumed than is contained in the product.[2]

Apparently in defense of the standard vision of the economic process, economists have set forth themes of their own. We may mention first the argument that

> the notion of an absolute limit to natural resource availability is untenable when the definition of resources changes drastically and unpredictably over time. . . .
> A limit may exist, but it can be neither defined nor specified in economic terms. [3, 7, 11]

We also read that there is no upper limit even for arable land because "arable is infinitely indefinable" [55, 22]. The sophistry of these arguments is flagrant. No one would deny that we cannot say *exactly* how much coal, for example, is accessible. Estimates of natural resources have constantly been shown to be too low. Also, the point that metals contained in the top mile of the earth's crust may be a million times as much as the present known reserves [4, 338; 58, 331] does not prove the inexhaustibility of resources, but, characteristically, it ignores both the issues of accessibility and disposability.[3] Whatever resources or arable land we may need at one time or another, they will consist of accessible low entropy and accessible land. *And since all kinds together are in finite amount, no taxonomic switch can do away with that finiteness.*

The favorite thesis of standard and Marxist economists alike, however, is that the power of technology is without limits [3; 4; 10; 49; 51; 74; 69]. We will always be able not only to find a substitute for a resource which has become scarce, but also to increase the *productivity* of any kind of energy and material. Should we run out of some resources, we will always think up something, just as we have continuously done since the time of Pericles [4, 332–334]. Nothing, therefore, could ever stand in the way of an increasingly happier existence of the human species. One can hardly think of a more blunt form of linear thinking. By the same logic, no healthy young human should ever become afflicted with rheumatism or any other old-age ailments; nor should he ever die. Dinosaurs, just before they disappeared from this very same planet, had behind them not less than one hundred and fifty million years of truly prosperous existence. (And they did not pollute environment with industrial waste!) But the logic to be truly savored is Solo's [73, 516]. If entropic degradation is to bring mankind to its knees sometime in the future, it should have done so sometime after A.D. 1000. The old truth of Seigneur de La Palice has never been turned around—and in such a delightful form.[4]

In support of the same thesis, there also are arguments directly pertaining to its substance. First, there is the assertion that only a few kinds of resources are "so resistant to technological advance as to be incapable of eventually yielding extractive products at constant or declining cost" [3, 10] More recently, some have come out with a specific law which, in a way, is the contrary of Malthus' law concerning resources. The idea is that technology improves exponentially [4, 236; 51, 664; 74, 45]. The superficial justification is that one technological advance induces another. This is true, only it does not work cumulatively as in population growth. And it is terribly wrong to argue, as Maddox does [59, 21], that to insist on the existence of a limit to technology means to deny man's power to influence progress. Even if technology continues to progress, it will not necessary exceed any limit; an increasing sequence may have an upper limit. In the case of technology this limit is set by the theoretical coefficient of efficiency. . . . If progress were indeed exponential, then the input i per unit of output would follow in time the law $i = i_0 (1 + r)^{-t}$ and would constantly approach zero. Production would ultimately become incorporeal and the earth a new Garden of Eden.

Finally, there is the thesis which may be called the fallacy of endless substitution: "Few components of the earth's crust, including farm land, are so specific as to defy economic replacement; . . . nature imposes particular scarcities, not an inescapable general scarcity" [3, 10f].[6] Bray's protest notwithstanding [10, 8], this *is* "an economist's conjuring trick." True, there are only a few "vitamin" elements which play a totally specific role such as phosphorus plays in living organisms. Aluminum, on the other hand, has replaced iron and copper in many, although not in all uses.[7] However, *substitution within a finite stock of accessible low entropy* whose irrevocable degradation is speeded up through use cannot possibly go on forever.

In Solow's hands, substitution becomes the key factor that supports technological progress even as resources become increasingly scarce. There will be, first, a substitution within the spectrum of consumer goods. With prices reacting to increasing scarcity, consumers will buy "fever resource-intensive goods and more of other things" [74, 47].[8] More recently, he extended the same idea to production, too. We may, he argues, substitute "other factors for natural resources" [75, 11]. One must have a very erroneous view of the economic process as a whole not to see that there are no material factors other than natural resources. To maintain further that "the world can, in effect, get along without natural resources" is to ignore the difference between the actual world and the Garden of Eden.

More impressive are the statistical data invoked in support of some of the foregoing theses. The data adduced by Solow [74, 44f] show that in the United States between 1950 and 1970 the consumption of a series of mineral elements per unit of GNP decreased substantially. The exceptions were attributed to substitution but were expected to get in line sooner or later. In strict logic, the data do not prove that during the same period technology necessarily progressed to a greater economy of resources. The GNP may increase more than any input of minerals even if technology remains the same, or even if it deteriorates. But we also know that during practically the same period, 1947–1967, the consumption per capita of basic materials increased in the United States. And in the world, during only one decade, 1957–1967, the consumption of steel per capita grew by 44 percent [12, 198–200]. What matters in the end is not only the impact of technological progress on the consumption of resources per unit of GNP, but especially the increase in the rate of resource depletion, which is a side effect of that progress.

Still more impressive—as they have actually proved to be—are the data used by Barnett and Morse to show that, from 1870 to 1957, the ratios of labor and capital costs to net output decreased appreciably in agriculture and mining, both critical sectors as concerns depletion of resources [3, 8f, 167–178]. In spite of some arithmetical incongruities,[9] the picture emerging from these data cannot be repudiated. Only its interpretation must be corrected.

For the environmental problem it is essential to understand the typical forms in which technological progress may occur. A first group includes the *economy-innovations,* which achieve a *net* economy of low entropy—be it by a

more complete combustion, by decreasing friction, by deriving a more intensive light from gas or electricity, by substituting materials costing less in
energy for others costing more, and so on. Under this heading we should also
include the discovery of how to use new kinds of accessible low entropy. A
second group consists of *substitution-innovations,* which simply substitute
physico-chemical energy for human energy. A good illustration is the innovation of gunpowder, which did away with the catapult. Such innovations generally enable us not only to do things better but also (and especially) to do things
which could not be done before—to fly in airplanes, for example. Finally,
there are the *spectrum-innovations,* which bring into existence new consumer
goods, such as the hat, nylon stockings, etc. Most of the innovations of this
group are at the same time substitution-innovations. In fact, most innovations
belong to more than one category. But the classification serves analytical
purposes.

Now, economic history confirms a rather elementary fact—the fact that the
great strides in technological progress have generally been touched off by a
discovery of how to use a new kind of accessible energy. On the other hand, a
great stride in technological progress cannot materialize unless the corresponding innovation is followed by a great mineralogical expansion. Even a
substantial increase in the efficiency of the use of gasoline as fuel would pale
in comparison with a manifold increase of the known, rich oil fields.

This sort of expansion is what has happened during the last one hundred
years. We have struck oil and discovered new coal and gas deposits in a far
greater proportion than we could use during the same period. Still more
important, all mineralogical discoveries have included a substantial proportion
of *easily* accessible resources. This exceptional bonanza by itself has sufficed
to lower the real cost of bringing mineral resources *in situ* to the surface.
Energy of mineral source thus becoming cheaper, substitution-innovations
have caused the ratio of labor to net output to decline. Capital also must have
evolved toward forms which cost less but use more energy to achieve the same
result. What has happened during this period is a modification of the cost
structure, the flow factors being increased and the fund factors decreased.[10]
By examining, therefore, only the relative variations of the fund factors during
a period of exceptional mineral bonanza, we cannot prove either that the
unitary total cost will always follow a declining trend or that the continuous
progress of technology renders accessible resources almost inexhaustible—as
Barnett and Morse claim [3, 239].

Little doubt is thus left about the fact that the theses examined in this section
are anchored in a deep-lying belief in mankind's immortality. Some of their
defenders have even urged us to have faith in the human species: such faith
will triumph over all limitations.[11] But neither faith nor assurance from some
famous academic chair [4] could alter the fact that, according to the basic law
of thermodynamics, mankind's dowry is finite. Even if one were inclined to
believe in the possible refutation of these principles in the future, one still

must not act on that faith now. We must take into account that evolution does not consist of a linear repetition, even though over short intervals it may fool us into the contrary belief.

A great deal of confusion about the environmental problem prevails not only among economists generally (as evidenced by the numerous cases already cited), but also among the highest intellectual circles simply because the sheer entropic nature of all happenings is ignored or misunderstood. Sir Macfarlane Burnet, a Nobelite, in a special lecture considered it imperative "to prevent the progressive destruction of the earth's irreplaceable resources" [quoted, 15, 1]. And a prestigious institution such as the United Nations, in its Declaration on the Human Environment (Stockholm, 1972), repeatedly urged everyone "to improve the environment." Both urgings reflect the fallacy that man can reverse the march of entropy. The truth, however unpleasant, is that the most we can do is to prevent any unnecessary depletion of resources and any unnecessary deterioration of the environment, but without claiming that we know the precise meaning of "unnecessary" in this context.

• • •

THE STEADY STATE: A TOPICAL MIRAGE

Malthus, as we know, was criticized primarily because he assumed that population and resources grow according to some simple mathematical laws. But this criticism did not touch the real error of Malthus (which has apparently remained unnoticed). This error is the implicit assumption that population may grow beyond any limit both in number and time *provided that it does not grow too rapidly*.[12] An essentially similar error has been committed by the authors of *The Limits,* by the authors of the nonmathematical yet more articulate "Blueprint for Survival," as well as by several earlier writers. Because, like Malthus, they were set exclusively on proving the impossibility of growth, they were easily deluded by a simple, now widespread, but false syllogism: since exponential growth in a finite world leads to disasters of all kinds, ecological salvation lies in the stationary state [42; 47; 62, 156–184; 6, 3f, 8, 20].[13] H. Daly even claims that "the stationary state economy is, therefore, a necessity" [21, 5].

This vision of a blissful world in which both population and capital stock remain constant, once expounded with his usual skill by John Stuart Mill [64, bk. 4, ch. 6], was until recently in oblivion.[14] Because of the spectacular revival of this myth of ecological salvation, it is well to point out its various logical and factual snags. The crucial error consists in not seeing that not only growth, but also a zero-growth state, nay, even a declining state which does not converge toward annihilation, cannot exist forever in a finite environment. The error perhaps stems from some confusion between finite stock and finite flow rate, as the incongruous dimensionalities of several graphs suggest [62,

62, 64f, 124ff; 6, 6]. And contrary to what some advocates of the stationary state claim [21, 15], this state does not occupy a privileged position vis-à-vis physical laws.

To get to the core of the problem, let S denote the actual amount of accessible resources in the crust of the earth. Let P_i and s_i be the population and the amount of depleted resources per person in the year i. Let the "amount of total life," measured in years of life, be defined by $L = \Sigma P_i$, from $i = 0$ to $i = \infty$. S sets an upper limit for L through the obvious constraint $\Sigma P_i s_i \leq S$. For although s_i is a historical variable, it cannot be zero or even negligible (unless mankind reverts sometime to a berry-picking economy). Therefore, $P_i = 0$ for i greater than some finite n, and $P_i > 0$ otherwise. That value of n is the maximum duration of the human species [31, 12f; 32, 304].

The earth also has a so-called carrying capacity, which depends on a complex of factors, including the size of s_i.[15] This capacity sets a limit on any single P_i. But this limit does not render the other limits, of L and n, superfluous. It is therefore inexact to argue—as the Meadows group seems to do [62, 91f]—that the stationary state can go on forever as long as P_i does not exceed that capacity. The proponents of salvation through the stationary state must admit that such a state can have only a finite duration—unless they are willing to join the "No Limit" Club by maintaining that S is inexhaustible or almost so—as the Meadows group does in fact [62, 172]. Alternatively, they must explain the puzzle of how a whole economy, stationary for a long era, all of a sudden comes to an end.

Apparently, the advocates of the stationary state equate it with an open *thermodynamic* steady state. This state consists of an *open* macrosystem which maintains its entropic structure constant through material exchanges with its "environment." As one would immediately guess, the concept constitutes a highly useful tool for the study of biological organisms. We must, however, observe that the concept rests on some special conditions introduced by L. Onsager [50, 89–97]. These conditions are so delicate (they are called the principle of *detailed* balance) that in actuality they can hold only "within a deviation of a few percent" [50, 140]. For this reason, a steady state may exist in fact only in an approximated manner and over a finite duration. This impossibility of a macrosystem not in a state of chaos to be perpetually durable may one day be explicitly recognized by a new thermodynamic law just as the impossibility of perpetual motion once was. Specialists recognize that the present thermodynamic laws do not suffice to explain all nonreversible phenomena, including especially life processes.

Independently of these snags there are simple reasons against believing that mankind can live in a perpetual stationary state. The structure of such a state remains the same throughout; it does not contain in itself the seed of the inexorable death of all open macrosystems. On the other hand, a world with a stationary population would, on the contrary, be continually forced to change its technology as well as its mode of life in response to the inevitable decrease of resource accessibility. Even if we beg the issue of how capital may change qualitatively and still remain constant, we could have to assume that the unpredictable decrease in accessibility will be miraculously compensated by the right innovations at the right time. A stationary world may for a while be interlocked with the changing environment through a system of balancing feedbacks analogous to those of a living organism during one phase of its life. But as Bormann reminded us [7, 707], the miracle cannot last forever; sooner or later the balancing system will collapse. At that time, the stationary state will enter a crisis, which will defeat its alleged purpose and nature.

One must be cautioned against another logical pitfall, that of invoking the Prigogine principle in support of the stationary state. This principle states that the minimum of the entropy produced by an Onsager type of open thermodynamic system is reached when the system becomes steady [50, ch, xvi]. It says nothing about how this last entropy compares with that produced by other open systems.[16]

The usual arguments adduced in favor of the stationary state are, however, of a different, more direct nature. It is, for example, argued that in such a state there is more time for pollution to be reduced by natural processes and for technology to adapt itself to the decrease of resource accessibility [62, 166]. It is plainly true that we could use much more efficiently today the coal we have burned in the past. The rub is that we might not have mastered the present efficient techniques if we had not burned all that coal "inefficiently." The point that in a stationary state people will not have to work additionally to accumulate capital (which in view of what I have said in the last paragraphs is not quite accurate) is related to Mill's claim that people could devote more time to intellectual activites. "The trampling, crushing, elbowing, and trading on each other's heel" will cease [64, 754]. History, however, offers multiple examples —the Middle Ages, for one—of quasi stationary societies where arts and sciences were practically stagnant. In a stationary state, too, people may be busy in the fields and shops all day long. Whatever the state, free time for intellectual progress depends on the intensity of the pressure of population on resources. Therein lies the main weakness of Mill's vision. Witness the fact that—as Daly explicitly admits [21, 6–8]—its writ offers no basis for determining even in principle the optimum levels of population and capital. This brings to light the important, yet unnoticed point, that *the necessary conclusion of the arguments in favor of that vision is that the most desirable state is not a stationary, but a declining one.*

Undoubtedly, the current growth must cease, nay, be reversed. But anyone who believes that he can draw a blueprint for the ecological salvation of the human species does not understand the nature of evolution, or even of history —which is that of permanent struggle in continuously novel forms, not that of a predictable, controllable physico-chemical process, such as boiling an egg or launching a rocket to the moon.

SOME BASIC BIOECONOMICS[17]

Apart from a few insignificant exceptions, all species other than man use only *endosomatic* instruments—as Alfred Lotka proposed to call those instruments (legs, claws, wings, etc.) which belong to the individual organism *by birth*. Man alone came, in time, to use a club, which does not belong to him by birth, but which extended his endosomatic arm and increased its power. At that point in time, man's evolution transcended the biological limits to include also (and primarily) the evolution of *exosomatic* instruments, i.e., of instruments produced by man but not belonging to his body.[18] That is why man can now fly in the sky or swim under water even though his body has no wings, no fins, and no gills.

The exosomatic evolution brought down upon the human species two fundamental and irrevocable changes. The first is the irreducible social conflict, which characterizes the human species [29, 98–101; 32, 306–315, 348f]. Indeed, there are other species which also live in society, but which are free from such conflict. The reason is that their "social classes" correspond to some clear-cut biological divisions. The periodic killing of a great part of the drones by the bees is a natural, biological action, not a civil war.

The second change is man's addiction to exosomatic instruments—a phenomenon analogous to that of the flying fish which became addicted to the atmosphere and mutated into birds forever. It is because of this addiction that mankind's survival presents a problem entirely different from that of all other species [31; 32, 302–305]. It is neither only biological nor only economic. It is bioeconomic. Its broad contours depend on the multiple asymmetries existing among the three sources of low entropy which together constitute mankind's dowry—the free energy received from the sun, on the one hand, and the free energy and the ordered material structures stored in the bowels of the earth, on the other.

The *first* asymmetry concerns the fact that the terrestrial component is a *stock*, whereas the solar one is a *flow*. The difference needs to be well understood [32, 226f]. Coal *in situ* is a stock because we are free to use it all today (conceivably) or over centuries. But at no time can we use any part of a future flow of solar radiation. Moreover, the flow rate of this radiation is wholly beyond our control; it is completely determined by cosmological conditions, including the size of our globe.[19] One generation, whatever it may do, cannot alter the share of solar radiation of any future generation. Because of the priority of the present over the future and the irrevocability of entropic degradation, the opposite is true for the terrestrial shares. These shares are affected by how much of the terrestrial dowry the past generations have consumed.

Second, since no practical procedure is available at human scale for transforming energy into matter. . . , accessible material low entropy is by far the most critical element from the bioeconomic viewpoint. True, a piece of coal burned by our forefathers is gone forever, just as is part of the silver or iron, for instance, mined by them. Yet future generations will still have their inalienable share of solar energy (which, as we shall see next, is enormous). Hence, they will be able, at least, to use each year an amount of wood equivalent to the annual vegetable growth. For the silver and iron dissipated by the earlier generations there is no similar compensation. This is why in bioeconomics we must emphasize that every Cadillac or every Zim—let alone any instrument of war—means fewer plowshares for some future generations, and implicitly, fewer future human beings, too [31, 13; 32, 304].

Third, there is an astronomical difference between the amount of the flow of solar energy and the size of the stock of terrestrial free energy. At the cost of a decrease in mass of 131×10^{12} tons, the sun radiates annually 10^{13} Q—one single Q being equal to 10^{18} BTU! Of this fantastic flow, only some 5,300 Q are intercepted at the limits of the earth's atmosphere, with roughly one half of that amount being reflected back into outer space. At our own scale, however, even this amount is fantastic; for the total world consumption of energy currently amounts to no more than 0.2 Q annually. From the solar energy that reaches the ground level, photosynthesis absorbs only 1.2 Q. From waterfalls we could obtain at most 0.08 Q, but we are now using only one tenth of that potential. Think also of the additional fact that the sun will continue to shine with practically the same intensity for another five billion years (before becoming a red giant which will raise the earth's temperature to 1,000°F). Undoubtedly, the human species will not survive to benefit from all this abundance.

Passing to the terrestrial dowry, we find that, according to the best estimates, the initial dowry of fossil fuel amounted to only 215 Q. The outstanding recoverable reserves (known and probable) amount to about 200 Q. These reserves, therefore, could produce only two weeks of sunlight on the globe.[20] If their depletion continues to increase at the current pace, these reserves may support man's industrial activity for just a few more decades. Even the reserves of uranium-235 will not last for a longer period if used in the ordinary reactors. Hopes are now set on the breeder reactor, which, with the aid of uranium-235, may "extract" the energy of the fertile but not fissionable elements, uranium-238 and thorium-232. Some experts claim that this source of energy is "essentially inexhaustible" [83, 412]. In the United States alone, it is believed, there are large areas covered with black shale and granite which contain 60 grams of natural uranium or thorium per metric ton [46, 226f]. On ths basis, Weinberg and Hammond [83, 415f] have come out with a grand plan. By stripmining and crushing all these rocks, we could obtain enough nuclear fuel for some 32,000 breeder reactors distributed in 4,000 offshore parks and capable of supplying a population of twenty billion for millions of years with twice as much energy per capita as the current consumption rate in the USA. The grand plan is a typical example of linear thinking, according to which all that is needed for the existence of a population, even "considerably larger than twenty billion." is to increase all supplies proportionally.[21] Not that the authors deny that there also are nontechnical issues; only, they play them down with noticeable zeal [83, 417f]. The most important issue, of whether a social organization compatible with the density of population and the nuclear manipulation at the grand level can be achieved, is brushed aside by Weinberg as "transscientific" [82].[22] Technicians are prone to forget that due to their own successes, nowadays it may be easier to move the mountain to Mohammed than to induce Mohammed to go to the mountain. For the time being, the snag is far more palpable. As responsible forums openly admit, even one breeder still presents substantial risks of nuclear catastrophes, and the problem of safe transportation of nuclear fuels and especially that of safe storage of the radioactive garbage still await a solution even for a moderate scale of operations [35; 36; especially 39 and 67].

There remains the physicist's greatest dream, controlled thermonuclear reaction. To constitute a real breakthrough, it must be the deuterium-deuterium reaction, the only one that could open up a formidable source of terrestrial energy for a long era.[23] However, because of the difficulties alluded to earlier . . . , even the experts working at it do not find reasons for being too hopeful.

For completion, we should also mention the tidal and geothermal energies, which, although not negligible (in all 0.1 Q per year), can be harnessed only in very limited situations.

The general picture is now clear. The terrestrial energies on which we can rely effectively exist in very small amounts, whereas the use of those which exist in ampler amounts is surrounded by great risks and formidable technical obstacles. On the other hand, there is the immense energy from the sun which reaches us without fail. Its direct use is not yet practiced on a significant scale, the main reason being that the alternative industries are now much more efficient economically. But promising results are coming from various directions [37; 41]. What counts from the bioeconomic viewpoint is that the feasibility of using the sun's energy directly is not surrounded by risks or big question marks; it is a proven fact.

The conclusion is that mankind's entropic dowry presents another important differential scarcity. From the viewpoint of the extreme longrun, the terrestrial free energy is far scarcer than that received from the sun. The point exposes the foolishness of the victory cry that we can finally obtain protein from fossil fuels! Sane reason tells us to move in the opposite direction, to convert vegetable stuff into hydrocarbon fuel—an obviously natural line already pursued by several researchers [22, 311–313].[24]

Fourth, from the viewpoint of industrial utilization, solar energy has an immense drawback in comparison with energy of terrestrial origin. The latter is available in a concentrated form, in some cases, in a too concentrated form. As a result, it enables us to obtain almost instantaneously enormous amounts of work, most of which could not even be obtained otherwise. By great contrast, the flow of solar energy comes to us with an extremely low intensity, like a very fine rain, almost a microscopic mist. The important difference from true rain is that this radiation rain is not collected naturally into streamlets, then into creeks and rivers, and finally into lakes from where we could use it in a concentrated form, as is the case with waterfalls. Imagine the difficulty one would face if one tried to use *directly* the kinetic energy of some microscopic rain drops as they fall. The same difficulty presents itself in using solar energy directly (i.e., not through the chemical energy of green plants, or the kinetic energy of the wind and waterfalls). But as was emphasized a while ago, the difficulty does not amount to impossibility. [Editor's note: Georgescu-Roegen's more recent writings are less sanguine about the prospects for direct use of solar energy. See his "Energy Analysis and Economic Valuation," *Southern Economic Journal*, April 1979.]

Fifth, solar energy, on the other hand, has a unique and incommensurable advantage. The use of any terrestrial energy produces some noxious pollution, which, moreover, is irreducible and hence cumulative, be it in the form of thermal pollution alone. By contrast, any use of solar energy is *pollution-free*. For, whether this energy is used or not, its ultimate fate is the same, namely, to become the dissipated heat that maintains the thermodynamic equilibrium between the globe and outer space at a propitious temperature.[25]

The *sixth* asymmetry involves the elementary fact that the survival of every species on earth depends, directly or indirectly, on solar radiation (in addition to some elements of a superficial environmental layer). Man alone, because of his exosomatic addiction, depends on mineral resources as well. For the use of these resources man competes with no other species; yet his use of them usually endangers many forms of life, including his own. Some species have in fact been brought to the brink of extinction merely because of man's exosomatic needs or his craving for the extravagant. But nothing in nature compares in fierceness with man's competition for solar energy (in its primary or its by-product forms). Man has not deviated one bit from the law of the jungle; if anything, he has made it even more merciless by his sophisticated exosomatic instruments. Man has openly sought to exterminate any species that robs him of his food or feeds on him—wolves, rabbits, weeds, insects, microbes, etc.

But this struggle of man with other species for food (in ultimate analysis, for solar energy) has some unobtrusive aspects as well. And, curiously, it is one of these aspects that has some far-reaching consequences in addition to supplying a most instructive refutation of the common belief that every technological innovation constitutes a move in the right direction as concerns the economy of resources. The case pertains to the economy of modern agricultural techniques.

• • •

Justus von Liebig observed that "civilization is the economy of power" [32, 304]. At the present hour, the economy of power in all its aspects calls for a turning point. Instead of continuing to be opportunistic in the highest degree and concentrating our research toward finding more economically efficient ways of tapping mineral energies—all in finite supply and all heavy pollutants —we should direct all our efforts toward improving the direct uses of solar energy—the only clean and essentially unlimited source. Already known techniques should without delay be diffused among all people so that we all may learn from practice and develop the corresponding trade.

An economy based primarily on the flow of solar energy will also do away, though not completely, with the monopoly of the present over future generations, for even such an economy will still need to tap the terrestrial dowry, especially for materials. Technological innovations will certainly have a role in this direction. But it is high time for us to stop emphasizing exclusively—as all platforms have apparently done so far—the increase of supply. Demand can also play a role, an even greater and more efficient one in the ultimate analysis.

It would be foolish to propose a complete renunciation of the industrial comfort of the exosomatic evolution. Mankind will not return to the cave or, rather, to the tree. But there are a few points that may be included in a minimal bioeconomic program.

First, the production of all instruments of war, *not only of war itself,* should be prohibited completely. It is utterly absurd (and also hypocritical) to continue growing tobacco if, avowedly, no one intends to smoke. The nations which are so developed as to be the main producers of armaments should be able to reach a consensus over this prohibition without any difficulty if, as they claim, they also possess the wisdom to lead mankind. Discontinuing the production of all instruments of war will not only do away at least with the mass killings by ingenious weapons but will also release some tremendous productive forces for international aid without lowering the standard of living in the corresponding countries.

Second, through the use of these productive forces as well as by additional well-planned and sincerely intended measures, the underdeveloped nations must be aided to arrive as quickly as possible at a good (not luxurious) life. Both ends of the spectrum must effectively participate in the efforts required by this transformation and accept the necessity of a radical change in their polarized outlooks on life.[26]

Third, mankind should gradually lower its population to a level that could be adequately fed only by organic agriculture.[27] Naturally, the nations now experiencing a very high demographic growth will have to strive hard for the most rapid possible results in that direction.

Fourth, until either the direct use of solar energy becomes a general convenience or controlled fusion is achieved, all waste of energy—by overheating, overcooling, overspeeding, overlighting, etc.—should be carefully avoided, and if necessary, strictly regulated.

Fifth, we must cure ourselves of the morbid craving for extravagant gadgetry, splendidly illustrated by such a contradictory item as the golf cart, and for such mammoth splendors as *two-garage* cars. Once we do so, manufacturers will have to stop manufacturing such "commodities."

Sixth, we must also get rid of fashion, of "that disease of the human mind," as Abbot Fernando Galliani characterized it in his celebrated *Della moneta* (1750). It is indeed a disease of the mind to throw away a coat or a piece of furniture while it can still perform its specific service. To get a "new" car every year and to refashion the house every other is a bioeconomic crime. Other writers have already proposed that goods be manufactured in such a way as to be more durable [e.g. 43, 146]. But it is even more important that consumers should reeducate themselves to despise fashion. Manufacturers will then have to focus on durability.

Seventh, and closely related to the preceding point, is the necessity that durable goods be made still more durable by being designed so as to be repairable. (To put it in a plastic analogy, in many cases nowadays, we have to throw away a pair of shoes merely because one lace has broken.)

Eighth, in a compelling harmony with all the above thoughts we should cure ourselves of what I have been calling "the circumdrome of the shaving machine," which is to shave oneself faster so as to have more time to work on a machine that shaves faster so as to have more time to work on a machine that shaves still faster, and so on *ad infinitum.* This change will call for a great deal of recanting on the part of all those professions which have lured man into this empty infinite regress. We must come to realize that an important prerequisite for a good life is a substantial amount of leisure spent in an intelligent manner.

Considered on paper, in the abstract, the foregoing recommendations would on the whole seem reasonable to anyone willing to examine the logic on which they rest. But one thought has persisted in my mind ever since I became interested in the entropic nature of the economic process. Will mankind listen to any program that implies a constriction of its addiction to exosomatic comfort? Perhaps, the destiny of man is to have a short, but fiery, exciting and extravagant life rather than a long, uneventful and vegetative existence. Let other species—the amoebas, for example—which have no spiritual ambitions inherit an earth still bathed in plenty of sunshine.

NOTES

1. A specific suggestion implying entropy bootlegging is Harry Johnson's: it envisages the possibility of reconstituting the stores of coal and oil "with enough ingenuity" [49, 8]. And if he means with enough energy as well, why should one wish to lose a great part of that energy through the transformation?

2. How incredibly resilient is the myth of energy breeding is evidenced by the very recent statement of Roger Revelle [70, 169] that "farming can be thought of as a kind of breeder reactor in which much more energy is produced than consumed." Ignorance of the main laws governing energy is widespread indeed.

3. Marxist economists also are part of this chorus. A Romanian review of [32], for example, objected that we have barely scratched the surface of the earth.

4. To recall the famous old French quatrain: "Seigneur de La Palace / fell in the battle for Pavia. / A quarter of an hour before his death / he was still alive." (My translation.) See *Grand Dictionnaire Universel du XIX-e Siècle,* vol. X, p. 179.

5. Even some natural scientists, e.g., [1], have taken this position. Curiously, the historical fact that some civilizations were unable "to think up something" is brushed aside with the remark that they were "relatively isolated" [3, 6]. But is not mankind, too, a community completely isolated from any external cultural diffusion and one, also, which is unable to migrate?

6. Similar arguments can be found in [4, 338f; 59, 102; 74, 45]. Interestingly, Kaysen [51, 661] and Solow [74, 43], while recognizing the finitude of mankind's entropic dowry, pooh-pooh the fact because it does not "lead to any very interesting conclusions." Economists, of all students, should know that the finite, not the infinite, poses extremely interesting questions. The present paper hopes to offer proof of this.

7. Even in this most cited case, substitution has not been as successful in every direction as we have generally believed. Recently, it has been discovered that aluminum electrical cables constitute fire hazards.

8. The pearl on this issue, however, is supplied by Maddox [59, 104]: "Just as prosperity in countries now advanced has been accompanied by an actual decrease in the consumption of bread, so it is to be expected that affluence will make societies less dependent on metals such as steel."

9. The point refers to the addition of capital (measured in *money terms*) and labor (measured in *workers employed*) as well as the computation of net output (by subtraction) from physical gross output [3, 167f].

10. For these distinctions, see [27, 512–519; 30, 4; 32, 223–225].

11. See the dialogue between Preston Cloud and Roger Revelle quoted in [66, 416]. The same refrain runs through Maddox's complaint against those who point out mankind's limitations [59, vi, 138, 280]. In relation to Maddox's chapter, "Man-made Men," see [32, 348–359].

12. Joseph J. Splenger, a recognized authority in this broad domain, tells me that indeed he knows of no one who may have made the observation. For some very penetrating discussions of Malthus and of the present population pressure, see [76; 77].

13. The substance of the argument of *The Limits* beyond that of Mill's is borrowed from Boulding and Daly [8; 9; 20; 21].

14. In *International Encyclopedia of the Social Sciences,* for example, the point is mentioned only in passing.

15. Obviously, any increase in s_i will generally result in a decrease of L and of n. Also, the carrying capacity in any year may be increased by a greater use of terrestrial resources. These elementary points should be retained for further use. . . .

16. The point recalls Boulding's idea that the inflow from nature into the economic process, which he calls "throughput," is "something to be minimized rather than

maximized" and that we should pass from an economy of flow to one of stock [8, 9f; 9, 359f]. The idea is more striking than enlightening. True, economists suffer from a flow-complex [29, 55, 88]; also, they have little realized that the proper analytical description of a process must include *both flows and funds* [30; 32, 219f, 228–234]. Entrepreneurs, as far as Boulding's idea is concerned, have at all times aimed at minimizing the flow necessary to maintain their capital funds. If the present inflow from nature is incommensurate with the safety of our species, it is only because the population is too large and part of it enjoys excessive comfort. Economic decisions will always forcibly involve both flows and stocks. Is it not true that mankind's problem is to economize S (a stock) for as large an amount of life as possible, which implies to minimize s_i (a flow) for some "good life"?

17. I saw this term used for the first time in a letter from Jiří Zeman.

18. The practice of slavery, in the past, and the possible procurement, in the future, of organs for transplant are phenomena akin to the exosomatic evolution.

19. A fact greatly misunderstood: Ricardian land has economic value for the same reason as a fisherman's net. Ricardian land catches the most valuable energy, roughly in proportion to its total size [27, 508; 32, 232].

20. The figures used in this section have been calculated from the data of Daniels [22] and Hubbert [46]. Such data, especially those about reserves, vary from author to author but not to the extent that really matters. However, the assertion that "the vast oil shales which are to be found all over the world [would last] for no less than 40,000 years" [59, 99] is sheer fantasy.

21. In an answer to critics (*American Scientist*, LVIII, no. 6, p. 610), the same authors prove, again linearly, that the agro-industrial complexes of the grand plan could easily feed such a population.

22. For a recent discussion of the social impact of industrial growth, in general, and of the social problems growing out of a large scale use of nuclear energy, in particular, see [78], a monograph by Harold and Margaret Sprout, pioneers in this field.

23. One percent only of the deuterium in the oceans would provide 10^8 Q through that reaction, an amount amply sufficient for some hundred millions of years of very high industrial comfort. The reaction deuterium-tritium stands a better chance of success because it requires a lower temperature. But since it involves lithium-6, which exists in small supply, it would yield only about 200 Q in all.

24. It should be of interest to know that during World War II in Sweden, for one, automobiles were driven with the poor gas obtained by heating charcoal with kindlings in a container serving as a tank!

25. One necessary qualification: even the use of solar energy may disturb the climate if the energy is released in another place than where collected. The same is true for a difference in time, but this case is unlikely to have any practical importance.

26. At the Dai Dong Conference (Stockholm, 1972), I suggested the adoption of a measure, which seems to me to be applicable with much less difficulty than dealing with installations of all sorts. My suggestion, instead, was to allow people to move freely from any country to any other country whatsover. Its reception was less than lukewarm. See [2, 72].

27. To avoid any misinterpretation, I should add that the present fad for organic foods has nothing to do with this proposal. . . .

REFERENCES

1. Abelson, Philip H., "Limits to Growth." *Science*, 17 March 1972, 1197.

2. Artin, Tom, *Earth Talk: Independent Voices on the Environment*. New York: Grossman, 1973.

3. Barnett, Harold J., and Chandler Morse, *Scarcity and Growth*. Baltimore: Johns Hopkins Press, 1963.

4. Beckerman, Wilfred, "Economists, Scientists, and Environmental Catastrophe." *Oxford Economic Papers*, November 1972, 327–344.

5. Blin-Stoyle, R. J., "The End of Mechanistic Philosophy and the Rise of Field Physics," in *Turning Points in Physics*, edited by R. J. Blin-Stoyle et al. Amsterdam: North-Holland, 1959, pp. 5–29.

6. "A Blueprint for Survival." *The Ecologist*, January 1972, 1–43.

7. Bormann, F. H., "Unlimited Growth: Growing, Growing, Gone?" *BioScience*, December 1972, 706–709.

8. Boulding, Kenneth, "The Economics of the Coming Spaceship Earth," in *Environmental Quality in a Growing Economy*, edited by Henry Jarrett. Baltimore: Johns Hopkins Press, pp. 3–14.

9. Boulding, Kenneth, "Environment and Economics," in [66], pp. 359–367.

10. Bray, Jeremy, *The Politics of the Environment*, Fabian Tract 412. London: Fabian Society, 1972.

11. Bridgman, P. W., "Statistical Mechanics and the Second Law of Thermodynamics," in *Reflections of a Physicist*, 2d ed. New York: Philosophical Library, 1955, pp. 236–268.

12. Brown, Harrison, "Human Materials Production as a Process in the Biosphere." *Scientific American*, September 1970, 195–208.

13. Brown, Lester R., and Gail Finsterbusch, "Man, Food and Environment," in [66], pp. 53–69.

14. Cannon, James, "Steel: The Recyclable Material." *Environment*, November 1973, 11–20.

15. Cloud, Preston, ed., *Resources and Man*. San Francisco: W. H. Freeman, 1969.

16. Cloud, Preston, "Resources, Population, and Quality of Life," in *Is There an Optimum Level of Population?*, edited by S. F. Singer. New York: McGraw-Hill, 1971, pp. 8–31.

17. Cloud, Preston, "Mineral Resources in Fact and Fancy," in [66], pp. 71–88.

18. Commoner, Barry, *The Closing Circle*. New York: Knopf, 1971.

19. Culbertson, John M., *Economic Development: An Ecological Approach*. New York: Knopf, 1971.

20. Daly, Herman E., "Toward a Stationary-State Economy," in *Patient Earth*, edited by J. Hart and R. Socolow. New York: Holt, Rinehart and Winston, pp. 226–244.

21. Daly, Herman E., *The Stationary-State Economy*. Distinguished Lecture Series No. 2, Department of Economics, University of Alabama, 1971.

22. Daniels, Farrington, *Direct Use of the Sun's Energy*. New Haven: Yale University Press, 1964.

23. Einstein, Albert, and Leopold Infeld, *The Evolution of Physics*. New York: Simon and Schuster, 1938.

24. "The Fragile Climate of Spaceship Earth." *Intellectual Digest*, March 1972, 78–80.

25. Georgescu-Roegen, Nicholas, "The Theory of Choice and the Constancy of Economic Laws." *Quarterly Journal of Economics*, February 1950, 125–138. Reprinted in [29], pp. 171–183.

26. Georgescu-Roegen, Nicholas, "Toward a Partial Redirection of Econometrics," Part III, *Review of Economics and Statistics*, 34, 3 (August, 1952), pp. 206–211.

27. Georgescu-Roegen, Nicholas, "Process in Farming versus Process in Manufacturing: A Problem of Balanced Development," in *Economic Problems of Agriculture in Industrial Societies*, Ugo Papi and Charles Nunn, eds. London: Macmillan; New York: St. Martin's Press, 1969, pp. 497–528.

28. Georgescu-Roegen, Nicholas, "Further Thoughts on Corrado Gini's *Dellusioni dell' econometria*," *Metron*, 25, 104 (1966), pp. 265–279.

29. Georgescu-Roegen, Nicholas *Analytical Economics: Issues and Problems*. Cambridge: Harvard University Press, 1966.

30. Georgescu-Roegen, Nicholas, "The Economics of Production," *American Economic Review*, 40, 2 (May, 1970), pp. 1–9.

31. Georgescu-Roegen, Nicholas, "The Entropy Law and the Economic Problem." Reprinted in this volume.

32. Georgescu-Roegen, Nicholas, *The Entropy Law and the Economic Process*. Cambridge: Harvard University Press, 1971.

33. Georgescu-Roegen, Nicholas, "Process Analysis and the Neoclassical Theory of Production," *American Journal of Agricultural Economics*, 54, 2, (May, 1972), pp. 279–294.

34. Gillette, Robert, "The Limits to Growth: Hard Sell for a Computer View of Doomsday." *Science*, 10 March 1972, 1088–1092.

35. Gillette, Robert, "Nuclear Safety: Damaged Fuel Ignites a New Debate in AEC." *Science*, 28 July 1972, 330–331.

36. Gillette, Robert, "Reactor Safety: AEC Concedes Some Points to Its Critics." *Science*, 3 November 1972, 482–484.

37. Glaser, Peter E., "Power from the Sun: Its Future." *Science*, 22 November 1968, 857–861.

38. Goeller, H. E., "The Ultimate Mineral Resource Situation." *Proceedings of the National Academy of Science, USA*, October 1972, 2991–2992.

39. Gofman, John W., "Time for a Moratorium." *Environmental Action,* November 1972, 11–15.

40. Haar, D. ter, "The Quantum Nature of Matter and Radiation, " in *Turning Points in Physics,* [5], pp. 30–44.

41. Hammond, Allen L., "Solar Energy: A Feasible Source of Power?" *Science,* 14 May 1971, 660.

42. Hardin, Garrett, "The Tragedy of the Commons." *Science,* 13 December 1968, 1234–1248.

43. Hibbard, Walter R., Jr., "Mineral Resources: Challenge or Threat?" *Science,* 12 April 1968, 143–145.

44. Holdren, John, and Philip Herera, *Energy.* San Francisco: Sierra Club, 1971.

45. Hotelling, Harold, "The Economics of Exhaustible Resources." *Journal of Political Economy,* March–April 1931, 137–175.

46. Hubbert, M. King, "Energy Resources," in [15], pp. 157–242.

47. Istock, Conrad A., "Modern Environmental Deterioration as a Natural Process." *International Journal of Environmental Studies,* 1971, 151–155.

48. Jevons, W. Stanley, *The Theory of Political Economy,* 2d ed. London: Macmillan, 1879.

49. Johnson, Harry G., *Man and His Environment,* London: The British-North American Committee, 1973.

50. Katchalsky, A., and Peter F. Curran, *Nonequilibrium Thermodynamics in Biophysics.* Cambridge, Mass.: Harvard University Press, 1965.

51. Kaysen, Carl, "The Computer that Printed Out W*O*L*F*." *Foreign Affairs,* July 1972, 660–668.

52. Kneese, Allen, and Ronald Ridker, "Predicament of Mankind." *Washington Post,* 2 March 1972.

53. Laplace, Pierre Simon de, *A Philosophical Essay on Probability.* New York: Wiley, 1902.

54. Leontief, Wassily, "Theoretical Assumptions and Nonobservable Facts." *American Economic Review,* March 1971, 1–7.

55. "Limits to Misconception." *The Economist,* 11 March 1972, 20–22.

56. Lovering, Thomas S., "Mineral Resources from the Land," in [15], pp. 109–134.

57. MacDonald, Gordon J. F., "Pollution, Weather and Climate," in [66], pp. 326–336.

58. Maddox, John, "Raw Materials and the Price Mechanism." *Nature,* 14 April 1972, 331–334.

59. Maddox, John, *The Doomsday Syndrome.* New York: McGraw-Hill, 1972.

60. Marshall, Alfred. *Principles of Economics,* 8th ed. London: Macmillan, 1920.

61. Marx, Karl. *Capital*. 3 vols. Chicago: Charles H. Kerr, 1906–1933.

62. Meadows, Donella H. et al., *The Limits to Growth*. New York: Universe Books, 1972.

63. Metz, William D., "Fusion: Princeton Tokamak Proves a Principle." *Science*, 22 December 1972, 1274B.

64. Mill, John Stuart, *Principles of Political Economy*, in *Collected Works*, vols. II–III. Edited by J. M. Robson, Toronto: University of Toronto Press, 1965.

65. Mishan, E. J., *Technology and Growth: The Price We Pay*. New York: Praeger, 1970.

66. Murdoch, William W., ed., *Environment: Resources, Pollution and Society*. Stamford, Conn.: Sinauer, 1971.

67. Novick, Sheldon, "Nuclear Breeders." *Environment*, July–August 1974, 6–15.

68. Pigou, A. C., *The Economics of Stationary States*. London: Macmillan, 1935.

69. *Report on Limits to Growth*. Mimeographed. A Study of the Staff of the International Bank for Reconstruction and Development, Washington, D.C., 1972.

70. Revelle, Roger, "Food and Population." *Scientific American*, September 1974, 161–170.

71. Schrödinger, Erwin, *What is Life?* Cambridge, England: The University Press, 1944.

72. Silk, Leonard, "On the Imminence of Disaster." *New York Times*, 14 March 1972.

73. Solo, Robert A., "Arithmomorphism and Entropy." *Economic Development and Cultural Change*, April 1974, 510–517.

74. Solow, Robert M., "Is the End of the World at Hand?" *Challenge*, March–April 1973, 39–50.

75. Solow, Robert M., "The Economics of Resources or the Resources of Economics." Richard T. Ely Lecture, *American Economic Review*, May 1974, 1–14.

76. Spengler, Joseph J., "Was Malthus Right?" *Southern Economic Journal*, July 1966, 17–34.

77. Spengler, Joseph J. "Homosphere, Seen and Unseen: Retreat from Atomism." *Proceedings of the Nineteenth Southern Water Resources and Pollution Control Conference*, 1970, pp. 7–16.

78. Sprout, Harold, and Margaret Sprout, *Multiple Vulnerabilities*. Mimeographed. Research Monograph No. 40, Center of International Studies, Princeton University, 1974.

79. Summers, Claude M., "The Conversion of Energy." *Scientific American*, September 1971, 149–160.

80. Wallich, Henry C., "How to Live with Economic Growth." *Fortune*, October 1972, 115–122.

81. Weinberg, Alvin M., "Breeder Reactors." *Scientific American*, January 1960, 82–94.

82. Weinberg, Alvin M., "Social Institutions and Nuclear Energy." *Science,* 7 July 1972, 27–34.

83. Weinberg, Alvin M., and R. Philip Hammond, "Limits to the Use of Energy." *American Scientist,* July–August 1970, 412–418.

5

LIMITS TO EXPLOITATION OF NONRENEWABLE RESOURCES

Earl Cook

Nonrenewable resources consist of geochemical concentrations of naturally occurring elements and compounds that can or may be exploited at a profit. The concentrations that are at present exploitable at a profit range from slightly more than twice to several thousand times the average crustal abundance of the desired element (Table 5.1). Rates of concentration into ore bodies or oil pools appear to be slow compared to the pace of human history. Moreover, the formation of deposits of ores and mineral fuels appears to require unusual to extraordinary geologic conditions; consequently, such deposits are unevenly distributed in space and time, and they commonly occupy very small portions of the lithic prisms in which they are found.

Almost 70 percent of proved crude-oil reserves are in the Middle East, and five countries produce more than 65 percent of the world's copper. These nonuniform distributions are real and do not merely reflect differences in

From *Science*, Vol. 191, pp. 677–682, 20 February, 1976. Copyright © 1976 by the American Association for the Advancement of Science. Reprinted by permission of the author and the publisher.

TABLE 5.1

Ratio of cutoff grade (the lowest concentration economically recoverable in 1975) to crustal abundance for selected elements. Except for carbon, which is from Mason (27), crustal abundances are from Lee and Yao (28). Values are parts per million (ppm).

Element	Crustal abundance (ppm)	Cutoff grade (ppm)	Ratio
Mercury	0.089	1,000	11,200
Tungsten	1.1	4,500	4,000
Lead	12	40,000	3,300
Chromium	110	230,000	2,100
Tin	1.7	3,500	2,000
Silver	0.075	100	1,330
Gold	0.0035	3.5	1,000
Molybdenum	1.3	1,000	770
Zinc	94	35,000	370
Uranium	1.7	700	350
Carbon	320	100,000	310
Lithium	21	5,000	240
Manganese	1,300	250,000	190
Nickel	89	9,000	100
Cobalt	25	2,000	80
Phosphorus	1,200	88,000	70
Copper	63	3,500	56
Titanium	6,400	100,000	16
Iron	58,000	200,000	3.4
Aluminum	83,000	185,000	2.2

exploration effort. Many of the most common ore deposits appear genetically and spatially related to the boundaries of crustal plates (*1*). Other ore deposits not associated with crustal-plate margins may be localized by uplift of the crust over thermal plumes (*2*). Petroleum as well as metallogenic provinces exist, and the world's coal deposits are strikingly concentrated in the temperate belt of the Northern Hemisphere.

Not only are geologic resources distributed unevenly over the surface of the globe, they are concentrated in the outermost part of the earth's continental crust. Mechanisms that concentrate chemical elements operate most effectively on and near the earth's surface: weathering, erosion, sorting during transport, groundwater leaching, and supergene enrichment are effective only in the upper few hundred meters of the continents. Hot metal-bearing solutions encounter the precipitating effect of colder meteoric waters and find relatively high permeability only in the upper few thousand meters of the crust. Oil and gas formation, migration, and entrapment take place within the thin and discontinuous sedimentary skin of the continents. There is a hoary myth among old prospectors that ore bodies widen and get rich downward. In fact, they generally do just the opposite. The rich gold and silver deposits of the American cordillera are notorious for bottoming at depths of a few tens to a thousand meters. The Comstock Lode and the several ore bodies at Guanajuato (3) are excellent examples. The mineral-fuel analog is the transition zone in a reservoir rock between crude oil and water, a zone commonly only a meter or two thick; the world's greatest oil well, Cerro Azul No. 4 in Mexico, after producing more than 50 million barrels of oil, suddenly produced only salt water.

The limited nature of individual deposits, the difficulty of seeing through rock, and the history of many mining districts and oil fields have led to many forecasts of depletion and exhaustion. But, as old deposits have become exhausted and new ones have become harder to find, world mineral and fossil-fuel production paradoxically has continued to increase. There is a wide difference of opinion now on the question of limits to the exploitation of nonrenewable resources.

THREE KINDS OF LIMITS

To the mining or petroleum engineer, the profit of exploitation is defined by the difference between the price received for his product and the pecuniary costs of recovering the natural material and turning it into a salable product. To society, however, the profit from mining (including oil and gas extraction) can be defined either as an energy surplus, as from the exploitation of fossil and nuclear fuel deposits, or as a work saving, as in the lessened expenditure of human energy and time when steel is used in place of wood in tools and structures. In this context, the exploitation of earth resources for display, adornment, or monetary backing is a deficit operation, financed by energy profits from other kinds of mining.

The ultimate limit to exploitation of earth resources then is the limit of net energy profit (or work savings). When it takes more energy to find, recover, process, and transport the fossil fuels than can be gotten from them in useful form, there will be no more oil, gas, or coal resources. When it takes so much energy or work to produce a nonenergy material that one must sacrifice other, more needed, items or services to pay for it, there will be no more resources of that material. Short of this energetic limit, one or both of two other limits may intervene. First is the limit of comparable utility. A resource is a resource only while it can be used to perform a function desired by man better or more cheaply than can another substance. If the energy cost of an earth resource such as crude oil rises to a level at which another substance, such as synthetic crude oil from coal, can be substituted in adequate volume at a lower cost for comparable utility, substitution will take place, with the first resource reverting to a mere geochemical anomaly and the source of the replacing substance becoming a resource.

The limit to a resource also may be determined by the unwillingness of society to pay the cost of its exploitation, even though an energy surplus (or saving) might be obtained thereby. According to Sahlins (4) many primitive societies preferred to take their energy surplus in leisure rather than in goods (stored energy or work) and deliberately abstained from exploiting available potential resources that could have increased their surplus. Some primitive agricultural societies still do this. Rappaport (5) has described a New Guinean society in which agricultural surplus is taken in leisure when the option of taking it in meat or goods is clearly open. A modern decision to forgo the calculable energy benefits of the breeder-reactor power plant would again invoke this limit of living-level degradation, a limit that comes into play when a society is not willing to pay the total costs of production—because so doing would, it is judged, lower the level of living more than would forgoing use of the resource.

EFFECTS OF TECHNOLOGY AND CHEAP ENERGY

To some, the history of nonrenewable resource exploitation seems to contradict the idea of an energetic limit short of mining common rock and "burning" seawater (6). During the past 150 years large increases in the earth-resource base of industrialized society have been attained. By increasing the efficiencies of discovery, recovery, processing, and application of such resources, we have been able to find and exploit leaner, deeper, and more remote deposits. By discovering and developing new methods of utilizing previously worthless materials we have created resources where none existed. Important in this rapid technologic advance has been a progressive lowering of the cost of energy per unit of work or useful heat obtained. Cheaper energy, along with technological ingenuity and discovery, has greatly extended the availability of nonenergy resources. In 1900 the lowest grade of copper ore economically minable was about 3 percent; today the economic cutoff has fallen to about 0.35 percent; at that grade each ton of refined copper produced requires the breaking, transport, and milling of almost 300 tons of rock and, in addition, the removal of perhaps an equal amount of waste or barren rock. A great deal of energy—about 26,000 kilowatt-hours (7), the equivalent of the energy in about 4 metric tons of Wyoming coal—is required to produce a metric ton of copper today, but the cost of that energy is still low compared to the cost of supporting the equivalent in men and mules.

Many past forecasts of the exhaustion of one or more earth resources have come to appear almost wildly inaccurate in the light of later production. Forty

TABLE 5.2

Comparison of the ratio of reserves to production (R/P) in 1934 with the same ratio and the ratio of reserves to primary consumption (R/Cp) in 1974 for five major earth resources. Figures are for the United States. Figures for copper, iron ore, lead, and zinc are in thousands of metric tons; for crude oil, in millions of barrels. The 1974 statistics, except for crude oil, are from the Bureau of Mines (29); values have been converted to metric tons. Crude oil production and reserve figures are from (9), net imports and primary consumption from (30). The 1934 approximate R/P figures are from Leith (8).

Resource	1934 R/P approx-imate	1974 Do-mestic mine (well) pro-duction	1974 Net imports (primary and second-ary)	1974 Do-mestic second-ary supply	1974 Do-mestic reserves (R)	1974 R/P	1974 Do-mestic primary con-sumption (Cp)	1974 R/Cp
Copper	40	1,441	391	455	81,800	57	1,640	50
Iron ore	18	83,000	46,000	NA*	2,000,000	24	140,500	14
Lead	15–20	615	82	564	53,600	87	800	67
Zinc	15–20	447	655	77	27,300	61	1,150	24
Crude oil	15–20	3,043	1,268	NA*	34,250	11.2	4,447	7.7

*NA, not applicable.

years ago, geologist C. K. Leith, for example, called attention to the coming exhaustion of U.S. mineral resources, claiming (8, p. 169) that "despite a magnificent endowment [of metals and fuels], depletion is further advanced than even mining men generally realize." At the time Leith wrote, proved reserves of crude oil, zinc, and lead in the United States were 15 to 20 times larger than annual production rates, the Lake Superior iron ores appeared to have less than 20 years of measured supply remaining, and known copper reserves were about 40 times the 1934 production. Leith went on:

> Further discovery and the use of the lower grade resources will extend the life of most of these resources, but the range of possibilities is now pretty well under-stood, and with maximum allowance for such extension, the figures are suffi-ciently small, when compared with what we hope will be the life of the nation, as to be matters of public concern. . . . Discovery has not stopped, but the rate has been slowing. . . . Of 33 metal-mining districts that have yielded the greatest wealth to date only 5 have been discovered since 1900 and none at all since 1907. . . . The rate of discovery of oil and gas continues high . . . but the chances of finding another East Texas or Kettleman Hills are not promising.

Well, what happened? Since 1935, the United States has produced more zinc than it did before that year. In 1974 the U.S. mine production of zinc (Table 5.2) could have been maintained for 61 years on the then-known re-serves; the ratio of domestic reserves to primary consumption (defined as domestic demand less the recycled or secondary supply) stood at 24, despite the fact that demand had soared.

Although U.S. lead production since 1935 does not equal the pre-1936 total, the ratio of measured reserves to primary consumption in 1974 was 67, and the 1974 mine production could have continued for 87 years without further discovery.

The Lake Superior iron ore of Leith's day has been virtually exhausted, but it has been largely replaced by taconite, a low-grade iron-bearing rock not considered to be ore in 1935. The 1974 ratio of measured reserves to U.S. iron-ore consumption was 14, and at the 1974 rate of U.S. mine production, the reserves would last about 24 years.

Since 1935, more copper has been mined in the United States than before. Based on 1974 figures, the ratio of reserves to primary consumption was 50, and U.S. mine production could have continued at the 1974 level for 57 years without new discoveries.

More recoverable crude oil (77.3 billion barrels) has been discovered since 1935 than was produced from 1857 through 1934 (62.0 billion barrels). At the end of 1974, however, the ratio of proved reserves to 1974 production was only about 11. Perhaps more significantly, the ratio of proved reserves to 1974 consumption (of both domestic and foreign petroleum) was only 7.7.

In regard to these major earth resources, the United States in 1975 was substantially worse off than it was in 1935 only in crude oil. Despite large increases in consumption rates over the past 40 years, we now have many more "years" of lead reserves than we did 40 years ago, as well as about 25 percent more years of copper and zinc reserves—even if we were abruptly deprived of all imports of these metals. With continued imports, our iron-ore reserve position is much better than it was 40 years ago; without imports, we have lost only 4 years of reserves in 40 years.

In the short term, and except for oil, Leith appears to have been wrong. The continuous-creation school of resource analysts would classify him as a doom-sayer of the past whose forecasts went awry for the same reason that those of the present-day Cassandras will miss the mark, a lack of understanding of the impact on reserves of continuously improving technology, which geologists Nolan (*10*) once called "the inexhaustible resource."

The view that advances in technology, stimulated by the market economy, will prolong the availability of a mineral commodity almost indefinitely or will provide adequate substitutes when rising cost begins to slow demand, has much evidence in its favor and many strong adherents (*11*). There is currently an oversupply of both copper and crude oil in the world, and the supply of ores of iron and aluminum, despite enormous increases in the production and consumption of both during the past 50 years, seems almost boundless.

Why, then, do some (*12*) persist in the opposite view, that physical limits will slow or halt the development and utilization of most earth resources long before crustal concentrations can be regarded as reserves? Perhaps it is because they are impressed by the steepness of the geochemical gradients at the margins of most ore and fossil-fuel deposits, by the fact that such deposits do not show a compensating increase in tonnage of reserves (calculated as recoverable metal or fuel) as grade decreases, by the environmental limitations on their origin, and by the fact that the energy or work cost of recovery increases exponentially with decreasing grade of the ore or with increasing cumulative recovery in the case of crude oil.

EXAMPLES OF EXPLOITATION LIMITS

The so-called porphyry copper mines, which now produce more than half the world's copper, are worth looking at in the context of exploitation limits. Although differing considerably in detail, they have certain features in common (13, 14). They are sharply restricted in age of formation to three periods, or pulses, within the range of 30 million to 200 million years ago. They are associated with small intrusive bodies of stocklike form, averaging 1200 by 2000 meters in outcrop. The ore bodies tend to be pipelike and oval in plan, with dimensions of approximately 1000 by 2000 meters. Mineralization is in concentric zones (15), with the copper content in the center of the body reaching ten times that at the outer edge of metallization (16). Vertical dimensions can reach 3000 meters, but the pipe narrows downward. If, as Sillitoe (17) believes, the porphyry copper deposit spans the boundary between the plutonic and volcanic environments, it occupies a very special geologic position indeed, sharply limited in both time and space.

The Toquepala and Cuajone mines in Peru are typical of the porphyry coppers (18, 19). The mass of mineralized rock in these deposits has the shape of an inverted and truncated cone, within which the copper content ranges from 1.32 percent to less than 0.45 percent, the present cutoff grade, below which mining and processing would be unprofitable. Rock containing between 0.20 and 0.45 percent copper is, however, being mined and stockpiled for later leaching by sulfuric acid. Below an average of about 1 percent copper, the copper content of the ore (Table 5.3) decreases sharply as the grade drops. The deposits, although the ore minerals are irregularly disseminated through them, have rather sharp geochemical boundaries, and the diameter of the mineralized cone decreases downward. The energy cost, per kilogram or ton of refined copper, of mining and milling the ore increases inversely with grade and directly with depth.

At Cuajone, if the ore cutoff grade were to fall from the present 0.45 percent to 0.20 percent (the upper and lower boundaries of the 102 million tons that average 0.32 percent), the total copper recovery would be increased by only 7 percent. At Toquepala, a similar lowering of the cutoff grade would increase recoverable copper by less than 4 percent. Because economies of scale appear to have been exploited fully, and because energy costs are rising,

TABLE 5.3

Relations of ore grade, copper content, and mining and milling energy at Cuajone mine, Peru. Values in the last column are Δ per short ton of copper, where Δ is the energy required to mine and mill a short ton of 1.00 percent copper ore. To convert short tons of metric tons, divide by 1.1023.

Average grade (%)	Tonnage (short tons) ($\times 10^3$)	Copper content (short tons) ($\times 10^3$)	Energy needed to mine and mill (Δ/ton)
1.32	20,000	264	0.76
0.99	430,000	4,257	1.01
0.32	102,000	326.4	3.13
< 0.20*	1,057,000	66.6*	> 16,000

*Mostly barren overburden of post-ore volcanic rocks; calculated at crustal abundance for copper content and energy needed.

it does not appear likely that the ore reserves in these mines will be extended much either by technological advances or rises in the price of copper.

A tonnage-grade analysis of known North American porphyry copper deposits (*20*) indicates that 70 percent of the copper metal is in deposits above 0.7 percent copper; lower-grade deposits do not represent increasingly larger amounts of copper, but the reverse. Analyses of the known deposits of the two other principal types of copper deposits, strata-bound and massive sulfide, suggest similar tonnage-grade relations (*21; 22*, p. 167). Significant, too, is the fact that the rate of additions to reserves of copper metal appears to have been falling off since 1960, during a period when the price of copper has risen strongly; here it is important to distinguish between tonnage of ore and tonnage of contained metal. Many more deposits will need to be found, at a faster pace than recently, if copper production is to continue at high levels into the coming century. Furthermore, there appears to be a geochemical barrier to copper recovery at about 0.1 percent copper (16 times the geochemical background), below which most copper is in solid solution in common silicate minerals and is not amenable to selective physical or chemical extraction (*22*, p. 129).

The basic question in forecasting earth-resource exhaustion is whether or not the energy-profit limit will be reached, or demand will cease, short of attempts to extract the desired resource from ordinary rock and seawater. For some resources, we can say with assurance that the energy-profit limit will be reached long before ordinary rock can be mined profitably. The fossil fuels are the best and most important examples. The energy potential represented by the average concentration of carbon in the earth's crust is 2.9 kilowatt-hours per metric ton, not nearly enough to crush and grind it to liberate the carbon for use. In large modern copper-ore mills, grinding and classification (separation)

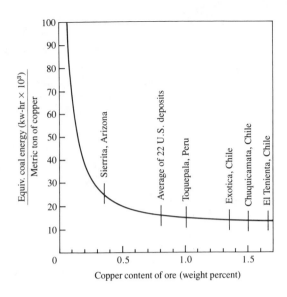

FIGURE 5.1

Equivalent coal energy requirements for different grades of copper sulfide ores. Grades of some copper deposits are shown (25, figure 2).

alone require about 26 kilowatt-hours (coal equivalent) per metric ton of ore milled. We can thus be sure that the sharp physical boundaries that characterize coal and petroleum deposits are also economic boundaries. In fact, for most petroleum deposits the economic limit of exploitation lies within the deposit rather than at its margins; oil clings so tenaciously to the pore walls of reservoir rocks that to flush it all out would require more energy than can be gotten from it. The curve of incremental recovery against energy cost is steeply exponential for so-called tertiary recovery techniques, and to achieve an average cumulative recovery ratio of even 40 percent from American reservoirs will require much higher prices for oil than can now be foreseen (23).

On the other hand, there are very large low-grade deposits of uranium in which the potential energy is more than sufficient to break, transport, and pulverize the rock, and then to recover the uranium. Breeder reactors converting 60 percent of the potential energy of uranium to thermal energy and 40 percent of that to electricity could produce more than 5500 kilowatt-hours per metric ton of average crustal rock, which might allow an energy profit to be returned. The question here is the amount of energy required for mining and milling very low grade ore. Not only does the tonnage of ore necessary to produce 1 ton of metal increase hyperbolically as the grade decreases (24; 25, p. 10) (Figure 5.1), but the energy input per ton of ore ground increases as the size required to liberate small particles of ore decreases (26). As ore grade decreases, the percentage of the valuable metal recovered in milling decreases; this falling off in recovery efficiency has the effect of increasing the energy cost per unit of refined metal. Finally, the ore generally gets harder to break and more expensive to lift as mining goes deeper; therefore, the energy costs of mining (per ton of recovered metal) tend to increase as exploitation continues.

The energy required to produce refined metal from low-grade ores becomes extremely high at grades that, except for iron and aluminum, are well above the corresponding crustal abundances.

Except in the cases of strip-mined coal and Persian Gulf oil, the energy costs of obtaining useful energy are rising as found sources grow deeper, leaner, and more recalcitrant or refractory and as income sources become limited. Coal exploitable by stripping and Persian Gulf oil are clearly finite, and production of both is likely to wane within 25 to 40 years. Increased costs of obtaining useful energy and higher work costs of exploiting leaner or more refractory materials will tend to raise present ore cutoff limits and thereby to reduce reserves, while technologists continue the struggle to lower cutoff grades and augment reserves. Only a breakthrough of provident technology that results in a substantial lowering of energy costs would reverse what appears to be a tightening of the drawstring on nature's bag of nonenergy resources. The breeder reactor may represent such a breakthrough.

DEPLETION HISTORIES

The history of a mining district of an oil field has a beginning and an end, separated by a productive period. Some histories end abruptly, others are drawn out. Resurrection is rare. The history of the Comstock silver lode (Figure 5.2) illustrates a simple depletion pattern characteristic of high-grade, sharply bounded, vertically limited mineral deposits. The Comstock vein system, a candelabrum with tabular branches, is typical of fractures that fill with ore minerals at shallow depths; the system is rich and intricate near the surface, barren and simple a few thousand feet below. Its production history shows three distinct stages. In the first stage, during which the greatest part of the lode's total value was extracted, high-grade ore was mined at a fast rate. In the second stage, it became possible because of technological improvements to mine lower-grade material bepassed in the first stage. In the final stage, waste material and some very low grade ore were processed by a new technology, but little was added to the value already produced.

Somewhat different from the history of the Comstock is that of the Lake Superior iron district. Depletion of the rich "direct shipping" ores of that district is almost complete (Figure 5.3). These ores, created by a geologic process related to groundwater levels and to the particular geologic configurations of the district, had sharp physical boundaries that coincided with economic limits. In the waning stage of production, upgrading of low-grade mate-

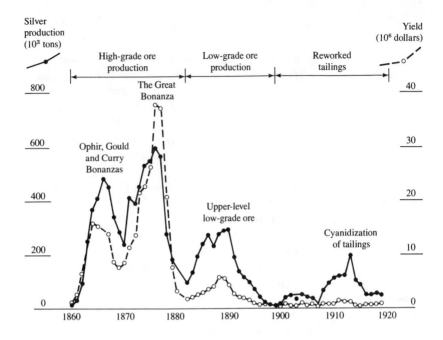

FIGURE 5.2

Production history of the Comstock Lode in Nevada. The data for 1860–1881 are from Lord (*31*); the data for 1882–1920 are from Smith (*32*).

rial into shippable concentrates added substantially to total production, but delayed exhaustion by only a few years. However, the Lake Superior district has been revived through a technological breakthrough that created a very large resource out of a previously worthless iron-bearing rock called taconite. Such provident technology can be effective only where there is a deposit, already concentrated by natural processes, characterized by a refractory host or reservoir rock. Taconite production, now in its youthful stage, will also pass through maturity to exhaustion.

Iron and aluminum are abundant elements in the earth's crust. For each, there are several kinds of geologic concentrations that represent actual or potential resources; consequently, for each we may expect the depletion history to consist of a series of production-history curves, as availability and cost dictate a steplike descent from high-grade hematite to taconite to iron-rich intrusive bodies, and from bauxite to alunite to high-alumina clays.

When we move in scale from an individual mining district to a country, we find fewer examples of complete production cycles. Mercury, however, is an essentially exhausted resource within the United States, and its production history shows some significant relations to price (Figure 5.4). Exploitation of mercury went through three phases: a waxing phase, during which increases in production caused the price to fall; a mature phase, during which price and

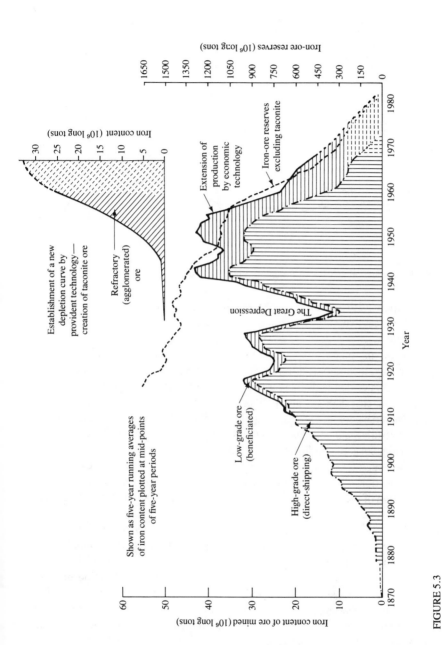

FIGURE 5.3

Depletion history of Lake Superior district iron ore, showing overlapping stages of depletion of a mining region.

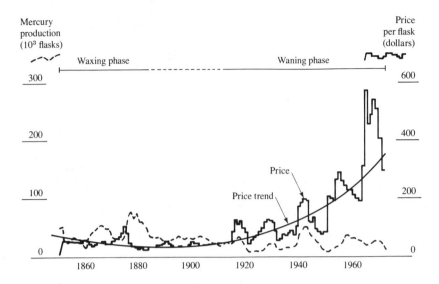

FIGURE 5.4

Production and price history of mercury in the United States (33).

production were more or less in equilibrium; and a waning phase, during which successive surges in price evoked progressively weaker responses in production.

The waxing phase represents a period when real cost falls because of new discoveries, technological improvements, and economies of scale. The falling cost stimulates demand. Increased production hastens the exhaustion of high-grade, low-cost deposits and puts pressure on technology to counter increasingly adverse geologic and geographic conditions. When technology begins to lose the battle, real cost rises and the waning phase is entered. Prices rise with increasing costs of production and demand falls. Sharply rising prices stimulate the search for a substitute, either imports of the same substance or domestic production of a replacement material; if a substitute is found, domestic production of the resource ceases; if not, it is stretched out, diminishing slowly as demand wanes.

The relation of production and price curves for U.S. silver is similar to that for mercury (19, p. 21) and the curves for crude oil are developing in like fashion. During the waxing phase of U.S. oil production, gluts of oil drove the price down to or below the actual cost of production. Proliferation of automobiles and trucks was stimulated by cheap fuel, and demand grew. The passage to the waning phase, about 1971, was abrupt because of the large cost differential between domestic and foreign crude oil at a time of strongly rising demand, a differential that forces a rapid shift from domestic production to imports. Current, artificially high, world crude-oil prices have encouraged exploration for new domestic reserves and have stimulated new efforts to recover more oil from existing wells. It is almost certain, however, that we shall not see a production response equivalent to the price rise because the costs of finding and recovering crude oil (and natural gas) increase exponentially with depletion. If the present cartel of oil exporting countries collapses and world oil prices fall sharply, the end of the U.S. production curve will be abrupt. If the cartel does not collapse, but an adequate supply of substitute energy, say from coal or oil shale, is developed at or near the present price of crude oil, the end of U.S. crude production will be slower but similarly assured.

CONCLUSION

In view of the geologic and geochemical constraints on the occurrence of economic deposits of minerals and energy resources, and the advanced nature of present exploitation techniques, we must conclude that such resources are finite. The "endlessly retreating" interface between ore and almost-ore that some optimists have described could be validated only if the cost of useful energy would endlessly and acceleratingly decrease. On the other hand, the question "When will we run out?" bespeaks a misunderstanding of geologic resource limits. The world will not run out of geologic resources. They will merely become more expensive. As they become more expensive their utility will diminish, either by human decision or by failure to achieve an energetic profit. How expensive a geologic resource becomes, and how fast its real cost rises, will depend on a combination of geologic and technological factors. Depletion (rise in cost) is swift for those materials found mainly in sharply bounded, highly concentrated deposits—especially swift if they cannot be recycled after use. Depletion is slow for abundant materials found mainly in deposits of relatively low geochemical concentration with gradational boundaries—especially slow if they can be recycled after use.

• • •

Our society and economy are growth- and production-oriented.* Goods and services are produced but do not accumulate indefinitely; coincident with production is waste or entropy increase (the dispersion of materials and the degration of energy toward useless heat), which *does* accumulate indefinitely. The ultimate constraint on a growth society is entropic.

Mineral and energy deposits have low entropy relative to average rock. At considerable energy cost, their entropy is further lowered by concentration and refining. No energy profit can be made by reducing entropy; when we do it, we save human energy at the expense of fossil energy. In application or use, most geologic resources are degraded: their entropy increases. The fossil

---

*This section reprinted from *Technology Review*, June 1975, with permission of the publisher.

fuels, the agricultural chemicals, many of the construction minerals, and some of the metals are degraded beyond energetic recall. On the other hand, the low entropy of metals used in structures, machines, pipes, wires, and batteries may be conserved for recycling.

Two critical elements in the conservation of geologic resources as they become scarce and costly will be the development of economic ways to reduce or delay entropy increase; and the social rationing of depletion. The first subject has been treated in evocative fashion by Nicholas Georgescu-Roegen, while the latter has been explored by Herman Daly. Because actual recycling and reforming of materials can be done with only a relatively small fraction of the material used by an industrial society, increased attention is likely to be given to forming structural elements so that they can be rehabilitated in place or recovered for use elsewhere; and, of course, common materials will be used wherever practicable in place of scarce ones. Eventually, dissatisfaction with the market as the allocating mechanism for the social benefits of resource use is apt to bring depletion rationing of those resources which can be neither recycled nor reused and for which demand exceeds supply. Barring a breakthrough in the technology of energy, the present industrialized nations will have severe readjustments to make in the next 50 years.

If we neglect to conserve the remaining natural subsidy of the fossil fuels, there may be little hope for the nonindustrialized countries, except through luck or aggression, to supply their citizens with needed minerals, for without a substantial energy surplus that can be allocated to their exploitation, the nonenergy mineral resources do not exist, no matter how much mineral is in the ground. Industrialized nations may be compelled to uncommon ingenuity in use of common materials to avoid devolution into a retrograde agricultural society.

The dynamics and ethics of our production-oriented society will make thermodynamic thrift very difficult to achieve. The government now proposes tax cuts and other incentives to stimulate the U.S. public to buy more things, in order to "get America rolling again." High on the list of things we are urged to buy is the automobile, a machine that merits inclusion in *The Guinness Book of World Records* as the champion resource wastrel of the modern era. In the push to get workers back to the assembly line, government has not taken into account the realistic *need* for the product or the cost to future generations in nonrenewable resources depleted and entropy irrevocably increased by the production of unneeded machines. I consider most new cars unneeded because it is patent that the majority of citizens can get by with the cars they now have, perhaps for several years, with no decrease in actual transport utility.

Sometime in the not-too-distant future, Americans will look back with astonishment at our ignorance of the world we live in. Because of diminishing resources and continued population growth, we are heading for a planned, managed society. Just how restraining or undemocratic that society will become may depend in large measure on how quickly and successfully we move to minimize entropy increase and resource depletion—which, after all, are the same thing.

• • •

SUMMARY

Despite the fact that strongly positive geochemical anomalies are relatively small and rare and appear to be restricted to the outermost part of continental crusts, the history of economic exploitation of nonrenewable resources over the past 200 years is, in general, one of decreasing costs and increasing reserves. However, the direct energy or work costs of recovery have been rising, slowly for a long while, then more rapidly as the number of tons of ore required to produce a ton of refined metal has started to rise more steeply with decreasing ore grade. The seeming paradox of decreasing total costs and increasing work costs is explained by a long record of decreasing real costs of the energy used to extract and process nonrenewable resources. Now that energy resources themselves are beginning to cost more in work, now that the efficiencies of energy conversion appear to be nearing limits dictated by the strength of materials and the laws of thermodynamics, and now that the work costs of recovery, at least for some resources, are moving up the steeper parts of exponential curves, the nature of the limits to exploitation of nonrenewable resources is beginning to be recognized.

NOTES

1. P. W. Guild, *Schriftenr. Erdwiss. Komm. Osterr. Akad. Wiss.* 1, 10 (1974).

2. J. F. Dewey and K. Burke, *EOS* 54, 239 (1973).

3. W. H. Gross, *Econ. Geol.* 70, 1175 (1975).

4. M. Sahlins, *Stone Age Economics* (Aldine-Atherton, Chicago, 1972).

5. R. A. Rappaport, in *Energy and Power* (W. H. Freeman and Company, San Francisco, 1971), pp. 69–80.

6. D. B. Brooks and P. W. Andrews, for example, claim that "it is simply not true that average rock will never be mined" [*Science* 185, 15 (1975)].

7. J. C. Agarwal and J. R. Sinek, in *Energy Use and Conservation and the Metals Industry*, Y. A. Chang, W. M. Danver, J. M. Cigan, Eds. (Metallurgical Society of the AIME, New York, 1975), pp. 122, 124. The reader will note that this estimate exceeds that implied by the curve of Figure 5.1

8. C. K. Leith, *Science* 82, 109 (1935); reprinted in *Man and His Physical Environment*, G. D. McKenzie and R. O. Utgard, eds. (Burgess, Minneapolis, 1975), pp. 168–171.

9. *Reserves of Crude Oil, Natural Gas Liquids, and Natural Gas in the United States and Canada and United States Productive Capacity as of December 31, 1974* American Gas Association, Arlington, Va., American Petroleum Institute, Washington, D.C., Canadian Petroleum Association, Calgary, Alberta, May 1975).

10. T. B. Nolan, in *Perspectives on Conservation,* H. Jarrett, ed. (Johns Hopkins Press, Baltimore, 1958), p. 49.

11. See, for examples, H. J. Barnett, in *The Survival Equation,* R. Revelle, A. Khosla, M. Vinovskis, eds. (Houghton Mifflin, Boston, 1971), pp. 180–186; V. McKelvey, *U.S. Geol. Surv. Prof. Pap. 820* (1973), pp. 9–19.

12. Articulate exponents of this point of view include T. S. Lovering, in *Resources and Man,* P. Cloud, ed. (W. H. Freeman and Company, San Francisco, 1969), pp. 109—134; P. Cloud, in *Environment,* W. W. Murdoch, ed. (Sinauer, Sunderland, Mass., 1975), pp. 97—120.

13. A. H. James, *Econ. Geol.* 66, 43 (1971).

14. J. D. Lowell, ibid. 69, 601 (1974).

15. J. D. Lowell and J. M. Guilbert, ibid. 65, 373 (1970).

16. A. W. Rose, ibid., p. 920.

17. R. H. Sillitoe, ibid. 68, 799 (1973); ibid. 70, 1190 (1975).

18. Some of this section is taken from Cook (*19*).

19. E. Cook, *Technol. Rev.* 77 (No. 7), 14 (1975).

20. J. W. Whitney, *Econ. Geol.* 70, 527 (1975).

21. D. A. Singer, D. P. Cox, L. J. Drew, *U.S. Geol. Surv. Prof. Pap. 907-A* (1975).

22. Committee on Mineral Resources and the Environment, National Research Council, *Mineral Resources and the Environment* (National Academy of Sciences, Washington, D.C., 1975).

23. *Oil Gas J.* 73, 26 (17 November 1975).

24. Page and Creasy (*25*) show that the tonnage of rock required to produce 1 ton of metal increases very sharply below a metal content of 1 percent . . . and that there is a similar sharp inversion in the energy-cost curve for refined copper at about 0.3 percent ore. They believe that there is a demonstrable energy limit to the exploitation of copper sulfide ores, at or above 0.2 percent ore.

25. N. J. Page and S. C. Creasy, *J. Res. U.S. Geol. Surv.* 3, 10 (1975).

26. An empirical equation developed by R. J. Charles [*Trans. AIME* 208, 87 (1957)] expresses this relation. The equation, as revised by R. Schuhmann, Jr. [ibid. 217, 22 (1960)] is $E = AK^a$, in which E is the energy input per unit volume of material, A is a constant, K is the size modulus, and a is the distribution modulus. See also L. M. Berlioz and D. W. Fuerstenau [ibid. 238, 282 (1967)].

27. B. Mason, *Principles of Geochemistry* (Wiley, New York, 2nd ed., 1958).

28. T. Lee and C. Yao, *Int. Geol. Rev.* 12, 778 (1970).

29. U.S. Bureau of Mines, *Commodity Data Summaries* (Bureau of Mines, Washington, D.C., 1975).

30. U.S. Department of the Interior, Bureau of Mines, "U.S. energy use down in 1974 after two decades of increases," press release, 3 April 1975.

31. E. Lord, *Comstock Mining and Miners* (U.S. Geological Survey, Washington, D.C., 1883), p. 416.

32. G. H. Smith, *Univ. Nev. Bull.* 37 (No. 3), 297 (1943).

33. E. H. Bailey, A. L. Clark, R. M. Smith, in *United States Mineral Resources,* D. A. Brobst and W. P. Pratt, Eds. (U.S. Geological Survey, Washington, D.C., 1973), figure 46, p. 404.

6

THE TRAGEDY OF THE COMMONS

Garrett Hardin

At the end of a thoughtful article on the future of nuclear war, Wiesner and York[1] concluded that:

> "Both sides in the arms race are . . . confronted by the dilemma of steadily increasing military power and steadily decreasing national security. *It is our considered professional judgment that this dilemma has no technical solution.* If the great powers continue to look for solutions in the area of science and technology only, the result will be to worsen the situation.

I would like to focus your attention not on the subject of the article (national security in a nuclear world) but on the kind of conclusion they reached, namely that there is no technical solution to the problem. An implicit and almost universal assumption of discussions published in professional and semipopular scientific journals is that the problem under discussion has a technical solution. A technical solution may be defined as one that requires a

"The Tragedy of the Commons." From *Science*, Vol. 162, pp. 1243–1248, 13 December 1968. Copyright 1968 by the American Association for the Advancement of Science. Reprinted by permission of the author and the publisher.

change only in the techniques of the natural sciences, demanding little or nothing in the way of change in human values or ideas of morality.

In our day (though not in earlier times) technical solutions are always welcome. Because of previous failures in prophecy, it takes courage to assert that a desired technical solution is not possible. Wiesner and York exhibited this courage; publishing in a science journal, they insisted that the solution to the problem was not to be found in the natural sciences. They cautiously qualified their statement with the phrase, "It is our considered professional judgment. . . ." Whether they were right or not is not the concern of the present article. Rather, the concern here is with the important concept of a class of human problems which can be called "no technical solution problems," and, more specifically, with the identification and discussion of one of these.

It is easy to show that the class is not a null class. Recall the game of tick-tack-toe. Consider the problem "How can I win the game of tick-tack-toe?" It is well known that I cannot, if I assume (in keeping with the conventions of game theory) that my opponent understands the game perfectly. Put another way, there is no "technical solution" to the problem. I can win only by giving a radical meaning to the word "win." I can hit my opponent over the head; or I can drug him; or I can falsify the records. Every way in which I "win" involves, in some sense, an abandonment of the game, as we intuitively understand it. (I can also, of course, openly abandon the game—refuse to play it. This is what most adults do.)

The class of "no technical solution problems" has members. My thesis is that the "population problem," as conventionally conceived, is a member of this class. How it is conventionally conceived needs some comment. It is fair to say that most people who anguish over the population problem are trying to find a way to avoid the evils of overpopulation without relinquishing any of the privileges they now enjoy. They think that farming the seas or developing new strains of wheat will solve the problem—technologically. I try to show here that the solution they seek cannot be found. The population problem cannot be solved in a technical way, any more than can the problem of winning the game of tick-tack-toe.

WHAT SHALL WE MAXIMIZE?

Population, as Malthus said, naturally tends to grow "geometrically," or, as we would now say, exponentially. In a finite world this means that the per capita share of the world's goods must steadily decrease. Is ours a finite world?

A fair defense can be put forward for the view that the world is infinite; or that we do not know that it is not. But, in terms of the practical problems that we must face in the next few generations with the foreseeable technology, it is clear that we will greatly increase human misery if we do not, during the immediate future, assume that the world available to the terrestrial human population is finite. "Space" is no escape.[2]

A finite world can support only a finite population; therefore, population growth must eventually equal zero. (The case of perpetual wide fluctuations above and below zero is a trivial variant that need not be discussed.) When this condition is met, what will be the situation of mankind? Specifically, can Bentham's goal of "the greatest good for the greatest number" be realized?

No—for two reasons, each sufficient by itself. The first is a theoretical one. It is not mathematically possible to maximize for two (or more) variables at the same time. This was clearly stated by von Neumann and Morgenstern,[3] but the principle is implicit in the theory of partial differential equations, dating back at least to D'Alembert (1717–1783).

The second reason springs directly from biological facts. To live, any organism must have a source of energy (for example, food). This energy is utilized for two purposes: mere maintenance and work. For man, maintenance of life requires about 1600 kilocalories a day ("maintenance calories"). Anything that he does over and above merely staying alive will be defined as work, and is supported by "work calories" which he takes in. Work calories are used not only for what we call work in common speech; they are also required for all forms of enjoyment, from swimming and automobile racing to playing music and writing poetry. If our goal is to maximize population it is obvious what we must do: We must make the work calories per person approach as close to zero as possible. No gourmet meals, no vacations, no sports, no music, no literature, no art. . . . I think that everyone will grant, without argument or proof, that maximizing population does not maximize goods. Bentham's goal is impossible.

In reaching this conclusion I have made the usual assumption that it is the acquisition of energy that is the problem. The appearance of atomic energy has led some to question this assumption. However, given an infinite source of energy, population growth still produces an inescapable problem. The problem of the acquisition of energy is replaced by the problem of its dissipation, as J. H. Fremlin has so wittily shown.[4] The arithmetic signs in the analysis are, as it were, reversed; but Bentham's goal is still unobtainable.

The optimum population is, then, less than the maximum. The difficulty of defining the optimum is enormous; so far as I know, no one has seriously tackled this problem. Reaching an acceptable and stable solution will surely require more than one generation of hard analytical work—and much persuasion.

We want the maximum good per person; but what is good? To one person it is wilderness, to another it is ski lodges for thousands. To one it is estuaries to nourish ducks for hunters to shoot; to another it is factory land. Comparing one good with another is, we usually say, impossible because goods are incommensurable. Incommensurables cannot be compared.

Theoretically this may be true; but in real life incommensurables *are* commensurable. Only a criterion of judgment and a system of weighting are needed. In nature the criterion is survival. Is it better for a species to be small and hideable, or large and powerful? Natural selection commensurates the incommensurables. The compromise achieved depends on a natural weighting of the values of the variables.

Man must imitate this process. There is no doubt that in fact he already does, but unconsciously. It is when the hidden decisions are made explicit that the arguments begin. The problem for the years ahead is to work out an acceptable theory of weighting. Synergistic effects, nonlinear variation, and difficulties in discounting the future make the intellectual problem difficult, but not (in principle) insoluble.

Has any cultural group solved this practical problem at the present time, even on an intuitive level? One simple fact proves that none has: there is no prosperous population in the world today that has, and has had for some time, a growth rate of zero. Any people that has intuitively identified its optimum point will soon reach it, after which its growth rate becomes and remains zero.

Of course, a positive growth rate might be taken as evidence that a population is below its optimum. However, by any reasonable standards, the most rapidly growing populations on earth today are (in general) the most miserable. This association (which need not be invariable) casts doubt on the optimistic assumption that the positive growth rate of a population is evidence that it has yet to reach its optimum.

We can make little progress in working toward optimum population size until we explicitly exorcize the spirit of Adam Smith in the field of practical demography. In economic affairs, *The Wealth of Nations* (1776) popularized the "invisible hand," the idea that an individual who "intends only his own gain," is, as it were, "led by an invisible hand to promote . . . the public interest."[5] Adam Smith did not assert that this was invariably true, and perhaps neither did any of his followers. But he contributed to a dominant tendency of thought that has ever since interfered with positive action based on rational analysis, namely, the tendency to assume that decisions reached individually will, in fact, be the best decisions for an entire society. If this assumption is correct it justifies the continuance of our present policy of laissez-faire in reproduction. If it is correct we can assume that men will control their individual fecundity so as to produce the optimum population. If the assumption is not correct, we need to reexamine our individual freedoms to see which ones are defensible.

THE TRAGEDY OF FREEDOM IN A COMMONS

The rebuttal to the invisible hand in population control is to be found in a scenario first sketched in a little-known pamphlet[6] in 1833 by a mathematical amateur named William Forster Lloyd (1794–1852). We may well call it "the tragedy of the commons," using the word "tragedy" as the philosopher White-head used it:[7] "The essence of dramatic tragedy is not unhappiness. It resides in the solemnity of the remorseless working of things." He then goes on to say, "This inevitableness of destiny can only be illustrated in terms of human life by incidents which in fact involve unhappiness. For it is only by them that the futility of escape can be made evident in the drama."

The tragedy of the commons develops in this way. Picture a pasture open to all. It is to be expected that each herdsman will try to keep as many cattle as possible on the commons. Such an arrangement may work reasonably satis-factorily for centuries because tribal wars, poaching, and disease keep the numbers of both man and beast well below the carrying capacity of the land. Finally, however, comes the day of reckoning, that is, the day when the long-desired goal of social stability becomes a reality. At this point, the inherent logic of the commons remorselessly generates tragedy.

As a rational being, each herdsman seeks to maximize his gain. Explicitly or implicitly, more or less consciously, he asks, "What is the utility to *me* of adding one more animal to my herd?" This utility has one negative and one positive component.

1. The positive component is a function of the increment of one animal. Since the herdsman receives all the proceeds from the sale of the additional animal, the positive utility is nearly $+1$.

2. The negative component is a function of the additonal overgrazing created by one more animal. Since, however, the effects of overgraz-ing are shared by all the herdsmen, the negative utility for any particular decision-making herdsman is only a fraction of -1.

Adding together the component partial utilities, the rational herdsman con-cludes that the only sensible course for him to pursue is to add another animal to his herd. And another; and another. . . . But this is the conclusion reached by each and every rational herdsman sharing a commons. Therein is the tragedy. Each man is locked into a system that compels him to increase his herd without limit—in a world that is limited. Ruin is the destination toward which all men rush, each pursuing his own best interest in a society that believes in the freedom of the commons. Freedom in a commons brings ruin to all.

Some would say that this is a platitude. Would that it were! In a sense, it was learned thousands of years ago, but natural selection favors the forces of psychological denial.[8] The individual benefits as an individual from his ability to deny the truth even though society as a whole, of which he is a part, suffers. Education can counteract the natural tendency to do the wrong thing, but the inexorable succession of generations requires that the basis for this knowledge be constantly refreshed.

A simple incident that occurred a few years ago in Leominster, Massachusetts, shows how perishable the knowledge is. During the Christmas shopping season the parking meters downtown were covered with plastic bags that bore tags reading: "Do not open until after Christmas. Free parking courtesy of the mayor and city council." In other words, facing the prospect of an increased demand for already scarce space, the city fathers reinstituted the system of the commons. (Cynically, we suspect that they gained more votes than they lost by this retrogressive act.)

In an approximate way, the logic of the commons has been understood for a long time, perhaps since the discovery of agriculture or the invention of private property in real estate. But it is understood mostly only in special cases which are not sufficiently generalized. Even at this late date, cattlemen leasing national land on the western ranges demonstrate no more than an ambivalent understanding, in constantly pressuring federal authorities to increase the head count to the point where overgrazing produces erosion and weed dominance. Likewise, the oceans of the world continue to suffer from the survival of the philosophy of the commons. Maritime nations still respond automatically to the shibboleth of the "freedom of the seas." Professing to believe in the "inexhaustible resources of the oceans," they bring species after species of fish and whales closer to extinction.[9]

The National Parks present another instance of the working out of the tragedy of the commons. At present, they are open to all, without limit. The parks themselves are limited in extent—there is only one Yosemite Valley —whereas population seems to grow without limit. The values that visitors seek in the parks are steadily eroded. Plainly, we must soon cease to treat the parks as commons or they will be of no value to anyone.

What shall we do? We have several options. We might sell them off as private property. We might keep them as public property, but allocate the right to enter them. The allocation might be on the basis of wealth, by the use of an auction system. It might be on the basis of merit, as defined by some agreed-upon standards. It might be by lottery. Or it might be on a first-come, first-served basis, administered to long queues. These, I think, are all the reasonable possibilities. They are all objectionable. But we must choose—or acquiesce in the destruction of the commons that we call our National Parks.

POLLUTION

In a reverse way, the tragedy of the commons reappears in problems of pollution. Here it is not a question of taking something out of the commons, but of putting something in—sewage, or chemical, radioactive, and heat wastes into water; noxious and dangerous fumes into the air; and distracting and unpleasant advertising signs into the light of sight. The calculations of utility are much the same as before. The rational man finds that his share of the cost of the wastes he discharges into the commons is less than the cost of purifying his wastes before releasing them. Since this is true for everyone, we are locked into a system of "fouling our own nest," so long as we behave only as independent, rational, free-enterprisers.

The tragedy of the commons as a food basket is averted by private property, or something formally like it. But the air and waters surrounding us cannot readily be fenced, and so the tragedy of the commons as a cesspool must be prevented by different means, by coercive laws or taxing devices that make it cheaper for the polluter to treat his pollutants than to discharge them untreated. We have not progressed as far with the solution of this problem as we have with the first. Indeed, our particular concept of private property, which deters us from exhausting the positive resources of the earth, favors pollution. The owner of a factory on the bank of a stream—whose property extends to the middle of the stream—often has difficulty seeing why it is not his natural right to muddy the waters flowing past his door. The law, always behind the times, requires elaborate stitching and fitting to adapt it to this newly perceived aspect of the commons.

The pollution problem is a consequence of population. It did not much matter how a lonely American frontiersman disposed of his waste. "Flowing water purifies itself every ten miles," my grandfather used to say, and the myth was near enough to the truth when he was a boy, for there were not too many people. But as population became denser, the natural chemical and biological recycling processes became overloaded, calling for a redefinition of property rights.

HOW TO LEGISLATE TEMPERANCE?

Analysis of the pollution problem as a function of population density uncovers a not generally recognized principle of morality, namely: *the morality of an act is a function of the state of the system at the time it is performed.*[10] Using the commons as a cesspool does not harm the general public under frontier conditions, because there is no public; the same behavior in a metropolis is unbearable. A hundred and fifty years ago a plainsman could kill an American bison, cut out only the tongue for his dinner, and discard the rest of the animal. He was not in any important sense being wasteful. Today, with only a few thousand bison left, we would be appalled at such behavior.

In passing, it is worth noting that the morality of an act cannot be determined from a photograph. One does not know whether a man killing an elephant or setting fire to the grassland is harming others until one knows the total system in which his act appears. "One picture is worth a thousand words," said an ancient Chinese; but it may take 10,000 words to validate it. It is as tempting to ecologists as it is to reformers in general to try to persuade others by way of the photographic shortcut. But the essence of an argument cannot be photographed: it must be presented rationally—in words.

That morality is system-sensitive escaped the attention of most codifiers of ethics in the past. "Thou shalt not . . ." is the form of traditional ethical directives which make no allowance for particular circumstances. The laws of our society follow the pattern of ancient ethics, and therefore are poorly suited to governing a complex, crowded, changeable world. Our epicyclic solution is to augment statutory law with administrative law. Since it is practically impossible to spell out all the conditions under which it is safe to burn trash in the back yard or to run an automobile without smog-control, by law we delegate the details to bureaus. The result is administrative law, which is rightly feared for an ancient reason—*Quis custodiet ipsos custodes?*—"Who shall watch the watchers themselves?" John Adams said that we must have "a government of laws and not men." Bureau administrators, trying to evalute the morality of acts in the total system, are singularly liable to corruption, producing a government by men, not laws.

Prohibition is easy to legislate (though not necessarily to enforce); but how do we legislate temperance? Experience indicates that it can be accomplished best through the mediation of administrative law. We limit possibilities unnecessarily if we suppose that the sentiment of *Quis custodiet* denies us the use of administrative law. We should rather retain the phrase as a perpetual reminder of fearful dangers we cannot avoid. The great challenge facing us now is to invent the corrective feedbacks that are needed to keep custodians honest. We must find ways to legitimate the needed authority of both the custodians and the corrective feedbacks.

FREEDOM TO BREED IS INTOLERABLE

The tragedy of the commons is involved in population problems in another way. In a world governed solely by the principle of "dog eat dog"—if indeed there ever was such a world—how many children a family had would not be a matter of public concern. Parents who bred too exuberantly would leave fewer descendants, not more, because they would be unable to care adequately for their children. David Lack and others have found that such a negative feedback demonstrably controls the fecundity of birds.[11] But men are not birds, and have not acted like them for millenniums, at least.

If each human family were dependent only on its own resources; *if* the children of improvident parents starved to death; *if*, thus, overbreeding brought its own "punishment" to the germ line—*then* there would be no public interest in controlling the breeding of families. But our society is deeply committed to the welfare state,[12] and hence is confronted with another aspect of the tragedy of the commons.

In a welfare state, how shall we deal with the family, the religion, the race, or the class (or indeed any distinguishable and cohesive group) that adopts overbreeding as a policy to secure its own aggrandizement?[13] To couple the concept of freedom to breed with the belief that everyone born has an equal right to the commons is to lock the world into a tragic course of action.

Unfortunately this is just the course of action that is being pursued by the United Nations. In late 1967, some thirty nations agreed to the following:[14]

> The Universal Declaration of Human Rights describes the family as the natural and fundamental unit of society. It follows that any choice and decision with regard to the size of the family must irrevocably rest with the family itself, and cannot be made by someone else.

It is painful to have to deny categorically the validity of this right; denying it, one feels as uncomfortable as a resident in of Salem, Massachusetts, who denied the reality of witches in the seventeeth century. At the present time, in liberal quarters, something like a taboo acts to inhibit criticism of the United Nations. There is a feeling that the United Nations is "our last and best hope," that we shouldn't find fault with it; we shouldn't play into the hands of the archconservatives. However, let us not forget what Robert Louis Stevenson said: "The truth that is suppressed by friends is the readiest weapon of the enemy." If we love the truth we must openly deny the validity of the Universal Declaration of Human Rights, even though it is promoted by the United Nations. We should also join with Kingsley Davis[15] in attempting to get Planned Parenthood-World Population to see the error of its ways in embracing the same tragic ideal.

CONSCIENCE IS SELF-ELIMINATING

It is a mistake to think that we can control the breeding of mankind in the long run by an appeal to conscience. Charles Galton Darwin made this point when he spoke on the centennial of the publication of his grandfather's great book. The argument is straightforward and Darwinian.

People vary. Confronted with appeals to limit breeding, some people will undoubtedly respond to the plea more than others. Those who have more children will produce a larger fraction of the next generation than those with more susceptible consciences. The difference will be accentuated, generation by generation.

In C. G. Darwin's words: "It may well be that it would take hundreds of generations for the progenitive instinct to develop in this way, but if it should do so, nature would have taken her revenge, and the variety *Homo contracipiens* would become extinct and would be replaced by the variety *Homo progenitivus.*"[16]

The argument assumes that conscience or the desire for children (no matter which) is hereditary—but hereditary only in the most general formal sense. The result will be the same whether the attitude is transmitted through germ cells, or exosomatically, to use A. J. Lotka's term. (If one denies the latter possibility as well as the former, then what's the point of education?) The argument has here been stated in the context of the population problem, but it applies equally well to any instance in which society appeals to an individual exploiting a commons to restrain himself for the general good—by means of his conscience. To make such an appeal is to set up a selective system that works toward the elimination of conscience from the race.

PATHOGENIC EFFECTS OF CONSCIENCE

The long-term disadvantage of an appeal to conscience should be enough to condemn it; but it has serious short-term disadvantages as well. If we ask a man who is exploiting a commons to desist "in the name of conscience," what are we saying to him? What does he hear?—not only at the moment but also in the wee small hours of the night when, half asleep, he remembers not merely the words we used but also the nonverbal communication cues we gave him unawares? Sooner or later, consciously or subconsciously, he senses that he has received two communications, and that they are contradictory: (1, the intended communication) "If you don't do as we ask, we will openly condemn you for not acting like a responsible citizen"; (2, the unintended communication) "If you *do* behave as we ask, we will secretly condemn you for a simpleton who can be shamed into standing aside while the rest of us exploit the commons."

Everyman then is caught in what Bateson has called a "double bind." Bateson and his co-workers have made a plausible case for viewing the double bind as an important causative factor in the genesis of schizophrenia.[17] The double bind may not always be so damaging, but it always endangers the mental health of anyone to whom it is applied. "A bad conscience," said Nietzsche, "is a kind of illness."

To conjure up a conscience in others is tempting to anyone who wishes to extend his control beyond the legal limits. Leaders at the highest level succumb to this temptation. Has any President during the past generation failed to call on labor unions to moderate voluntarily their demands for higher wages, or to steel companies to honor voluntary guidelines on prices? I can recall none. The rhetoric used on such occasions is designed to produce feelings of guilt in noncooperators.

For centuries it was assumed without proof that guilt was a valuable, perhaps even an indispensable, ingredient of the civilized life. Now, in this post-Freudian world, we doubt it.

Paul Goodman speaks from the modern point of view when he says:

> No good has ever come from feeling guilty, neither intelligence, policy, nor compassion. The guilty do not pay attention to the object but only to themselves, and not even to their own interests, which might make sense, but to their anxieties.[18]

One does not have to be a professional psychiatrist to see the consequences of anxiety. We in the Western world are just emerging from a dreadful two-centuries-long Dark Ages of Eros that was sustained partly by prohibition laws, but perhaps more effectively by the anxiety-generating mechanisms of education. Alex Comfort has told the story well in *The Anxiety Makers;*[19] it is not a pretty one.

Since proof is difficult, we may even concede that the results of anxiety may sometimes, from certain points of view, be desirable. The larger question we should ask is whether, as a matter of policy, we should ever encourage the use of a technique the tendency (if not the intention) of which is psychologically pathogenic. We hear much talk these days of responsible parenthood; the coupled words are incorporated into the titles of some organizations devoted to birth control. Some people have proposed massive propaganda campaigns to instill responsibility into the nation's (or the world's) breeders. But what is the meaning of the word responsibility in this context? Is it not merely a synonym for the word conscience? When we use the word responsibility in the absence of substantial sanctions are we not trying to browbeat a free man in a commons into acting against his own interest? Responsibility is a verbal counterfeit for a substantial *quid pro quo*. It is an attempt to get something for nothing.

If the word responsibility is to be used at all, I suggest that it be in the sense Charles Frankel uses it.[20] "Responsibility," says this philosopher, "is the product of definite social arrangements." Notice that Frankel calls for social arrangements—not propaganda.

MUTUAL COERCION MUTUALLY AGREED UPON

The social arrangements that produce responsibility are arrangements that create coercion, of some sort. Consider bank robbing. The man who takes money from a bank acts as if the bank were a commons. How do we prevent such action? Certainly not by trying to control his behavior solely by a verbal appeal to his sense of responsibility. Rather than rely on propaganda we follow Frankel's lead and insist that a bank is not a commons; we seek the definite social arrangements that will keep it from becoming a commons. That we thereby infringe on the freedom of would-be robbers we neither deny nor regret.

The morality of bank robbing is particularly easy to understand because we accept complete prohibition of this activity. We are willing to say "Thou shalt not rob banks," without providing for exceptions. But temperance also can be created by coercion. Taxing is a good coercive device. To keep downtown shoppers temperate in their use of parking space we introduce parking meters for short periods, and traffic fines for longer ones. We need not actually forbid a citizen to park as long as he wants to; we need merely make it increasingly expensive for him to do so. Not prohibition, but carefully biased options are what we offer him. A Madison Avenue man might call this persuasion; I prefer the greater candor of the word coercion.

Coercion is a dirty word to most liberals now, but it need not forever be so. As with the four-letter words, its dirtiness can be cleansed away by exposure to the light, by saying it over and over without apology or embarrassment. To many, the word coercion implies arbitrary decisions of distant and irresponsible bureaucrats; but this is not a necessary part of its meaning. The only kind of coercion I recommend is mutual coercion, mutually agreed upon by the majority of the people affected.

To say that we mutually agree to coercion is not to say that we are required to enjoy it, or even to pretend we enjoy it. Who enjoys taxes? We all grumble about them. But we accept compulsory taxes because we recognize that voluntary taxes would favor the conscienceless. We institute and (grumblingly) support taxes and other coercive devices to escape the horror of the commons.

An alternative to the commons need not be perfectly just to be preferable. With real estate and other material goods, the alternative we have chosen is the institution of private property coupled with legal inheritance. Is this sytem perfectly just? As a genetically trained biologist I deny that it is. It seems to me that, if there are to be differences in individual inheritance, legal possession should be perfectly correlated with biological inheritance—that those who are biologically more fit to be the custodians of property and power should legally inherit more. But genetic recombination continually makes a mockery of the doctrine of "like father, like son" implicit in our laws of legal inheritance. An idiot can inherit millions, and a trust fund can keep his estate intact. We must admit that our legal system of private property plus inheritance is unjust—but we put up with it because we are not convinced, at the moment, that anyone has invented a better system. The alternative of the commons is too horrifying to contemplate. Injustice is preferable to total ruin.

It is one of the peculiarities of the warfare between reform and the status quo that it is thoughtlessly governed by a double standard. Whenever a reform measure is proposed it is often defeated when its opponents triumphantly discover a flaw in it. As Kingsley Davis has pointed out,[21] worshippers of the status quo sometimes imply that no reform is possible without unanimous agreement, an implication contrary to historical fact. As nearly as I can make out, automatic rejection of proposed reforms is based on one of two unconscious assumptions: (1) that the status quo is perfect; or (2) that the choice we face is between reform and no action; if the proposed reform is imperfect, we presumably should take no action at all, while we wait for a perfect proposal.

But we can never do nothing. That which we have done for thousands of years is also action. It also produces evils. Once we are aware that the status quo is action, we can then compare its discoverable advantages and disadvantages with the predicted advantages and disadvantages of the proposed reform, discounting as best we can for our lack of experience. On the basis of such a comparison, we can make a rational decision which will not involve the unworkable assumption that only perfect systems are tolerable.

RECOGNITION OF NECESSITY

Perhaps the simplest summary of this analysis of man's population problems is this: the commons, if justifiable at all, is justifiable only under conditions of low-population density. As the human population has increased, the commons has had to be abandoned in one aspect after another.

First we abandoned the commons in food gathering, enclosing farm land and restricting pastures and hunting and fishing areas. These restructions are still not complete throughout the world.

Somewhat later we saw that the commons as a place for waste disposal would also have to be abandoned. Restrictions on the disposal of domestic sewage are widely accepted in the Western world; we are still struggling to close the commons to pollution by automobiles, factories, insecticide sprayers, fertilizing operations, and atomic energy installations.

In a still more embryonic state is our recognition of the evils of the commons in matters of pleasure. There is almost no restriction on the propagation of sound waves in the public medium. The shopping public is assaulted with mindless music, without its consent. Our government is paying out billions of dollars to create supersonic transport which will disturb 50,000 people for every one person who is whisked from coast to coast three hours faster. Advertisers muddy the airwaves of radio and television and pollute the view of travelers. We are a long way from outlawing the commons in matters of pleasure. Is this because our Puritan inheritance makes us view pleasure as something of a sin, and pain (that is, the pollution of advertising) as the sign of virtue?

Every new enclosure of the commons involves the infringement of somebody's personal liberty. Infringements made in the distant past are accepted because no contemporary complains of a loss. It is the newly proposed infringements that we vigorously oppose; cries of "rights" and "freedom" fill the air. But what does "freedom" mean? When men mutually agreed to pass laws against robbing, mankind became more free, not less so. Individuals locked into the logic of the commons are free only to bring on universal ruin; once they see the necessity of mutual coercion, they become free to pursue other goals. I believe it was Hegel who said, "Freedom is the recognition of necessity."

The most important aspect of necessity that we must now recognize, is the necessity of abandoning the commons in breeding. No technical solution can rescue us from the misery of overpopulation. Freedom to breed will bring ruin to all. At the moment, to avoid hard decisions many of us are tempted to propagandize for conscience and responsible parenthood. The temptation must be resisted, because an appeal to independently acting consciences selects for the disappearance of all conscience in the long run, and an increase in anxiety in the short.

The only way we can preserve and nurture other and more precious freedoms is by relinquishing the freedom to breed, and that very soon. "Freedom is the recognition of necessity"—and it is the role of education to reveal to all the necessity of abandoning the freedom to breed. Only so, can we put an end to this aspect of the tragedy of the commons.

NOTES

1. J. B. Wiesner and H. F. York, *Scientific American* 211 (No. 4), 27 (1964). Offprint 319.

2. G. Hardin, *J. Hered.* 50, 68 (1959); S. von Hoernor, *Science* 137, 18 (1962).

3. J. von Neumann and O. Morgenstern. *Theory of Games and Economic Behavior* (Princeton Univ. Press, Princeton, N.J., 1947), p. 11.

4. J. H. Fremlin, *New Sci.*, No. 415 (1964), p. 285.

5. A. Smith, *The Wealth of Nations* (Modern Library, New York, 1937), p. 423.

6. W. F. Lloyd, *Two Lectures on the Checks to Population* (Oxford Univ. Press, Oxford, England, 1833) reprinted (in part) in G. Hardin, ed., *Population, Evolution, and Birth Control*, 2nd ed. (W. H. Freeman and Company, San Francisco, 1969), p. 28.

7. A. N. Whitehead, *Science and the Modern World* (Mentor, New York, 1948), p. 17.

8. G. Hardin, ed., *Population, Evolution, and Birth Control*, 2nd ed. (W. H. Freeman and Company, San Francisco, 1969), p. 46.

9. S. McVay, *Scientific American* 216 (No. 8), 13 (1966). Offprint 1046.

10. J. Fletcher, *Situation Ethics* (Westminster, Philadelphia, 1966).

11. D. Lack, *The Natural Regulation of Animal Numbers* (Clarendon Press, Oxford, 1954).

12. H. Girvetz, *From Wealth to Welfare* (Stanford Univ. Press, Stanford, Calif., 1950).

13. G. Hardin, *Perspec. Biol. Med.* 6, 366 (1963).

14. U. Thant, *Int. Planned Parenthood News,* No. 168 (February 1968), p. 3.

15. K. Davis, *Science* 158, 730 (1967).

16. S. Tax, ed., *Evolution after Darwin* (Univ. of Chicago Press, Chicago, 1960), vol. 2, p. 469.

17. G. Bateson, D. D. Jackson, J. Haley, J. Weakland, *Behav. Sci.* 1, 251 (1956).

18. P. Goodman, *New York Rev. Books* 10 (8), 22 (23 May 1968).

19. A. Comfort, *The Anxiety Makers* (Nelson, London, 1967).

20. C. Frankel, *The Case for Modern Man* (Harper, New York, 1955), p. 203.

21. J. D. Roslansky, *Genetics and the Future of Man* (Appleton-Century-Crofts, New York, 1966), p. 177.

7

SECOND THOUGHTS ON "THE TRAGEDY OF THE COMMONS"

Garrett Hardin

A scholar who ventures outside his own field can confidently expect soon to be informed that his pronouncements are not as original as he has supposed. So much have I learned in publishing "The Tragedy of the Commons." Though officially trained only in microbiology (and in only a micropart of that vast field), in writing "Tragedy" I did not hesitate to make assertions that impinged on the fields of economics, political science, human behavior, and ethics. I was soon informed that there was a considerable literature on "common pool resources" in economics and that Aristotle long ago had said, "What is common to the greatest number gets the least amount of care." So what is new in my essay?

Just this, I think: the *emphasis* on the tragedy of the situation. Aristotle's statement is as bland as a bureaucrat's: It hardly impels one to take action. Yet action is what we must have now that the world is overcrowded—action in the form of rejecting the commons as a distribution system. Failing that, a tragic end is our fate.

No fate is intrinsically inevitable; rather, each fate is contingent upon the mechanism that produces it. How overpopulation leads to a disastrous end was clearly set forth by an English geologist and minister, Joseph Townsend (1739–1816), in *A Dissertation on the Poor Laws,* published in 1786, a decade after Adam Smith's *Wealth of Nations.* The essential passage follows:

In the South Seas there is an island, which from the first discoverer is called Juan Fernandez. In this sequestered spot, John Fernando placed a colony of goats, consisting of one male, attended by his female. This happy couple finding pasture in abundance, could readily obey the first commandment, to increase and multiply, till in process of time they had replenished their little island. In advancing to this period they were strangers to misery and want, and seemed to glory in their numbers: but from this unhappy moment they began to suffer hunger; yet continuing for a time to increase their numbers, had they been endued with reason, they must have apprehended the extremity of famine. In this situation the weakest first gave way, and plenty was again restored. Thus they fluctuated between happiness and misery, and either suffered want or rejoiced in abundance, according as their numbers were diminished or increased; never at a stay, yet nearly balancing at all times their quantity of food. This degree of aequipoise was from time to time destroyed, either by epidemical diseases or by the arrival of some vessel in distress. On such occasions their numbers were considerably reduced; but to compensate for this alarm, and to comfort them for the loss of their companions, the survivors never failed immediately to meet returning plenty. They were no longer in fear of famine: they ceased to regard each other with an evil eye; all had abundance, all were contented, all were happy. Thus, what might have been considered as misfortunes, proved a source of comfort; and, to them at least, partial evil was universal good.

When the Spaniards found that the English privateers resorted to this island for provisions, they resolved on the total extirpation of the goats, and for this purpuse they put on shore a greyhound dog and bitch. These in their turn increased and multiplied, in proportion to the quantity of the food they met with; but in consequence, as the Spaniards had foreseen, the breed of goats diminished. Had they been totally destroyed, the dogs likewise must have perished. But as many of the goats retired to the craggy rocks, where the dogs could never follow them, descending only for short intervals to feed with fear and circumspection in the vallies, few of these, besides the careless and the rash, became a prey; and none but the most watchful, strong, and active of the dogs could get a sufficiency of food. Thus a new kind of balance was established. The weakest of both species were among the first to pay the debt of nature; the most active and vigorous preserved their lives. It is the quantity of food which regulates the numbers of the human species. In the woods, and in the *savage state,* there can be few inhabitants; but of these there will be only a proportionable few to suffer want. As long as food is plenty they will continue to increase and multiply; and every man will have ability to support his family, or to relieve his friends, in proportion to his activity and strength. The weak must depend upon the precarious bounty of the strong; and, sooner or later, the lazy will be left to suffer the natural consequence of their indolence. Should they introduce a community of goods, and at the same time leave every man at liberty to marry, they would at first increase their numbers, but not the sum total of their happiness, till by degrees, all by being equally reduced to want and misery, the weakly would be the first to perish.

Ashley Montagu, commenting on this passage, says: "Townsend recounts the story of what is purported to have happened on Robinson Crusoe's island."

The word *purported* belittles the moral of the story. Whether or not Townsend's tale is historically correct, the moral is nonetheless supported by empirical facts. In our time, David Klein's study of the reindeer on St. Matthew Island tells essentially the same story and points to the same moral. A population of 29 animals, minus predators, released on this remote island off the coast of Alaska, multiplied to 6,000 animals in 19 years and then, through starvation, "crashed" to 42 in three years. The 42 were in miserable condition and probably all sterile. This may well be the end of the story, though it is possible that the population might later "fluctuate between happiness and misery," as supposed by Townsend. In any case, a predator-free population, multiplying freely and enjoying "a community of goods," can know only transient happiness as it races toward overpopulation.

Stability and happiness are possible only if the positive feedback of natural biological reproduction—interest earning interest, *compound interest* in economic terms—finds a countervailing force in negative feedback. To use other terms, *runaway feedback* must be opposed by *corrective feedback* to produce a stable system. Wolves could have been the corrective feedback on St. Matthew Island, but the human beings who stocked the island did not think to include predators. Bacteria and other disease organisms can act as micropredators and hence as negative feedbacks. So also can starvation, when worst comes to worst. How much fluctuation there is in the size of the population of the *propositus* population (reindeer, in this case) depends on the particularities of the life cycles in the organisms involved—prey, macropredators, micropredators, and food organisms (lichens). If the time constants of the interacting species are wrong, even a system with negative feedback may collapse. Complexities and discontinuities in the environment—the "craggy rocks" of Townsend's model—may also be required for persistence of the demographic system. Real demography is not simple, not even among nonhuman species.

The human species has freed itself of all macropredators and bids fair soon to do the same for all micropredators. What effective controls remain? There are only three substantial possibilities: the "misery and vice" (the "positive checks") of the first edition of Malthus's essay—starvation and human conflict, in which man is his own predator—and the "preventive checks" of the second edition. The only acceptable preventive checks, in Malthus's mind, fell under the heading of "moral restraint"—delay in the age of marriage and considerable sexual continence in marriage (hopefully coupled with complete continence outside). We latter-day Malthusians (though not Malthus himself) also regard contraception as a genuinely moral restraint. Whatever its definition, moral restraint raises political problems of great difficulty.

It is in the nature of biological reproduction that it anticipates no limit: In every species the exponential curve of unopposed population growth soars off toward infinity. Population is prevented from reaching this goal by countervailing forces that are extrinsic to the propositus species—predators and the like. The coexistence of all the forces produces a more or less precise population equilibrium. By removing the countervailing forces of predators and disease from the population of our own species, we have created a disequilibrium that can persist for only a moment, as time is reckoned geologically. If utter misery is to be avoided, *Homo sapiens* must create and maintain new countervailing forces that are intrinsic to his own species—contraception and continence, to mention the most acceptable. (Less acceptably, war and genocide can perform the same funtion.) The adoption and enforcement of intrinsic controls necessarily involve policy. Who is to be controlled? By what means? What do we do with noncooperators? How do we superintend education so as to minimize noncooperation and the problems it creates? These are all political questions.

It is astonishing how the inescapably political nature of human population control is ignored by the political establishment. The United States government annually finances several hundred million dollars of research that is labeled *population research* in official summaries. From the titles of the projects I would estimate that at least 98 percent of them are either pedestrian surveys of the most unproductive sort or attempts to improve the technology of contraception. But we already have a nearly perfect system of birth control, and a perfect system of birth control merely permits people to have the number of children they want. It is an empirical fact that in every country in the world the number of children wanted by the average family is greater than the number needed to produce population equilibrium in that nation. Theoretically, this is perfectly understandable. Human psychology has evolved in an environment that included extrinsic countervailing forces which human ingenuity has only lately removed. Some mating couples internalize effective control forces, but not all do so. Population problems are created by those who cannot, or will not, internalize the necessary controls.

In the absence of extrinsic population controls, a totally voluntary control system selects for its own failure. Even a partial abandonment of voluntarism in the United States will require difficult political adjustments. With government money, it is perilous even to study the possibilities of change. How can a going political concern finance its own (partial) dissolution? Our exceptional Constitution makes change more practicable than it is for most nations, but even for us it is not easy.

Before significant political change can be instituted, there must be a fundamental improvement in the theory and practice of economics, which needs to be firmly tied down to the sort of conservation laws that have proven essential to the progress of the natural sciences. The idea of a conservation law is much older than science. Basically it is this—that in any equation that stands for before-and-after, what is on the left side of the equation must equal what is on the right side. This is the spirit behind double-entry bookkeeping, known to exist (in Genoa) as far back as the year 1340. In the investigation of nature, a lack of the discipline of balancing income and outgo kept alchemy from achieving any significant insights into chemical processes. It was Lavoisier, on the eve of the French Revolution, who changed alchemy to chemistry by the discipline of the mandatory balanced equation. A similar advance was made in physics in the middle of the nineteenth century with the explicit statement of the law of the conservation of energy. This signal advance was momentarily imperiled when in 1896 Becquerel discovered the spontaneous fluorescence of uranium, which seemed to mean that we could get something (radiant energy) for nothing (no known energy input). The anomaly was resolved nine years later when Einstein wrote an equation that conserved matter and energy jointly. Since then, conservation principles have reigned supreme in physics and chemistry. It is hard to see how these sciences could have progressed otherwise.

What about economics? There is some ambivalence here. On the one hand, economists constantly remind their students that there is no such thing as a free lunch. On the other, in many public areas, particularly when politically pressed, some economists act on the nonconservative assumption that demand creates supply. In a limited economic context there is a quasi-truth in this doctrine, but not in any rigorous sense. Unfortunately, the rapid progress of technology during the past two centuries has repeatedly expanded the area of known supplies, thus making it difficult to denote the explicit limits of conservation in everyday affairs. Faced with threats of limited supplies, politicians and economists, like Dickens's Mr. Micawber, optimistically intone "Something will turn up." Unfortunately, under the impetus of science, something quite often does, and this undeserved good fortune encourages economist-advisers to sound more like alchemists than scientists, or even good book-keepers.

The basic conservative concept of ecologists is the idea of *carrying capacity*, which defines that population of the propositus species that can be supported by a given territory year after year without degrading the environment —that is, without lowering its carrying capacity subsequently. Transgressing the carrying capacity even for a short time can set in train degradative processes (such as soil erosion) that operate by the rule of positive feedback (runaway feedback). For this reason, transgressing the carrying capacity even momentarily is an error of the most serious sort. The degraded environment of the southern and eastern shores of the Mediterranean is a permanent monument to transgressions committed two thousand years ago. Because carrying capacity varies seasonally in a predictable way, and unpredictably over longer periods of time, conservative management dictates that the operating figure for carrying capacity always be kept well below the momentary actual carrying capacity by an amount that we can call the *margin of safety*.

Even with these refinements, determining the carrying capacity for the animal populations that people exploit is fairly straightforward; for people themselves this is not so. We must first face the reality that this carrying capacity has, for a long time, been slowly moved upward by technology. Should we base the political and economic decisions of today on the increase in carrying capacity anticipated for tomorrow? The true conservative would say *no;* but few economists in the twentieth century have been conservatives. Conservatives are satisfied to postpone the spending of tomorrow's (possible) income until tomorrow; that way they do not risk transgressing the carrying capacity.

For human beings, carrying capacity is ineluctably tied to the desired standard of living, which is a political decision. Some people want to include meat in their diet, recreational vehicles in their life, and the delights of wilderness and uncrowded areas in which "unimproved" land creates a "waste" of natural resources. (The quotation marks surround the implicit value judgments of those of the opposite persuasion.) By political decisions, such high-standard people define the carrying capacity of their land at a lower figure than that agreed upon by those who want food only to live and are willing to sacrifice all recreational values to the support of more human lives. The contradiction between these two carrying capacities is a political contradiction, not a fact of natural science. If the two political views are allowed to compete with each other under laissez-faire rules, those people who accept lower standards will displace those who desire (but will not fight for) higher standards, in a sort of Gresham's Law of Living Standards. But whatever the standards—whatever the quantitative definition of carrying capacity—the transgression of carrying capacity must not be allowed because it leads to ruin.

In retrospect, I see the revival of Lloyd's image of the commons and the use of this metaphor in the formulation of conservation laws as necessary measures in putting the policy sciences on the path toward a rigorous grounding in conservation principles. To the extent that we achieve this goal, we will discover that much of the vagueness and prolixity that now afflict the policy sciences will disappear. The goal is worth pursuing.

REFERENCES

Garrett Hardin, "Carrying Capacity as an Ethical Concept," *Soundings* 59(1): 120–137 (1976). Reprinted in Hardin, *Stalking the Wild Taboo,* 2nd ed. Los Altos, Calif.: Kaufmann, 1978.

David R. Klein, "The Introduction, Increase, and Crash of Reindeer on St. Matthew Island," *Journal of Wildlife Management* 32: 350–367 (1968).

Joseph Townsend, *A Dissertation on the Poor Laws, by a Well-Wisher to Mankind,* Berkeley: University of California Press, 1971, pp. 8, 36–38 (originally published 1786).

II

ETHICS: THE ULTIMATE END AND VALUE CONSTRAINTS

The western world is now suffering from the
limited moral outlook of the three previous
generations. . . .

The two evils are: one, the ignoration of the
true relation of each organism to its environment;
and the other, the habit of ignoring the intrinsic
worth of the environment which must be allowed
its weight in any consideration of final ends.

ALFRED NORTH WHITEHEAD, *Science and the Modern World,* 1925

INTRODUCTION

Herman E. Daly

Humanity, craving for the infinite, has been corrupted by the temptation to satisfy an insatiable hunger in the material realm. Turn these stones into bread, urges Satan, and modern man sets to it, even to the extent of devising energy-intensive schemes for grinding up ordinary rock for minerals—to eat the spaceship itself! But Jesus' answer to the same temptation was more balanced: man does not live by bread alone. The proper object of economic activity is to have *enough* bread, not infinite bread, not a world turned into bread, not even vast storehouses full of bread. The infinite hunger of man, his moral and spiritual hunger, is not to be satisfied, is indeed exacerbated, by the current demonic madness of producing more and more things for more and more people. Afflicted with an infinite itch, modern man is scratching in the wrong place, and his frenetic clawing is drawing blood from the life-sustaining circulatory systems of his spaceship, the biosphere.

It is important to be very clear on the paramount importance of the moral issue. We could opt to scratch ourselves to death, destroying the spaceship in an orgy of procreation and consumption. The *only* arguments against doing this are religious and ethical: the obligation of stewardship for God's creation, the extension of brotherhood to future generations, and of some lesser degree of brotherhood to the subhuman world.

The essays in this section give particular, though not exclusive, attention to the upper or ends segment of the ends-means spectrum discussed in the Introduction (p. 9). In "The Age of Plenty," E. F. Schumacher discusses the Ultimate End from an explicitly Christian perspective, taking St. Ignatius Loyola's "Foundation" as a basic principle by which sufficiency may be distinguished from excess of worldly goods. At what point does our use of the things of the earth cease to aid and begin to hinder us in the attainment of the end for which we were created? Those who do not accept the Christian view of the end for which humanity was created must nevertheless face a similar question. In his article "Buddhist Economics," Schumacher arrived at much the same practical conclusions starting from a Buddhist view of the purpose of human life. Schumacher himself was a Christian, and it is somewhat ironic that his article on Buddhist economics has attracted so much more attention than his economic writings from an explicitly Christian perspective.

"The Presumptions of Science," by biologist Robert L. Sinsheimer, questions what seems the implicit answer of modern scientific secularism, that "the highest purpose available to humanity is the acquisition of knowledge, and in particular scientific knowledge." Might there not be knowledge which, though not permanently forbidden, would be so inopportune under the existing state of social and moral development as to be fatal to the very scientific civilization that produced it? The biblical quotation "Know the truth and the truth shall make you free" is frequently carved on laboratory lintels as high sanction for pulling apart anything that arouses someone's curiosity. But the quotation is badly out of context. The full quotation reads, "Jesus said to the Jews who had believed in him, 'If you continue in my word, you are truly my disciples, and you will know the truth and the truth will make you free' " (John 8:31). The statement is decidedly conditional, subject to prior religious commitment and moral discipline, and the freedom referred to is freedom from sin, not from ignorance. Some other authority must be appealed to for justification of the unlimited pursuit of knowledge. Sinsheimer is far from denying the value of knowledge; he merely questions the presumption of many scientists that knowledge always merits first place among values.

In "Ecology, Ethics, and Theology," theologian John Cobb considers the extension of brotherhood to the subhuman world and develops the thesis that our ethics should be based on feeling and on a perception of the hierarchy of feeling in the biotic pyramid. Nonhuman feeling, Cobb contends, must be considered valuable, though its value is not on an equal footing with human feeling. Human beings may be the apex of the biotic pyramid from which they evolved, but an apex with no pyramid underneath is a dimensionless point.

The reader may be forgiven the cynical question that since brotherhood has not yet been extended to all people existing at the same time in the same society, is it not premature to speak of extending it to the future and to animals and rocks? Does not true brotherhood require more growth for the sake of the poor, not less?

Certainly the first extension of brotherhood must be to presently existing people. This is agreed by all. But it does not follow that this extension requires more, rather than less, growth. Past economic growth has not eliminated poverty, since distribution has remained very unequal and since population has grown rapidly, especially the poorer populations of the world. Distribution is a moral problem, as is population control, and we lack the moral resources to solve these problems because our limited energies have been overwhelmingly devoted to material growth. We thought we could grow our way out of poverty and injustice, but we were wrong. There is just not room for that much growth. Brotherhood means sharing what we have *now,* not the exponentially swollen sum we hope to have in the future.

The final essay, "The Abolition of Man," by C. S. Lewis, the late British professor of literature, lay theologian, and writer of science fiction, was first published in 1947, long before the wave of environmental concern had swelled. When, as in this case, the relevance of the article increases with time, it is a good indication the author has based his arguments upon something very solid. Controlling nature, as Lewis shows, becomes after some point a very dangerous undertaking, and if carried to the limit, the whole enterprise blows up in our face—"Man's conquest of Nature turns out, in the moment of its consummation, to be Nature's conquest of Man."

8

THE AGE OF PLENTY: A CHRISTIAN VIEW

E. F. Schumacher

On all sides, the future of industrial society is being called into question. Not many years ago we were told that we had never had it so good; as time moved on we would have it better still. And the same would hold for all the world's people, particularly those who, for one reason or another, had been left behind in mankind's onward march into the Age of Plenty. The backward countries were politely and optimistically named the "developing countries," and the nineteen-sixties were to be known as the "Development Decade." If there was one thing on which everybody was expected to agree it was this: that at long last the problem of production had been solved. Modern science and technology had done it; western civilisation had done it; and the unique and dazzling achievements of this civilisation were now destined to spread across the globe in a very short time.

Originally published in pamphlet form by The Saint Andrew Press, Edinburgh, 1974. Reprinted here by permission of the late Dr. Schumacher's widow, Verena Schumacher.

THE GLORY OF THE MODERN ACHIEVEMENT

We may recall the claims that were made—and indeed are still being made in some quarters—for the power and glory of the modern achievement. Theologians told us that God was dead: there was now no more need for this hypothesis; and high academics announced that man, the naked ape, emancipated and come-of-age, had now, at long last, taken possession of His seat of omnipotence. This was said to be the meaning of the Second Industrial Revolution, of the Nuclear Age, the Space Age, the Age of Automation. Energy would be forever cheap and plentiful; man was no longer confined to this miserable planet called the Earth; nor would he continue to have to labour for his living: automation and cybernetics would finally remove the curse allegedly put on Adam after the Fall. If there was a remaining problem, it was the problem of how to educate ourselves for endless leisure.

How is it that the mood has changed so suddenly and so profoundly, even though hardly a week passes without announcements of new, astonishing scientific or technological breakthroughs? The late President Kennedy set a target: that by the end of the sixties man would visit the moon—*and he did.* The week of this fantastic feat was referred to by President Nixon as "the greatest week since Genesis." It cannot be said that science and technology have suddenly lost their power. But somehow the glory is gone. At the height of success there is a smell of bankruptcy.

You may accuse me of overdramatisation—and you are quite right. The materialistic optimism of ten or twenty years ago did not possess all the people all the time. There was the awesome threat of the Atom Bomb; but we were advised to keep our cool; if we learned to "live with the Bomb" all would be well. Also, most of our artists did seem rather unhappy. The painters insisted on painting pictures which suggested the dissolution, if not the abolition, of man. The most gifted writers and composers did much the same in words and sounds. But this was interpreted as "experimentation in new art forms," indicating liberation from outdated restraints and an upsurge of creative vitality. Warning voices were raised also by people involved in agriculture, industry, and general economic affairs; but these were minority opinions, easily decried as "unbalanced," "irresponsible," or "unrealistic."

Today, however, those minority opinions of a few years ago are having a wide impact even on official utterances. The limits-to-growth debate is in full swing. The possibility of severe fuel shortages in many parts of the world, which only a few years ago was laughed out of court, is becoming a reality. Concern over environmental degradation and the dangers of ecological breakdown is no longer confined to a few minority groups. Most important of all, many people are beginning to take an overall view of the condition and prospects of life in industrial society and to feel that we may be moving into a real crisis of survival.

It is not easy to take an overall view, because such a view can be obtained only from a considerable height. But what is higher and what is lower? How could we measure this kind of height, and, if it cannot be measured has it any meaning? We cannot get an overall view merely by assembling more and more facts. By themselves, facts mean nothing, prove nothing, and lead to no conclusions. Facts need to be evaluated, that is to say fitted into a value system, to be of use. What, then, is our value system? Only from the height of a value system can we obtain a meaningful overall view.

A CHRISTIAN VIEW

That is why I have written into my subject title the words: "a Christian view." This is meant to indicate the value system which, as I think, rules what I have to say. Unfortunately, there is no unanimity today as to what constitutes a Christian point of view when it comes to such mundane matters as our economic life. I resort, therefore, to what a great Christian saint called "The Foundation." This is what he said:

> Man was created to praise, reverence, and serve God
> our Lord, and by this means to save his soul;
> And the other things on the face of the earth were
> created for man's sake, and in order to aid him in the
> prosecution of the end for which he was created.
> *Whence it follows*
> That man ought to make use of them just so far as they
> help him to attain his end,
> And that he ought to withdraw himself from them just
> so far as they hinder him.[1]

The logic of this statement is unshakeable; it is in fact the kind of logic we invariably try to apply in our everyday affairs, whether it be business, or science, or engineering, or politics. We first try to clarify what we want to achieve; we then study the means at our disposal; and we then use those means *just so far* as—in our judgment—they help us to attain our objective, and when it appears that we are overdoing things we withdraw from these means *just so far* as they hinder us.

When applied to mankind's presentday economic situation, the statement also seems eminently realistic. It implies that where people do not have enough means to attain their ends they should have more, and where they have more than enough they should "withdraw" from that which is excessive.

We can say therefore that the statement—"The Foundation"—is distinguished by both implacable logic and genial common sense. Anybody who is prepared to accept the two premises cannot possibly refuse to accept the conclusions. The question is: Does a Christian accept the two premises, namely, first, that man was created to "save his soul" and, second, that all the other things were created in order to aid him?

Obviously, some of us might wish to formulate these propositions slightly differently; but it hardly seems possible that a Christian should reject their essential meaning.

All the same, the more we look at this statement, and the more deeply we ponder the meaning of its artless syllogism, offered as "The Foundation" on which all our thinking, policy-making, and acting should be built, the more incredible, remote, impractical, irritating it must seem to us; something completely out of keeping with what we actually think, plan, and do. We might feel this is something only for hermits or monks, but not for ordinary Christian householders like ourselves.

Are we then saying that salvation is only for hermits and monks? Surely not. How can we extricate ourselves from this disturbing logic? We might say: This statement, called "The Foundation," is indeed irrefutable as an ideal; but as ordinary mortals we cannot attain the ideal. Fair enough. The validity of an ideal, or goal, or objective depends on its inherent Truth, not on the number of people who actually attain it or live up to it. And those who accept it, while they cannot promise attainment, undertake to walk in one particular direction and not in any other. It would appear, therefore, that the Christian, as far as the goods of this world are concerned, is called upon to *strive* to use them *just so far* as they help him to attain salvation, and that he should *strive* to withdraw himself from them *just so far* as they hinder him.

If this is "The Foundation" from which the Christian obtains his overall view, we may now proceed to a consideration of the future of industrial society.

A CHRISTIAN LOOKS AT THE FUTURE

From this point of view it can be seen right away that we cannot be the least bit interested in purely quantitative concepts, such as economic growth *or* non-growth appplied to that mysterious aggregate, GNP (Gross National Product) or, even more mysterious, GWP (Gross World Product). That which is good and helpful ought to be growing and that which is bad and hindering ought to be diminishing; whether aggregation of these two processes yields a higher grand total or a lower one is of no interest whatever. In fact, the aggregation itself is quite meaningless. We therefore need, above all else, qualitative concepts: concepts that enable us to choose the right direction of our movement and not merely to measure its speed.

The future of industrial society will depend on the development and adoption of such qualitative concepts. This, of course, is a somewhat arid way of expressing oneself. Let us look at some of the living details of which the overall picture is made up. We all know that, economically speaking, mankind is not a reasonably homogeneous group but is most unreasonably split between, on the one hand, about one quarter who (as conventionally measured) are immensely rich, and, on the other hand, about three-quarters who (similarly measured) are immensely poor. The gap between the rich and the poor, worldwide, is quite enormously large, and there are not many people situated, as it were, in the middle. A *normal* distribution curve would show most people in the middle and relatively few at the two extremes. But this distribution curve, classifying people in accordance with their income, is highly "abnormal," almost an inverted image of a normal distribution curve: with the extremes—of great poverty and of great affluence—heavily populated and the middle almost empty. This striking abnormality suggests that there is something seriously wrong. What ought to be—and used to be—one world, has broken up into two worlds, neither of which is normal and healthy. This split grievously afflicts many countries internally. They have lost all internal cohesion, reflecting the world situation in miniature: "dual societies" with the extremes of poverty and of wealth heavily represented and the middle relatively empty, again almost an inverted image of normal distribution.

From the point of view of "The Foundation" this indicates a seriously pathological condition, because the rich evidently use too much and the poor use too little, and the golden mean is being achieved only by a minority.

THE RICH SOCIETY NORM

What makes the world situation particularly abnormal and even alarming is the almost universally held idea that the rich societies set the norm and demonstrate what can and ought to be achieved by everybody. It does not require deep insight, nor extensive factual knowledge, to realise that his idea is mischievous and unsupportable. Let us take the allegedly most "advanced" society of the modern age, the United States of America, which President Nixon calls "the hope of the world." It contains 5.6 percent of the world's population and absorbs something approaching 40 percent of the world's output of raw materials, many of which are non-renewable. To obtain its supplies, the United States, in spite of the vastness of its superbly endowed territory, has had to extend its commercial tentacles into every corner of the globe.

How, then, could a life style that makes such exorbitant demands upon world resources serve as a normal or a model for development? The very idea that "the problem of production" has been solved by the achievements of modern science and technology is based on a most astonishing oversight, namely, that the whole edifice of modern industry is built on non-renewable energy resources.

In short, the poor countries, which assuredly need development to regain some kind of economic health, have to evolve a life-style for which America or for that matter Japan or any other "advanced" country cannot serve as a model, and the so-called advanced countries have the even more difficult task of achieving some basis of existence which is compatible with peace and permanence.

As I have mentioned already, it is not only the problem of resources that has, suddenly and somewhat belatedly, moved into the centre of discussion; there is also the problem of pollution and of ecological breakdown. In addition, we do not need to look far afield to realize that modern industrial society is involved in some kind of human crisis which manifests itself in inflation, various types of unrest, rising crime rates, drug addiction, and so on. All this suggests that there is something wrong at the root of things—as indeed a Christian would be inclined to think. What is being called into question, so it seems, is not our *technical* competence but our value system and the very aims and objects we are pursuing.

However, we cannot leave the matter there. Many people, particularly among the young, are only too ready to agree with any criticism that can be made of modern society's aims and objects; they are only too anxious to adopt less materialistic and (shall we say) more idealistic aims for their own lives; but they are at a loss what to do. "The system," they find, is geared to a certain set of values, it can produce "growth" but it cannot produce justice; it can improve the quality of goods but not the quality of people; it can find money for the development of Concorde, moon rockets, and heart transplants, but not for adequate housing, public transport, school or hospital building. As Professor Galbraith complained about the richest country in the world, it produces private affluence and public squalor. Are they then to "drop out of the system"? But they have nothing sensible to drop into. It appears that any substantial re-setting of aims and objects implies or even presupposes a re-setting of the "system." How is that to be done and who can do it?

EFFICIENT PRODUCTION

Etienne Gilson once said that only the professors of philosophy speak of ideas; a true philosopher speaks always of things.[2] So let us try to be true philosophers. The "things" we might speak about are the methods of production, both technical and social, which the modern world mainly employs. We may note that these methods are chosen and developed primarily from the point of view of efficiency, and this is of course as it should be. No one in his senses favours inefficiency. The concept of efficiency, however, has become quite uncannily narrow and exclusive: it relates only to the material side of things and only to profit. It certainly does not relate to people, the actual persons involved in the process of production. If I said: "This process is efficient, because it makes the worker a happy man," I should be accused of talking sentimental nonsense, unless I could demonstrate that the worker's happiness actually led to increased output, better quality output, and above all to more profitable output. What the work does to the worker is not recognised as a decisive criterion of efficiency. Among all the machines engaged in the productive process there are also workers to fill certain gaps of mechanisation or automation. Pope Pius XI described the situation thus:

> With the leaders of business abandoning the true path, it was easy for the working class also to fall at times into the same abyss; all the more so because very many employers treated their workmen as mere tools, without the slightest thought of spiritual things. . . . And so bodily labour, which even after original sin was decreed by Providence for the good of man's body and soul, is in many instances changed into an instrument of perversion; for from the factory dead matter goes out improved, whereas men there are corrupted and degraded.[3]

This is the outcome of a concept of efficiency which relates to goods and not to people. And the damage cannot be undone by paying the worker higher wages or treating him with respect or in some other way trying to compensate him. Compensation never compensates: it can never undo the damage that has been done, but can merely try to mitigate some of the consequences.

From the point of view of this kind of material efficiency, there always appear to be so-called "economies of scale," and every increase in scale offers opportunities for the introduction of more specialised equipment, while at the same time forcing the worker into a greater division of labour. So the production units become ever bigger, more complex, more expensive, and also in a special sense more violent. Although it is, of course, society that produces the production system, once a particular system has come into existence it begins to mould society: it, as it were, insists that the members of society respect the immanent logic of the system and adapt to it by accepting its implicit aims as their own. Man then becomes the captive of the system whether he approves of its aims or not, *and he cannot effectively adopt different aims or values unless he takes steps to alter the system of production.*

NEW CONCEPTS REQUIRED

In other words, ideas can change the world only by some process of "incarnation." The prevailing concept of efficiency rules the modern world not by itself, but by the type of technology and organisation it has produced. A mere change of the concept remains wishful thinking until new technologies and types of organisation have been evolved.

This is of decisive importance. It shows that appeals for good behaviour and the teaching of ethical or spiritual principles, necessary as they always are, invariably stay, as it were, *inside* the system and are powerless to alter it:

unless and until the preaching leads to significant *new types of work* in the physical world.

It is true, indeed, that in the beginning is the word. But the word remains ineffectual unless it comes into this world; in the words of the Gospel: unless it is made flesh and dwells among us. It may then, of course, not be recognised and accepted by the established order; it may be looked upon as impractical and subversive. Whether it will eventually succeed in changing the world will depend not just on its truth, but on the work it manages to get done "in the flesh."

What kind of work? Since the prevailing system has been shaped by a technology that drives it into giantism, infinite complexity, vast expensiveness, and violence, it would seem to follow that we should engage the best of our intelligence to devise a technology that moves in the opposite direction —towards smallness, simplicity, cheapness, and non-violence. With the help of such a technology it would be possible, I am sure, to create an economic system to serve man, in the place of the present system which enslaves him. But this is said from a Christian point of view, where "serving man" means something different from what it may mean when the point of view is modern materialism.

BACK TO THE HUMAN SCALE

To strive for smallness means to try to bring organisations and units of production back to a human scale. This is not a field in which precise definitions are possible, nor are they needed. When we feel that things have become too large for human comfort, let's see if we cannot make them smaller. There are many reasons for favoring smallness. Small units of production can use small resources—a very important point when concentrated, large resources are becoming scarce or inaccessible. Small units are ecologically sounder than big ones: the pollution or damage they may cause has a better chance of fitting into nature's tolerance margins. Small units can be used for decentralised production, leading to a more even distribution of the population, a better use of space, the avoidance of congestion and of monster transport. Most important of all: small units, of which there can be a great number, enable more people "to do their own thing" than large units of which there can only be a few. Smallness is also conductive to simplicity.

Simplicity, from a Christian point of view, is a value in itself. Making a living should not absorb all or most of a man's attention, energy, or time, as if it were the primary purpose of his existence on earth. Complexity forces people to become so highly specialised that it is virtually impossible for them to attain to wisdom or higher understanding. As Thomas Aquinas said: "The smallest knowledge of the highest things is more to be desired than the most certain knowledge of the lower things." A life-style full of complexity and specialisation, while conducive to the acquisition of knowledge of the lower things, normally involves such agitation and constant strain that it tends to act as a complete barrier against the acquisition of any higher knowledge.

Giantism and complexity bring it about that the capital required for production grows to fantastic proportions. Only people already rich and powerful can gain access to it. All other people are excluded; they cannot create a job for themselves, but must try to find one created by the rich. The effect is that, as has been said, capital employs labor, instead of labor employing capital. If the rich have not created enough job opportunities to employ all job seekers, the latter have no practicable opportunities for self-help and self-reliance. Not surprisingly, the poor countries, caught in the net of gigantic, complex, immensely expensive technology, used for even the simplest tasks, are saddled with mass unemployment, which affects mainly school leavers and other young people and makes all exhortations to self-reliance a mockery.

NON-VIOLENCE

From a Christian point of view, non-violence is also a value in itself. It flows from man forming a true view of himself: seeing himself not as creator but as a creature which has been sent into life for a purpose. The smallest mosquito, as St. Thomas Aquinas said, is more wonderful than anything man has produced and will ever produce. So man must never lose his sense of the marvellousness of the world around and inside him—a world which he has not made and which, assuredly, has not made itself. Such an attitude engenders a spirit of non-violence, which is a form or aspect of wisdom. With all the great powers man has recently acquired through his science and technology, it seems certain that he is now far too clever to be able to survive without wisdom.

As with so many other things, perfect non-violence may not be attainable in this imperfect world. But it *does* make a difference in which direction we *strive*. A system of production and a style of living, or a concept of efficiency, which advance steadily in the direction of violence, which refuse to recognize non-violence as a valid criterion of success, move on a disaster course. And the warning signals are appearing all around us. We call them pollution, environmental degradation, ugliness, intolerable noise, rapid exhaustion of resources, social disintegration and so forth. In other words, I do not think of violence only in the context of man's relation to other men, but in the context of all his relations including those with animate and inanimate nature.

It is sometimes said that modern man's ruthlessness vis-à-vis the rest of creation stems from the teaching in the first book of the Bible according to which God gave man "dominion" over all creatures of the earth. This is an excessively superficial view. Man, the noblest of all creatures, has indeed been given "dominion" over the rest, but he is not entitled to forget that *noblesse oblige*.

In more mundane terms: what is non-violence? We can say, for instance, that biologically and ecologically sound farming systems, with "good husbandry" and the careful observance of the Law of Return (recycling of all organic materials) represent a non-violent approach, whereas the ever intensifying warfare against nature of highly chemicalised, industrialised, computerised farming systems represents violence. Some people say: "The choice is between these violent systems and hunger. Look how productive, how efficient, these systems are. We need them to feed the growing populations of the world." The question is: Is this true? An immensity of R & D (research and development) expenditure has gone into the development of these violent systems, which completely depend on a vast chemical and pharmaceutical industry, which in turn completely depends on non-renewable oil. How much R & D has gone into the development of non-violent systems? Apart from a few private efforts, such as those of the Soil Association, hardly any. Even so, there are thousands of farmers around the world who are obtaining excellent yields and making a good living without resort to chemical fertilizers, insecticides, herbicides, fungicides, etc. Would it not be right to take these alternatives seriously and support them consciously, instead of putting all our eggs into the basket of violence?

There are many other directions in which the idea of non-violence can and should be developed. In medicine, we can say that prevention is essentially non-violent, compared with cure. Somebody once asked the question: "If an ancestor of long ago visited us today, what would he be more astonished at, the skill of our dentists or the rottenness of our teeth?" We should not need the violent interferences we get from our skillful dentists if we had maintained the health of our teeth the way other peoples have.

POSSIBILITIES OF CHANGE

It will be apparent that the four criteria of smallness, simplicity, capital-cheapness, and non-violence are closely interconnected, and I do not need to spell out all the interconnections. Can they become criteria for *action?* Indeed they can. It would, of course, be a violent approach if one suggested that all of a sudden the direction of progress should be changed one hundred percent. The "withdrawal symptoms" would be too severe, but there can be experimentation and gradual change. Why this prevailing immobilism? If only a few percent of our scientific, technical, intellectual, and financial effort and resources were diverted into a systematic search for

smallness

simplicity

capital saving and

non-violence

as concerns our industrial and farming systems—and many other fields of activity as well—it would emerge that a viable future can be attained. One does not even have to be a Christian to countenance and promote such a marginal diversion of effort. Do we not all, as good householders, use a small proportion of our income for insurance against calamities, some of which might never happen?

Smallness, simplicity, capital saving, and non-violence, *as a direction of conscious striving,* by means of very practical, down-to-earth work, commend themselves also from a social and political point of view. Good human relations, in my experience, are extremely difficult, if not impossible, to attain in large units, whether these are schools, universities, offices, or factories. Participation, so rightly demanded in industry and elsewhere, cannot become a reality when units are so large and complex that people cannot know each other as people and the minds of ordinary men and women cannot encompass the meaning and the ramifications of the whole.

PEOPLE DO MATTER

The future of industrial, technological society must be a future in which every man and woman, even "the least among my brethren," can be *persons,* can see themselves and be seen by their children as real people, not as cogs in vast machines and gap-fillers in automated processes, employed solely because, occasionally, the human machine is calculated to be a cheaper "means of production" than a mindless device.

It seems to me that, when looking at the future of industrial society from a Christian point of view, one is looking at it from a realistic point of view—as against a certain "crackpot realism" (as, I believe, Veblen called it) which is based on the implicit assumptions that people really do not matter; that we are masters of nature which can be ravaged and mutilated with impunity; that some Divine Improvidence has endowed a finite world with infinite material resources; and that consumption is the be-all and end-all of human life on earth. And it also seems to me that we *can* get off the hook of crackpot realism if we, as it were, *remember ourselves,* if we remember that we have a purpose in life that goes beyond the material; in other words, if we remember "The Foundation" which I have quoted.

As more and more people realize the predicament of modern technological society and the dangers it is facing, I can see the formation of a new battle-line. One the one side, there will be what we might call the people of the forward stampede, with the slogan: "A break-through a day keeps the crisis at bay." On the other side there will be—what shall we call them?—the home-comers: people striving to lead things back to their proper place and function, realizing that when it is said that man has dominion over the rest of creatures the reference is to man as a child of God, not to man as a higher animal. They believe that the spiritual has dominion over the material, which it is called upon to use *just so far* as it is needed for the attainment of spiritual ends, and no further.

It must be admitted that the people of the forward stampede, like the devil, have all the best—or at least all the most catchy—tunes. But the homecomers have the most exalted texts on which to base their patient and painstaking *practical* work; texts such as this one: "Seek ye first the Kingdom of God and all these other things—which you also need—will be added unto you."

The extraordinary thing about our period is the *great convergence*. The language of spiritual wisdom can now be understood also as the language of practical sanity, showing the road to survival in this world as well as to salvation in the next.

NOTES

1. W. H. Longridge, *The Spiritual Exercises of St. Ignatius of Loyola.* A. R. Mowbray, London and Oxford, 1922.

2. Etienne Gilson, *God and Philosophy.* Yale University Press, New Haven, 1941.

3. Pius IX, *Quadragesimo Anno,* 134.

9

BUDDHIST ECONOMICS

E. F. Schumacher

"Right Livelihood" is one of the requirements of the Buddha's Eightfold Path. It is clear, therefore, that there must be such a thing as Buddhist Economics.

Buddhist countries, at the same time, have often stated that they wish to remain faithful to their heritage. So Burma: "The New Burma sees no conflict between religious values and economic progress. Spiritual health and material well-being are not enemies: they are natural allies."[1] Or: "We can blend successfully the religious and spiritual values of our heritage with the benefits of modern technology."[2] Or: "We Burmans have a sacred duty to conform both our dreams and our acts to our faith. This we shall ever do."[3]

All the same, such countries invariably assume that they can model their economic development plans in accordance with modern economics, and they call upon modern economists from so-called advanced countries to advise them, to formulate the policies to be pursued, and to construct the grand design for development, the Five-Year Plan or whatever it may be called. No one seems to think that a Buddhist way of life would call for Buddhist

"Buddhist Economics" from *Resurgence*, Vol. 1, No. 11, January-February 1968. Reprinted by permission of the author and publisher.

economics, just as the modern materialist way of life has brought forth modern economics.

Economists themselves, like most specialists, normally suffer from a kind of metaphysical blindness, assuming that theirs is a science of absolute and invariable truths, without any presuppositions. Some go as far as to claim that economic laws are as free from "metaphysics" or "values" as the law of gravitation. We need not, however, get involved in arguments of methodology. Instead, let us take some fundamentals and see what they look like when viewed by a modern economist and a Buddhist economist.

There is universal agreement that the fundamental source of wealth is human labor. Now, the modern economist has been brought up to consider labor or work as little more than a necessary evil. From the point of view of the employer, it is in any case simply an item of cost, to be reduced to a minimum if it cannot be eliminated altogether, say, by automation. From the point of view of the workman, it is a "disutility": to work is to make a sacrifice of one's leisure and comfort, and wages are a kind of compensation for the sacrifice. Hence the ideal from the point of view of the employer is to have output without employees, and the ideal from the point of view of the employee is to have income without employment.

The consequences of these attitudes both in theory and in practice are, of course, extremely far-reaching. If the ideal with regard to work is to get rid of it, every method that "reduces the work load" is a good thing. The most potent method, short of automation, is the so-called division of labor and the classical example is the pin factory eulogized in Adam Smith's *Wealth of Nations*. Here it is not a matter of ordinary specialization, which mankind has practised from time immemorial, but of dividing up every complete process of production into minute parts, so that the final product can be produced at great speed without anyone having had to contribute more than a totally insignificant and, in most cases, unskilled movement of his limbs.

WORK

The Buddhist point of view takes the function of work to be at least threefold: to give a man a chance to utilize and develop his faculties; to enable him to overcome his ego-centredness by joining with other people in a common task; and to bring forth the goods and services needed for a becoming existence. Again, the consequences that flow from this view are endless. To organize work in such a manner that it becomes meaningless, boring, stultifying, or nerve-racking for the worker would be little short of criminal; it would indicate a greater concern with goods than with people, an evil lack of compassion and a soul-destroying degree of attachment to the most primitive side of this worldly existence. Equally, to strive for leisure as an alternative to work would be considered a complete misunderstanding of one of the basic truths of human existence, namely, that work and leisure are complementary parts of the same living process and cannot be separated without destroying the joy of work and the bliss of leisure.

From the Buddhist point of view, there are therefore two types of mechanization which must be clearly distinguished: one that enhances a man's skill and power and one that turns the work of man over to a mechanical slave, leaving man in a position of having to serve the slave. How to tell the one from the other? "The craftsman himself," says Ananda Coomaraswamy, a man equally competent to talk about the Modern West as the Ancient East, "the craftsman himself can always, if allowed to, draw the delicate distinction between the machine and the tool. The carpet loom is a tool, a contrivance for holding warp threads at a stretch for the pile to be woven round them by the craftsman's fingers; but the power loom is a machine, and its significance as a destroyer of culture lies in the fact that it does the essentially human part of the work."[4] It is clear, therefore, that Buddhist economics must be very different from the economics of modern materialism, since the Buddhist sees the essence of civilization not in a multiplication of wants but in the purification of human character. Character, at the same time, is formed primarily by a man's work. And work, properly conducted in conditions of human dignity and freedom, blesses those who do it and equally their products. The Indian philosopher and economist J. C. Kumarappa sums the matter up as follows:

> If the nature of the work is properly appreciated and applied, it will stand in the same relation to the higher faculties as food is to the physical body. It nourishes and enlivens the higher man and urges him to produce the best he is capable of. It directs his freewill along the proper course and disciplines the animal in him into progressive channels. It furnishes an excellent background for man to display his scale of values and develop his personality.[5]

If a man has no chance of obtaining work he is in a desperate position, not simply because he lacks an income but because he lacks this nourishment and enlivening factor of disciplined work which nothing can replace. A modern economist may engage in highly sophisticated calculations on whether full employment "pays" or whether it might be more "economic" to run an economy at less than full employment so as to ensure a greater mobility of labor, a better stability of wages, and so forth. His fundamental criterion of success is simply the total quantity of goods produced during a given period of time. "If the marginal urgency of goods is low," says Professor Galbraith in *The Affluent Society,* "then so is the urgency of employing the last man or the last million men in the labor force." And again: "If . . . we can afford some unemployment in the interest of stability—a proposition, incidentally, of impeccably conservative antecedents—then we can afford to give those who are unemployed the goods that enable them to sustain their accustomed standard of living."[6]

From a Buddhist point of view, this is standing the truth on its head by considering goods as more important than people and consumption as more important than creative activity. It means shifting the emphasis from the worker to the product of work, that is, from the human to the subhuman, a surrender to the forces of evil. The very start of Buddhist economic planning would be a planning for full employment, and the primary purpose of this would in fact be employment for everyone who needs an "outside" job: it would not be the maximization of employment nor the maximization of production. Women, on the whole, do not need an outside job, and the large-scale employment of women in offices or factories would be considered a sign of serious economic failure. In particular, to let mothers of young children work in factories while the children run wild would be as uneconomic in the eyes of a Buddhist economist as the employment of a skilled worker as a soldier in the eyes of a modern economist.

While the materialist is mainly interested in goods, the Buddhist is mainly interested in liberation. But Buddhism is 'the Middle Way' and therefore in no way antagonistic to physical well-being. It is not wealth that stands in the way of liberation but the attachment to wealth; not the enjoyment of pleasurable things but the craving for them. The keynote of Buddhist economics, therefore, is simplicity and nonviolence. From an economist's point of view, the marvel of the Buddhist way of life is the utter rationality of its pattern—amazingly small means leading to extraordinarily satisfactory results.

THE STANDARD OF LIVING

For the modern economist this is very difficult to understand. He is used to measuring the standard of living by the amount of annual consumption, assuming all the time that a man who consumes more is "better off" than a man who consumes less. A Buddhist economist would consider this approach excessively irrational: since consumption is merely a means to human well-being, the aim should be to obtain the maximum of well-being with the minimum of consumption. Thus, if the purpose of clothing is a certain amount of temperature comfort and an attractive appearance, the task is to attain this purpose with the smallest possible effort, that is, with the smallest annual destruction of cloth and with the help of designs that involve the smallest possible input of toil. The less toil there is, the more time and strength is left for artistic creativity. It would be highly uneconomic, for instance, to go in for complicated tailoring, like the modern West, when a much more beautiful effect can be achieved by the skillful draping of uncut material. It would be the height of folly to make material so that it should wear out quickly and the height of barbarity to make anything ugly, shabby or mean. What has just been said about clothing applies equally to all other human requirements. The ownership and the consumption of goods is a means to an end, and Buddhist economics is the systematic study of how to attain given ends with the minimum means.

Modern economics, on the other hand, considers consumption to be the sole end and purpose of all economic activity, taking the factors of production —land, labor, and capital—as the means. The former, in short, tries to maximize human satisfactions by the optimal pattern of consumption, while the latter tries to maximize consumption by the optimal pattern of productive effort. It is easy to see that the effort needed to sustain a way of life which seeks to attain the optimal pattern of consumption is likely to be much smaller than the effort needed to sustain a drive for maximum consumption. We need not be surprised, therefore, that the pressure and strain of living is very much less in, say, Burma than it is in the United States, in spite of the fact that the amount of labor-saving machinery used in the former country is only a minute fraction of the amount used in the latter.

THE PATTERN OF CONSUMPTION

Simplicity and nonviolence are obviously closely related. The optimal pattern of consumption, producing a high degree of human satisfaction by means of a relatively low rate of consumption, allows people to live without great pressure and strain and to fulfill the primary injunction of Buddhist teaching: "Cease to do evil; try to do good." As physical resources are everywhere limited, people satisfying their needs by means of a modest use of resources are obviously less likely to be at each other's throats than people depending upon a high rate of use. Equally, people who live in highly self-sufficient local communities are less likely to get involved in large-scale violence than people whose existence depends on worldwide systems of trade.

From the point of view of Buddhist economics, therefore, production from local resources for local needs is the most rational way of economic life, while dependence on imports from afar and the consequent need to produce for export to unknown and distant peoples is highly uneconomic and justifiable only in exceptional cases and on a small scale. Just as the modern economist would admit that a high rate of consumption of transport services between a man's home and his place of work signifies a misfortune and not a high standard of life, so the Buddhist economist would hold that to satisfy human wants from far-away sources rather than from sources nearby signifies failure rather than success. The former might take statistics showing an increase in the number of ton/miles per head of the population carried by a country's transport system as proof of economic progress, while to the latter—the Buddhist economist—the same statistics would indicate a highly undesirable deterioration in the *pattern* of consumption.

NATURAL RESOURCES

Another striking difference between modern economics and Buddhist economics arises over the use of natural resources. Bertrand de Jouvenel, the eminent French political philosopher, has characterized "Western man" in words which may be taken as a fair description of the modern economist:

> He tends to count nothing as an expenditure, other than human effort; he does not seem to mind how much mineral matter he wastes and, far worse, how much living matter he destroys. He does not seem to realize at all that human life is a dependent part of an ecosystem of many different forms of life. As the world is ruled from towns where men are cut off from any form of life other than human, the feeling of belonging to an ecosystem is not revived. This results in a harsh and improvident treatment of things upon which we ultimately depend, such as water and trees.[7]

The teaching of the Buddha, on the other hand, enjoins a reverent and nonviolent attitude not only to all sentient beings but also with great emphasis, to trees. Every follower of the Buddha ought to plant a tree every few years and look after it until it is safely established, and the Buddhist economist can demonstrate without difficulty that the universal observance of this rule would result in a high rate of genuine economic development independent of any foreign aid. Much of the economic decay of Southeast Asia (as of many other parts of the world) is undoubtedly due to a heedless and shameful neglect of trees.

Modern economics does not distinguish between renewable and nonrenewable materials, as its very method is to equalize and quantify everything by means of a money price. Thus, taking various alternative fuels, like coal, oil, wood or water power: the only difference between them recognized by modern economics is relative cost per equivalent unit. The cheapest is automatically the one to be preferred, as to do otherwise would be irrational and "uneconomic." From a Buddhist point of view, of course, this will not do; the essential difference between nonrenewable fuels like coal and oil on the one hand and renewable fuels like wood and waterpower on the other cannot be simply overlooked. Nonrenewable goods must be used only if they are indispensable, and then only with the greatest care and the most meticulous concern for conservation. To use them heedlessly or extravagantly is an act of violence, and while complete nonviolence may not be attainable on this earth, there is nonetheless an ineluctable duty on man to aim at the idea of nonviolence in all he does.

Just as a modern European economist would not consider it a great economic achievement if all European art treasures were sold to America at attractive prices, so the Buddhist economist would insist that a population basing its economic life on nonrenewable fuels is living parasitically, on capital instead of income. Such a way of life could have no permanence and could therefore be justified only as a purely temporary expedient. As the world's resources of nonrenewable fuels—coal, oil and natural gas—are exceedingly unevenly distributed over the globe and undoubtedly limited in quantity, it is clear that their exploitation at an ever increasing rate is an act of violence against nature which must almost inevitably lead to violence between men.

THE MIDDLE WAY

This fact alone might give food for thought even to those people in Buddhist countries who care nothing for the religious and spiritual values of their heritage and ardently desire to embrace the materialism of modern economics at the fastest possible speed. Before they dismiss Buddhist economics as nothing better than a nostalgic dream, they might wish to consider whether the path of economic development outlined by modern economics is likely to lead them to places where they really want to be. Towards the end of his courageous book *The Challenge of Man's Future,* Professor Harrison Brown of the California Institute of Technology gives the following appraisal:

> Thus we see that, just as industrial society is fundamentally unstable and subject to reversion to agrarian existence, so within it the conditions which offer individual freedom are unstable in their ability to avoid the conditions which impose rigid organization and totalitarian control. Indeed, when we examine all of the foreseeable difficulties which threaten the survival of industrial civilization, it is difficult to see how the achievement of stability and the maintenance of individual liberty can be made compatible.[8]

Even if this were dismissed as a long-term view—and in the long term, as Keynes said, we are all dead—there is the immediate question of whether modernization, as currently practised without regard to religious and spiritual values, is actually producing agreeable results. As far as the masses are concerned, the results appear to be disastrous—a collapse of the rural economy, a rising tide of unemployment in town and country, and the growth of a city proletriat without nourishment for either body or soul.

It is in the light of both immediate experience and long-term prospects that the study of Buddhist economics could be recommended even to those who believe that economic growth is more important than any spiritual or religious values. For it is not a question of choosing between "modern growth" and "traditional stagnation." It is a question of finding the right path of development, "The Middle Way" between materialist heedlessness and traditionalist immobility, in short, of finding "Right Livelihood."

That this can be done is not in doubt. But it requires much more than blind imitation of the materialist way of life of the so-called advanced countries.[9] It requires above all, the conscious and systematic development of a "Middle Way in technology," as I have called it.[10] A technology more productive and powerful than the decayed technology of the ancient East, but at the same time nonviolent and immensely cheaper and simpler than the labor-saving technology of the modern West.

NOTES

1. *Pyidawtha, The New Burma* (Economic and Social Board, Government of the Union of Burma, 1954, p. 10).

2. *Ibid.*, p. 8.

3. *Ibid.*, p. 128.

4. Ananda K. Coomaraswamy. *Art and Swadeshi* (Ganesh and Co., Madras, p. 30).

5. J. C. Kumarappa. *Economy of Preformance* (Sarva-Seva-Sangh-Publication, Rajghat, Kashi, 4th ed., 1958, p. 117).

6. J. K. Galbraith. *The Affluent Society* (Penguin, 1962, pp. 272–273).

7. Richard B. Gregg. *A Philosophy of Indian Economic Development* (Navajivan Publishing House, Ahmedabad, 1958, pp. 140–141).

8. Harrison Brown. *The Challenge of Man's Future* (The Viking Press, New York, 1954, p. 255).

9. E. F. Schumacher, "Rural Industries" in *India at Midpassage* (Overseas Development Institute, London, 1964).

10. E. F. Schumacher. "Industrialization through Intermediate Technology" in *Minerals and Industries.*, Vol. 1, no. 4 (Calcutta, 1964). Vijay Chebbi and George McRobie. *Dynamics of District Development* (SIET Institute, Hyderabad, 1964).

10

THE PRESUMPTIONS OF SCIENCE

Robert L. Sinsheimer

Can there be "forbidden"—or, as I prefer, "inopportune" knowledge? Could there be knowledge, the possession of which, at a given time and stage of social development, would be inimical to human welfare—and even fatal to the further accumulation of knowledge? Could it be that just as the information latent in the genome of a developing organism must be revealed in an orderly pattern, else disaster ensue, so must our knowledge of the universe be acquired in a measured order, else disaster ensue?

Biological organisms are equipped with many sensors essential to their survival, sensors for heat, cold, pain, thirst, hunger. Social organisms similarly need sensors of peril, particularly as they evolve into new domains—and for these we must use our intelligence, limited as it may be.

Discussion of the possible restraint of inquiry touches a most sensitive nerve in the academic community. If one believes that the highest purpose available to humanity is the acquisition of knowledge (and in particular of

Reprinted by permission of author and publisher from *Daedalus*, Spring 1978.

scientific knowledge, knowledge of the natural universe), then one will regard any attempt to limit or direct the search for knowledge as deplorable—or worse.

If, however, one believes that there may be other values to be held even higher than the acquisition of knowledge—for instance, general human welfare—and that science and possible other modes of knowledge acquisition should subserve these higher values, then one is willing to (indeed, one must) consider such issues as: the possible restriction of the rate of acquisition of scientific knowledge to an "optimal" level relative to the social context into which it is brought; the selection of certain areas of scientific research as more or less appropriate for that social context; the relative priorities at a given time of the acquisiton of scientific knowledge or of other knowledge such as the effectiveness of modes of social integration, or of systems of justice, or of educational patterns.

In short, if one does not regard the acquisition of scientific knowledge as an unquestioned ultimate good, one is willing to consider its disciplined direction. One may, of course, still have grave doubt as to whether mankind can know enough to be able intelligently to guide the rate or direction of the scientific endeavor, but at least one will then accept that we have a responsibility to seek answers—if there be any—to such questions.

THE IMPACT OF SCIENCE

In 1930 Robert A. Millikan, Nobel Prize winner, founder and long-time leader of Caltech, wrote in an article entitled "The Alleged Sins of Science" that one may "sleep in peace with the consciousness that the Creator has put some foolproof elements into his handiwork, and that man is powerless to do it any titanic physical damage."[1]

To what was Millikan referring? Stimulated by the recombinant DNA controversy, I have looked back to see if there were any similar admonitions or premonitions with respect to the possible consequences of nuclear energy. And there were. Millikan, in 1930, was responding to an earlier writing of Frederick Soddy. In a book entitled *Science and Life* Soddy, who had been a collaborator of Rutherford, had written:

> Let us suppose that it became possible to extract the energy which now oozes out, so to speak, from radioactive material over a period of thousands of millions of years, in as short a time as we pleased. From a pound weight of such substance one could get about as much energy as would be obtained by burning 150 tons of coal. How splendid. Or a pound weight could be made to do the work of 150 tons of dynamite. Ah, there's the rub. . . . It is a discovery that conceivably might be made tomorrow in time for its development and perfection, for the use or destruction, let us say, of the next generations, and, which it is pretty certain, will be made by science sooner or later. Surely it will not need

this actual demonstration to convince the world that it is doomed if it fools with the achievements of science as it has fooled too long in the past.

War, unless in the meantime man has found a better use for the gifts of science, would not be the lingering agony it is today. Any selected section of the world, or the whole of it if necessary, could be depopulated with a swiftness and dispatch that would leave nothing to be desired.[2]

Millikan commented, just prior to his statement quoted above,

Since Mr. Soddy raised the hobgoblin of dangerous quantities of available subatomic energy [science] has brought to light good evidence that this particular hobgoblin—like most of the hobgoblins that crowd in on the mind of ignorance—was a myth. . . . The new evidence born of further scientific study is to the effect that it is highly improbable that there is any appreciable amount of available subatomic energy to tap.[3]

So much for scientific prophecy. But it is indeed instructive and also troubling to recognize that our scientific endeavor truly does rest upon unspoken, even unrecognized, faith—a faith in the resilience, even the benevolence, of nature as we have probed it, dissected it, rearranged its components in novel configurations, bent its forms and diverted its forces to human purpose. Scientific endeavor rests upon the faith that our scientific probing and our technological ventures will not displace some key element of our protective environment and thereby collapse our ecological niche. It is a faith that nature does not set booby traps for unwary species.

Our bold scientific thrusts into *new* territories uncharted by experiment and unencompassed by theory must rely wholly upon our faith in the resilience of nature. In the past that faith has been justified and rewarded, but will it always be so? The faith of one era is not always appropriate to the next, and an unexamined faith is unworthy of science. Ought we step more cautiously as we explore the deeper levels of matter and life?

Most states of nature are quasiequilibria, the outcome of competing forces. Small deviations from equilibrium, the result of natural processes or human intervention, are most often countered by an opposing force and the equilibrium restored, at some rate dependent upon the kinetics of the processes, the sizes of the relevant natural pools of components, and other factors. Although we may therefore speak of the resilience of nature, this restorative capacity is finite and is limited in rate.

For example, if the ozone layer of the atmosphere is lightly and transiently depleted by a nuclear explosion or the atmospheric release of fluorocarbons, the natural processes which generate the ozone layer can restore it to the original level within a brief period. However, should the ozone layer be massively depleted—as by extended, large-scale release of fluorocarbons —many decades would be required for its renewal by natural processes, even if the release of fluorocarbons ceased.

Similarly, the populations of most living creatures can achieve an equilibrium level dependent upon birth rates and upon death rates from various causes. Most species have an excess capacity for reproduction, so that minor additions to the process of their removal (as by the harvesting of fish) cannot appreciably influence the equilibrium population. Patently however, excessive harvesting removing numbers beyond the reproductive capacity of the species will in time bring about its extinction.

In a similar manner lakes and rivers and air basins can absorb and dispose of limited amounts of pollutant but can be overwhelmed by masses beyond their capacity. Once overwhelmed the very agents responsible for disposal of pollution in small quantities may be destroyed, leaving a "dead" sea.

The concept of resilience extends to the planet as a whole and to the impact upon the manifold equilibria upon which the network of life forms depends as we continue to expand our intensive monoculture agriculture, as we continue to increase the total of human energy consumption (the man-made release of energy in the Los Angeles basin is now estimated at about 5 percent of the solar input), as we continue to raise the atmospheric level of CO_2 by combustion of fossil fuel, and so forth.

Because human beings (and most creatures) are adapted by evolution to the near equilibrium states, the resilience provided by the restorative forces of nature has appeared to us to be not only benevolent, but unalterable. Less overt than our faith in the resilience of nature is the faith with which we have relied upon the resilience of our social institutions and their capacity to contain the stress of change and to adapt the knowledge gained by science—and the power inherent in that knowledge—to the benefit of society, more than to its detriment. The fragility of the equilibria underlying social institutions is even more apparent than of the equilibria of nature. Political, economic, and cultural balances have shifted drastically in human history under the impact of new technologies, or new ideologies or religions, of invading peoples, of resource exhaustion, and other changes. Our faith in the resilience of both natural and man-made phenomena is increasingly strained by the acceleration of technical change and the magnitude of the powers deployed.

Physics and chemistry have given us the power to reshape the physical nature of the planet. We wield forces comparable to, even greater than those of, natural catastrophes. And now biology is bringing to us a comparable power over the world of life. The recombinant DNA technology, while significant and potentially a grievous hazard in itself (through the conceivable production, by design or by inadvertance, of new human, animal, or plant pathogens or of novel forms capable of disrupting important biological equilibria), must be seen as a portent of things to come.

The present recombinant DNA technology, which permits the addition or replacement of a few genes in living cells, is but the first prototype of genetic engineering. More powerful means involving cell fusion or chromosome transfer are already close to hand; even more sophisticated future developments appear assured. Since genes determine the basic structures and biological potentials of all living forms, the ultimate potential of genetic engineering for the modification and redesign of plants and animals to meet human needs and desires seems virtually unlimited.

Such capabilities will pose major questions as to the extent to which mankind will want to assume the responsibility for the life forms of the planet. Further, there is no reason to believe the same technology will not be applicable to mankind as well; the capability of human genetic engineering will raise profound questions of values and judgment for human societies.

It seems pradoxical that a living organism emergent from the evolutionary process after billions of years of blind circumstance should undertake to determine its own future evolution. The process is perhaps analogous to that of the mind seeking to understand itself. In both cases it is uncertain whether the attempt can possibly be successful. Nonetheless, at this point perhaps we had best step back and reconsider what it is we are about.

For four centuries science has progressively expanded our knowledge and reshaped our perception of the world. In that same time technology has correspondingly reshaped the pattern of our lives and the world in which we live.

Most people would agree that the net consequence of these activities has been benign. But it may be that the conditions which fostered such a benign outcome of scientific advance and technological innovation are changing to a less favorable set. Changes in the nature of science or technology or in the external society—in either the scale of events or their temporal order—can affect the preconditions, the presumptions, of scientific activity, and can thus alter the future consequences of such activities.

Both quantitative and qualitative changes have surely affected the impact of science and technology upon society. Quantitatively, the exponential growth of scientific activity and the unprecedented magnitude of modern industrial ventures permit the introduction of new technologies (e.g., fluorocarbon sprays) on a massive scale within very brief periods often with unforeseen consequence. Qualitatively, science and technology have been directed increasingly to synthesis—to the formulation of new substances designed for specific human purpose. Thus we have synthetic atoms (plutonium, strontium-90), synthetic molecules (dioxin, kepone, DDT) and now synthetic microorganisms (recombinant DNA). In these activities we introduce wholly novel substances into the planetary environment, substances with which our evolution has not always prepared us to cope.

Can we continue to rely upon the past four centuries as a guide for scientific activity, given these changes? Other human activities of this same era are now increasingly seen in a different hue. The same period witnessed exponential increases in population and in the exploitation of natural resources for material wealth. Few would argue continuance of such trends will be benign.[4] The same era has witnessed the constant acceleration of the rate of change, the increasing dominance of technology in the affairs of men.

The constantly accelerating accretion of knowledge, therefore, may not always be counted as a good. Can circumstances change so as to devalue the net worth of new knowledge? Might a pause or slowdown for consolidation and reflection then be more in order? Indeed, could it be that some knowledge could, at this time, be positively malign? Hard questions, perhaps not answerable, perhaps not the right questions, but they are not answered for 1977 by involking Galileo or Darwin or Freud. I believe they demand our thought.

I would advance for consideration some propositions that frankly I'm not at all sure I entirely believe. I think that in order to find out what one does believe it is necessary to go beyond what one can readily accept—to explore honestly more extreme and more remote positions so that one's position is based upon intelligent choice, not simple ignorance.

The domain I propose to explore can be indicated by a question. The question is one I have actually raised within the administration at Caltech (and it could as well be raised elsewhere). Institutions such as Caltech and others devote much energy and effort and talent to the advancement of science. We raise funds, we provide laboratories, we train students, and so on. In so doing we apply essentially only one criterion—that it be good science as science —that the work be imaginative, skillfully done, in the forefront of the field. Is that, as we approach the end of the twentieth century, enough? As social institutions, do Caltech and others have an obligation to be concerned about the likely *consequences* of the research they foster? And if so, how might they implement such a responsibility?

For reasons which probably need no elaboration Caltech has been more than reluctant to come to grips with this question. And, indeed, it just may be —and I say this with real sorrow—that scientists are simply not the people qualified to cope with such a question. The basic tactic of natural science is analysis: fragment a phenomenon into its components, analyze each part and process in isolation, and thereby derive an understanding of the subject. In physics, chemistry, even biology, this tactic has worked splendidly.

To answer my question, however, the focus must not be inward but outward, not narrowed but broadened. The focus must be on all the ties of the sciences to society and culture and on the impact of scientific knowledge and technological advancement on all human, indeed all planetary, life.

Consider as an instance the recombinant DNA issue. The natural tendency of the scientist, if he will admit this a problem, is to break it down, to decompose it into individually analyzable situations. If there is a danger, quantitate it: what is the numerical chance of the organisms escaping, of their colonizing the gut, of their penetrating the intestinal epithelium, of their causing disease (what disease)? If you point out that there is a nearly infinite set of possible scenarios of misfortune—that accidents do happen and in unpredictable ways, that humans do err, that bacterial or viral cultures do become contaminated, that indeed aspects of this technology involve inherently unpredictable consequence and hence are not susceptible to quantitative analysis —you are regarded as unscientific.

The consequences of the interaction of known but foreign gene products with the complex contents of a bacteria cell would be difficult enough to predict, much less the consequences of the interactions of unknown gene products, as produced in "shotgun" experiments. Some of these consequences may well modify, in unpredictable ways, the likelihood of the organism's survival or persistence in various environments, its potential toxicity for a host or nearby life forms. It may alter, for instance, an organism's survival in an animal intestine, contrary to our expectations, for we have presumed that we know all factors important for survival there and that no new successful adaptations could emerge.

For complex reasons, consideration of the potential hazards from organisms with recombinant DNA has focused upon immediate medical concerns. That these organisms with unpredictable properties might have impact upon any of the numerous microbiological processes which are important components of our life support systems is simply dismissed as improbable. The fact that these organisms are evolutionary innovations and have within themselves, as do all living forms, the capacity (if they survive) for their own unpredictable future evolutionary development is ignored, or dismissed as mystical.

If you point out that the recombinant DNA issue simply cannot be effectively considered in isolation but must be viewed in perspective and in a larger context as a possible precursor to future technologies available to many elements of society (including totalitarian governments, the military, and terrorist factions) your remarks are regarded as irrelevant to science.

There is an intensity of focus in the scientific perspective which is both its immediate strength and its ultimate weakness. The scientific approach focuses rigorously upon the problem at hand, ignoring as irrelevant the antecedents of motive and the prospectives of consequence.

Viewed objectively such an approach can only make sense if either (1) the consequences are always trivial, which is patently untrue, or (2) the consequences are always benign, that is, if the acquisition of knowledge, of any knowledge at any time, is always good, a proposition one might find hard to defend, or (3) the dangers and difficulties inherent in any attempt to restrict the acquisition of knowledge are so great as to make the unhindered pursuit of science the lesser evil.

In thinking about the impacts of science, we should, perhaps, reflect upon the inverse of the uncertainty principle. Perhaps it might be called the certainty principle. The uncertainty principle is concerned with the inevitable impact of the observer upon the observed, which thereby alters the observed. Conversely, there is an effect of the observed upon the observer. The discovery of new knowledge, the addition of new certainty, which correspondingly diminishes the domain of uncertainty and mystery, inevitably alters the perspective of the observer. We do not see the world with the same eyes as a Newton or a Descartes, or even a Faraday or a Rutherford.

The acquisition of a discipline sharpens our vision in its domain, but too frequently it seems also to blind us to other concerns. Thus immersion in the world of science, with its store of accumulated and substantiated fact, can make the participant intolerant of, and impatient with the uncertainties and nonreproducibilities of the human world. Engrossed in the search for knowledge, scientists tend to adopt the position that more knowledge is the key to the solution to human problems. They may not see that the uses we make of knowledge or the ways in which we organize to use knowledge can, as well, be the limiting factors to the human condition, and they forget that even within science our knowledge and our theories are always human constructs. Moreover, we should always remember (lest we become too secure and even smug) that our knowledge and our theories are ever incomplete.

OF DUBIOUS MERIT

To make this discussion more specific let me consider three examples of research that I personally consider to be, on balance, of dubious merit. One is in an area of rather applied research, the second in a very speculative but surely basic area, and the third in the domain of biomedical research, which we most often conceive to be wholly benign.

The first I would cite is current research upon improved means for isotope fractionation. In one technique, one attempts to use sophisticated lasers[5] to activate selectively one isotope of a set. I do not wish to discuss the technology but rather the likely consequence of its success. To be sure, there are benign experiments that would be facilitated by the availability of less expensive, pure isotopes. For some years I wanted to do an experiment with oxygen 18 but was always deterred by the cost.

But does anyone doubt that the most immediate application of isotope fractionation techniques would be the separation of uranium isotopes? This country has recently chosen to defer, at least, if not in fact to abandon, the plutonium economy and the breeder reactor because of well-founded concern that plutonium would inevitably find its way into weapons. We are thus left with uranium-fueled reactors. But uranium 235 can also be made into a bomb. Its use for power is safer only because of the difficulty in the separation of uranium 235 from the more abundant uranium 238. If we supersede the complex technology of Oak Ridge, if we devise quick and ingenious means for isotope separation, then one of the last defenses against nuclear terror will be breached. Is the advantage worth the price?

A second instance I would cite of research of dubious merit, and one probably even more tendentious than the first, relates to the proposal to search for and contact extraterrestrial intelligence.[6] Recent proposals suggest that, using advanced electronic and computer technology, we could monitor a million "channels" in a likely region of the electromagnetic spectrum, "listening" over several years for signals with an "unnatural" regularity or complexity.

I am concerned about the psychological impact upon humanity of such contact. We have had the technical capacity to search for such postulated intelligence for less than two decades, an instant in cosmic terms. If such intelligent societies exist and if we can "hear" them, we are almost certain to be technologically less advanced and thus distinctly inferior in our development to theirs. What would be the impact of such knowledge upon human values?

Copernicus was a deep cultural shock to man. The universe did not revolve about us. But God works in mysterious ways and we could still be at the center of importance in His universe. Darwin was a deep cultural shock to man. But we were still number one. If we are closer to the animals than we thought before, and through them to the rocks and the sea, it does not really devalue man to revalue matter. To really be number two, or number 37, or in truth to be wholly outclassed, an inferior species, inferior on our own turf of intellect and creativity and imagination, would, I think, be very hard for humanity.

The impact of more advanced cultures upon less advanced has almost invariably been disastrous to the latter. We are well acquainted with such impacts as the Spanish upon the Aztecs and Incas or the British and French upon the Polynesians and Hawaiians. These instances were, however, compounded by physical interventions (warfare) and the introduction of novel diseases. I want to emphasize the purely cultural shock. Hard learned skills determinant of social usefulness and positions become quickly obsolete. Less advanced cultures quickly become derivative, seeking technological handouts. What would happen to *our* essential tradition of self-reliance? Would we be reduced to seekers of cosmic handouts?

The distance of the contacted society might, to some degree, mitigate its consequent impact. A contact with a round trip communication time of ten years would have much more effect than one with a thousand years. The likelihood of either is, however, a priori, unknown. Nor is it inconceivable that an advanced society could devise means for communication faster than light.

The proponents of such interactions have considered the consequences briefly. In a 427-page book *Communication with Extraterrestrial Intelligence*[7] sixteen pages comprise a chapter entitled "Consequences of Contact." Opinion therein ranges from "Our obligation is, I feel, to stress that in any sensible way this problem has no danger for human society. I believe we can give a full guarantee of this" to "If we come in contact with some superior civilization this would mean the end of our civilization, although that might take a while. Our period of culture would be finished."

How and by whom should such a momentous decision[8] be made—one that will clearly, if successful, have an impact upon all humanity? Somehow I cannot believe it should be left to a small group of enthusiastic radioastronomers.

My concern here does not extend so far that I would abolish the science of astronomy. If the astronomers in the course of their science come across phenomena that can only be understood as the product of intelligent activity, so be it. But I do not believe that is the same as deliberately setting out to look for such activity with overt pretentions of social benefit.

The third example of research I consider of dubious merit concerns the aging process. I would suggest this subject exemplifies in supreme degree the eternal conflict between the welfare of the individual and the welfare of society and, indeed, the species. Obviously, as individuals, we would prefer youth and continued life. Equally obviously, on a finite planet, extended individual life must restrict the production of new individuals and that renewal which provides the vitality of our species.

The logic is inexorable. In a finite world the end of death means the end of birth. Who will be the last born?

If we propose such research we must take seriously the possibility of its success. The impact of a major extension of the human life span upon our entire social order, upon the life styles, mores, and adaptations associated with "three score and ten," upon the carrying capacity of a planet already facing overpopulation would be devastating. At this time we hardly need such enormous additional problems. Research on aging seems to me to exemplify the wrong research on the wrong problem in the wrong era. We need that talent elsewhere.

IS RESTRAINT FEASIBLE?

If one concedes, however reluctantly, that restraint of some directions of scientific inquiry is desirable, it is appropriate to ask if it is feasible and, if so, at what cost.

Some of my colleagues, not only in biology but in other fields of science as well, have indicated to me that they too increasingly sense that our curiosity, our exploration of nature, may unwittingly lead us into an irretrievable disaster. But they argue we have no alternative.[9] Such a position is, of course, a self-fulfilling prophecy.

I would differentiate among what might be called physical feasibility, logical feasibility, and political feasibility.

I believe that actual physical restraint is in principle feasible. There are two evident avenues of control: the power of the purse and access to instruments. Control of funding is indeed already a powerful means for control of the directions of inquiry for better or worse. To the extent that there exists a multiciplity of sources of support, such control is porous and incomplete, but it is clearly a first line of restraint.

Research today cannot be done with household tools. It is difficult to imagine, for instance, any serious research on aging that would not require the use of radioisotopes or an ultracentrifuge or an electron microscope. The use of isotopes is already regulated for other reasons. Access to electron microscopes could, in principle, be regulated, albeit at very real cost to our current concepts of intellectual freedom.

An immediately related, important aspect of any policy of restraint concerns the distinctions to be made about the nature of research. Can we logically differentiate research on aging from general basic biologic studies? I expect we cannot in any simple, absolute sense. Yet obviously the people who established the National Institute of Aging must have believed that there is a class of studies which deserves specific support under that rubric. Indeed, distinctions of ths sort are made all the time by the various institutes of National Institutes of Health in deciding which grant applications are potentially eligible for their particular support. Pragmatically, and with some considerable margin of error, such distinctions can be and are made.

It is frequently claimed that the "unpredictability" of the outcome of research makes its restraint, for social or other purpose, illogical and indeed futile. However, the unpredictability of a research outcome is not an absolute but is both quantitatively and qualitatively variable.

In more applied research within a field with well-defined general principles, the range of possible outcomes is surely circumscribed. In more fundamental research, in wholly new fields remote from prior human experience—as in the cosmos, or the subatomic world, or the core of the planet—wholly novel phenomena may be discovered. But, for instance, even in a fundamental science such as biology, most of the overt phenomena of life have been long known.

The basic principles of heredity were discovered by Mendel a century ago and were elaborated by Morgan and others early in this century. The understanding of genetic mechanism, the reduction of genetics to chemistry, had to await the advent of molecular biology. This understanding of mechanism has now provided the potential for human interventions, for genetic engineering, but it has not significantly modified our comprehension of the genetic basis of biological process.[10]

The path of modern biology will surely lead to further understanding of biological mechanism, with subsequent application to medicine and agriculture (and accompanying social impact). But it would seem likely that only within the central nervous system may there be the potential for wholly novel—and correspondingly wholly unpredictable—process. Even there, the facts of human psychology and the subjective realities of human consciousness have long been familiar to us, albeit the underlying mechanisms are indeed obscure.

Political feasibility is, of course, another question. The constituency most immediately affected is, of course, the scientific. And despite our protestations and alarms this community does have real political influence. It would seem unlikely to me that a policy of scientific restraint could be adopted in any sector unless a major portion of the scientific community came to believe it desirable.

For this to happen, that community will clearly have to become far more alert to, and aware of, and responsible for the consequences of their activities. The best discipline is self-discipline. Scientists are keenly sensitive to the evaluations of their peers. The scientific community and the leaders of our scientific and technical institutions will have to develop a collective conscience; they will have to let it be known certain types of research are looked upon askance, much as biological warfare research is today; it needs to be understood that such research will not be weighed in considerations of tenure and promotions; societies need to agree not to sponsor symposia on such topics. All of these and similar measures short of law could indeed be very effective.

I am well aware of the dangers implicit in such forms of cultural restraint. But I think we really must look at the dangers we face in the absence of self-restraint. Do we accept only the restraint of catastrophe?

If we are to consider this position, we must do so in a forthright manner. We must be willing to explore the vistas exposed if we lower conventional taboos and sanctions. We may not at first enjoy what we see, but at least we will have a better perception of the available alternatives. Any attempt to limit the freedom of scientific inquiry will surely involve what will appear, at least at first, to be quite arbitrary distinctions—judgmental decisions, the establishment of boundaries in gray and amorphous terrain. These are, however, familiar processes in our society, in the courts, in the legislatures. Indeed, most of us are familir with such problems in our educational activities. The selection of new faculty, the award of tenure, the assignment of grades are clearly judgmental decisions.

In science we try with some success to elude the necessity for such very human judgments. Indeed, one suspects that many persons go into science precisely to avoid the necessity for such complex decisions—in search of a domain of unique and unequivocal answers of enduring validity. And it is painful to see the sanctuary invaded.

Admittedly it is difficult to achieve consensus on the criteria for judgmental decisions. Such consensus is all the more difficult in the sphere of international activities such as science which involve participants from diverse cultures and traditions.

Conversely there are many persons who prefer the more common, perhaps the more human world of ambiguity and compromise and temporally valid judgments and who resist the seemingly brutal, life and death, cataclysmic types of decision increasingly imposed upon society by the works of science. And science and scientists cannot stand wholly aloof from these latter dilemmas—for science is a human activity and scientists live in the human society. We cannot expect the adaptation to be wholly one-sided.

Even if, at best, we can only slow the rate of acquisition of certain areas of knowledge, such a tactic would give us more time to prepare for social adaptation—if we mobilize ourselves to use that time.

THE CASE FOR RESTRAINT

The view one exposes by lifting that sanction we label freedom of inquiry is frankly gloomy. It would seem that we are asked to make thorny decisions and delicate differentiations, to relinquish long-cherished rights of free inquiry, to forego clear prospects of technological progress. And it would seem that all these concessions stem ultimately from recognition of human frailty and from recognition of the limitations of human rationality and foresight, of human adaptability and even good will. Just such recognitions have already spawned many of our institutions and professions—religions, the law, government, United Nations—yet all of these are as imperfect as the world they are designed to restrain and improve.

At such level of human activity, whether individual, group, or national, we continually struggle to find acceptable compromises between the freedom to pursue varied courses and goals and the conflicts that arise when one person's actions run contrary to another's. In a crude sense the greater the power available to an entity, the more limitations must be imposed upon its freedom if conflict is to be averted. Ideally such limits are internalized through education and conscience, but we all understand the inadequacy of that process.

In short, we must pay a price for freedom, for the toleration of diversity, even eccentricity. That price may require that we forego certain technologies, even certain lines of inquiry where the likely application is incompatible with the maintenance of other freedoms. If this is so and if we can recognize and understand this, perhaps we can, as scientists, be more accepting.

Some will argue that knowledge simply provides us with more options and thus that the decision point should not be at the acquisition of knowledge but at its application.

Such a view, however ideal, overlooks the difficulty inherent in the restriction of application of new knowledge, once that knowledge has become available in a free society. Does anyone really believe, for instance, that knowledge permitting an extension of the human life span would not be applied once it were available?

One must also recognize again that the very acquisition of knowledge can change both the perceptions and the values of the acquirer. Could, for instance, deeper knowledge of the realities of human genetics affect our commitment to democracy?

It may be argued that the cost, however it may be measured, of impeding research would be greater to a society than the cost of impeding application. Perhaps so. This issue could be debated, but it must be debated in realistic terms with regard for the nature of real people and real society and with full understanding that knowledge is indeed power.

Although the nature of the measures necessary to restrict the application of knowledge has seldom been analyzed, the measures needed would surely be dependent upon the size of investment required to apply the knowledge, as well as on the form of and the need for the potential benefits of the knowledge, among other things. The compatibility of such restrictive measures with the principles of a democratic society would need to be considered. Restriction of nuclear power may be a case in point.

Alvin Weinberg has developed the concept of the technological fix as the simple solution to cut the Gordian knot of complex social problems. However, we seem to be discovering that the application of one technological fix seems to lead us into another technological fix. For example, the development of antibiotics and other triumphs of modern medicine has led to the tyranny of overpopulation. In efforts to cope with overpopulation by more intensive agriculture, we develop pesticides, herbicides and other chemicals which increase the level of environmental carcinogenesis. And so on.

The moral is that we cannot ignore the social and cultural context within which the technology is deployed. In retrospect we can see that in the cultural and social context of the seventeenth, eighteenth, and nineteenth centuries the consequences of technological innovation were most often benign. Whether because of change in the society and culture or change in the nature and effectiveness of technology, at some time in the twentieth century the balance began to shift and by now our addiction to technology begins to assume an unpleasant cast.

We are indeed addicted to technology. We rely ever more upon it and thus become its servant as well as its master. It has led to human populations insupportable without its aid. Further, new technologies shape our perceptions; they spawn expectations of change or stir deep fears of disaster. They dissociate us from the past and becloud the shape of the future. Even the oldest boundary conditions of humanity fall as we leave the planet and as we plan to reshape our genes.

Our academic institutions and our professional societies foster and promote science. To some degree they also have concern for its consequences, but it is a minor aspect. The principle that one should separate agencies which promote and agencies which regulate may apply here.

But where then is the balance, the necessary check to the force of scientific progress? Is the accumulation of knowledge unique among human activities —an unmitigated good that needs no counterweight? Perhaps that was true when science was young and impotent, but hardly now. Yet we lack the institutional mechanisms for regulation.

Our experience with constraint upon science has hardly been encouraging. From the Inquisition to Lysenko such constraint has been the work of bigots and charlatans. Obviously, if it is to be done to a good purpose, any restraint must be informed, both as to science and as to the larger society in which science impacts.

The acquisition of knowledge is a human, a social, enterprise. If we, through the relentless, single-minded pursuit of new knowledge so destabilize society as to render it incapable—or unwilling—to continue to support the scientific enterprise, then we will have, through our obsession, defeated ourselves.

At Caltech and the many other academic institutions, we have now, *culturally,* cloned Galileo a millionfold. We have nurtured this Galilean clone well; we award prizes and honors to those most like the original. No doubt this clone has been most beneficial for humanity, but perhaps there is a time for Galileos. Perhaps we need in this time to start another clone.

NOTES

1. R. A. Millikan, "Alleged Sins of Science," *Scribners Magazine,* 87 (2) (1930): 119–130.

2. Frederick Soddy, *Science and Life* (London: John Murray, 1920).

3. Precisely what evidence Dr. Millikan had in mind is uncertain. However, it was generally appreciated that the efficiency of nuclear transformation by the charged particles in use was so low that there was no significant prospect of a net release of energy. No practical chain reaction could yet be envisaged.

4. A. V. Hill in his presidential address to the British Association for the Advancement of Science in 1952, referring to the population problem, said, "If ethical principles deny our right to do evil in order that good may come, are we justified in doing good when the foreseeable consequence is evil?"

5. See A. S. Krass, "Laser Enrichment of Uranium: The Proliferation Connection," *Science,* 196 (1977): 721–731; also B. M. Casper, "Laser Enrichment: A New Path to Proliferation?" *Bulletin of Atomic Scientists,* 33 (1) (1977): 28–41.

6. See T. B. H. Kuiper and M. Morris, "Searching for Extraterrestrial Civilizations," *Science;* 196 (1977): 616–621; also B. Murray, S. Gulkis, and R. E. Edelson, "Extraterrestrial Intelligence: An Observational Approach," *Science,* in press.

7. C. Sagan (ed.), *Communication with Extraterrestrial Intelligence (EETC)* (Cambridge, Mass.: MIT Press, 1973).

8. Conceivably, we might not be given this choice if an advanced civilization were determined to contact us. At present however, it would seem to be our option.

9. This is not a new perception. "The world is now faced with a self-evolving system which it cannot stop. There are dangers and advantages in this situation. . . . Modern science has imposed upon humanity the necessity for wandering. Its progressive thought and its progressive technology make the transition through time, from generation to generation, a true migration into uncharted seas of adventure. The very benefit of wandering is that it is dangerous and needs skill to avert evils. We must expect, therefore, that the future will disclose dangers. It is

the business of the future to be dangerous; and it is the merit of science that it equips the future for its duties," wrote A. W. Whitehead in *Science and the Modern World*.

10. Indeed the failure to discover a new class of phenomena underlying genetics has been most disappointing to some. See Gunther S. Stent, "That Was the Molecular Biology That Was." *Science*, 160 (1968): 390–395.

11

ECOLOGY, ETHICS, AND THEOLOGY

John Cobb

Western ethics, like Western thought generally, has been radically anthro-pocentric. But the disruptions of ecological systems which have brought the world to crisis have called our attention to the need for adopting different patterns of behavior with respect to our environment. Ecological crisis opens the question of whether the moral necessity of behavioral changes follows from the same anthropocentric principles we have had in the past or whether our ethical principles themselves are partly at fault and need alteration. If the latter, on what ground can such alteration be effected? Surely ultimate ethical principles cannot be altered only because we do not like their results.

There are two basic elements in almost any ethical theory, although one or the other is often more implicit than explicit. We require some judgment as to what is good or desirable, and we require some principles of right action. Those who concentrate on the first of these elements, developing a theory of

"Ecology, Ethics, and Theology." Published by permission of the author, with additions written especially for this volume.

value, often assume that when their work is done the answer to the question of how we ought to act is self-evident. That is, having determined good or desirable values, they suppose that we ought to maximize those values. But this ignores the complex question of exactly what our obligation is if maximization presents conflicts. Should we maximize values in general or our own values? Should we maximize present values or be equally concerned about future values? Are there any acts that we should not perform regardless of the value of their consequences? Is the relation of our present action to past commitments a relevant factor in deciding how we ought now to act? Answering these questions is not a further development of a theory of value but a treatment of the formal questions that belong to ethics proper.

VALUE THEORY

In a value theory it is customary to distinguish types of values. One important distinction is between intrinsic value and instrumental value. An automobile is of instrumental value to me in that it enables me to get places and thereby to have experiences that I would otherwise be denied. Perhaps it may also be instrumentally valuable to me as an object of aesthetic contemplation or as contributory to my feeling of power. So long as its value is only instrumental it must be measured by its potential for contributing to the intrinsic value of my feeling of beauty and power, and by that alone. Hence intrinsic value is our primary consideration.

Although the distinction between instrumental and intrinsic values is important, it should not be exaggerated or misunderstood. There may be some things whose *only* value is instrumental, but there is nothing whose only value is intrinsic. That is, everything or every event has consequences for other things or events. These consequences can be evaluated as relatively favorable or unfavorable. Hence, though not everything can be evaluated in terms of its intrinsic value, everything does have its instrumental value.

It is my contention that whereas everything has instrumental value, only feeling is the locus of intrinsic value. The existence or nonexistence of something that has no feeling seems to me a matter of indifference unless it somehow contributes to the feeling belonging to something else, either actually or potentially. That is to say, what has no feeling has no intrinsic value and its instrumental value is a function of its contribution to something that does feel. Feeling, on the other hand, is intrinsically valuable, while it also has instrumental value in its relation to other feelings.

This doctrine is not far removed from common sense or from traditional theories of value. Utilitarianism proposed to regard only pleasure (and pain) as valuable (and disvaluable). Pleasure is of course a matter of feeling. Critics of utilitarianism have rightly complained that either the notion of pleasure must be taken very broadly or else it must be recognized that men find other feelings beside pleasure valuable. But in general they agree that the focus of intrinsic value is in the sphere of feeling.

However, it is noteworthy that despite a passing reference to the value of feelings of other sentient beings by John Stuart Mill in Chatper II of *Utilitarianism,* utilitarians limited the feeling that is valuable to the feeling humans have, a restriction most value theorists have tended to leave unquestioned. To be concerned about the feelings of other animals has appeared sentimental, and philosophers are even more eager than most men not to appear sentimental.

The most famous opposition to this restriction came from G. E. Moore. It is striking that in order to oppose it he thought he had to give up the locus of value in feeling. In place of *feeling,* Moore argues that *good,* a nonnatural property, is an objective ingredient in states of affairs. When we contemplate alternative states of affairs, he argues, we recognize one as better than the other, but our judgment is not based on the amount of pleasure present in these alternative states of affairs.

Moore proposes, in Section 50 of his *Principia Ethica,* that we consider two "worlds" in the following way.

> Let us imagine one world exceedingly beautiful. Imagine it as beautiful as you can; put into it whatever on this earth you most admire—mountains, rivers, the sea; trees, and sunsets, stars and moon. Imagine all these combined in the most exquisite proportions, so that no one thing jars against another, but each contributes to increase the beauty of the whole. And then imagine the ugliest world you can possibly conceive. Imagine it simply one heap of filth, containing everything that is most disgusting to us, for whatever reason, and the whole, as far as may be, without one redeeming feature.

In order to separate out the question of the value of these worlds in themselves from their value for a human observer, Moore asks that we suppose that no human being can ever *see* either world. Do we not, he then asks, still believe that it is better for the beautiful world to exist rather than the ugly one?

Moore, however, has not been very convincing. At least he has not convinced me. The beauty and ugliness of which he speaks are relational qualities, that is, they do not exist apart from the way certain formal patterns are apprehended by the human observer. Even though he asks us to imagine them as existing apart from observation or the possibility of observation, we are still visualizing them. But we are asked to suppose they have no effect, actual or potential, on any visualizing activity at all. In that case it simply has no meaning to say that one is beautiful and the other ugly.

My view of value can be sharply juxtaposed to Moore's by introducing into the ugly world something from the filth heap that has not been previously included: a number of worms and insects that men agree are utterly repulsive. Let us suppose that we had purposely excluded such life from the beautiful world. And let us assume further that the ugly world constitutes a suitable environment for our insects and worms, that these are able to secure adequate food and are free from excessive pain. In that case I would contend the ugly world had more value than the beautiful one. For in the ugly world there exist feelings of a level excluded from the beautiful world, namely, the feelings of the worms and insects. Since men are excluded in principle from both worlds, the fact that men would prefer to see and live in the beautiful world is irrelevant. If, on the other hand, we characteristically fill the beautiful world with birds and animals, and restrict residence in the ugly one to insects and worms, I would affirm much greater value to the beautiful world, not because it would appear beautiful to men, which of course it would, but because the feelings of birds and animals are more valuable than those of insects and worms. This I believe is more realistic because there is in fact considerable correlation between what *we* find beautiful and the sort of environment hospitable to higher forms of life.

Thus, whereas I reject Moore's position, I wish strongly to affirm with him, against the anthropocentric tendencies of most value theory, that values do exist apart from man's knowledge of them. If I contemplate two situations which I suppose no man to be cognizant of or affected by, one in which a dog is thoroughly enjoying life and the other in which it is suffering agony from a broken leg, I have no difficulty in judging between them. Enjoyment is an intrinsic good, and agony is an intrinsic evil, whether or not men know about it.

How far does intrinsic value extend beyond man? The question requires us to consider how far feeling extends beyond human feeling. To suppose that only men have feelings is surely arbitrary and contrary to the clear implications of our evolutionary connection with other forms of animal life. The reasonable issue is only how far to extend the category *feeling* or *experience*. Do unicellular organisms feel? What about the individual cells in multicellular organisms? Can a sharp line be drawn between cells and subcellular entities? My own view is that no line at all can be drawn, that wherever one deals with actual unitary entities one is dealing with feelings. But of course much that is most important in human feeling depends on such a high evolutionary product as consciousness, and I doubt that there is consciousness where there is no central nervous system. Hence, the feeling we can attribute to lower forms of life and *a fortiori* to so-called inanimate entities like molecules and submolecular forms, is very different from human feeling.

The major basis in the West of drawing sharp lines separating what is valuable in itself from what is not has been the doctrine of the psyche or soul. For Aristotle psyche was the principle of life and hence was attributed to plants and animals as well as to man. Even so, he made a distinction between the vegetable, animal, and rational souls, limiting the last to man. Christian theology stressed the uniqueness of the rational soul, associated it with the image of God, which in Genesis is attributed only to man, and viewed it as the object of divine redemption. From a religious and ethical point of view that made absolute the gulf between human souls and souls at other levels. Indeed, the term *soul* came to refer self-evidently to human soul. The hierarchy of levels of soul gave way to the dualism of ensouled man and soul-less animals.

Evolutionary views of living things should have reintroduced a more hierarchical conception. The human psyche as we now know it must have developed from simpler forms of life similar to those now found among other animals. Because of the differences between men and other animals, and because of the now traditional restriction of usage of the word *soul,* we may continue to limit soul terminologically to human soul if we like. But we must avoid the too apparent implication of a radical and abrupt difference. Functions and subjective experiences analogous to human psychic life are attributable to other complex animals as well.

Utilitarianism affirmed that each human being should count for as much as every other. This is a laudably democratic principle, but it has highly questionable features even when applied to humans. It is not really evident that the advantage of a mongoloid idiot or human vegetable should count equally with that of a healthy child. Also there is no objective way of determining the point in development at which a fertilized ovum should count equally with an adult. And the principle cannot function at all when we recognize that there are subhuman intrinsic values as well. It would be quite arbitrary to count a dog's pleasure or pain as equally important with that of a human being. If we extended such a principle to microorganisms the absurdity would become still more apparent. Hence the extension of intrinsic value beyond man to the subhuman world forces consideration of criteria for appraising values.

Utilitarianism did, of course, have criteria. Pleasure is good and pain is bad. What it assumed was that the state of feeling of any person could be plotted somewhere along the continuum between optimal pleasure and maximal pain. It ignored the fact that among persons there may be significant differences in the degree of feeling present. For example, there may be a very intense experience in which the factors of extreme pleasure and extreme pain are so nearly balanced that the utilitarian calculus would yield a negligible value either way. There may be another experience at very low ebb of feeling in which such minimal feeling as is present is purely pleasurable. This would be assigned a top plus score on the utilitarian calculus. The distortion thus introduced would be immeasurably magnified when the subjects compared were a man and a unicellular organism.

For a satisfactory theory of intrinsic value we require initially a quite different measure than pain and pleasure. It must be a quantitative measure of the experience as such rather than of its pleasurableness. A man enjoys *more* experience than do paramecia. How can this "more" be interpreted? One measure is intensity of feeling. We can distinguish between experiences according to their intensity, and other things being equal, we can meaningfully assert that more is happening in the more intense experience than in the less intense experience. But intensity may be gained at the expense of breadth and inclusiveness: how much is included in an experience and how different factors harmonize within it are also meaningful in comparing experiences. Of two experiences one may be more intense and the other more inclusive. Between these a judgment of which is "more" of an experience would be difficult to come by. However, we can judge that an experience in which inclusiveness *and* intensity are combined involves more feeling than would an experience consisting of either in isolation. Thus intensity and inclusiveness and their ideal combination can function as norms for ranking the experiences of men in relation to subhuman forms of life as well as in relation to each other.

There is a high degree of correlation between the amount of pleasure present in an experience and the amount of inclusiveness and intensity. The more broadly we conceive pleasure the more closely we can correlate it with inclusiveness and intensity. Yet the correlation of pleasure with harmony and intensity of experience is not perfect; as for pain the lack of correlation is much too great to be overlooked. Pain, therefore, must be introduced as a distinct factor in the value appraisal. Physical pain or spiritual anguish may be so intense that the annihilation of one experience and even of the possibility for future experiences may be preferable to the continuation of a relatively intense painful experience.

Suffice it to say that a fully developed value theory would have to relate the negative value of pain and suffering to the positive values of inclusiveness and intensity in some coherent way. For purposes of this paper the problem is only indicated.

ETHICS PROPER

With this sketchy indication of the locus of value and criteria of evaluation, we come to the question of ethics proper. Are we obligated to act so as to maximize value? If so, whose value? Are there other considerations that weigh upon ethical choices?

One major question is whether there is any meaning at all in sentences that state obligations, but let us simply assume here that statements of ethical obligation do have meaning. Our task is to decide which general statement, from among several alternatives is correct. Consider the following:

1. So act as to maximize value for yourself in the present.

2. So act as to maximize value for yourself for the rest of your life.

3. So act as to maximize value for all men for the indefinite future.

4. So act as to maximize value in general.

Of these the first would hardly be viewed as an ethical principle. There are those who suppose that in fact this describes human behavior and that the ethical call to consider a wider sphere is useless. But this is an exceedingly doubtful judgment. Most would recognize that we act with some regard to some future consequences of our actions at least to ourselves.

The second principle is the maxim of prudence. This is recognizably ethical in character. Against the tendency to consider only short-run consequences it calls for full consideration of long-term consequences. Yet it, too, is highly questionable. First, it cannot be defended as describing actual human behavior. There is no clear evidence that men do consider the consequences of their actions for themselves in the distant future more seriously than they consider more immediate consequences to their friends and children. If they do not maximize value for themselves for the rest of their lives, on what grounds can we say they *should?* The argument is sometimes made that consideration of long-term consequences is the one *rational* basis for making decisions. But such a view entails many questionable assumptions. It assumes absolute self-identity through time and absolute separation between one self and all other selves. I believe this is psychologically and metaphysically false, and hence I cannot see how the ethics based upon it can be regarded as uniquely rational.

The third principle is the familiar utilitarian one. An ethical action is one that seeks the greatest good for the greatest number of men. This is profoundly plausible and attractive to all who have been shaped by the Judeo-Christian tradition. Indeed it is a restatement of the fundamental teaching that we should love our neighbors as ourselves.

The basic utilitarian assumption is that it is right to increase value, a principle I accept. That does not mean that people do in fact act in the way such a principle requires. But it means that the sense of rightness points toward this kind of action. I may disregard my neighbor's good and seek only my own, but insofar as I realize that my neighbor's good is in fact, objectively, just as important as my own, I recognize a disproportion between my action and what would be objectively appropriate. I see my action as irrational and hence morally wrong.

My present point, however, is not to defend this view of morality in detail but to point out its instability. If the reason I should seek the greatest good of the greatest number of persons is that it is right to increase value, then limiting this action to human value is arbitrary. It could be justified only if subhuman entities had no intrinsic value. Since the denial of intrinsic value to subhuman entities is false, excluding subhuman entities from the influence of the third principle is without justification. Therefore, only the fourth principle is sufficiently encompassing to be stable and acceptable.

The calculation of pleasure and pain and the multiplication by the number of persons affected, called for by utilitarianism, has never been predictable in detail. Although it has provided a rough and useful guide for making decisions, the extension of such calculations to the subhuman world would be impossibly complex. To be at all functional, we require an image of that state of affairs in which some optimum of value obtains.

We are helped toward an image for this state of affairs by the idea of the biotic pyramid, a concept that describes the movement of life from the soil and the microorganisms therein through vegetation, through the herbivores, and to the carnovores and primates. The total amount of value in a pyramid is roughly correlative with the richness of the base, the number of levels, the diversity of forms and total numbers at each level, and the complexity of living forms at the top. These measures correlate closely with each other.

The more valuable biotic pyramids would clearly place man at the top. Hence the biotic pyramid does not provide an antihuman view of value. Nevertheless, up to a considerable, not yet determined point, man, unlike any other species, can increase his numbers at the top of the pyramid by reducing the number of levels in the pyramid and the diversity of life at each level. For the rich biotic community of the American prairie, man substituted the wheat field and thereby fed a much larger human population. Hence there is a tension between the comprehensive biotic model that is inclusive of man and specialized biotic models in which man's needs alone are better satisfied.

We are warned today that the highly specialized biotic communities produced by man are more precarious than we had previously supposed and that for man's own survival it is important he modify them. However, that is not now the issue before us. *Without* such specializations the total human population would have to be much smaller than it can be *with* such specializations. There is therefore also a tension between what is optimal for man alone and what is optimal when viewed in terms of the biotic pyramid. The problem we face is how to balance these optimalities. If we count only human values, the levels and diversity in the biotic pyramid will be relevant only insofar as they support economic and aesthetic values in human experience, that is, they will be relevant *only* instrumentally. Unless we deny altogether the hierarchical ranking of values, a ranking reflected in the pyramid itself, we cannot discount the great increase of value a larger human population gives so long as population size does not impair the quality of human life. But if we take seriously the fact that all forms of life have value, we cannot ignore the loss of value entailed by man's simplification of the pyramid.

This discussion points to the need for moderating, without renouncing, man's structuring of the world around his own needs. He must of course develop a more realistic view of his actual long-term needs and seek to practice the utilitarian ethic more wisely. When he does so, the value of the biotic pyramid will be more adequately conserved than it is now. But the force of the present argument is that ethical action will require still further moderation of man's actions so as to give greater scope to the biotic pyramid. He must learn to balance his values against the others rather than to judge the others as only instrumental to his. Practically, this points, for example, to the moral obligation to preserve wilderness even beyond the values accruing to man from it.

Thus far the ethical principles considered have been oriented entirely to consequences. There is another tradition in philosophical ethics that is sharply critical of exclusive attention to the consequences of actions, a tradition which interests itself instead in the intrinsic rightness of actions. The most famous spokesman of this tradition is Kant.

Kant's position is extreme. He seems to say, incorrectly, I believe, that the advantages accruing from actions are irrelevant to ethical judgment. However, analysis of his thought indicates that there are two important considerations introduced by his approach which are neglected in the utilitarian approach followed above.

First, Kant points out that an ethical action must be in some way generalizable. It is not enough to calculate that the probable consequences of one's acting in a certain way will increase value. One must also ask what the consequences would be if people in general acted in that way. For example, I might calculate that there would be more increase in value by picking and taking home some wildflowers than by leaving them in the woods. But that would not make this action ethically right unless I could also decide that value would be increased in general by others who picked wildflowers and took them home under similar circumstances. What Garrett Hardin pointed out in "The Tragedy of the Commons" graphically illustrates this principle in relation to the ecological crisis. Since the reader can follow Hardin's logic in another part of this volume, I will not develop it here.

Second, Kant shows that the judgment of the rightness of an action must include consideration of its relationship to the past as well as to the future. If I have made a serious promise, I should not simply ignore that fact when I later face a decision impinging on it. Kant is so convinced of this that he makes extreme—and I think false—judgments about the absolute moral necessity of living up to promises. Most of us could agree that there are many circumstances under which I ought not fulfill a promise no matter how solemnly I made it. But that is not to say that the fact of my having made the promise should have no weight in deciding what to do. If that were the case, as Kant notes, the very notion of a promise would be destroyed.

I have selected the notion of promise as an example. Kant stresses truthtelling. The very nature of society presupposes some kind of mutual commitment to truthfulness except when there are overriding reasons against it. Society presupposes other commitments as well. The acceptance of a job entails implicit as well as explicit commitments. The legal enforcement of contracts is intended to support their moral weight. Marriage is based on mutual vows. Bringing children into the world is understood to entail obligations to them.

My point is that in general what happened at some time before making a decision sets a context for reflection on what one should do on the decision.

This is complicated by the fact that what others have done for us may be as important as what we have ourselves done. For me to ignore the great generosity previously extended me by another man when I make a present decision that affects him would be morally wrong. However, what one's debts *really* are cannot be determined by examining's one's *feelings* of gratitude.

There is no simple objective way of determining what commitments one makes in his life, what debts one incurs, and how all of these are to be balanced against each other. Much of the anguish of the ethically sensitive person comes from his realization of the impossibility of living up to all his commitments and repaying all his debts. Further, giving too much consideration to the way in which present action should relate to these "givens" from the past can block fresh and creative action in the present that is oriented to the production of new and greater values in the future.

THEOLOGY

At this point I find myself forced across the threshold from ethics proper to theology. How can a man deal with the inescapable experience of guilt that is engendered by ethical sensitivity? Should he desensitize himself? Or can he persuade himself that he is in fact not guilty? Or can he satisfy himself by balancing the scales and then tipping them toward the side of virtue? Or must he constantly defend himself from the self-accusation of guilt that he projects into every criticism directed toward him by others, however gentle? Or can he experience both the reality and the forgiveness of guilt?

These are all important questions, but they are not the ones that can be appropriately treated here. For our present purposes other functions of theology are more pertinent.

First, since there are no objective bases for determining exactly what commitments one has made and how his indebtedness is to be evaluated, how one defines his basic perspective on life and his fundamental self-understanding become crucial. One man may see himself as self-made, owing little or nothing to society and family. Another man may see society chiefly as a corrupt institution and a corrupting force, and he may locate any power that works for good in the virtue of individual men. A third man may see all that is most valuable in his own life as given to him through society and he may deplore his own tendencies toward ingratitude and violation of the rules of society. Evaluation of these several judgments, so important for the functioning of the ethical principles we discussed earlier, belongs to theology.

The most important theological question for our discussion is whether men have any commitments or debts beyond the limits of human society. Now the theological diversity becomes still clearer. Certainly Kant had no perception of such a relation of ethics to the natural environment. And in this respect his position is typical of that of Western ethics in general. But there are exceptions.

It is possible to see one's life neither as self-made nor as the product of human society alone but as a gift of the total evolutionary process. If I view myself primarily in this way, then it is appropriate for my response to be one of gratitude. The fitting ethical action then is service of that to which I find myself so comprehensively indebted. To serve the evolutionary process can be understood to mean furthering its inclusive work. One would then strive in general to contribute to the progress or growth of life in all its diversity of forms, beginning with human life but by no means limiting oneself to it.

This religious objective is thus far stated very vaguely. Its clarification is a theological task. What is the "total evolutionary process"? And how should we understand it? It would, of course, be possible to understand evolution in such a way that commitment to it would have quite opposite effects from those I have listed. For example, if one's vision of evolution is dominated by the notion of "survival of the fittest" then he might rejoice in man's continuing success in stamping out all competitive forms of life. He might also encourage ruthless competition among human individuals and societies so as to accelerate the evolutionary process if evolution were understood in this way.

I suggest that far more basic to the evolutionary process than survival of the fittest is the urge for survival itself. In living things there is an urge for life, for continued life, for more and better life. Theories of evolution describe the results of this pervasive urge, which certainly produces competition as well as cooperation. But theories of evolution presuppose the urge, apart from which there would be nothing to compete for. But I think this urge itself, rather than the formulae which describe aspects of its consequences, is what one may reasonably feel indebted to for his existence.

If this urge works toward more and better life, one must have some criteria for understanding what that means. Here we can return generally to the theory of value with which we began. More and better life is that in which there is enhancement of feeling. Feeling is enhanced when it can be more inclusive and intense and when pain is not excessive. Consciousness marks and enriches higher levels of feeling. A man may reasonably understand the very rich potentiality of feeling that is his as the product of millions of years of evolutionary development in which the urge for more and better life has been at work. One's sense of what is ethically appropriate can be deeply affected by this vision.

Even here, however, the implications can be ambiguous. Since the values of human experience represent the consummate achievement of the evolutionary process, one might still deduce that evolution's lesser achievements are of trivial importance for the furtherance of the evolutionary process. One might suppose that it is appropriate for ethics to be instrumental in furthering the development, through the human species, of superhuman forms of life. The question here is how to appraise the rich variety of the products of the evolutionary process. Is there value in the variety as such, apart from the relatively minor value that most evolutionary products have for human contemplation, exploitation, and study. Does the evolutionary process in some way prize its own products?

The importance of this question can be seen if we consider again the kind of intrinsic value that variety can have. We have seen that inclusiveness enriches the value of experience. Reducing what is available for inclusion thus reduces the potential value of subsequent experience. Thus reduction of the number of species of living things on the earth would mean some reduction also of potential for future value. Yet the great variety of species now existing has but trivial relevance for most human experience, and if the value of variety is based on consideration of relevance alone, it would count but little.

When we say we feel variety has great value, we tend to think of this variety in terms of an inclusive perspective. We conceive of the biota of the planet earth not as life viewed by man but as life viewed by a larger, more inclusive perspective. When we do so, we attribute a value to the whole that is greatly enriched by all the complex contrasts and interrelations of the parts, man being one of those parts.

Is the perspective from which this rich value can be contemplated a real perspective? The *idea* of an inclusive perspective is a real idea, but if it is only an idea in the minds of men, the values a *real* perspective would generate do, in fact, not obtain, and the prizing of variety of life is then mostly sentimental.

If, however, reality is such that there *is* an inclusive perspective in addition to the limited ones which are human, the value of the variety of life is real. And our callous disregard of the values of the whole for the sake of values of parts is a violation and desecration that has great ethical importance. To believe this is to believe, implicitly if not explicitly, in God.

Theology has yet another importance to an ecological ethics, and in this connection theology and ecological ethics relate to each other much the way theology relates to purely humanistic ethics, but it is worthwhile to consider this additional relation in the context of ecological ethics: ethical theory focuses attention on clearly conscious decision-making, telling us how we should balance the factors on which we reflect when making such decisions. Conscious decision-making depends on calculations of probable consequences of alternative actions and on the relation of action to behavior shaped by past commitments and obligations.

I do not want to disparage ethical behavior. In comparison with the widespread tendency to thoughtless selfishness, mere conventionalism, and compulsiveness, ethical behavior is of utmost desirability. Yet ethical living or ethical behavior also has its problems and limitations. We can take time to note only two.

First, life is a constant series of subtle decisions, many of them unconscious, and it is therefore easy to exaggerate the importance of what are really rather rare instances calling for reflective decision-making. To extend reflective decision-making as a norm too far toward trivial decisions would be to make wholesome living impossible.

Second, ethical reflection necessarily operates with the knowledge that is presently available. The decision must be made in terms of the expectation of consequences established by this limited knowledge. This is inevitable. That part of this knowledge which can be easily and articulately expressed also takes precedence over less easily expressible sensitivites and implicit understandings. The subtle lure of as yet unimagined values has little opportunity to play its role. Ethical action is almost always conservative.

The problem can be seen in human history. It can be illustrated in the characteristic tensions between art and morality. Moral principles tend to formulate and enforce practices supportive of fully apprehended goods, i.e., those values recognized and established in the community. The artist is often exploring the fringes of his sensibility in ways that cannot be but destructive of the established order of values.

If we place these considerations in the still wider context of the whole evolutionary process they become still more important. The urge toward continued, increased, and enhanced life has pushed and pulled living things through hundreds of millions of years toward new and unforeseeable forms. Unforeseeable ends cannot come into the calculation of the utilitarian ethicist. Hence, to serve the evolutionary process cannot be simply identical with making ethical decisions calculated to further it. We need to work with the process rather than only to manipulate it.

What then is the alternative? The alternative, I think, would be sensitivity to the urge toward life as it operates both within oneself and in the entire world. The alternative would be attunement of the self to that creative process. And this can lead to a spontaneity that is informed by rational ethics but at the same time transcends rational ethics.

CAN BIBLICAL FAITH HELP?

But what is the relation of all this to the dominant religious traditions of the West—those rooted in the Bible? Lynn White, Jr., has argued that the roots of our ecological crisis lie in the attitudes fostered in Western Europe by the reading of the Bible. His point is that Western culture, shaped by the Bible, pictured human beings as separated from all other creatures and dominating them. Westerners felt a divine imperative to master nature both technologically and scientifically. We see now that this mastery was also over our own bodies and by males over females. Instead of committing ourselves to God as the One who evokes and enhances life in us and in all things, we have understood faith in God as the expression of our transcendence of nature and of our rightful imposition of our own purposes upon it.

There is much truth in this picture of Western Christianity. It has widely fostered a hierarchical view in which God is above us and nature below, and it has tended, especially in its nineteenth- and twentieth-century forms, to associate itself with philosophies that are radically anthropocentric. Even though science as a whole has cut its ties to Christianity, the drive for intellectual mastery which it expresses is an inheritance from medieval Christianity. Even today typical Christian ways of thinking are as much a part of the ecological problem as a help toward its solution. It has not been a mistake to look away from modern Christian theology and toward American Indians and ancient Taoists for a vision of the interdependence of humanity and the remainder of nature.

Nevertheless, a fresh look at the Bible shows us that the opposition of nature and history, so prominent in recent Protestant theology, is not present in the Bible itself. The Bible is not anthropocentric but theocentric, and the God who is the center of all things is the creator of all nature, not only of human beings. God declares the plants and animals good quite independently of the creation of human beings. God knows and cares for plants and animals as well as for human beings. In short, God is the Creator of all life.

In the New Testament it is clear that God is not only the remote and transcendent power who externally imposes order upon things. God creates and redeems by entering in the world. This is the incarnational view which is the heart of Christianity. The life in the world expresses the divine presence. Note how this is formulated in the immensely influential prologue to John's gospel:

> When all things began Word already was. The Word dwelt with God, and what God was, the Word was. The Word, then, was with God at the beginning, and through him all things came to be; no single thing was created without him. *All that came to be was alive with his life* . . . So the Word became flesh. (New English Bible, John 1:1—4a, 14a. Emphasis mine)

If we Christians take seriously the idea that the Word, which is Christ, and which fully became flesh in Jesus, is also found in the life of all living things, we will cease to be part of the problem and will be freed to participate in the healing of a suffering biosphere. Our service to God as Christ will be the commitment to God as the urge and call to life and its enhancement and not an orientation away from the natural world toward a purely human and transcendent sphere. We will love and serve the God who cares about the grasses of the field and the death of a sparrow and not one who treats nature as a mere stage on which the human drama is enacted.

If philosophy, science, and biblical faith are defined in terms of their dominant expressions in the recent past, all are enemies of the future. They have shared in blinding us to our continuity with the natural world and our obligations to it. They have set us on a course which leads to catastrophe for human beings as well as other creatures.

But philosophy and science are not committed to repeat their major past expressions. To do so is not philosophical or scientific. The commitment to truth demands revision in the light of evidence which, while far from new, has new power of conviction.

Likewise, biblical faith is not committed to repeat the forms it has taken in recent centuries. There is nothing in the Bible itself that requires the dualism, the anthropocentrism, and the human arrogance which have blinded us to the inherent value of other creatures. Commitment to Christ as the Way, Truth, and Life (John 14:6) requires instead that we follow the way of openness to truth in the service of life. The cross is not a club with which to destroy other living things but a symbol of willingness even to suffer that others may live. We know now that the others are not only human beings but, as the Hindus and Buddhists say, all sentient beings or, as the Old Testament says, all flesh. A penitent Christianity transformed by an authentic recovery of its own normative sources can contribute depth and vision to the profound reorientation needed in our public life.

12

THE ABOLITION OF MAN

C. S. Lewis

It came burning hot into my mind, whatever he said
and however he flattered, when he got me to his
house, he would sell me for a slave.
JOHN BUNYAN

"Man's conquest of Nature" is an expression often used to describe the progress of applied science. "Man has Nature whacked" said someone to a friend of mine not long ago. In their context the words had a certain tragic beauty, for the speaker was dying of tuberculosis. "No matter," he said, "I know I'm one of the casualties. Of course there are casualties on the winning as well as on the losing side. But that doesn't alter the fact that it is winning." I have chosen this story as my point of departure in order to make it clear that I do not wish to disparage all that is really beneficial in the process described as "Man's conquest," much less all the real devotion and self-sacrifice that has gone to make it possible. But having done so I must proceed to analyse this conception a little more closely. In what sense is Man the possessor of increasing power over Nature?

Let us consider three typical examples: the aeroplane, the wireless, and the contraceptive. In a civilized community, in peacetime, anyone who can pay for them may use these things. But it cannot strictly be said that when he does so he is exercising his own proper or individual power over Nature. If I pay you to carry me, I am not therefore myself a strong man. Any or all of the three things I have mentioned can be withheld from some men by other men—by those who sell, or those who allow the sale, or those who own the sources of production, or those who make the goods. What we call Man's power is, in reality, a power possessed by some men which they may, or may not, allow other men to profit by. Again, as regards the powers manifested in the aeroplane or the wireless, Man is as much the patient or subject as the possessor, since he is the target both for bombs and for propaganda. And as regards contraceptives, there is a paradoxical, negative sense in which all possible future generations are the patients or subjects of a power wielded by those already alive. By contraception simply, they are denied existence; by contraception used as a means of selective breeding, they are, without their concurring voice, made to be what one generation, for its own reasons, may choose to prefer. From this point of view, what we call Man's power over Nature turns out to be a power exercised by some men over other men with Nature as its instrument.

It is, of course, a commonplace to complain that men have hitherto used badly, and against their fellows, the powers that science has given them. But that is not the point I am trying to make. I am not speaking of particular corruption and abuses which an increase of moral virtue would cure. I am considering what the thing called, "Man's power over Nature" must always and essentially be. No doubt, the picture could be modified by public ownership of raw materials and factories and public control of scientific research. But unless we have a world state this will still mean the power of one nation over others. And even within the world state or the nation it will mean (in principle) the power of majorities over minorities, and (in the concrete) of a government over the people. And all long-term exercises of power, especially in breeding, must mean the power of earlier generations over later ones.

The latter point is not always sufficiently emphasized, because those who write on social matters have not yet learned to imitate the physicists by always including Time among the dimensions. In order to understand fully what Man's power over Nature, and therefore the power of some men over other men, really means, we must picture the race extended in time from the date of its emergence to that of its extinction. Each generation exercises power over its successors: and each, insofar as it modifies the environment bequeathed to it and rebels against tradition, resists and limits the power of its predecessors. This modifies the picture which is sometimes painted of a progressive emancipation from tradition and a progressive control of natural processes resulting in a continual increase of human power. In reality, of course, if any one age really attains, by eugenics and scientific education, the power to make its descendants what it pleases, all men who live after it are the patients of that power. They are weaker, not stronger: for though we may have put wonderful machines in their hands we have preordained how they are to use them. And if, as is almost certain, the age which had thus attained maximum power over posterity were also the age most emancipated from tradition, it would be engaged in reducing the power of its predecessors almost as drastically as that of its successors. And we must also remember that, quite apart from this, the later a generation comes—the nearer it lives to that date at which the species becomes extinct—the less power it will have in the forward direction, because its subjects will be so few. There is therefore no question of a power vested in the race as a whole steadily growing as long as the race survives. The last men, far from being the heirs of power, will be of all men most subject to the dead hand of the great planners and conditioners and will themselves exercise least power upon the future. The real picture is that of one dominant age—let us suppose the hundredth century A.D.—which resists all previous ages most successfully and dominates all subsequent ages most irresistibly, and thus is the real master of the human species. But even within this master generation (itself an infinitesimal minority of the species) the power will be exercised by a minority smaller still. Man's conquest of Nature, if the dreams of some scientific planners are realized, means the rule of a few hundreds of men over billions upon billions of men. There neither is nor can be any simple increase of power on Man's side. Each new power won *by* man is a power *over* man as well. Each advance leaves him weaker as well as stronger. In every victory, besides being the general who triumphs, he is also the prisoner who follows the triumphal car.

I am not yet considering whether the total result of such ambivalent victories is a good thing or a bad. I am only making clear what Man's conquest of Nature really means and especially that final stage in the conquest, which, perhaps, is not far off. The final stage is come when Man by eugenics, by prenatal conditioning, and by an education and propaganda based on a perfect applied psychology, has obtained full control over himself. *Human* nature will be the last part of Nature to surrender to Man. The battle will then be won. We shall have "taken the thread of life out of the hand of Clotho" and be henceforth free to make our species whatever we wish it to be. The battle will indeed be won. But who, precisely, will have won it?

For the power of Man to make himself what he pleases means, as we have seen, the power of some men to make other men what *they* please. In all ages, no doubt, nurture and instruction have, in some sense, attempted to exercise this power. But the situation to which we must look forward will be novel in two respects. In the first place, the power will be enormously increased. Hitherto the plans of educationalists have achieved very little of what they attempted and indeed, when we read them—how Plato would have every infant "a bastard nursed in a bureau," and Elyot would have the boy see no men before the age of seven and, after that, no women,[1] and how Locke wants children to have leaky shoes and no turn for poetry[2]—we may well thank the beneficent obstinacy of real mothers, real nurses, and (above all) real children for preserving the human race in such sanity as it still possesses. But the man-moulders of the new age will be armed with the powers of an omni-competent state and an irresistible scientific technique: we shall get at last a race of conditioners who really can cut out all posterity in what shape they please. The second difference is even more important. In older systems both the kind of man the teachers wished to produce and their motives for produc-ing him were prescribed by the *Tao*—a norm to which the teachers themselves were subject and from which they claimed no liberty to depart.[3] They did not cut men to some pattern they had chosen. They handed on what they had received: they initiated the young neophyte into the mystery of humanity which overarched him and them alike. It was but old birds teaching young birds to fly. This will be changed. Values are now mere natural phenomena. Judgments of value are to be produced in the pupil as part of the conditioning. Whatever *Tao* there is will be the product, not the motive, of education. The conditioners have been emancipated from all that. It is one more part of Nature which they have conquered. The ultimate springs of human action are no longer, for them, something given. They have surrendered—like electric-ity: it is the function of the Conditioners to control, not to obey them. They know how to *produce* conscience and decide what kind of conscience they will produce. They themselves are outside, above. For we are assuming the last stage of Man's struggle with Nature. The final victory has been won. Human nature has been conquered—and, of course, has conquered, in what-ever sense those words may now bear.

The Conditioners, then, are to choose what kind of artificial *Tao* they will, for their own good reasons, produce in the Human race. They are the motiva-tors, the creators of motives. But how are they going to be motivated them-selves? For a time, perhaps, by survivals, within their own minds, of the old "natural" *Tao*. Thus at first they may look upon themselves as servants and guardians of humanity and conceive that they have a "duty" to do it "good." But it is only by confusion that they can remain in this state. They recognize the concept of duty as the result of certain processes which they can now control. Their victory has consisted precisely in emerging from the state in which they were acted upon by those processes to the state in which they now use them as tools. One of the things they now have to decide is whether they will, or will not, so condition the rest of us that we can go on having the old idea of duty and the old reactions to it. Now can duty help them to decide that? Duty itself is up for trial: it cannot be also the judge. And "good" fares no better. They know quite well how to produce a dozen different conceptions of good in us. The question is which, if any, they should produce. No conception of good can help them to decide. It is absurd to fix on one of the things they are comparing and make it the standard of comparison.

To some it will appear that I am inventing a factitious difficulty for my Conditioners. Other, more simpleminded, critics may ask "Why should you suppose they will be such bad men?" But I am not supposing them to be bad men. They are, rather, not men (in the old sense) at all. They are, if you like, men who have sacrificed their own share in traditional humanity in order to devote themselves to the task of deciding what "Humanity" shall henceforth mean. "Good" and "bad," applied to them, are words without content: for it is from them that the content of these words is henceforward to be derived. Nor is their difficulty factitious. We might suppose that it was possible to say "After all, most of us want more or less the same things—food and drink and sexual intercourse, amusement, art, science, and the longest possible life for individuals and for the species. Let them simply say, This is what we happen to like, and go on to condition men in the way most likely to produce it. Where's the trouble?" But this will not answer. In the first place, it is false that we all really like the same things. But even if we did, what motive is to impel the Conditioners to scorn delights and live laborious days in order that we, and posterity, may have what we like? Their duty? But that is only the *Tao,* which they may decide to impose on us, but which cannot be valid for them. If they accept it, then they are no longer the makers of conscience but still its subjects, and their final conquest over Nature has not really happened. The preservation of the species? But why should the species be preserved? One of the questions before them is whether this feeling for posterity (they know well how it is produced) shall be continued or not. However far they go back, or down, they can find no ground to stand on. Every motive they try to act on becomes at once a *petitio*. It is not that they are bad men. They are not men at all. Stepping outside the *Tao,* they have stepped into the void. Nor are their subjects necessarily unhappy men. They are not men at all: they are artifacts. Man's final conquest has proved to be the abolition of Man.

Yet the Conditioners will act. When I said just now that all motives fail them, I should have said all motives except one. All motives that claim any validity other than that of their felt emotional weight at a given moment have failed them. Everything except the *sic volo, sic jubeo* has been explained away. But what never claimed objectivity cannot be destroyed by subjectivism. The impulse to scratch when I itch or to pull to pieces when I am inquisitive is immune from the solvent which is fatal to my justice, or honour, or care for posterity. When all that says "it is good" has been debunked, what says "I want" remains. It cannot be exploded or "seen through" because it never had any pretensions. The Conditioners, therefore, must come to be motivated simply by their own pleasure. I am not here speaking of the corrupting influence of power nor expressing the fear that under it our Conditioners will degenerate. The very words *corrupt* and *degenerate* imply a doctrine of value and are therefore meaningless in this context. My point is that those who stand outside all judgments of value cannot have any ground for preferring one of their own impulses to another except the emotional strength of that impulse. We may legitimately hope that among the impulses which arise in minds thus emptied of all "rational" or "spiritual" motives, some will be benevolent. I am very doubtful myself whether the benevolent impulses, stripped of that preference and encouragement which the *Tao* teaches us to give them and left to their merely natural strength and frequency as psychological events, will have much influence. I am very doubtful whether history shows us one example of a man who, having stepped outside traditional morality and attained power, has used that power benevolently. I am inclined to think that the Conditioners will hate the conditioned. Though regarding as an illusion the artificial conscience which they produce in us their subjects, they will yet perceive that it creates in us an illusion of meaning for our lives which compares favourably with the futility of their own: and they will envy us as eunuchs envy men. But I do not insist on this, for it is mere conjecture. What is not conjecture is that our hope even of a "conditioned" happiness rests on what is ordinarily called "chance"—the chance that benevolent impulses may on the whole predominate in our Conditioners. For without the judgment "Benevolence is good"—that is, without reentering the *Tao*—they can have no ground for promoting or stabilizing their benevolent impulses rather than any others. By the logic of their position they must just take their impulses as they come, from chance. And Chance here means Nature. It is from heredity, digestion, the weather, and the association of ideas, that the motives of the Conditioners will spring. Their extreme rationalism, by "seeing through" all "rational" motives, leaves them creatures of wholly irrational behavior. If you will not obey the *Tao,* or else commit suicide, obedience to impulse (and therefore, in the long run, to mere "nature") is the only course left open.

At the moment, then, of Man's victory over Nature, we find the whole human race subjected to some individual men, and those individuals subjected to that in themselves which is purely "natural"—to their irrational impulses. Nature, untrammelled by values, rules the Conditioners and, through them, all humanity. Man's conquest of Nature turns out, in the moment of its consummation, to be Nature's conquest of Man. Every victory we seemed to win has led us, step by step, to this conclusion. All Nature's apparent reverses have been but tactical withdrawals. We thought we were beating her back when she was luring us on. What looked to us like hands held up in surrender was really the opening of arms to enfold us forever. If the fully planned and conditioned world (with its *Tao* a mere product of the planning) comes into existence, Nature will be troubled no more by the restive species that rose in revolt against her so many millions of years ago, will be vexed no longer by its chatter of truth and mercy and beauty and happiness. *Ferum victorem cepit:* and if the eugenics are efficient enough there will be no second revolt, but all snug beneath the Conditioners, and the Conditioners beneath her, till the moon falls or the sun grows cold.

My point may be clearer to some if it is put in a different form. Nature is a word of varying meanings, which can best be understood if we consider its various opposites. The Natural is the opposite of the Artificial, the Civil, the Human, the Spiritual, and the Supernatural. The Artificial does not now concern us. If we take the rest of the list of opposites, however, I think we can get a rough idea of what men have meant by Nature and what it is they oppose to her. Nature seems to be the spatial and temporal, as distinct from what is less fully so or not so at all. She seems to be the world of quantity, as against the world of quality: of objects as against consciousness: of the bound, as against the wholly or partially autonomous: of that which knows no values as against that which both has and perceives value: of efficient causes (or, in some modern systems, of no causality at all) as against final causes. Now I take it that when we understand a thing analytically and then dominate and use it for our own convenience we reduce it to the level of "Nature" in the sense that we suspend our judgments of value about it, ignore its final cause (if any), and treat it in terms of quantity. This repression of elements in what would otherwise be our total reaction to it is sometimes very noticeable and even painful: something has to be overcome before we can cut up a dead man or a live animal in a dissecting room. These objects *resist* the movement of the mind whereby we thrust them into the world of mere Nature. But in other instances too, a similar price is exacted for our analytical knowledge and manipulative power, even if we have ceased to count it. We do not look at trees either as Dryads or as beautiful objects while we cut them into beams: the first man who did so may have felt the price keenly, and the bleeding trees in Virgil and Spenser may be far-off echoes of that primeval sense of impiety. The stars lost their divinity as astronomy developed, and the Dying God has no place in chemical agriculture. To many, no doubt, this process is simply the gradual discovery that the real world is different from what we expected and the old opposition to Galileo or to "body-snatchers" is simply obscurant-ism. But that is not the whole story. It is not the greatest of modern scientists who feel most sure that the object, stripped of its qualitative properties and reduced to mere quantity, is wholly real. Little scientists, and little unscien-tific followers of science, may think so. The great minds know very well that the object, so treated, is an artificial abstraction, that something of its reality has been lost.

From this point of view the conquest of Nature appears in a new light. We reduce things to mere Nature *in order that* we may "conquer" them. We are always conquering Nature, because "Nature" is the name for what we have, to some extent, conquered. The price of conquest is to treat a thing as mere Nature. Every conquest over Nature increases her domain. The stars do not become Nature till we can weigh and measure them: the soul does not become Nature till we can psychoanalyze her. The wresting of powers *from* Nature is also the surrendering of things *to* Nature. As long as this process stops short of the final stage we may well hold that the gain outweighs the loss. But as soon as we take the final step of reducing our own species to the level of mere Nature, the whole process is stultified, for this time the being who stood to gain and the being who has been sacrificed are one and the same. This is one of the many instances where to carry a principle to what seems its logical conclusion produces absurdity. It is like the famous Irishman who found that a certain kind of stove reduced his fuel bill by half and thence concluded that two stoves of the same kind would enable him to warm his house with no fuel at all. It is the magician's bargain: give up our soul, get power in return. But once our souls, that is, ourselves, have been given up, the power thus conferred will not belong to us. We shall in fact be the slaves and puppets of that to which we have given our souls. It is in Man's power to treat himself as a mere "natural object" and his own judgments of value as raw material for scientific manipulation to alter at will. The objection to his doing so does not lie in the fact that his point of view (like one's first day in a dissecting room) is painful and shocking till we grow used to it. The pain and the shock are at most a warning and a symptom. The real objection is that if man chooses to treat himself as raw material, raw material he will be; not raw material to be manipulated, as he fondly imagined, by himself, but by mere appetite, that is, mere Nature, in the person of his dehumanized Conditioners.

We have been trying, like Lear, to have it both ways: to lay down our human prerogative and yet at the same time to retain it. It is impossible. Either we are rational spirit obliged forever to obey the absolute values of the *Tao,* or else we are mere nature to be kneaded and cut into new shapes for the pleasures of masters who must, by hypothesis, have no motive but their own "natural" impulses. Only the *Tao* provides a common human law of action which can overarch rulers and ruled alike. A dogmatic belief in objective value is necessary to the very idea of a rule which is not tyranny or an obedience which is not slavery.

I am not here thinking solely, perhaps not even chiefly, of those who are our public enemies at the moment. The process which, if not checked, will abolish Man, goes on apace among Communists and Democrats no less than among Fascists. The methods may (at first) differ in brutality. But many a mild-eyed scientist in pince-nez, many a popular dramatist, many an amateur philosopher in our midst, means in the long run just the same as the Nazi rulers of Germany. Traditional values are to be "debunked" and mankind to be cut out into some fresh shape at the will (which must, by hypothesis, be an arbitrary will) of some few lucky people in one lucky generation which has learned how to do it. The belief that we can invent "ideologies" at pleasure, and the consequent treatment of mankind as mere υλη, specimens, preparations, begins to affect our very language. Once we killed bad men: now we liquidate unsocial elements. Virtue has become *integration* and diligence *dynamism,* and boys likely to be worthy of a commission "potential officer material." Most wonderful of all, the virtues of thrift and temperance, and even of ordinary intelligence, are *sales resistance.*

The true significance of what is going on has been concealed by the use of the abstraction Man. Not that the word Man is necessarily a pure abstraction. In the *Tao* itself, as long as we remain within it, we find the concrete reality in which to participate is to be truly human: the real common will and common reason of humanity, alive, and growing like a tree, and branching out, as the situation varies, into ever new beauties and dignities of application. While we speak from within the *Tao* we can speak of Man having power over himself in a sense truly analogous to an individual's self-control. But the moment we step outside and regard the *Tao* as a mere subjective product, this possibility has disappeared. What is now common to all men is a mere abstract universal, an H.C.F., and Man's conquest of himself means simply the rule of the Conditioners over the conditioned human material, the world of post-humanity which, some knowingly and some unknowingly, nearly all men in all nations are at present labouring to produce.

Nothing I can say will prevent some people from describing this lecture as an attack on science. I deny the charge, of course: and real Natural Philosophers (there are some now alive) will perceive that in defending value I defend *inter alia* the value of knowledge, which must die like every other when its roots in the *Tao* are cut. But I can go further than that, I even suggest that from Science herself the cure might come. I have described as a "magician's bargain" that process whereby man surrenders object after object, and finally himself, to Nature in return for power. And I meant what I said. The fact that the scientist has succeeded where the magician failed has put such a wide contrast between them in popular thought that the real story of the birth of Science is misunderstood. You will even find people who write about the sixteenth century as if Magic were a medieval survival and Science the new thing that came to sweep it away. Those who have studied the period know better. There was very little magic in the Middle Ages: the sixteenth and seventeenth centuries are the high noon of magic. The serious magical endeavour and the serious scientific endeavour are twins: one was sickly and died, the other strong and throve. But they were twins. They were born of the same impulse. I allow that some (certainly not all) of the early scientists were actuated by a pure love of knowledge. But if we consider the temper of that age as a whole we can discern the impulse of which I speak. There is something which unites magic and applied science while separating both from the "wisdom" of earlier ages. For the wise men of old the cardinal problem had been how to conform the soul to reality, and the solution had been knowledge, self-discipline, and virtue. For magic and applied science alike the problem is how to subdue reality to the wishes of men: the solution is a technique; and both, in the practice of this technique, are ready to do things hitherto regarded as disgusting and impious—such as digging up and mutilating the dead. If we compare the chief trumpeter of the new era (Bacon) with Marlowe's Faustus, the similarity is striking. You will read in some critics that Faustus has a thirst for knowledge. In reality, he hardly mentions it. It is not truth he wants from his devils, but gold and guns and girls. "All things that move between the quiet poles shall be at his command" and "a sound magician is a mighty god."[4] In the same spirit Bacon condemns those who value knowledge as an end in itself: this, for him, is to use as a mistress for pleasure what ought to be a spouse for fruit.[5] The true object is to extend Man's power to the performance of all things possible. He rejects magic because it does not work,[6] but his goal is that of the magician. In Paracelsus the characters of magician and scientist are combined. No doubt those who really founded modern science were usually those whose love of truth exceeded their love of power; in every mixed movement the efficacy comes from the good elements not from the bad. But the presence of the bad elements is not irrelevant to the direction the efficacy takes. It might be going too far to say that the modern scientific movement was tainted from its birth: but I think it would be true to say that it was born in an unhealthy neighborhood and at an inauspicious hour. Its triumphs may have been too rapid and purchased at too high a price; reconsideration, and something like repentance, may be required.

Is it, then, possible to imagine a new Natural Philosophy, continually conscious that the "natural object" produced by analysis and abstraction is not reality but only a view, and always correcting the abstraction? I hardly know what I am asking for. I heard rumours that Goethe's approach to nature deserves fuller consideration—that even Dr. Steiner may have seen something that orthodox researchers have missed. The regenerate science which I have in mind would not do even to minerals and vegetables what modern science threatens to do to man himself. When it explained it would not explain away. When it spoke of the parts it would remember the whole. While studying the *It* it would not lose what Martin Buber calls the *Thou*-situation. The analogy between the *Tao* of Man and the instincts of an animal species would mean for it new light cast on the unknown thing, Instinct, by the inly known reality of conscience and not a reduction of conscience to the category of Instinct. Its followers would not be free with the words *only* and *merely*. In a word, it would conquer Nature without being at the same time conquered by her and buy knowledge at a lower cost than that of life.

Perhaps I am asking impossibilities. Perhaps, in the nature of things, analytical understanding must always be a basilisk which kills what it sees and only sees by killing. But if the scientists themselves cannot arrest this process before it reaches the common Reason and kills that too, then someone else must arrest it. What I most fear is the reply that I am "only one more" obscurantist, that this barrier, like all previous barriers set up against the advance of science, can be safely passed. Such a reply springs from the fatal serialism of the modern imagination—the image of infinite unilinear progression which so haunts our minds. Because we have to use numbers so much we tend to think of every process as if it must be like the numeral series, where every step, to all eternity, is the same kind of step as the one before. I implore you to remember the Irishman and his two stoves. There are progressions in which the last step is *sui generis*—incommensurable with the others—and in which to go the whole way is to undo all the labor of your previous journey. To reduce the *Tao* to a mere natural product is a step of that kind. Up to that point, the kind of explanation which explains things away may give us something, though at a heavy cost. But you cannot go on "explaining away" forever: you will find that you have explained explanation itself away. You cannot go on "seeing through" things forever. The whole point of seeing through something is to see something through it. It is good that the window should be transparent, because the street or garden beyond it is opaque. How if you saw through the garden too? It is no use trying to "see through" first principles. If you see through everything, then everything is transparent. But a wholly transparent world is an invisible world. To "see through" all things is the same as not to see.

NOTES

1. Sir Thomas Elyot, *The Boke Named the Governour* (1531), I, iv: "All men except physitions only shulde be excluded and kepte out of the norisery." I. vi: "After that a childe is come to seuen yeres of age . . . the most sure counsaile is to withdrawe him from all company of women."

2. John Locke, *Some Thoughts concerning Education* (1693), § 7: "I will also advise his *Feet to be wash'd* every Day in cold Water, and to have his Shoes so thin that they might leak and *let in Water,* whenever he comes near it." § 174: "If he have a poetick vein, 'tis to me the strangest thing in the World that the Father should desire or suffer it to be cherished or improved. Methinks the Parents should labour to have it stifled and suppressed as much as may be." Yet Locke is one of our most sensible writers on education.

3. [*Tao* means "The Way," the path of virtuous conduct in Confucianism, the ultimate principle of the universe in Taoism. As close synonyms for his usage of *Tao,* Lewis elsewhere suggests "natural law or traditional morality or the first principles of practical reason."—*Ed.*]

4. Christopher Marlowe, *Dr. Faustus* (1588), 77–90.

5. Francis Bacon, *Advancement of Learning* (1605), Bk. I (p. 60 in Ellis and Spedding, 1905; p. 35 in Everyman Ed.).

6. Francis Bacon, *Filum Labyrinthi* (1953), i.

III

ECONOMICS: INTERACTION OF ENDS AND MEANS

It is very arguable that the science of political economy as studied in its first period after the death of Adam Smith (1790), did more harm than good. . . . It riveted on men a certain set of abstractions which were disastrous in their influence on modern mentality. It dehumanized industry. . . . It fixes attention on a definite group of abstractions, neglects everything else, and elicits every scrap of information and theory which is relevant to what it has retained. This method is triumphant, provided that the abstractions are judicious. But, however triumphant, the triumph is within limits. The neglect of these limits leads to disastrous oversights.

ALFRED NORTH WHITEHEAD, *Science and the Modern World*, 1925

INTRODUCTION

Herman E. Daly

In the first article of this part, "Economics and the Challenge of Environmental Issues," Canadian economist Peter A. Victor gives a general survey of how economics has responded to the challenge of environmental issues. The neoclassical paradigm, the Marxist paradigm, and their environmental modifications are discussed, and the two paradigms are compared.

A historical perspective is provided next by Gerald Alonzo Smith, who, in "The Teleological View of Wealth: A Historical Perspective," reviews the ideas of the great critics of the industrial growth-oriented economy: Sismondi, Ruskin, Hobson, and Tawney. These thinkers refused to follow the trend of the emerging "positive economics" in divorcing themselves from the larger questions of purpose and insisted upon an explicitly teleological view of wealth. Well-defined ends never require infinite means for their fulfillment, whereas ill-defined ends seem, in their vagueness, always to require more resources. In terms of the ends-means spectrum discussed in the Introduction (see p. 9), the thinkers surveyed by Smith are concerned mainly with the upper half of the spectrum, arguing from the top down.

In the next article, "On Economics as a Life Science," the influence of Ruskin and Hobson is again present, although the argument that I present is mainly in terms of the bottom half of the ends-means spectrum—with what A. J. Lotka called the "biophysical foundations of economics" or what Hobson called the "groundwork for conscious valuation." The close analogies between biology and economics are discussed both in their short-term steady-state aspects and in their long-term evolutionary aspects. The human economy is considered in ecological perspective with the aid of an expanded input-output model.

Kenneth Boulding's classic article on "The Economics of the Coming Spaceship Earth" develops the important vision of the economy as an open system that maintains some structure in the midst of an entropic flow or throughput. As Boulding writes, "The essential measure of the success of the economy is not throughput, but the extent, quality and complexity of the total capital stock"—in other words, of the structure maintained by the throughput. For this book Boulding has added "Spaceship Earth Revisited," some further thoughts on space colonization, a theme taken up again in my "Postscript."

British economist E. J. Mishan, following in the tradition of his countrymen Ruskin, Hobson, and Tawney, offers some insight into the seeming paradox of "The Growth of Affluence and the Decline of Welfare." Mishan examines the crucial premises by which economists invest "real GNP" with a significance for welfare, as well as the relation to human welfare of growth, equality, mobility, education, and permissiveness. Most significantly, he analyzes the dire consequences for freedom inherent in the crumbling of the moral consensus of society—an analysis that clearly supports C. S. Lewis's remark, so prescient and so disagreeable to the modern temperament, that "A dogmatic belief in objective value is necessary to the very idea of a rule which is not tyranny or an obedience which is not slavery."

The following article by Bruce Hannon on "Energy Use and Moral Restraint" is hard to classify. Cast in the form of an imaginary and insightful exchange of letters between Malthus and Carnot the article contrasts the "views of the economist and the engineer on the use of finite resources." The piece is so imaginatively written that one must occasionally remind one's self that one is reading Hannon, not Malthus or Carnot. Though full of references to the issues of the times in which Malthus and Carnot lived, the article obviously aims to elucidate modern issues in terms of historical parallel, and especially to foster a closer conceptual friendship between economics and thermodynamics by creating an imaginary friendship between the first thermodynamicist and the first holder of a university chair of political economy.

The article by Talbot Page, "The Severance Tax as an Instrument of Intertemporal Equity," shifts attention back to the issue of policy, making use of the framework of neoclassical analysis to argue for the ad valorem severance tax as a means of limiting the total volume of throughput in the interest of intergenerational equity. Page points out the limitations of the present value criterion and discusses the relation of the steady state to intergenerational equity.

In "The Steady-State Economy: Toward a Political Economy of Biophysical Equilibrium and Moral Growth," I attempt to pull together the case for a steady-state economy and suggest some policies. Three institutional reforms are presented as necessary for a steady-state economy: (1) limits to inequality in the form of a minimum income combined with a maximum income and wealth; (2) a system of transferrable birth quotas for limiting population; (3) a system of depletion quotas, auctioned by the government, in order to limit total throughput according to ecological and ethical criteria while allowing market allocation of the limited total among competing firms and individuals. This last institution should be compared with Talbot Page's suggestion for an ad valorem severance tax and with Bruce Hannon's energy tax plus rebate proposal. The depletion quota plan has the long-run advantage of controlling throughput more rigorously and of forcing the recognition of a biophysical budget constraint. The severance tax has the short-run advantage of requiring less administrative change and of being politically more acceptable. Perhaps the best strategy would be to go first for the severance tax, and then, on the basis of experience with it, debate the advisability of moving to a depletion quota system at at later time.

Further issues, replies to critics, and second thoughts are considered in my Postscript.

13

ECONOMICS AND THE CHALLENGE OF ENVIRONMENTAL ISSUES

Peter A. Victor

I stepped out into the night air that nobody had yet found out how to option. But a lot of people were probably trying. They'd get around to it.
PHILIP MARLOWE, in RAYMOND CHANDLER'S *The Little Sister*

THE NEO-CLASSICAL PERSPECTIVE

Perhaps the most significant event of the nineteenth century was the establishment of the self-regulating market as the predominant institution in the industrial world. For the first time in history, economic activity became identifiable as something distinct from the rest of man's social life. Paralleling this development was the growth of economics as a system of thought designed to comprehend these new arrangements.

Reprinted from *Ecology versus Politics in Canada*, edited by William Leiss, by permission of University of Toronto Press. © University of Toronto Press 1979.

Despite the collapse of the self-regulating market, as witnessed in the twentieth century, one lasting result of developments in the nineteenth century is the popular view that there is an important set of issues which are economic rather than political, social, or environmental. Economic growth, inflation, balance of payments, productivity, are some of the "economic" issues that are commonly given priority over issues that are "social" and "environmental." The choice of priority is regarded as "political." We are assured, for example, that we must have a healthy, growing economy if we are to afford anti-poverty programs, pollution control, and the means to defend our political freedoms.

The fact of the matter is that the modern institutions of business, labour, and government, and the problems to which they give rise, are just as much political and social as they are economic. It is essential that this be recognized in an attempt to understand the present and possible futures of contemporary society, not least with respect to man's interaction with the rest of nature.

One of the most notable and influential attempts to understand the society of his day, and to prescribe for its future, was that of Adam Smith. The year 1976 marked the two hundredth anniversary of the publication of Smith's *Inquiry into the Nature and Causes of the Wealth of Nations*. This was by no means the first treatise on economics, but it was the first to organize the subject matter into categories that modern economists still find extremely familiar. Production, consumption, distribution, trade, prices, employment, and growth each receive due attention within an integrated framework of fact and theory. The comprehensive nature of Smith's work is impressive particularly when compared with the narrow vision exemplified in the typical journal article that today's professional economist is obliged, by his peers, to write.

One result of the undue degree of specialization within economics, as in so many other disciplines, is the neglect of some important aspects of economic and social processes. A few notable exceptions apart, until the late 1960s economists ignored the environmental issues of pollution and resource depletion which are so intimately related to the functioning of the economy. As the decade turned, the "environment" became the focus of considerable public concern. Since then, a growing number of economists have addressed these environmental issues, principally with the analytical tools and professional biases developed in dealing with the more established parts of economics.

There now exist numerous books and papers by economists on environmental management, pollution as an externality, public "bads," input-output and residuals analysis, and on benefit-cost analysis of the use of land, air, water, and mineral resources. It has become common for introductory textbooks on economics to include at least a chapter on the environment and fewer newcomers to economics are being exposed to the myth, so widely taught by economists only a few years ago, that air and water are free because they are abundant.

This increase in the interest of economists in environmental issues has been only a small part of the total academic and governmental response, which has been impressive if only for the time and money it has involved. All sorts of government environmental agencies have been established, new legislation for environmental protection has been enacted, and environmental degree programs have been devised in an attempt to integrate the ideas and information generated by the older and more firmly established academic disciplines.

Now, after a flourish, things have quietened down. The flood of publications on pollution control and resource depletion has moderated and it is an opportune moment for an assessment of how well economists, particularly of the "neo-classical" variety, have met the challenge of environmental issues.

The argument to be presented in this chapter is that, by and large, economists have failed to come to grips with many of the fundamentals that underlie pollution and resource depletion. Certainly their diagnosis and policy advice have received a cool reception from environmentalists and government alike. Moreover, it will be shown that this failure has implications not only for the contribution of economists to the environmental debate but for the whole fabric of contemporary, "neo-classical" economics.

The main thrust of this paper is that there are several premises upon which the economic analysis of environmental issues is built that are incompatible with the premises of other participants in the debate, and which preclude economists from perceiving some of the root causes of the problem. As a preface to the main argument, the neo-classical analysis of pollution and resource depletion and the policies that follow from this analysis will be outlined. A critique and suggestions for a new direction follow.

The Neo-Classical Theory of Pollution

The neo-classical explanation of environmental pollution is very straightforward. Essentially, it points out that in a market economy based upon the private ownership of the factors or means of production, the self-interested owners of these resources will be induced to do the best for others by doing the best for themselves. Government may be required to ensure that the conditions for competition prevail by anti-trust measures, and it is definitely required to guarantee for all the property rights of each. Given these conditions the neo-classical economy will commit privately owned resources to their most productive uses.

In the conspicuous case of air and to a lesser extent water, the property rights on which the efficiency of a capitalist economy depends generally do not exist. This gives rise to what neo-classical economists refer to as "externalities." Although the precise definition of an externality is still a matter of debate among economists, it may be thought of as an effect of economic activity that lies outside the normal control of market processes. For example, people exposed to the effects of air pollution caused by the industrial production of goods made and sold for profit, have no recourse through the market to obtain financial compensation. This would not be the case if people owned a marketable right to clean air since, under those circumstances, industrialists wishing to pollute the air in their quest for profit would have to buy the right to do so in the same way as they must buy the right to use the other resources that are necessary for production. In the absence of such rights the market cannot properly regulate activities that pollute and there is a *prima facie* case for some form of governmental intervention.

The Neo-Classical Theory of Natural Resources

The question of property rights and externalities applies equally well to the neo-classical analysis of the depletion of natural resources. Resource economists of this school hold the view that privately owned stocks of resources will automatically be conserved if resource owners foresee future shortages, since it will be profitable for them to restrict the rate of depletion in order to sell later at the expected higher price. According to this analysis the trouble begins when some element of common property exists: for example, if two oil companies drill wells into the same deposit each company has an incentive to withdraw the oil as rapidly as possible for fear that the other is doing just that. Overfishing is merely an extension of these common property circumstances to a renewable resource. Since fishermen do not own the fish until they have caught them, no individual fisherman can sensibly decide to refrain from fishing to allow the fish to grow and to breed. If this view is widely shared by the competing fishermen the very real problem of stock depletion arises.

Neo-Classical Environmental Policies

The environmental policies arising out of the neo-classical analysis of pollution and resource depletion stem directly from the concepts of externality and common property. Externalities can be "internalized" by the imposition of effluent charges, which many economists argue are more efficient than effluent standards. This approch to pollution control utilizes the incentives that drive the market economy and only indirectly does it affect the property relations in society. However, some economists suggest that these relations should be changed directly to cope with common property situations.[1] For example, to control the effluent discharged into a lake it has been proposed that the regulatory agency should issue saleable rights permitting the owner of the right to discharge a specified quantity of effluent in the lake. Initially a limited quantity of discharge rights would be sold or given away by this agency, thus establishing the maximum amount of effluent that could be discharged into the lake from all sources. Once all the rights were allocated, any company, municipality, or individual wishing to discharge effluent into the lake would be obliged to purchase the necessary rights from those who already owned them. In this way the market would regulate the use of the lake as a recipient of effluent with all the advantages of economic efficiency that are normally claimed for market processes.

The importance of externalities in the neo-classical analysis of environmental issues has raised the question of their magnitude, particularly when environmental policies are being formulated and reviewed. This empirical concern has been met by an increase in the use of benefit-cost analysis for simulating market values for environmental quality. Benefit-cost analysis allows monetary values to be attributed to externalities. For example, the cost of air pollution might be assessed in terms of such items as extra laundry costs, extra house maintenance costs, increased medical bills, and incomes forgone due to illness and premature death. On this basis projects involving an increase in air pollution may be evaluated not only by those costs and benefits that are normally registered in the market but also by accounting for the social costs and benefits caused by externalities associated with such projects.

Material/Energy Balance

This brief summary represents the core of the neo-classical response to the environmental challenge. All of the ideas embodied in this analysis were, of course, well established in economics long before the upsurge of interest in environmental issues. There has been only one apparently new analytical idea which neo-classical economists have introduced and this is the notion of materials and energy balance to which Kenneth Boulding drew attention in his widely reprinted paper, "The Economics of the Coming Spaceship Earth."[2] He pointed out that the economic activities of consumption, production, and trade involve a rearrangement of matter and not a creation of new material. He likened the Earth to a spaceship consisting of a fixed quantity of material subject to a single source of external energy provided by the sun. With this as his perspective, Boulding argued that the Earth's resources should be husbanded with as much care as the supplies of a spaceship.

Since 1966, a number of other economists have taken up Boulding's ideas concerning material flows and material balances and have used them to emphasize the pervasiveness of externalities.[3] Empirical work has begun on the study of the flow of materials and energy through economic processes at all levels and this has highlighted the essential physical links between the depletion of natural resources and pollution.[4]

This new approach to economic activites is particularly insightful for analysing environmental issues. It may be surprising to discover, therefore, that in fact it is not really a new approach at all. Economists as distinct in their orientation as Alfred Marshall and Karl Marx devoted substantial passages in their respective treatises to a description of economic activity in precisely these terms. Marshall, for example, opened Chapter III of his *Principles of Economics* with the statement that:

Man cannot create material things. . . . His efforts and sacrifices result in changing the form or arrangement of matter to adapt it better for the satisfaction of his wants. . . . As his production of material products is really nothing more than a rearrangement of matter which gives it new utilities, so his consumption of them is nothing more than a disarrangement of matter, which diminishes or destroys its utilities.[5]

Marx, in whose work this theme recurs time and again, cites a statement published in 1773 by the Italian economist, Pietro Verri:

All the phenomena of the universe, whether produced by the hand of man or by the general laws of physics, are not in fact *newly-created* but result solely from a transformation of existing material. *Composition* and *division* are the only elements, which the human spirit finds again and again when analysing the notion of reproduction; and this is equally the case with the reproduction of value. . . . and of riches, when earth, air, and water become transformed into corn in the fields, or when through the hand of man the secretions of an insect turn into silk, or certain metal parts are arranged to construct a repeating watch.[6]

Marshall must be credited with having anticipated an idea which has since attracted the attention of many of his intellectual grandchildren, but at the same time the materials-balance principle is merely an appendage to the main body of neo-classical economics which retains its emphasis on production costs and consumers' preferences. In the contrary case of Marx, the self-described materialist, this view of economic activity permeates his entire theoretical structure.

This is only one of several aspects of Marx's economic structure which differ from that of the neo-classical economists and which are more consistent with the assumptions made in the various non-economic analyses of environmental issues. This matter will be explored further after the following critique of the neo-classical response to the environmental challenge.

GAPS IN THE PARADIGM

This section will be divided into three areas which are by no means unrelated to each other: (*a*) the theory of value, (*b*) social relations, (*c*) the state and the economy.

Value

"Value," says Joan Robinson, "is just a word." It is a word that expresses "one of the great metaphysical ideas in economics." Just what that idea is, Robinson is not too sure. She tells us that value "does not mean usefulness—the good that goods do us, nor does it mean market price."[7] In her brief historical survey of economists' theories of value she notes the so-called paradox of value which bothered the classical economists who had difficulty in explaining why the price of diamonds was so much higher than the price of water when the latter was clearly of much greater importance to man. The marginal "revolution" of the 1870s resolved this issue by emphasizing scarcities and the significance of the last or marginal unit of a commodity consumed in determining its price.

Robinson also discussed Marx's labour theory of value on which his analysis of exploitation is founded. Writing in 1937, Maurice Dobb expressed an important distinction between what he described as these "two major value-theories which have contested the economic field" when he said that they have each

> sought to rest their structure on a quantity which lay outside the system of price-variables, and independent of them; in the one case, an objective element in productive activity (that is, labour power), in the other case, a subjective factor underlying consumption and demand (that is, utility).[8]

Initially utility theory was founded in Bentham's principle of utility by which is meant "that principle which approves or disapproves of every action whatsoever, according to the tendency which it appears to have to augment or diminish the happiness of the party whose interest is in question."[9] Despite the failure of Bentham or anyone else to establish an empirical measure of utility, economic theorists continued to presume that the utility which guided man's economic behaviour was something that, in principle, lent itself to quantification. This notion of "cardinal utility" was supplanted by a view of utility as an entity which could not be added or subtracted but which could be placed in order of greater and less. Economists determined that this concept of "ordinal utility" was a sufficient basis for virtually all of the analytical results that had previously been obtained with cardinal utility. More recently still, economists have discarded the concept altogether by establishing a pure theory of choice which requires only that the participants in a market have preferences which satisfy a small number of fundamental axioms.[10] It is this theory which lies at the centre of modern welfare economics and which provides the normative foundation for economists' recommendations for public policy, including environmental policy.

Preferences   One of the implications of the replacement of cardinal utility by preferences is that economists have virtually precluded themselves from any interest in the reasons people may have for their preferences. At least with cardinal utility people could be said to prefer things for the utility or satisfaction that they expected to derive from their consumption. Obviously, this allows for the possibility that the expected utility on which people base their desires or preferences might be very different from that which they actually do derive in the process of consumption. If this should happen, the achievement of market equilibrium becomes complicated because people will change their preferences as they learn that the commodities they desired and purchased do not give them the utility on which that desire was based. Unless expected and actual utility finally merge for each person in the economy, equilibrium will not be attained and relative prices will continue to change in a way that is inexplicable in the absence of additional assumptions about people's learning processes.

Marshall and his successor at Cambridge, Pigou, each recognized this problem and resolved it by identifying utility with both "the desires which prompt activity and the satisfactions that result from them." However, the very fact that they admitted this distinction permitted them to consider the dynamic relation between desires and satisfactions such as Marshall did in his brief chapter entitled "Wants in Relations to Activities"[11]

The assumption that Marshall and Pigou made—that utility is to be identified with desires and satisfactions—served the same purpose in their economic analysis as the assumption of unchanging preferences does in neo-classical economics. Preferences are fixed points on which the neo-classical system rests and, as such, they are essential for the determination of relative prices. Changing preferences, resulting from the disappointment of consumers who discover in the process of consumption that their preference was misguided, would cause changing relative prices. Since the determination of relative prices is one of the prime objective of the neo-classical system, it would seem necessary to incorporate a theory of how preferences change into the system. However, this is one area into which economists have seldom ventured.[12]

In summary, the neo-classical theory of value is a theory of relative prices. It is a theory which is built upon a system of individuals' preferences which are assumed, wrongly, to be given and unchanging. In the neo-classical world it is difficult to distinguish value from price. Value is not an explanation of price. It is not even an explanation of preferences. It may be something which people attribute to the things they prefer but it is certainly not a quality that is inherent in the things themselves waiting to be discovered and unlocked in a manner appropriate to the thing itself.

The relevance of all this to environmental issues is that virtually all environmentalists call into question the preferences of people as expressed in the workings of the economy.[13] Far from being content to take them as given, they consider the determination of preferences as an essential aspect of environmental problems.[14] As well, many environmentalists critize preferences and the action to which they lead, on grounds that are unacceptable to neo-classical economists. For example, it is suggested that the preferences of individuals and the behaviour based upon them are: (*a*) not in the best interests of the individuals concerned, and (*b*) not in the best interest of the environment.

A variety of arguments are used to support these statements and it would be a mistake to think that environmentalists have reached a consensus on these issues. Nevertheless, many environmentalists would subscribe to the following views on preferences, value, and the environment—views which are incompatible with the premises of neo-classical economics.

First of all, environmentalists think that people's preferences frequently do not reflect the very real benefits to be obtained from exposure to a healthy environment. In defense of this position, it may be argued that no one would question its validity with regard to children, or those designated as mentally ill, and even a substantial proportion of old people. Those comprising this large section of the population are constantly being told what is good for them by others who claim to know better and, significantly, who are in a position to impose their will. The argument continues that just as children, and other dependents in society, may prefer things which are not in their best interests, so may adults. In support of this position, René Dubos[15] has argued that in the course of man's biological evolution, a number of human requirements were developed. These are not only for nutrition, and protection from the hazards of nature, but also for contact with plants and animals, exposure to the wilderness, and a lifestyle that is consistent with man's hormonal and endocrinal daily, seasonal, and yearly rhythms. His critique of society is based on the observation that people fail to satisfy these requirements because they are too often guided by preferences that bear an imperfect relation to their needs.

The economists' view of value as subjective precludes any discussion of whether individuals' preferences are consistent with their needs. People are *presumed* to be the best judges of what contributes to their welfare. If they make mistakes, then they are to be judges of that also. In any case, the assumption that preferences are stable through time does not allow for mistakes of a sort which could lead to revisions of those preferences themselves. And relaxing this assumption does not really help since, if it is possible for a person to discover that what he preferred and chose failed to meet with his expectations, then it should be allowed that others could have predicted this occurrence. Such a prediction could very well rest on the observation that what individuals prefer or want does not coincide with their needs.

Information   There is perhaps one avenue open to neo-classical economists whereby a divergence between preferences and needs could be accommodated within an otherwise unaltered framework of economics. The discrepancy between the two could be attributed to a lack of information on the part of the individual.[16] But this creates as many problems as it solves. Is information just another commodity for which an individual may or may not have a preference even though he has a need for it? Is this discrepancy between a preference and a need for information also to be explained by a lack of information? If so, where does the process end? In addition to this difficulty, once economists admit qualifications to the significance they attribute to preferences, other criteria are automatically introduced into the debate. Such criteria, which by definition are external to or additional to the preferences of individuals, transcend the preferences on which the neo-classical system rests.

An Environmental Ethic   The normative significance of preferences is certainly a point of contention between economists and environmentalists. However, they differ even more fundamentally over the idea that actions can and should be assessed in terms of their value to the environment. Environmentalists do not agree with economists who insist that the environment has "value" for individuals only for its utility. They argue that preservation and improvement of the natural environment is important for its own sake and not merely because people wish to make use of "environmental services." In other words, they advocate a system of ethics which encompasses animate nature in its entirety and even inanimate nature as well. J. Bruce Falls poses the question: "And what of the plants and animals themselves? Who gave us the right to eliminate other species? Doesn't our moral responsibility extend to the whole of nature of which we are a part?"[17]

There seems to be no way of *integrating* this view of the environment's intrinsic value into the scheme of neo-classical economics. Once again it calls into question the proper place of individuals' preferences, particularly in the determination of environmental policy. Quite clearly, this is an important area of dispute between environmentalists and economists. At the very least, its resolution will require on the part of economists a recognition of the difference between preferences and needs, and an investigation into the empirical relationship between preferences, needs, and welfare within a specific social context. In the meantime, environmentalists will continue to resist the lessons of a system of economics which presumes that individuals' preferences are the only legitimate criterion for establishing and assessing environmental policy.

The Social Relation

The basic unit in modern economics is the individual, whereas in sociology it is the social relation.[18] The only social relation, that is, relation between poeple, that is fully recognized in economic theory is the market relation between self-interested buyers and sellers. Some economists have examined various implications of interdependence among people's "utility functions," but significantly all the theorems of welfare economics concerning the efficiency of markets are based on the assumption that these utility functions are not interdependent. Indeed, these theorems *require* the assumption that there are no other social relations except market relations. This is immediately relevant to environmental issues in two ways:

1. economists frequently attribute excessive pollution and resource depletion to market failure rather than to the breakdown of other forms of social relations;

2. the environmental policy recommendations of economists are usually recommendations either to extend the scope of the market where it

presently fails to operate, for example, by establishing pollution rights or effluent charges, or to simulate the market by benefit-cost analysis to that government can regulate what the market would declare if circumstances allowed it to function properly.

In neglecting other forms of social interaction, economists account for environmental problems in terms of the failure of market relations and recommend that the situation be remedied by a direct or indirect extension of the market for the regulation of environmental "resources." In contrast, environmentalists, to varying degrees, attribute this type of problem not to the limited scope of the market, but to its overpervasiveness in modern social life. They express the concern that market decisions may be too short-sighted or that the future will be too heavily discounted, or that advertising, which is an integral part of the market, encourages too much consumption and production of the wrong type of goods and services. Policy recommendations which emanate from this line of analysis usually call for greater restrictions on the market, say in the form of legislated regulations rather than the extension of the market, which economists are predisposed to favour. Such a line of thought also makes environmentalists tend to reject the assumption that all things of "value" are or should be for sale. For environmentalists the relevant question is often: "Should a person have the right to pollute?" Whereas an economist would ask: "If the right to pollute were saleable, what price would it fetch?"

The Market and the Dissolution of Non-Market Social Relations There is an interesting and dynamic side to the question of market and other types of social relations. Numerous examples exist of over-exploitation of the environment because of the collapse of social restraints based on traditon, myth, and custom following the geographic expansion of capitalist economies. Richard Cooley's study of the Alaskan salmon fishery shows how property rights and the ownership of a fishing site were held by specific tribes and clans.[19] The salmon were a group totem for the Alaskan Indians who identified their genealogical continuity with the migrating cycles of the salmon and so were particularly careful not to deplete the fish stock. Over-exploitation of the fishery began only when the Indians came into contact with the rest of North America and the fish became a marketable commodity. The cultural checks that historically had preserved the fishery were destroyed, giving rise to an example of what would currently be termed the "tragedy of the commons."[20] The same tragedy, caused by a complex of factors, afflicts our east coast fisheries.

The experience of the North American Indian clearly illustrates the way in which the spread of the market undermined traditional relationships between man and man and, hence, between man and environment.[21] S. L. Udall observed that

The land and the Indian were bound together by the ties of kinship and nature, rather than by an understanding of property ownership. . . . the Indian's title, based on the idea that he belonged to the land and was its son, was a charter to its use—to use in common with his clan or fellow tribesman, and not to *use up*.

With the growth of the fur trade in North America, E. B. Leacock noted

The new trade introduced new bases for both cohesion and fragmentation in Indian society. Trade for basic necessities loosened the economic basis for cohesion upon which the "stateless society" was based. The introduction of commodity exchange cut at the reciprocity of basic relations in Indian society and weakened the foundation for traditional forms of leadership.

H. Hickerson, who has investigated this process in considerable detail as it applied to the Chippewa of the Upper Great Lakes, emphasized three factors:

(1) Changes in social norms . . . related directly to the imposition of outside socio-economic and ideological systems that everywhere gathered momentum; (2) such outside systems were . . . exploitative and continue to be so; and (3) changes in organization . . . in the long run did not result in accommodation to real relations, that is, relations of exploitation.

He goes on to say that "One factor seems . . . of overriding importance and must apply at one time or another everywhere trade was instituted. This was a factor growing out of the very conditions of trade, at the same time generating its social relations. This is the factor of the *individualization of the distribution of food*."[22]

The North American experience of the spread of the market and its destructive influence on the rights and duties which had traditionally regulated man's relations with nature is useful because it is relatively easy to see how the process operated as European capitalism moved across the Ameircan continent. A less obvious but equally important example of a similar process is found in the enclosure of agricultural land in pre-industrial England. Prior to enclosure, which was based on the desire of the more prosperous farmers to produce for the growing city markets, the villagers farmed open fields. Each had access, restricted by kinship and village custom, to the common land for pasturing animals and obtaining firewood and building materials. When enclosure included the common land, it reduced the marginal cottagers and smallholders, who already sold any surplus produce on the market, to "simple wage labour. More than this; it transformed them and the labourers from upright members of a community, with a distinct set of *rights,* into inferiors dependent on the rich."[23]

Karl Polanyi, more than anyone else, has stressed the historical significance of the development and ultimate collapse of the self-regulating market. He made the following observations about the establishment of markets in labour and land in Europe during the eighteenth and nineteenth centuries: "To separate labour from other activities of life and to subject it to the laws of the market was to annihilate all organic forms of existence and to replace them by a different type of organization, an atomistic and individualistic one." And about land he said: "What we call land is an element of nature inextricably interwoven with man's institutions. To isolate it and form a market out of it was perhaps the weirdest of all undertakings of our ancestors."[24]

Polanyi's observations suggest that the market has been destructive of the various forms of non-market controls which served to regulate man's relation to man and to the environment in such a way that avoided the over-exploitation of communal land. Thus while the economist's analysis of the despoliation of common property resources has an undeniable relevance to today's world, it does not follow that, since the market and common property are incompatible, it is common property which has to go. These examples from history indicate that the expansion of the market system *created* the tragedy of the commons by weakening the traditional forms of social relations which had hitherto prevailed. It is the reconstruction of social structures such as these, combined with the propagation of an environmental ethic, that environmentalists argue is an essential ingredient in an effective environmental policy. Since the market tends to weaken and destroy such structures by undermining all social relations except those of purchase and sale, environmentalists look to control of the market rather than to market control as the proper framework for resolving environmental issues.

The State and the Economy

Neo-classical economic analysis is primarily concerned with the functioning of a market economy based on the private ownership of property. Its analysis shows that in the absence of certain conditions relating to the distribution of property and the level of expenditure in the economy, in addition to those conditions necessary for perfect competition, a capitalist economy will be inequitable, inefficient, and subject to unemployment and inflation. If these defects are to be remedied, it is the task of the public sector as prescribed in the theory of public finance.[25]

This theory of public finance, which has its origins in Smith's *Wealth of Nations,* is exclusively normative. It is a theory of what the state ought to do so as to improve the functioning of the economy. It is not a theory to explain the role of the state in capitalist societies, which is thought by neo-classical economists to be the proper concern of political scientists. In a structural sense, therefore, the state is exogenous to the neo-classical framework. Consequently, economists who analyse environmental problems in terms of market failures of one kind or another resort very readily to the recommendation of solutions to be imposed by the state.

In terms of practical politics, most environmentalists also look to the state to resolve the environmental issues with which they are concerned. However, they do this with varying degrees of scepticism about the impartiality of the state. Some adopt the position that the state is so intimately involved with the interests of private property that it cannot be relied upon to protect the environment if such protection is incompatible with the interests of private property.

Views such as this are derived from some notion of what the state is and how it functions in capitalist societies. These are issues to which economists of the neo-classical school have not traditionally addressed themselves. And yet, in taking for granted, as they do, that the state is exogenous to the market, these economists base their analysis of problems and recommendations for their solution on the underlying assumption that the state is independent and impartial—an assumption which is at variance with the views and the experience of many people. If economists are to improve their understanding of economic and environmental issues in this era of big government, it is necessary for them to incorporate into their analysis a theory of the state which goes well beyond the traditional one of public finance and the unduly simplistic assumptions of neo-classical economics.[26]

OLD ORIGINS, NEW DIRECTIONS

Whenever the mainstream of economic thought encounters difficulties, there is an opportunity for the ever-ready Marxist critique of "bourgeois" economics to surface. A case in point was *Business Week*'s publication of a review of Marxist analyses of inflation and depression in 1974, when it was clear that more conventional economists were floundering. It is significant, therefore, that there has been very little Marxist economic analysis of environmental problems.[27] The simplistic response typified by a leading Marxist economist, Ernest Mandel, is clearly inadequate: "The evil is private property and competition, that is, the market economy and capitalism. All catastrophes, including the irrational and inhuman roads that technology is led down, derive from this social base and from it alone."[28]

This particular form of reductionism is definitely a misrepresentation of those ideas of Marx which can be related quite easily to the environmental issues of today. It has already been noted that Marx gave considerable prominence to the materials-balance principle which has attracted the attention of many economist in recent years. Moreover, his broadly conceived analytical framework is not open to the same criticism about social relations and the state that can be levelled at the neo-classical framework. This section will highlight some of the major parts of Marx's analysis which are of particular importance in understanding environmental issues and which can provide a new direction for economics of the environment.

Marx's View of Man and Nature

As an indication of the relevance of some of Marx's ideas to environmental issues, consider his treatment of man's relation to nature. For Marx, this relationship is dialectical. Those who have wrestled with the problem of whether man is a part of nature or is apart from nature find it refreshing to discover Marx's view. He says that

> Man opposes himself to Nature as one of her own forces . . . in order to appropriate Nature's production in a form adapted to his own wants. By thus acting on the external world and changing it, he at the same time changes his own nature.[29]

There are two important ideas contained in this quotation: (1) man is regarded as a part of nature, albeit, that part of nature which is self-conscious; and (2) man changes the world by his labour and, at the same time, changes himself. Neither of these ideas are found or can be accommodated in the neo-classical framework. There the distinction between man and nature is so sharply made that it is customary for neo-classical economists to define economics in terms of human wants on the one hand and scarce resources on the other.[30] These wants or preferences are assumed to be immutable and usually insatiable, and nature is regarded as no more than a set of resources for satisfying these wants. In Marx's analysis, needs arising from people's natural requirements, which are more or less fixed, are distinguished from needs which have a social origin and are therefore subject to change. This distinction is consistent with the view of human needs to which environmentalists such as René Dubos subscribe.[31] Moreover, Marx is able to integrate it into his framework without the difficulties that changing needs and preferences involve for the neo-classical school. This is so because the cornerstone of Marx's economic analysis is not an abstract notion of need, utility, or preference, but labour, which for Marx represents a direct empirical interaction between man and nature.

The neo-classical view of nature as a set of resources for satisfying human wants is not only recognized by Marx as a view that is characteristic of the age of capitalism, but he seeks to explain it in those terms. Referring to the advent of capitalism, Marx says:

> Nature becomes for the first time simply an object for mankind, purely a matter of utility; it ceases to be recognized as a power in its own right; and the theoretical knowledge of its independent laws appears only as a strategem designed to subdue it to human requirements. Pursuing this tendency, capital has pushed beyond national boundaries and prejudices, beyond the deification of nature and the inherited self-sufficient satisfaction of existing needs confined within well-defined bounds, and the reproduction of the traditional way of life. It is destructive of all this, and permanently revolutionary, tearing down all obstacles that impede the development of productive forces, the expansion of needs, the diversity of production, and the exploitation and exchange of natural and intellectual forces.[32]

That quotation brings out another characteristic of Marx's analysis which sharply distinguishes it from neo-classical economics. His work is infused with a sense of history. He was concerned with uncovering the "laws of motion" of capitalist society and he emphasized the origins of capitalism as well as its basic instability and impermanence, which he claimed to have demonstrated. By analysing capitalism in its historical context, Marx discerned that capitalism transforms everything of value into commodities to be bought and sold, and this includes people as labour power and nature as resources. In contrast, the practice of neo-classical economists is to use the historically specific phenomenon of the all-pervasive market for analyzing contemporaory environmental issues and to search for a solution within the same restricted historical setting. Many environmentalists, for their part, do not presume that solutions are possible without far reaching socio-economic changes,[33] and this provides them with a common perspective with Marx on the *need* for societal change if not on its *inevitability*.[34]

Among Marx's other observations which are of direct relevance to environmental issues is the attention he devoted to the various forms of property that have occurred in history. He commented on the durable, common property arrangements amongst "Romans, Teutons, and Celts as well as Indians and Slavs." He also noted the environmental implications of the increasing urbanization of the population:

> Capitalist production, by collecting the population in great centres, and causing an ever increasing preponderance of town population, disturbs the metabolism of man and the earth, i.e. the return to the soil of its elements consumed by man in the form of food and clothing, and therefore, violates the eternal condition for the lasting fertility of the soil.[35]

This theme, which has since been taken up by Barry Commoner in *The Closing Circle,* was presented by Marx together with another pertinent observation of his. Having argued that capitalism transforms everything of value into commodities, including labour and nature. Marx goes on to say how both of these are exploited by the same process:

> All progress in capitalistic agriculture is a progress in the art, not only of robbing the labourer but of robbing the soil; all progress in increasing fertility of the soil for a given time is a progress toward ruining the lasting sources of that fertility. . . . Capitalist production, therefore, develops technology, and the combining together of various processes into a social whole, only by sapping the original sources of all wealth: soil and labourer.[36]

The Importance of Production

Apart from its obvious and explicit relevance to the economics of environmental issues, this last idea reflects what may be the single most significant feature of Marx's analysis for reformulating the economics of environmental issues, the emphasis on the process of production: "It is a distinctive feature of Marxist approach to economics—in common with the classical economists —that the central focus of its analysis is productive relations. . . ."[37] In recent years there has been a renewed effort by some economists to reinstate the analysis of production as the central theme in economics. The most significant analytical work has been that of P. Sraffa, whose economic analysis has been complemented at the philosophical level by the work of M. Hollis and E. J. Nell, who call for the abandonment of positivist, neo-classical economics and its replacement by a rationalist, classical-Marxian framework.[38]

The thrust of this Marxian approach is to establish the logical implications of a system of production comprising numerous interdependent productive activities. To provide a viable basis for any society, a system of production must be capable of reproducing itself. This means for example, that the production of each commodity in each year must be sufficient to meet the needs of the economy during the year and to replenish the initial stocks that existed at the start of the year. This is equivalent to Marx's schema of "simple reproduction."

It is easy to see the relevance of examining the conditions for a reproductive economic system in terms of environmental issues. One of the threats of resource depletion and environmental pollution is that an economic system which gives rise to these problems may be incapable of resolving them. This raises questions about the sources and nature of technological change and whether such change alleviates or aggravates the environmental obstacles to an economic system's capacity to reproduce itself. Technological change is part of the larger social process by which people respond to the situations with which they are confronted. One of the contributions by Forrester and Meadows[39] to the debate about the limits to growth was their success in drawing attention to the existence of positive and negative feedbacks within the socio-economic system which can either dampen or aggravate explosive trends. For example, if a growing city responds to traffic congestion by increasing the capacity of its transportation systems, then this will tend to increase the growth of the city and ultimately worsen the transportation problem.

Whereas Forrester and Meadows were primarily concerned with the behaviour of a given system, albeit the world system, their perspective is of even greater significance when we consider the evolution of interacting sub-systems within society. Economic growth in the modern era has required and encouraged an increasing mobility of labour. Despite improvements in communications, this has undermined the viability of the extended family, which used to perform many of the welfare functions that are now performed by the state. It is an open question whether or not the nuclear family is a self-sustaining social unit, and the experimentation in the past decade with various forms of communal life suggests that some people at least are trying to create circumstances in which they can have closer contact with a larger group of people than is possible within the nuclear family.

The lesson to be learned here is that, even if sustained economic growth is capable of continuing indefinitely via the successful substitution of new resources for old, it is unlikely to bring the social, political, and environmental stability that the advocates of growth argue can only be brought with increased wealth. Instead, the process of economic growth, with its requirements for narrowly defined economic efficiency, may preclude the decentralization of economic and political activity, towards which an increasing number of people are looking as a condition for coping with many of our contemporary social and environmental problems.[40] In other words, not only must the economic system be capable of reproducing itself, but it must do so in a way that is consistent with reasonably stable social systems. Whether or not this will be possible without once again submerging man's economy into his social relations remains to be seen.[41]

Steady-State Economics

It is ironical that Kenneth Boulding, who has spoken out publicly and indiscriminately against the economic theories of Marx, should have written the seminal paper for environmentalists, on what has come to be known as steady-state economics. He introduced to many the idea of materials throughput, which, as shown above, is entirely consistent with the Marxian perspective. Boulding questioned the viability of any economy as dependent as ours on using up the non-renewable resources provided by nature and he advocated a substantial shift to the use of renewable resources, particularly solar energy.[42]

More than a century before Boulding, the influential classical economist, John Stuart Mill, regarded the attainment of the stationary state not only as inevitable but as definitely desirable. He noted that

> It must always have been seen, more or less distinctly, by political economists, that the increase in wealth is not boundless: that at the end of what they term the progressive state lies the stationary state . . . [which] I am inclined to believe . . . would be, on the whole, a very considerable improvement on our present condition.[43]

How remote this vision from the current musings of neo-classical economists!

CONCLUSIONS: FROM THEORY TO POLICY[44]

The increasing pervasiveness of the market in human social life, which has had serious implications for people's interactions with one another and with the natural environment, has been the result of a complicated historical process rather than a conscious social decision. Neo-classical economists have provided striking insights into the market system without considering the means by which it became established. For many economists, not least those concerned with environmental issues, advocacy has followed analysis. Consequently these economists have helped carry forward, albeit in a small way, a historical process of which they are scarcely aware.

Despite the vigour with which economists have proposed market-based solutions to environmental problems, there is yet to be a deliberate and widespread extension of the market, and the mentality to which it gives rise, to regulate the use of the full range of "environmental resources." One reason for this may be that bureaucratic relations have begun to supersede market relations and those with bureaucratic power are reluctant to relinquish their decision-making authority to market processes which they do not fully understand and which they are less able to control.

It is of current concern, therefore, whether those aspects of man-environment relations which are outside the market at present should remain there or whether they should be brought directly or indirectly under market control. Decisions relating to the environment can be social and political rather than economic. Economic considerations can still play a part, but the institutional processes by which environmental decisions are made can allow for the generation and flow of information and a distribution of influence, power, and responsibility that differs significantly from that which prevails in the market.

In the past the extension of the market has been thrust upon people, sometimes in the face of their opposition and frequently with the support of the state. At this point in history an opportunity exists for making a conscious decision about the exclusion of the environment from the market system. A decision to continue its exclusion and even to extend it, so that, for example, the exploitation of natural resources might become subject to publicly determined quotas, presents opportunities for restructuring our social and political decision-making institutions.[45] Some attempts to do this in Canada are already in evidence with the establishment of some form of environmental assessment in each province and by the federal government, and the somewhat novel approaches to their tasks of such Commissions as the Berger Commission and the Royal Commission on Electric Power Planning. It is still to be seen whether these initiatives will serve only to bolster the existing institutional structures or whether they are capable of leading the way to institutional changes adequate to cope with the environmental problems with which we are confronted.

NOTES

1. J. Dales, *Pollution, Property & Prices* (Toronto, 1968).

2. Boulding, in H. Jarrett, ed., *Environmental Quality in a Growing Economy* (Baltimore, 1966).

3. R. U. Ayres and A. V. Kneese, "Production, Consumption and Externalities," *American Economic Review*, LIX (June 1969), 282–97. See also N. Georgescu-

Roegen, *The Entropy Law and the Economic Process* (Cambridge, Mass., 1972). This book is especially noteworthy in that it represents an attempt to reconcile economic activity with physical laws of the twentieth rather than the nineteenth century.

4. P. Victor, *Pollution: Economy and Environment* (Toronto, 1972).

5. Marshall, *Principles of Economics,* 8th ed. (London, 1920), 53, 54.

6. Marx, *Capital,* I (London, 1970), 43.

7. Robinson, *Economic Philosophy* (Middlesex, 1965), 47, 29.

8. Dobb, *Political Economy of Capitalism* (London, 1937), 12.

9. J. Bentham, *Introduction to the Principles of Morals and Legislation* (London, 1948), 1.

10. H. A. J. Green, *Consumer Theory* (Middlesex, 1971), 22–5.

11. Marshall, *Principles of Economics,* 78n, 73–7.

12. Cf. Green, *Consumer Theory,* 26: "Such considerations are peripheral to standard textbook discussions of consumer behaviour and for the most part remain so in this one."

13. See, for example, W. Leiss, *The Limits to Satisfaction* (Toronto, 1976).

14. Some economists, notably J. K. Galbraith, have addressed this issue but their work lies outside the mainstream of contemporary economics.

15. Dubos, *A God Within* (New York, 1972).

16. As implied by Green's comments on advertising, information, and preferences. *Consumer Theory,* 27.

17. Falls, "The Importance of Nature Reserves," in B. M. Littlesohn and D. M. Pimlott, eds., *Why Wilderness?* (Toronto, 1971), 26.

18. Marx's emphasis on social relations accounts for the much greater attention he receives from sociologists than from most contemporary economists.

19. Cooley, *Politics and Conservation* (New York, 1963).

20. G. Hardin, "The Tragedy of the Commons," *Science,* 162 (13 Dec. 1968), 1243–1248.

21. An excellent account of this process is given by Irene Spry in "The Great Transformation: The Disappearance of the Commons in Western Canada," *Man and Nature on the Prairies,* Canadian Plains Studies 6 (Regina 1976).

22. Udall, *The Quiet Crisis* (New York, 1963), 5–7 (emphasis in original); Leacock, *Introduction to North American Indians in Historical Perspective,* ed. Leacock and N. D. Lane (New York, 1971); Hickerson, "The Chippewa of the Upper Great Lakes: A Study in Sociopolitical Change," in *ibid.,* 183, 186 (emphasis in original).

23. E. J. Hobsbawm, *Industry and Empire* (Middlesex, 1968), 102 (emphasis in original).

24. Polanyi, *The Great Transformation* (Boston, 1944), 163, 178.

25. R. A. Musgrave, *The Theory of Public Finance* (New York, 1959).

26. See, for example, R. Miliband, *The State in Capitalist Society* (London, 1969).

27. Two items of note are H. Rothman, *Murderous Providence* (London, 1972), and R. England and B. Bluestone, "Ecology and Class Conflict," in H. Daly, ed., *Toward a Steady-State Economy* (San Francisco, 1973).

28. Mandel, "The Generalized Recession of the International Capitalist Economy," *Inprecor*, 16 Jan. 1975, p. 16.

29. Marx, *Capital*, I, 177.

30. L. Robbins, *An Essay on the Nature and Significance of Economic Science* (London, 1937).

31. See pages 42–43 above.

32. Marx, *Grundrisse* (Middlesex, 1974).

33. See, for example, "The Blueprint for Survival," *The Ecologist* (Jan. 1972). This document represents a modern example of what Marx referred to, somewhat disparagingly, as utopian socialism. Its omission of any mention of private property is striking.

34. Exponents of the "Limits to Growth" thesis do concur with Marx on the inevitability of collapse if certain harsh measures are not quickly introduced. They are notably less optimistic than Marx about the outcome of such a collapse should it occur.

35. Marx, *Capital*, I, 505.

36. Commoner, *The Closing Circle* (London, 1971); Marx, *ibid*. It should be noted that the somewhat favorable interpretation given here of the relevance of Marx's work to environmental analysis is at variance with Georgescu-Roegen's view that "both main streams of economic thought view the economic process as a no deposit, no return affair in relation to nature."

37. J. Eaton, *Political Economy* (New York, 1966), 7.

38. Sraffa, *Production of Commodities by Means of Commodities* (London, 1960); Hollis and Nell, *Rational Economic Man* (London, 1975).

39. D. Meadows et al., *The Limits to Growth* (London, 1972).

40. E. F. Schumacher, *Small Is Beautiful* (New York, 1973).

41. K. Polanyi, "Our Obsolete Market Mentality," reprinted in G. Dalton, ed., *Primitive, Archaic and Modern Economics* (Boston, 1968).

42. Public lecture at the University of York, and "The Economics of the Coming Spaceship Earth."

43. Mill, *Principles of Political Economy*, II (London, 1857), 320.

44. I am grateful to Abraham Rotstein for suggesting the logic of this conclusion.

45. See Daly, *Toward a Steady-State Economy*.

14

THE TELEOLOGICAL VIEW OF WEALTH: A HISTORICAL PERSPECTIVE

Gerald Alonzo Smith

The practice of medicine may require the prescription of an addictive stimulant for the sake of good health. The amount of the stimulant is finite and limited by the end. When, however, one takes a stimulant for its own sake, the desire for it becomes infinite since it is no longer limited by a final goal but is an end in itself. The same is true of the output of the economic process which, rather than being used for the sake of achieving the final goal of life, tends to become the final goal itself. Since output is then not limited by any final goal, the desire for it becomes infinite. We get hooked on economic growth. To paraphrase Descartes, such a lifestyle would be based on the philosophical foundation: I make and I buy, therefore I am.

Published by permission of the author. Financial support for this research was provided by the Rockefeller Brothers Fund.

In such a philosophical perspective man's reason becomes subject to the desires of the acquisitive side of his nature rather than being the dominant partner in the orientation and direction of his activities. To act irrationally comes to mean only that, given one's desires, one commits some action which is inconsistent with such desires. It makes no difference what one's desires are, because they are seen to be beyond the reach of reason. As long as he used the most efficient tools, the completely mad Captain Ahab was entirely rational in his search for the white whale. No less an economist than Frank Knight has remarked on such a view: "Living intelligently includes more than the intelligent use of means in realizing ends; it is fully as important to select the ends intelligently, for intelligent action directed toward wrong ends only makes evil greater and more certain."[1] More recently, Tibor Scitovsky has written about such activity, "This may well be an example of the higher irrationality of behavior governed by narrowly rational calculation."[2]

Most economists, however, have refused to follow Knight and Scitovsky in a discussion of how man's economic behavior affects the achievement of his final end. Indeed, the representative modern economist, having been weaned upon a quantitative and arithmomorphic methodology, probably does not even recognize that there is a relationship between the final end of man and his economic activity. Although some economists are more perceptive and recognize that there is a problem, they refuse to discuss the issue because they are quite aware of the pitfalls to which such normative judgments upon the legitimacy of the producer's and consumer's activity lead. Since most economists have never had the time, inclination, or training to formulate an authentic value system based upon a rational reflection of the final end of man, it is no wonder that they do not want to enter into that complex and delicate question. It is not hard to understand why such economists readily and mostly unconsciously tend to follow in the well-worn footsteps of their nineteenth-century predecessors who had found their answer to this question in the ethics of utilitarian philosophy. For them happiness implied good, and since every individual was the best judge of his own happiness, the individual's choice of economic goods had to be taken as given (that is, beyond analysis). No wonder the nineteenth-century economist felt an enthusiasm akin to religious fervor toward his economic theory. It helped unlock the door to the greatest happiness of the greatest number simply by making sure that the individual consistently followed out the dictates of his self-interested acquisitive nature.

We who live in the twentieth century are not so optimistic. We realize more clearly the consequences of such utilitarianism and individualism. We know the economists with their tremendous influence in helping to decide where to allocate resources can *not* avoid making a normative judgment on this important issue of the final end of man and economic behavior. The very decision to ignore the question of the hierarchy of natural needs by treating all effective demand as equal and given is in itself a value judgment and, by definition, makes of these demands ends in themselves. The easy way out is not always the right way. Such an analysis (or lack thereof) would not be too harmful, however, if it left only the economics profession in error. But the economics profession provides society with the image of economic society, and this image, in turn, notably affects the economic behavior of society.[3] As Warren Samuels has noted, "Economists should and do participate in the social valuational process, despite disclaimers to the contrary."[4] If the economics profession accepts as appropriate the image that the end of an economic system is to fulfill consumers' effective demands and beyond that nothing useful can be said about the legitimacy of demand either in the aggregate or in the particular, then such a judgment will penetrate in a very subtle manner throughout society and will, in turn, reinforce the economists in their original judgment.

There have, however, been economists during the modern era who have questioned this crucial valuational premise. They have refused to let go of the conclusions reached slowly and with great difficulty about the final end of man by the Greco-Judeo-Christian civilization and to uncritically accept in their place the conclusions proposed by the ethics of utilitarianism and the epistemology of positivism modified by individualism. J. C. L. Simonde de Sismondi in *Nouveaux principes d' 'economie politique,* John Ruskin in *Unto This Last,* J. A. Hobson in *Wealth and Life: A Study in Value,* and R. H. Tawney in *The Acquisitive Society* have each in his own way rejected the conventional economic wisdom which views increased production and consumption as an end in itself. Each of these humanistic economists looked upon increases in economic activity as a means rather than an end. Each investigated whether the increases in production and consumption experienced during their lifetime benefited man in achieving his final end, which, following the Greco-Judeo-Christian tradition, they defined as life in *all* its dimensions, especially in the higher immaterial dimensions.

J. C. L. SIMONDE DE SISMONDI (1773–1842)

Sismondi was the first economist of modern times to question the notion that growth in economic productivity was an end in itself or the same as growth in the public good. It is necessary to remember that Sismondi was writing in an era of transition from the craft system to the factory system and that his criticism was directed against the excesses of that transition period. Sismondi was well equipped for his role as a critic of the excesses of industrialism as he was one of the few economists of his generation who had the historical knowledge and acumen to observe the transitory nature of his era.

> We are, and this point cannot be sufficiently stressed, in an altogether new state of society, of which we have absolutely no experience. We tend to separate completely all sorts of ownership from all sorts of work, to break all connections between man and master, to deprive the former of all associations in the profits of the latter.[5]

In a very early age of industrialism Sismondi attempted to orient the economics profession from the rigid abstractions of economic man that ultimately come to be its hallmark. He wanted economics to describe and analyze a changing economic scene but to hold fast to the ancient truths about man. Instead, economics would declare that its concepts and abstractions were permanent and that it was the nature of man that was unknowable and fleeting.

Sismondi began his analysis of the economy by rejecting the view that the role of the economist was to maximize wealth in itself. For his view of the importance of wealth Sismondi turned back to the Greeks and especially to Aristotle for his inspiration. "But at least they [the Greeks] never lost sight of the fact that wealth had no other worth than what it contributed to the national happiness; and precisely because their treatment was less abstract, their point of view was oftentimes more just than ours."[6] In both his *Nouveaux principes* and his later *Etudes sur l'economie politique,* Sismondi is insistent throughout on the distinction which he obtained from Aristotle between the science of "chremastics," which treats of the accumulation of monetary wealth or items of exchange value for their own sake, and "political economy," which treats of the role that economic production and consumption should play in achieving the final goal of society.

> The chremastic science, or the study of the means of increasing wealth, in setting aside the purpose of this wealth, is a false science.[7]

> When one takes the increase of economic goods as the end of society, one necessarily sacrifices the end for the means. One obtains more of production, but such production is paid for dearly by the misery of the masses.[8]

Since Sismondi disagreed with the conventional premise that increase in wealth was the final goal of the newly emerging science of economics, it is not surprising that he differed in his resolution to the economic problems facing the society of his era. Simply put, the solution of the conventional economists for the massive social misery that was only too apparent during those early crises of the Industrial Revolution was to expand production. "It [the misery resulting from the economic crisis of 1818–1821] is not a consequence of production being too much increased. Increase it more."[9] According to the classical economics, the general growth of economic productivity presented only minor inconveniences and was overall a good thing in every respect. Did not Say's Law show that supply created its own demand and, therefore, if supply was increasing, demand must also be increasing? Sismondi rejects this line of reasoning as being too abstract:

> The science in their hands is so speculative, that it seems to be detached from all practice. It was believed at first that in extricating the theory from all the accessory circumstances, one ought to render it clearer and easier to seize, but the opposite is attained. The new English economists are quite obscure and can be understood only with great effort because our mind is opposed to admitting the abstractions demanded of us. This repugnance is in itself a warning that we

are turning away from the truth when, in moral science where everything is connected, we endeavor to isolate a principle and to see nothing but that principle.[10]

Sismondi, on the other hand, develops his analysis by comparing the former economic society in which the majority worked for themselves as craftsmen and tradesmen with the current industrial society in which most laborers worked for others. (It was Sismondi who coined the word *proletariat*.) Since the craftsman's reward was the fruits of his own labor, and the amount of this reward was determined by the natural order of things, he would stop producing when he had reached the point beyond which he would prefer leisure and the fruits of his past labor to the extra income to be had from further labor.

> For the laborer who works for himself there is a point reached in the accumulation of wealth beyond which it would appear as folly to accumulate still more, since such a laborer would not be able to increase his consumption in a proportional amount. But the needs of the laborer who works in an industrial society appear to be infinite. . . . No matter how many riches he has massed, there is no point at which he will say: "This is enough."
>
> Moreover this is a serious error into which have fallen most of the modern economists that they think that the act of consumption is unlimited and always ready to devour an infinite quantity of production. They do not cease from encouraging the nations to produce, to invent new machines, to improve their work so that the quantity of production achieved in the year will always surpass that of the preceding year: they are very distressed when they see the number of improductive workers to multiply, they would point out the idle for the indignant public, and in a nation where the power of the worker has been increased by a hundredfold, they want that everyone should work in order to live.[11]

How does it happen that the industrial laborer works beyond that point which he would in a more natural system? Sismondi answers:

> If all "les pompons de la richesse" were offered to the manual worker as a recompense for his assiduous travail of twelve and fourteen hours a day, as many do today, there is not one of these workers who would not choose less luxury and more of leisure, less of frivolous ornaments and more of liberty. Such should be the choice of the entire society, if only there was more equality in our society. Every craftsman who profits the total amount of his own industry, when he compares the almost imperceptible pleasure that he would receive from a slightly finer suit of clothes with the additional work that such a suit of clothes entails, would not wish to pay this price. Luxury is not possible except when it is paid for by the work of others. Assiduous and constant labor is able to be procured, not for the sake of frivolities, but only to gain the necessities of life.[12]

For Sismondi overproduction occurs when workers strain to produce more than they would in a system in which they received a larger share of the fruits of the productive process. Because the owners reaped where the laborers sowed, the decision to expand production was made by those who profited from production rather than by those who bore the real cost of labor required by expanded production. Sismondi wrote about the England of the early days of the Industrial Revolution when its laissez faire economic ideology and factory system engendered a transparent exploitation of the workers unknown to previous centuries. It is important to note that in this critical period of transition Sismondi was unwilling to glorify economic production for its own sake after the manner of the orthodox economists because he did not share their absolute faith in the salvific efficacy of Say's Law, which declared that since supply created its own demand, an increase in production was identical to an increased demand for such production. Sismondi instead asked a more fundamental question:

> What, then, is the object of human society? Is it to dazzle the eye with an immense production of useful and elegant things; to daunt the senses with the control which man exercises over nature, and with the precision or the speed with which a human work is executed by lifeless beings? Is it to cover the sea with vessels and the earth with railways which distribute in all directions the products of an ever increasing industry? . . . If such is the case, we have undoubtedly made immense progress as compared with our ancestors; we are rich in inventions, rich in activities, rich in scientific powers, rich in merchandise everywhere; for every nation has produced not only for itself but also for its neighbors. But, if the aim which society ought to accept, in encouraging labor and protecting the fruits of the labor of man, fruits which we call wealth—if these fruits, which consist of oral and intellectual goods as well as material goods, should be the means of improvement as well as of enjoyment, are we sure that we are approaching our goal?[13]

Sismondi's observation of the industrial system reminded him of the story of Gandalin.

> In the time of enchantment, Gandalin, who lodged a sorcerer in his home, noticed that every morning the sorcerer would take a broom handle and, saying a few magic words on it, he made out of it a water-carrier, who at once would get for him as many pails of water as he desired. One morning Ganadalin hid himself behind a door and listened with all his might to overhear the magic words which the sorcerer pronounced for his enchantment. He, however, did not hear what the sorcerer said next to undo it. As soon as the sorcerer went away, Gandalin repeated the experiment; he took the broom handle, pronounced the mysterious words and the broom water-carrier went forward to the river and returned with water, and then again went forward and came back with it, thus again and again; Gandalin's reservoir was already full and the water flooded the room. "It's enough!" cried he, "Stop!" But the machine-man neither saw nor heard; insensible and indefatigable, he would have brought all the water from the river. Gandalin, in his despair, took an axe and hit his carrier with repeated blows. Then he saw, the fragments of the broom, upon falling on the ground, immediately get up and reassume the magic form and run to the river. Instead of the carrier, he had now four, eight, sixteen; the more that he struck down the machine-men, the more machine-men got up to do his work in spite of him. The entire river would have passed into his home, if the sorcerer had not fortunately come back and destroyed his enchantment.[14]

Sismondi then comments that

> the water, however is a good thing. Water, just as much as work, just as much as capital, is necessary for life. But one is able to have too much, even of the

best things of life. . . . Each new application of science and the useful arts, similar to the axe of Gandalin knocking down the machine-men which the magic words had created, only to find soon two, four, eight, sixteen in its place; so the productivity continues to increase with a rapidity without measure. Has not the moment come, or at least is not the moment able to come, when one should say. This is too much?

According to the theory which is professed today in all the schools of political economy, this moment has not yet come, and it is never going to come.[15]

This story of Gandalin epitomizes Sismondi's view of his society—a society that was increasing economic production with a rapidity without measure, but for what? Sismondi's historical studies had taught him that there was more to a superior civilization than just increased material production. Such increased productivity, if brought about because of an unjust economic system, could well do more harm than good. As Sismondi grew older, he grew more pessimistic about his society that would not reduce its frenetic activity and orient its economic production and consumption by some final goal. On September 19, 1834, he wrote in his private journal:

I read in the *Westminster Review* a striking article on civilization, in which the author points out many of the bad effects of the present system, which hitherto I have been almost the only one to remark. There is much ability in this article, but it inspires one with a melancholy feeling, because the evils are so serious and one does not see the remedies; the *too much* of everything is the evil of the day.[16] (Emphasis is in the original.)

As we leave this perceptive observer of the transition age to modern industrialism and turn to a later age of greater production and abundance, we should not forget that it was Sismondi who first criticized the economic theorists for making the increase of production a national goal. In his time of massive exploitation of laboring men, women, and, let us not forget, children, he questioned whether the cost in human suffering was too great for the frivolous items being produced.

JOHN RUSKIN (1819–1900)

Though as late as 1848 John Stuart Mill questioned whether all of the inventions yet produced had "lightened the day's toil of any human being," he nevertheless thought that "they have not yet begun to effect those great changes in human destiny, which it is in their nature and futurity to accomplish."[17] At the same time that John S. Mill was writing these sentiments, another writer was beginning to investigate what effect these great changes in physical inventions and their expanding productivity were having on human destiny.

John Ruskin was born in 1819 into a moderately wealthy London merchant family. Though his family had experienced the power and pleasure that commercial success brought in its train, his puritanic and artistic parents made sure that he never judged the accumulation of wealth to be the main goal of his life. Ruskin was trained as an artist and art critic, and his reputation grew immensely with the successive volumes in his series *Modern Painters*. It was always, however, Ruskin's ambition to bring the beauties and inspiration of the intellectual and artistic world to the representative British worker. When the average British laborer failed to respond to his efforts, Ruskin set himself to the task of finding the cause of such blindness. His investigations into the life and society of the British laboring class rather quickly led him to believe that something was wrong with an economy that produced so much quantity of so little quality, yet brutalized so many people in doing it. Similar to other English critics of the industrial society, such as Coleridge, Cobbett, Carlyle, Dickens, Arnold, Morris, and many more, Ruskin soon denounced the commercial society of his time for its worship of Mammon, its "gospel of greed,"[18] and the conventional political economy which intellectually supported such a system. As the historian Asa Briggs has noted, "indeed, they [the poets] had probed far more deeply than the political economists into the inner meanings of the processes of change, had taken the world of nature as well as the world of men into the reckoning."[19] Yet of all these humanistic critics, only Ruskin attempted to challenge the economic theorists on their own ground by undertaking the task of thoroughly analyzing and exposing the errors of conventional political economy.

Like Sismondi, Ruskin began his analysis by distinguishing between the true science of political economy and that science which merely attempted to maximize economic productivity.

> The real science of political economy, which has yet to be distinguished from the bastard science, as medicine from witchcraft, and astronomy from astrology, is that which teaches nations to desire and labor for the things that lead to life; and which teaches them to scorn and destroy the things that lead to destruction.[20]

For Ruskin, "the ideal of human life is a union of Spartan simplicity of manners with Athenian sensibility and imagination."[21] Thus for his definition of wealth it was natural for Ruskin to turn back to the Greek Xenephon for his inspiration. Ruskin claimed that the *Economist* of Xenephon

> contains a flawless definition of wealth, and an explanation of its dependence for efficiency on the merits and faculties of its possessors;—a definition which cannot be bettered; and which must be the foundation of all true Political Economy among nations, as Euclid is to all time the basis of Geometry.[22]

Ruskin is referring to the first chapter of Xenephon's *Economist*, "The Management of Property, that is Whatever is of Use to a Man, But is of No Value to Such as Are Slaves to their Passions," where Xenephon is intent on showing that some economic possessions aid man in living and thus are true wealth or property, and some possessions, on the contrary, contribute to the destruction of man's nature. These latter possessions cannot be considered as

true wealth, but must be considered as the opposite of wealth or property
—*illth* was Ruskin's label for such possessions.

> Then the very same things are property to a man who knows how to use them,
> and not property to one who does not. For instance, a flute is property to a man
> who can play on it fairly; but to one who is wholly unskilled in its use it is no
> more property than mere useless stones would be—unless indeed he sold it.
> So it is clear to us that a flute in the hands of a man who does not know how to
> use it, is not property to him, unless he sells it. So long as he keeps it, it is not
> property. And indeed, Socrates, we shall thus have reasoned consistently, since
> we before decided that a man's property must be something that benefits him. If
> the man does not sell the flute, it is not property, for it is of no use; but if he sell
> it, it becomes property.
> To this Socrates answered, Yes, if he know how to sell it. But if he, again,
> were to sell it to a man who does not know how to use it, it would not be
> property even when sold, according to what you say.
> Your words, Socrates, seem to imply that not even money would be property
> unless a man knew how to use it.
> Well, you seem to agree with me that a man's property is only what benefits him.
> Suppose a man were to make this use of his money, to buy, say, a mistress, by whose
> influence his body would be worse, his soul worse, his household worse, how could
> we then say that his money was any benefit to him?
> We could not—unless, indeed, we are to count as property henbane, the herb
> that drives mad those who eat it.[23]

This is an important passage for Ruskin and one that he would return to
more often than to any other for his inspiration when pursuing problems in
political economy. One can see a glimpse of it in the following often-quoted
declaration of Ruskin: "And possession is in use only, which for each man is
sternly limited; so that such things, and so much of them as he can use, are,
indeed, well for him, or Wealth; and more of them, or any other things are ill
for him, or Illth."[24]

Thus the concept of wealth includes more than just the measurement of
one's actual possessions; it includes, secondly, the capability of utilizing them
in an appropriate and vital manner.

> "Having" is not an absolute, but a graduated, power; and consists not only in the
> quantity or nature of the thing possessed, but also (and in a greater degree) in its
> suitableness to the person possessing it and in his vital power to use it. . . .
> Wealth, therefore is "the possession of the valuable by the valiant."[25]

It is clear from this brief discussion of Ruskin's view of wealth that he could
not consider the mere accumulation of wealth to be the final goal of either the
individual or the nation. He contrasts the erroneous with the correct perception
of wealth in the following passage:

> There will be always a number of men who would fain set themselves to the
> accumulation of wealth as the sole object to their life. Necessarily, that class of
> men is an uneducated class, inferior in intellect, and more or less cowardly. It is
> physically impossible for a well-educated, intellectual, or brave man to make
> money the chief object of his thoughts; just as it is for him to make his dinner the

principal object of them. All healthy people like their dinners, but their dinner is not the main object of their lives. So all healthily-minded people like making money—ought to like it, and to enjoy the sensation of winning it; but the main object of their life is not money; it is something better than money.[26]

Ruskin taught that moderate wealth should be the goal. "A nation which desires true wealth, desires it moderately, and can therefore distribute it with kindness, and possess it with pleasure; but one which desires false wealth, desires it immoderately, and can neither dispense it with justice, nor enjoy it in peace."[27] Ruskin urged the individual to recognize that "the law of life is that a man should fix the sum he desires to make annually, as the food he desires to eat daily; and stay when he has reached the limit, refusing increase of business, and leaving it to others, so obtaining due freedom of time for better thoughts."[28] Hence his prescriptions for the running of a state: "I strongly suspect that in a well-organized state, the possession of wealth ought to incapacitate for public office,"[29] and "one of the most important conditions of a healthy system of social economy, would be the restraint of the properties and incomes of the upper classes within certain fixed limits."[30]

This call for moderation and restraint did not fall on fertile ground in Victorian England. James Sherburne has pointed out that

> Ruskin's final call for restraint was, perhaps, the most incomprehensible to his Victorian contemporaries. It lies in the sensitive area of social advancement or "getting-on." Ruskin denies the "gospel of whatever we've got, to get more" as vehemently as he does that of "wherever we are, to go somewhere else."[31]

The customary reaction was that expressed in a lead article by the *Manchester Examiner and Times on* October 2, 1860: "He [Ruskin] is not worth our powder and shot, yet, if we do not crush him, his wild words will touch the springs of action in some hearts, and ere we are aware a moral floodgate may fly open and drown us all."[32] For better or worse, the *Manchester Examiner and Times* and, one might add, the conventional political economists, were able to keep shut the moral floodgate that Ruskin's thought represented and thus to keep the Victorian economic theory on the dry road of amorality. Though one economist predicted in 1888 that future economic theory would be built with Ruskinian bricks rather than with Ricardian straw,[33] this prediction has simply not come true.

Yet Ruskin's wild words have touched deeply some minds and hearts. Such diverse individuals as the heretical English economist John A. Hobson,[34] the artist and craftsman Eric Gill,[35] the biologist Patrick Geddes,[36] the physical chemist Frederick Soddy,[37] the economic historian R. H. Tawney,[38] Richard T. Ely, a founder of the American Economic Association,[39] the English novelist and distributist G. K. Chesterton,[40] the French novelist Marcel Proust,[41] and Indian pacifist and political leader Mohandas Gandhi[42] have all paid homage to Ruskin and his ideas.

JOHN A. HOBSON (1858–1940)

Although John A. Hobson often claimed that he was Ruskin's disciple, and in many of his works indicated that he was merely attempting to fill in some of the gaps in Ruskin's "magnificent plunge" into economic theory which brought "whole civilizations to a grand assise,"[43] it is nonetheless true that John Hobson added to and modified as much as he kept intact from Ruskin's thought. Ewald Grether has described the relationship of Ruskin and Hobson in the following manner: "It is clear that it was neither a faith nor a creed that descended from Ruskin to Hobson, but primarily an attitude."[44] This inherited attitude was that of subjecting standard or conventional economic theory to the test of a humane assessment. Hobson, more than Ruskin, admitted that there was a place for the orthodox economic theory which took the narrow and more quantitative vision of simply allocating scarce resources efficiently among the perceived needs of individuals. Nonetheless, Hobson's plea for a "wider human assessment" of the output of the economic system marks him clearly as a Ruskinian. For both Ruskin and Hobson the discipline of economics had to be moderated by a social ethic and brought under the umbrella of a broader science—the art or science of human welfare.

Hobson began his analysis by pointing to an inconsistency in orthodox economic thought:

> Though everybody agreed that consumption was the final goal, this goal, as such, was nobody's concern. When goods passed through the hands of farmers, manufacturers, and traders, into the hands of consumers, they seemed to pass out of the economic system into a destructive process that took place in privacy and obscurity. . . . [And though] consumption remained the formal end of economic processes, production was the real end.[45]

Such an ostrich attitude toward the problems of evaluating the worth of final consumption could only lead to further error, implied Hobson.

> Only so far as current tastes and appetites are reliable indices of human utility, only so far as we can identify the desired with the desirable, is the evolution of customary standards of life a sound human art. But it is needless to cite the ample evidence of the errors and wastes that are represented in every human standard of consumption.[46]

In order to obviate such errors Hobson attempted to dispel some of the "privacy and obscurity" that surrounded the consumption of economic products; as he perceived the task, "some further adjustment is needed to assess the desired in terms of the desirable."[47]

Hobson first rejected the approach taken by standard economic textbooks when dealing with consumer behavior. Hobson saw behind the façade of effective demand.

But a study primarily directed to the ascertainment and measurement of elasticity of demand, does not yet accord the disinterested valuations of consumptive processes required by a theory in which consumption is the "sole end." For consumption here only enters the economic field as a factor in markets and the determination of prices, not as the means of realizing the purpose of which the whole economic system is directed.[48]

In order to realize the purpose toward which the whole economic system is directed, Hobson had to determine what it was that was desirable, or, in other words, what was the Ultimate End by which the economic system could be orientated and measured. Hobson's favorite phrase for such an ideal was "organic welfare," about which he once added, "Though in form a mere synonym for good life, it is by usage both more restricted and more precise."[49] In another study he was concerned to show that organic welfare had both a materialistic component and a nonmaterial or artistic, spiritual component. "The organic conception of *mens sana in corpore sano* still stands as the first principle of human welfare. . . . It finds its justification in the truth so strongly enforced by Aristotle that we must first have a livelihood and then practise virtue."[50]

What contributes to a *mens sana in corpore sano?* More specifically, what contribution does the economic process make to a *mens sana in corpore sano?* As Hobson notes, we are immediately "confronted by the question how far the actual economic conduct, with its accompanying desires and gratifications, can be taken as a safe index of the desirable or organic welfare in its true sense." His response is that "we cannot assume a full identity of the income of an individual or a community, expressed in terms of current satisfactions, with that income expressed in terms of human welfare." This is so because "the total process of consumption-production may contain large elements of human waste or error, in that the tastes, desires, and satisfactions which actively stimulate this wealth creation may not conform to the desirable."[51] Later Hobson is more explicit in his condemnation of using the satisfaction of current consumers' effective demand as the Ultimate End of economics. "We cannot admit as the objective of economic activities either the yield of material goods which these activities produce, or the 'psychic income' which they yield as assessed in terms of current deservedness or satisfaction, without reference to their intrinsic desirability." Hobson then echoes Ruskin by immediately adding "A material or a psychic income may contain 'illth' as an alloy to its wealth."[52]

The notion of excess production appears next in Hobson's analysis. His declaration that "mechanical production can easily outrun organic consumption" reminds one of both Ruskin's concept of "acceptant capacity" and Sismondi's strictures of the political economists "who treat consumption as an unlimited force, always ready to devour an unlimited production."[53]

After surveying the results of actual consumption patterns and the economist's analysis of such consumer behavior, Hobson concludes that "it cannot be said that any adequate study either of the evolution of actual standards of consumption, or of 'desirable' standards, has yet been made." Hobson also indicated the reason for such failure:

> Though much attention has been given to the economy of expenditure in equalizing "marginal utilities," it has not been clearly recognized that the several margins are themselves determined by processes of utilitarian calculations based on balances of organic requirements.

In Hobson's mind, this failure to recognize the determination of the "several margins" is due, at least partly, to the fact that economists fail "to realize adequately that the organic nature of man necessarily stamps itself on his standard of consumption, and that, therefore, the various items of consumption must be studied as contributions toward the organic whole."[54]

Though Hobson never fully resolved in his own mind the absolute value of the items of consumption, he was unwilling to agree with the "popular thinking that is apt to brush aside the questions with the remark that values are matters of individual tastes, and *quot homines tot sententiae*."[55] Hobson considered such a position to be false because "we know that there exists a substantial body of agreement as to the main constituents of welfare, and even as to the order of their evaluation."[56]

From his analysis of consumption behavior Hobson discovered that an industrial economy has a built-in bias toward excessive production and consumption of economic goods. "This charge of materialism made against the more advanced industrial communities . . . based on an over-stimulation of certain instincts for physical satisfactions, due to the innovating tendencies of modern capitalism with its elaborated apparatus of selling pressures." This leads to an excess which is due to "a hasty exploitation of newly roused tastes that absorb too much of human nature in economic processes. 'Getting and spending, we lay waste our powers.'"[57]

"Getting and spending, we lay waste our powers" is the poet's lament over the philosophy of materialism that seems to be the inevitable consequence of an industrial economy in which narrow-minded and tunnel-visioned economists only describe a minute portion of the social canvas. Such economists never take off their blinders, and though they may peek from time to time to the left, they never look above to the Ultimate End.

Hobson's solution to combat this inherent bias toward excessive production is the following:

> Human energy, therefore, increasingly demands that half the power of mechanical production shall be applied, not to producing more goods but more leisure, that is to say, to so liberating the producer from the strain and burden of specialized production that he may become a skilled consumer, with leisure and energy enough at his free disposal to assimilate the slower gains of scientific production, instead of being overwhelmed by them, while at the same time bringing his harmonised economic standard of living into proper relations with the non-economic activities and satisfactions of his life. This seems impracti-

cable so long as profiteering rules the economic system. For the profit-maker can only gain his end either by working his machines and his workers to their full capacity, and turning out goods so rapidly that his skilled marketeers must induce the general body of workers to take their share in increased goods, not in increased leisure and other non-economic satisfactions, or by restrictions of output that give a wasteful or excessive leisure.[58]

As a fitting summation of J. A. Hobson's contribution to the analysis of wealth and the economic system which produces such wealth, and, at the same time, an introduction to the thought of Richard Henry Tawney, the noted economic historian and student of the current economic scene who will be the subject of the next section, we can quote a passage from Tawney's quite favorable review of Hobson's *Wealth and Life*.

The essence of humanism, perhaps, is the attitude which judges the externals of life by their effect in assisting or hindering the life of the spirit. It is the conviction that the machinery of existence—property and material wealth, and industrial organization, and the whole fabric and mechanism of social institutions—is to be regarded as means to an end, and that this end is the growth towards perfection of individual human beings. In this sense, Mr. Hobson is the greatest of economic humanists. Undisturbed by the roar of the wheels, he approaches the engine with questions most of us are too clever, or too superficial, to condescend to ask. What is the thing for? In what way do its impressive gyrations minister to the dignity and happiness of mankind?[59]

RICHARD H. TAWNEY (1880–1962)

During a period of introspection and reflection Richard H. Tawney made a long entry into his diary on July 12, 1913:

As long as individuals think the attainment of moderate material comfort the chief end of life, so long will governments plead as an excuse for not doing this or that that they cannot afford it. If modern England and America are right in believing that the principal aim of man, what should be taught to children, what should serve as a rough standard of merit, what merits approbation and respect, is the attainment of a moderate—or even immoderate—standard of comfort, and that moral questions arise only after this has been attained; then they must be content to go without religion, literature, art, and learning. These are not hard to find for those who really seek them, or who seek them first. But if they are sought second they are never found at all. . . .

What I mean is that the failure of society to make the changes which are obviously important when regarded in bulk is due to the fact that individually we all have a false philosophy of life. We assume that the greatest misfortune which can befall a man is poverty—and that conduct which leads to the sacrifice of income is unwise, impractical, etc.; in short that a man's life should be judged by its yield of income, and a nation's life by its production of wealth. . . .

But supposing unearned incomes, rents, etc. are pooled, will not the world, with its present philosophy, do anything but gobble them up and look up with an impatient grunt for more? That is the real question. It will not be faced in my lifetime because as long as the working classes believe, and believe rightly, that their mentors rob them, so long will they look on the restoration of the booty as *the* great reform, and will impatiently waive aside more fundamental issues, as a traveller robbed by a highwayman declines to be comforted by being told that money, after all, does not buy happiness. But when their masters are off their backs they will still have to face the fact that you must choose between less and more wealth and less and more civilization. . . .

When three or four hundred years hence mankind looks back on the absurd preoccupation of our age with economic issues with the same wonder as, and juster contempt than, we look back on the theological discussions of the middle ages, the names which they will reverence will be those of men who stood out against the prevalent fallacy that the most important problems were economic problems, and who taught men to conquer poverty by despising riches.[60]

Six years later, after being interrupted by World War I and its aftermath, Tawney returned to this question of the final end of the economic system. He published his conclusions in *The Acquisitive Society,* which became one of the most controversial books of the 1920s, calling on the British people to reform their fundamental philosophy of life.

These are times which are not ordinary, and in such times it is not enough to follow the road. It is necessary to know where it leads and, if it leads nowhere, to follow another. The search for another involves reflection, which is uncongenial to the bustling people who describe themselves as practical. . . . But the practical thing for a traveler who is uncertain of his path is not to proceed with the utmost rapidity in the wrong direction: it is to consider how to find the right one.[61]

Tawney next pointed out that the road upon which England's industrial and economic leaders were leading her—the philosophical road that viewed economic productivity as its own end—had been tried in the past and had been found wanting.

When they desire to place their economic life on a better foundation, they repeat, like parrots, the word "Productivity," because it is the word that rises first in their minds; regardless of the fact that productivity is the foundation on which it is based already, that increased productivity is the one achievement of the age before the war, as religion was of the Middle Ages or art of classical Athens, and that it is precisely in the century which has seen the greatest increase in productivity since the fall of the Roman Empire that economic discontent has been most acute.[62]

Increased productivity alone will not cause social ills to disappear. Such a response is based upon an illusion.

Hence the idea, which is popular with rich men, that industrial disputes would disappear if only the output of wealth were doubled, and every one were twice as well off, not only is refuted by all practical experience, but is in its very nature founded upon an illusion. For the question is one not of amounts but of proportions; and men will fight to be paid $120 a week, instead of $80, as readily as they will fight to be paid $20 instead of $16.[63]

Leaders whose faith is that "riches are not a means but an end" and who imply "that all economic activity is equally estimable, whether it is subordinated to a social purpose or not,"[64] are "like a man who, when he finds that his shoddy boots wear badly, orders a pair two sizes larger instead of a pair of good leather, or who makes up for putting a bad sixpence in the plate on Sunday by putting in a bad shilling the next."[65]

Tawney pointed out the direction of the correct path by harkening back to a central theme of Ruskin's:

> The purpose of industry is obvious. It is to supply man with things which are necessary, useful or beautiful, and thus to bring life to body or spirit. In so far as it is governed by this end, it is among the most important of human activities. In so far as it is diverted from it, it may be harmless, amusing, or even exhilarating to those who carry it on, but it possesses no more social significance than the orderly business of ants and bees, the strutting of peacocks, or the struggles of carnivorous animals over carrion.[66]

The true political economist realizes that "all rights . . . are conditional and derivative. . . . They are derived from the end or purpose of the society in which they exist."[67]

Tawney notes that such a frenetic rush to produce without any guiding ultimate principle creates a situation where "part of the goods which are annually produced, and which are called wealth, is strictly speaking, waste . . . [which] should not have been produced at all."[68] And to those who clamor for increased productivity as the solution to society's ills, Tawney responds "Would not 'Spend less on private luxuries' be as wise a cry as 'Produce more'?" To do so, however, would be "to admit that there is a principle superior to the mechanical play of economic forces . . . and thus to abandon the view that all riches, however composed, are an end, and that all economic activity is equally justifiable."[69]

Tawney continues by comparing "Prussian militarism" to "English industrialism." Both of these ideologies have killed the souls of men by allowing a subordinate social system to dominate their societies. "When the Press clamors that the one thing needed to make this island an Arcadia is productivity, and more productivity, and yet more productivity, that is Industrialism. It is the confusion of means with ends."[70]

Tawney concludes *The Acquisitive Society* by declaring that what English society needs, therefore, is a purpose, a principle of limitation. Such a principle of limitation would divide "what is worth doing from what is not, and settles the scale upon which what is worth doing ought to be done. . . . Above all, it assigns to economic activity itself its proper place as the servant, not the master, of society."[71]

This is not the place to review the historical portion of Tawney's *Religion and the Rise of Capitalism*,[72] but it is appropriate to our analysis to review the conclusions which Tawney drew from his historical studies. J. D. Chambers has succinctly summarized the importance of Tawney's findings:

> As is well known, Tawney's main preoccupation was with the secularization of traditional Christian values in the sixteenth and seventeenth centuries—the

greatest secular event, he considered, in the history of Western civilization. It was the first step, in Tawney's view, on the way to the establishment of an acquisitive society based on competition, individualism, and the divine right of self-aggrandisement on the assumption that what is good for one is, in the long run, good for all.[73]

In the concluding chapter of *Religion and the Rise of Capitalism* Tawney returns to many of the concerns that had troubled him in the opening pages of *The Acquisitive Society*. He quotes Berkeley's aphorism "Whatever the world thinks, he who has not much meditated upon God, the human mind and the *summum bonum* may possibly make a thriving earthworm, but will most indubitably make a sorry patriot and a sorry statesman." He continues by noting that

> the most obvious facts are the most easily forgotten. Both the existing economic order, and too many of the projects advanced for reconstructing it, break down through their neglect of the truism that, since even quite common men have souls, no increase in material wealth will compensate them for arrangements which insult their self-respect and impair their freedom.[74]

Making economic wealth its own end, Tawney points out, goes against the thrust of much of history.

> The distinction made by the philosophers of classical antiquity between liberal and servile occupations, the medieval insistence that riches exist for man, not man for riches, Ruskin's famous outburst, "there is no wealth but life," . . . are different attempts to emphasize the instrumental character of economic activities by reference to an ideal which is held to express the true nature of man.[75]

As we conclude our review of Tawney's analysis of the function of wealth and the economic system, we are led around to the question of what is the "true nature of man." Though Tawney never defined the nature of man in so many words, late in his life he remarked that man, "as known to history, is a religious animal." And he considered modern industrialism and capitalism not as irreligious but as counterreligious with their "idolatry of riches and the idolatry of power."[76] In his diary he had written some twenty years earlier: "If it be asked what is your criterion: why do you condemn this and approve that? I answer that the standard which we apply is really a transcendental, religious, or mystical one."[77] The important thing for Tawney was not to define precisely the ideal—such an achievement was clearly impossible in any total or definitive sense—but to recognize the need to acknowledge the primary importance of such a standard or principle. As he wrote, ideals of religion, art, and understanding "are not hard to find for those who really seek them, or who seek them first. But if they are sought second they are never found at all." Indubitably, Tawney sought them first. Perhaps that is why another eminent British economic historian, T. S. Ashton, was able to write of Tawney that "students who had the good fortune to sit at his feet rose with the sense of having been in touch not only with scholarship, but with wisdom."[78]

CONCLUSION

Why could Professor Ashton conclude that students of Tawney were in touch not only with scholarship, but also with wisdom? Wisdom—what is it? In our Western epistemological tradition the most important key to wisdom, the understanding of reality, has been the concept of causation. As Aristotle stated, "Men do not think that they know a thing till they have grasped the 'why' of it." Aristotle pursued this investigation by showing that there are four conceptually distinct and essential causes for every rational human activity utilizing material resources; the *causa materialis,* the *causa efficiens,* the *causa formalis,* and the *causa finalis.* An example is the building of a house wherein the wood and other materials are the *causa materialis,* the carpenter's labor and the tools are the *causa efficiens,* the blueprint or plan in the carpenter's mind is the *causa formalis,* and the desire to have a home for shelter and comfort is the *causa finalis.* To fully understand this act of building home, one would have to investigate all four of these causes. Were the most satisfactory materials used? Were the carpenter and his tools efficient? Did he have a good plan or blueprint? Was his final goal consistent with the needs of his nature? All such questions are relevant to understanding this activity.

This same methodological approach has to be used when a social scientist investigates the economic system with the intention of fully comprehending it. In current methodology, however, in economics as well as in other theoretical sciences, two of the types of causes advanced by Aristotle have been largely omitted: the *causa materialis* and the *causa finalis.*[79] In its search for understanding and its quest for reform, economics has tended to utilize only the *causa efficines* and the *causa formalis,* and of these two it has emphasized the *causa efficiens* much more than the *causa formalis.* More accurately, the *causa formalis* is often submerged by the *causa efficiens.* As Phyllis Colvin has remarked, "theoretical science tends to meld these two fundamentals of explanation, concentrating far more on the *causa efficiens* than on the *causa formalis.*"[80] "Doing" becomes its own justification. We no longer ask "Doing what?", even less do we explore "Doing what for what?" or analyze the consequences of "Doing what for what and with what?"

To attempt to investigate the economic system of reasonable purposive beings and to neglect the *causa materialis* and *causa finalis* of such a system while merging the *causa formalis* into the *causa efficiens* would have appeared to Aristotle to be shirking one's intellectual responsibility and to ensure that one would end up with the most dangerous kind of knowledge —half-knowledge or, more accurately, quarter-knowledge.

The four economists reviewed in this study were aware of this limitation of much economic analysis, this blindered vision, and they endeavored to broaden the perspective of economists so that they would have to include a critical study of the *causa finalis* of the economic system within their analysis. They realized that only that analysis which can lead to appropriate *causa finalis* is destined to give satisfaction in fruition since only the appropriate *causa finalis* gives a fundamental unity to the problem of human behavior. Because of the loss of an appropriate *causa finalis,* there is an unsatisfied craving in modern man. Since he has lost control of the direction of himself, he attempts to regain what he has lost by an inordinate and frantic search for those commodities which will stimulate his senses and thus temporarily quiet his sense of lost direction, or by seeking that power which allows one to control the lives of others. This control over other things and other people becomes a surrogate for having control of one's own life. Lacking the power and ability (and the will) to submit the direction of one's own life to an appropriate final goal, one seeks the false remedy of gaining power over things and persons. Economic production and power become their own ends. In so doing, modern man aggravates, rather than resolves, the sickness of society. It is only by returning to first principles, to a study of man and his appropriate final goal, that this sickness can be healed. As R. G. Hawtrey has noted, "Even in exploring human motives and behavior a cognizance of right ends is the foundation of firm and confident conclusions."[81] If such an exploration of the appropriate *causa finalis* is omitted, then although one may show much scholarship by manipulating vast amounts of data with precision and rigor in the largest of computer models, one can question whether it leads to wisdom. Are our students in touch with scholarship or with wisdom?

NOTES

1. Frank Knight, *The Economic Organization* (Harper & Row, 1933), p. 4.

2. Tibor Scitovsky, *The Joyless Economy* (Oxford University Press, 1976), p. 236.

3. See Kenneth Boulding, *The Image: Knowledge in Life and Society* (University of Michigan Press, 1956) for a thorough discussion of the important role that such images play in society.

4. Warren J. Samuels, "Normative Premises in Regulatory Theory," *Journal of Post Keynesian Economics* 1 (1978):112.

5. J. C. L. Simonde de Sismondi, *Nouveaux principes d' économie politique ou de la richesse dans ses rapports avec la population,* 2nd ed. (Paris, 1827), vol. II, p. 434. (Translation by the author.)

6. *Nouveaux principes,* I, p. 20.

7. J. C. L. Simonde de Sismondi, *Etudes sur l'Economie politique* (Paris,1837–38), vol. I, p. 4. (Translation by the author.)

8. *Nouveaux principes,* II, p. 140.

9. J. R. McCulloch, "The Opinions of Messrs. Say, Sismondi, and Malthus, on the Effects of Machinery and Accumulation, Stated and Examined," Edinburgh Review 35 (1821):106–107. See also J. B. Say, *A Treatise of Political Economy* (1834), pp. 139, 140n.

10. *Nouveaux principes*, I, pp. 55–56.

11. *Nouveaux principes*, I, pp. 75–76.

12. *Nouveaux principes*, I, p. 79.

13. *Etudes sur l'Economie politique*, I, p. 27.

14. *Etudes sur l'Economie politique*, I, pp. 60–62.

15. *Etudes sur l'Economie politigue*, I, pp. 60–62.

16. "Extracts from the Private Journal and Letters of M. de Sismondi," *Political Economy and the Philosophy of Government: A Series of Essays from the Words of M. de Sismondi*, translated and edited by an anonymous author (London, 1847), pp. 450–451.

17. J. S. Mill, *The Principles of Political Economy* (1915 edition), p. 751.

18. "Our large trading cities bear to me very nearly the aspect of monastic establishments in which the roar of the millwheel and the crane takes the place of other devotional music; and in which the worship of Mammon or Moloch is conducted with a tender reverence and an exact propriety; the merchant rising to his Mammon matins with the self-denial of an anchorite, and expiating the frivolities into which he may be beguiled in the course of the day by late attendance at Mammom vespers." "A Joy For Ever," in *Works of Ruskin*, ed. by E. T. Cook and Alexander Wedderburn. (London: G. Allen, 1903–1912), vol. VI, p. 138.

19. Asa Briggs, *The Making of Modern England: 1783–1867* (New York, 1959), p. 401.

20. "Unto This Last," in *Works of Ruskin*, vol. XVII, p. 85.

21. "A Joy For Ever," in *Works of Ruskin*, vol. XVI, p. 134.

22. "The Economist of Xenephon," in *Works of Ruskin*, vol. XXXI, p. 27.

23. "The Economist of Xenephon," in *Works of Ruskin*, vol. XXXI, pp. 38–39.

24. "Munera Pulveris," in *Works of Ruskin*, vol. XVII, p. 168.

25. "Unto This Last," in *Works of Ruskin*, vol. XVII, pp. 87–88.

26. *Works of Ruskin*, vol. XVIII, p. 412.

27. "Munera Pulveris," in *Works of Ruskin*, vol. XVII, p. 144.

28. "Munera Pulveris," pp. 277–278.

29. *Works of Ruskin*, vol. XVII, p. xlvii.

30. "Time and Tide," in *Works of Ruskin*, vol. XVII, p. 322.

31. James C. Sherburne, *John Ruskin or the Ambiguities of Abundance* (Harvard University Press, 1972), p. 277.

32. Quoted in Preface to vol. XVII of *Works of Ruskin*, p. xxxi.

33. F. J. Stimson, "Ruskin as Political Economist," *Quarterly Journal of Economics* 2 (1888):74–109.

34. John A. Hobson, *John Ruskin: Social Reformer* (London, 1898).

35. Eric Gill, "John Ruskin," *It All Goes Together: Selected Essays* (New York, 1944), pp. 45–47.

36. Patrick Geddes, *John Ruskin: Economist* (Edinburgh, 1884).

37. See Frederick Soddy, *Wealth, Virtual Wealth and Debt* (London, 1933), pp. 93 ff.

38. R. H. Tawney, "John Ruskin," *Observer* (February 19, 1919). Reprinted in *The Radical Tradition*, ed. Rita Hinden (London, 1966), pp. 42–46.

39. See the introduction by Richard T. Ely in the 1901 edition of *Unto This Last* edited by Richard T. Ely. The copy of Ruskin's *Munera Pulveris* that was owned by Richard T. Ely (now in the possession of Louisiana State University) shows many jottings in Ely's handwriting.

40. G. K. Chesterton, *Poems of Ruskin with an Essay by the Author* (London: G. Routledge, 1906).

41. Jean Autret, *L'influence de Ruskin sur la vie, les idées et l'oeuvre de Marcel Proust (Genève, 1955)*.

42. Elizabeth T. McLaughlin, *Ruskin and Gandhi* (Bucknell University Press, 1974).

43. John A. Hobson, *Wealth and Life: A Study in Values* (London, 1929), p. viii.

44. Ewald T. Grether, "John Ruskin–John A. Hobson," in *Essays in Social Economics*, ed. Ewald T. Grether et al. (Freeport, N.Y., 1935), p. 163.

45. *Wealth and Life*, pp. 301–302.

46. *Wealth and Life*, p. 328.

47. *Wealth and Life*, p. vii. For Hobson the words *desired* and *desirable* had important and precise, though quite different, meanings. *Desired* signified what consumers actually wanted. *Desirable* stood for what they *should* want.

48. *Wealth and Life*, pp. 304–306.

49. John A. Hobson, *Work and Wealth: A Human Evaluation* (New York: Macmillan, 1914), p. 12.

50. *Wealth and Life*, p. 47.

51. *Wealth and Life*, pp. xxiii–xxiv.

52. *Wealth and Life*, p. 130.

53. *Nouveaux principes* I, p. 76.

54. *Wealth and Life*, p. 305. Hobson would undoubtedly appreciate the recent book by Tibor Scitovsky, *The Joyless Economy: An Inquity into Human Satisfaction and Consumer Dissatisfaction* (see note 2), which can be viewed precisely as a study of the standards of consumption and their contributions to man's "organic whole."

55. However many individuals, that many ideas.

56. *Wealth and Life*, p. 51.

57. *Wealth and Life*, p. 309.

58. *Wealth and Life*, p. 339.

59. R. H. Tawney, "Book Review of *Wealth and Life* by J. A. Hobson," *The Political Quarterly* I (1930):276–277.

60. *R. H. Tawney's Commonplace Book*, ed. J. M. Winter and D. M. Joslin (Cambridge, England: Cambridge University Press, 1972), pp. 60–62.

61. R. H. Tawney, *The Acquisitive Society* (New York, 1920) p. 2.

62. *The Acquisitive Society*, p. 62.

63. *The Acquisitive Society*, p. 42.

64. *The Acquisitive Society*, p. 37.

65. *The Acquisitive Society*, p. 5.

66. *The Acquisitive Society*, p. 8.

67. *The Acquisitive Society*, p. 51.

68. *The Acquisitive Society*, pp. 37–38.

69. *The Acquisitive Society*, p. 39.

70. *The Acquisitive Society*, p. 46.

71. *The Acquisitive Society*, pp. 182–183.

72. For such a review, see C. K. Wilber, "The 'New' Economic History Reexamined: R. H. Tawney on the Origins of Capitalism," *American Journal of Economics and Sociology* 33 (1974):249–258.

73. J. D. Chambers, "The Tawney Tradition," *Economic History Review* 24 (1971):356.

74. R. H. Tawney, *Religion and the Rise of Capitalism* (New York: Mentor, 1954), p. 233.

75. Tawney, *Religion and the Rise of Capitalism*, p. 233.

76. "A Note on Christianity and the Social Order" in *The Attack and Other Papers* (London, 1953), p. 191.

77. *R. H. Tawney's Commonplace Book*, p. 64.

78. T. S. Ashton, "Richard Henry Tawney (1880–1962)," *Proceedings of the British Academy* 48 (1962):479.

79. See Phyllis Colvin, "Ontological and Epistemological Commitments and Social Relations in the Sciences," in *The Social Production of Scientific Knowledge*, ed. E. Mendelsohn, P. Weingart, and R. Whitley (Boston, 1977), pp. 103–129. Also see Nicholas Georgescu-Roegen, *The Entropy Law and the Economic Process*, pp. 182–191 for an analysis of why the social sciences have neglected the study of the *causa finalis* and the harm that has resulted from such neglect. As for Georgescu-Roegen's appreciation for the importance of the *causa materialis*, one could argue that the whole point of *The Entropy Law and the Economic Process* was to show the need for including the *causa materialis* in one's economic analysis. What else is low-entropy matter-energy except the basic *causa materialis* of an economy?

Alfred N. Whitehead has expressed somewhat the same opinion: "For instance, the enterprises produced by the individualistic energy of the European people presuppose physical action directed to final causes. But the science which is employed in their development is based on a philosophy which asserts that physical causation is supreme and which disjoins the physical cause from the end." *Science and the Modern World*, p. 111.

80. Colvin, "Ontological and Epistemological Commitments," p. 109.

81. R. G. Hawtrey, "The Need for Faith," *The Economic Journal* 56 (1946):364.

15

ON ECONOMICS
AS A LIFE SCIENCE

Herman E. Daly

There is no wealth but life.
JOHN RUSKIN

All flesh is grass.
ISAIAH 40:6

I. INTRODUCTION

The purpose of this essay is to bring together some of the more salient similarities between biology and economics and to argue that, far from being superficial, these analogies are profoundly rooted in the fact that the ultimate subject matter of biology and economics is *one,* viz., *the life process.* Most of biology concentrates on the "within skin" life process, the exception being ecology, which focuses on the "outside skin" life process (Bates, 1960, pp. 12–13). Economics is the part of ecology which studies the outside-skin life process insofar as it is dominated by *commodities* and their interrelations. In

Reprinted by permission from *Journal of Political Economy,* Vol. 76, no. 3, May/June 1968, pp. 392–406.

what follows the traditional economic (outside skin) and the traditional biological (within skin) views of the total life process will be considered, both in their *steady-state* aspect and in their *evolutionary* aspect. Finally an approach to a more general "general equilibrium" model will be suggested by considering the human economy from an ecological perspective.

II. BIOLOGICAL ANALOGIES IN ECONOMICS

Analogy is so fundamental to our way of thinking that the ability to recognize analogies is generally considered one of the criteria of intelligence. While there is a vast difference between analogy on the one hand and logical proof and empirical verification on the other, it by no means follows that the former belongs only to poetry and not to science. Analogy is the essence of the inductive side of science. Furthermore, the dominant mode of thought in economics today is the "analytical simile" (Georgescu-Roegen, 1966, pp. 114–24), the mathematical or geometric model based on a Pythagorean analogy between fuzzy, dialectical reality and well-defined, analytic number. The fruitfulness of this analogy for all science is obvious—but it is an analogy nonetheless, with its roots in the same insight which inspired the mystical Pythagorean brotherhood. That economists have also found biological analogies useful is only slightly less obvious. The circular flow of blood and the circular flow of money, the many parallel phenomena of specialization, exchange, interdependence, homoeostasis, and evolution are well known. In the opposite direction, economic analogies in biology are also common, as witnessed by Malthus' influence on Darwin and by the very etymology of the word "ecology." Finally, an ultimately central place for biological analogies in economics has been claimed by no less an authority than Alfred Marshall in this famous statement, "The Mecca of the economist lies in economic biology rather than in economic dynamics" (Marshall, 1920, Preface, p. 14), and in his further statement that "in the later stages of economics, when we are approaching nearly to the conditions of life, biological analogies are to be preferred to mechanical" (Marshall, 1925, p. 317). Among current economic theorists it would appear that only the works of Kenneth Boulding (1950, 1958, 1966) and Nicholas Georgescu-Roegen (1966) (both freely drawn upon here) reveal a disposition to take Marshall seriously on this point.

Perhaps the intellectual genealogy of the ideas to be developed in this paper can be more specifically indicated by a pair of quotations from two seminal thinkers of the early part of this century—one a biologist (A. J. Lotka) and the other an economist (J. A. Hobson).

Lotka (1956) informs us that

> underlying our economic manifestations are biological phenomena which we share in common with other species; and . . . the laying bare and clearly

formulating of the relations thus involved—in other words the analysis of the biophysical foundations of economics—is one of the problems coming within the program of physical biology.

Just what these "biophysical foundations" are, and how they support the economic superstructure, is in large part the subject of Section V.

From Hobson (1929) we learn that

> all serviceable organic activities consume tissue and expend energy, the biological costs of the services they render. Though this economy may not correspond in close quantitative fashion to a pleasure and pain economy or to any conscious valuation, it must be taken as the groundwork for that conscious valuation. For most economic purposes we are well-advised to prefer the organic test to any other test of welfare, bearing in mind that many organic costs do not register themselves easily or adequately in terms of conscious pain or disutility, while organic gains are not always interpretable in conscious enjoyment.

The "groundwork for conscious valuation" and the "organic test of welfare" are ideas with close counterparts in Section III, to which we now turn.

III. THE STEADY-STATE ANALOGY

The close similarity of the basic within-skin life process of metabolism (anabolism and catabolism) with the outside-skin life process of economics (production and consumption) is evident from Figure 15.1.

In either process the only *material* output is *waste*. The purpose (value produced) of the metabolic process is the maintenance of life. The purpose (value produced) of the economic process is the maintenance and enjoyment of life. An accounting balance equation of the life process in value terms would state that the value of life enjoyment plus the value of material waste (zero) equals the sum of the values of all the matter and energy upon which the total life process is based. The total value of life (our subjective estimate thereof) is *imputed* to the total quantity of things necessary for its enjoyable maintenance.[1] The Austrian economists have taught us that this imputation also determines the *relative* values (prices) of individual things according to the principle of diminishing marginal utility, which for Böhm-Bawerk was "the key-stone of all economic theory" (1891, p. 149). Since commodities are priced according to their diminishing marginal utilities, the sum of all goods in the economy valued at their marginal utilities (or prices) would be very small relative to the total utility of all goods (total life value), which is probably infinite.[2] The infinite difference between the finite sum of prices of all goods and the infinite sum of total utility of all goods is an infinite "global consumers' surplus." Hence, insofar as economics concentrates on value in exchange (marginal utility) to the exclusion of value in use (total utility)—to that extent it is concerning itself with only an infinitesimal portion of total life value. This is not meant to minimize the importance of exchange values, since it is

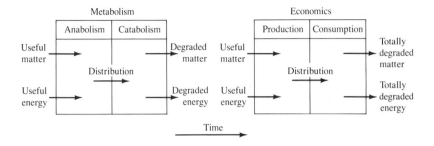

FIGURE 15.1

precisely by considering margins that we maximize totals. The point is that, while margins are reliable means for *maximizing* totals, they are very treacherous means for *evaluating* totals, as any student who has pondered the diamonds-water paradox must realize. Any sort of economic numerology which, with one-eyed devotion to Pythagoras, insists on glossing over this treachery deserves a thorough dunking in the satirical acid of Jonathan Swift's *A Modest Proposal*.[3] Perhaps Hobson's "organic test of welfare" is simply the idea that it is better to make imprecise statements about unmeasurable but relevant magnitudes (use value, total utility) than to make more precise statements about the measurable but irrelevant magnitude (for evaluating total welfare) of exchange value. Economists shy away from thinking too much about total utility mainly because it is unmeasurable and dependent on value judgments—both embarrassing for a "positive science." But perhaps, as Joan Robinson suggests (1962, p. 54), this aversion to total utility also stems from its tendency to make one question "an economic system in which so much of the good juice of utility is allowed to evaporate out of commodities by distributing them unequally"; furthermore "this egalitarian element in the doctrine was sterilized mainly by slipping from utility to physical output as the object to be maximized." But as we have seen, the ultimate *physical* output of the economic process is waste, and there is no sense in maximizing that!

There is also a balance equation of the life process in physical units, based on the law of conservation of matter-energy. But more significant than the physical balance, from an economic viewpoint, is the one-way, non-circular, irreversible nature of the flow of matter-energy through all divisions of the life process. Since useful (low-entropy) matter-energy is apparently finite, the total life process could be brought to a halt by what Boulding has called "the entropy trap." Thus one of the ultimate natural sources of scarcity, and hence of economic activity, is the second law of thermodynamics (Georgescu-Roegen, 1966, pp. 66–82). Indeed, if one were perversely to insist on a real-cost theory of value, it would seem that entropy, rather than labor or energy, should be the source of value. Even in the subjective theory of value, however, entropy, the common denominator of all forms of scarcity, determines the locations of the margins and hence enters into the determination of marginal utilities and exchange values.

Erwin Schroedinger (1945) has described life as a system in steady-state thermodynamic disequilibrium which maintains its constant distance from equilibrium (death) by feeding on low entropy from its environment—that is, by exchanging high-entropy outputs for low-entropy inputs. *The same statement would hold verbatim as a physical description of the economic process.* A corollary of this statement is that an organism cannot live in a medium of its own waste products. With this principle in mind, one can better appreciate the significance of the following recent observation by J. J. Spengler (1966) in his presidential address to the American Economic Association, "Witness here in America the endless dumping of trash (four pounds per person per day). . . . Indeed, some hold, J. K. Galbraith had better labeled ours an effluent society than an affluent one." This four pounds per person per day does not disappear —it becomes a part of the physical environment in which we must live. Great stress has been put on the reciprocal nature of the relation of fitness between organism and environment by L. J. Henderson (1958). If the organism fits the environment, then it is also the case that the environment is fit for the organism. Henderson argues that there must have been some not-yet-understood process of physical evolution prior to the emergence of life in order for the environment to attain the rather exacting preconditions for supporting life. Thus man's newly acquired ability to degrade his material environment at the rate of four pounds per person per day is likely to be even more dangerous than commonly realized, in view of our ignorance of ecological relations.

How do the economic and metabolic processes fit together? Clearly metabolism is partly contained within the economic subprocess of consumption. Many of the material inputs into metabolism are economic products, and some outputs of metabolism are generally not totally degraded and thus can be further consumed—for example, manure fertilizer and carbon dioxide. But the ultimate physical output of the economic process *is* totally degraded matter-energy, in Marx's term, "devil's dust." Continuing in Chinese-box fashion, the total economic process is itself a subprocess on the consuming side of the total ecological life process, the producing side of the latter consisting mainly of photosynthesis carried on by green plants, which draw their inputs from the physical environment of air, soil, water, and sunlight.

Both the within-skin and outside-skin life processes have a permanently maintained physical basis which undergoes continual replacement over relatively short time periods (steady-state aspect) and which is capable of qualitative change and reorganization over long periods (evolutionary aspect). In other words "capital" represents "exosomatic organs" and biological organs represent "endosomatic capital." In each case, we observe both short-term depreciation and replacement and long-term technological change. Physical capital is essentially matter that is capable of trapping energy and channeling it to human purposes. Hence, in a very real sense the entire physical environment is capital, since it is only through the agency of air, soil, and water that plant life is able to capture the solar energy upon which the whole hierarchy of life (and value) depends. Should not these elements receive the same care we bestow upon our other machines? And is not any theory of value that leaves them out rather like a theory of icebergs that fails to consider the submerged 90 per cent?

IV. THE EVOLUTIONARY ANALOGY

The material basis of the life process grows when the rate of production (anabolism) exceeds the rate of consumption (catabolism). Growth merges into development as alteration in the rates of increase of different parts give rise to new proportions, new qualitative relations, and new technologies. Although development is not well understood by either science, the subtle influence of size on organization has led both biologists and economists to the concept of a proper or optimum scale for a given organizational plan. That Marx, who emphasized this dialectic interplay of quantity and quality, also tended to view economics as a part of natural history is evident in the following quotation (1967, I, 372):

> Darwin has interested us in the history of Nature's Technology, that is, in the formation of the organs of plants and animals, which organs serve as instruments of production for sustaining life. Does not the history of the productive organs of man, of organs that are the material basis of all social organization, deserve equal attention?

The same idea has been expressed by Lotka (1956, p. 208), viz., "Man's industrial activities are merely a highly specialized and greatly developed form of the general biological struggle for existence," and further in a passage (1956, p. 369) that would have pleased Marx:

> The most singular feature of the artificial extensions of our natural body is that they are shared in common by a number of individuals. When the sick man consults the physician, who, we will say, makes a microscopic examination, for example, the patient is virtually hiring a pair of high power eyes. When you drop a nickel into a telephone box, you are hiring the use of an ear to listen to your friend's voice five or ten miles distant. When the workingman accepts a wage of forty dollars for his weekly labor, he is in fact paying to his employers an undetermined amount for the privilege of using his machines as artificial members to manufacture marketable wares.
> The modern development of artificial aids to our organs and faculties has exerted two opposing influences.
> On the one hand, it has in a most real way bound men together into one body: so very real and material is the bond that society might aptly be described as one huge multiple Siamese twin.
> On the other hand, since the control over certain portions of this common body is unevenly distributed among the separate individuals, certain of them may be said in a measure to own parts of the bodies of others, holding them a species of

refined slavery, and though neither of the two parties concerned may be clearly conscious of the fact, it is often resented in a more or less vague way by the one less favored.

In biological evolution genes transmit the "knowledge" of organic forms over time, and gene mutations introduce occasional modifications, resulting in the success of the forms best suited to the environment. In economic evolution, culture transmits knowledge over time, and new ideas produce mutant organizations from which competition again determines the fittest. Indeed, Teilhard de Chardin (1959) argues that "cultural evolution" is simply a new evolutionary mechanism that superseded the old mechanism in importance.

A natural history of economic evolution might be built around the theme of "economic surplus" and its progressive growth and cultivation. The original surplus was produced by plants, since they capture more solar energy than that necessary for their own maintenance. Animal life depends on this surplus, and perhaps man's greatest discovery was that he could cultivate and expand that upon which his existence depended, thus "exploiting niggardly nature."[4]

As soon as this primary activity became efficient enough to produce a surplus above the maintenance needs of those engaged in primary production, it became possible to evolve secondary economic activities, etc. Although economic activity moves far away from direct contact with nature, the "biophysical foundations of economics" remain ever present in the background, and it is to these foundations that we now direct our attention.

V. THE HUMAN ECONOMY IN ECOLOGICAL PERSPECTIVE

Although the life process is essentially one, it seems that for many analytical purposes the most convenient boundary by which to divide the process is the natural boundary of skin. The outside-skin life process is the subject of ecology, but ecologists abstract from the human economy and study only natural interdependences, while economists abstract from nature and consider only interdependences among commodities and man. But what discipline systematically studies the interdependences which clearly exist between the natural and human parts of the outside-skin life process? Marston Bates, a biologist, addresses himself to this point in the following quotation (1960, p. 247):

> Then we come to man and his place in the system of life. We could have left man out, playing the ecological game of "let's pretend man doesn't exist." But this seems an unfair as the corresponding game of the economists, "let's pretend that nature doesn't exist." The economy of nature and ecology of man are inseparable and attempts to separate them are more than misleading, they are dangerous. Man's destiny is tied to nature's destiny and the arrogance of the engineering mind does not change this. Man may be a very peculiar animal, but he is still a part of the system of nature.

Any attempt to isolate a segment of reality is always somewhat misleading, but not for that reason less necessary. Our purposes dictate the manner in which we abstract from reality, and as economists well know, many useful purposes can be served by partial analysis—that is, studying one industry in abstraction from its matrix of interconnections with the rest of the economy. While this is a useful procedure for studying the peanut industry, no economist would want to study the automobile industry under such limitations. Too many important feedbacks from the rest of the economy would be left out. Until recently the economy of man was "peanuts" in the total economy of nature. Now it is more like the automobile industry, and to continue *ceteris paribus* treatment of nature (even in general-equilibrium analysis) is indeed dangerous to our purpose if that purpose is to say something about how human wants can best be served.

A rather dramatic example of this kind of danger has been indicated by Dr. Edward Teller (1965), who pointed out that since the Industrial Revolution the tremendous consumption of carbon fuels has resulted in an increased concentration of carbon dioxide in the atmosphere. Since this gas increases the heat retention of the atmosphere, thus raising the average temperature, it may well be that the ultimate effect of the Industrial Revolution will be the melting of the polar ice cap and the inundation of large parts of the world. The more concrete case of the unintentional destruction wrought on the environment by chemical insecticides has been forcefully documented by Rachel Carson (1962). Also, we know that the entire chain of life depends heavily on bacteria —for example, nitrogen fixation and decomposition of dead organisms. Is it not possible that some export from the human economy (for example, detergents) could prove lethal to certain of these organisms? Conversely, might not some human exports be highly beneficial to the propagation of particular disease-causing bacteria? And one need only mention the problem of radioactive fallout. At a less dramatic but increasingly serious level, we have ubiquitous instances of air and water pollution plaguing the world's cities, not to mention the problems of deforestation, soil erosion, and noise.

Such phenomena have long been recognized (grudgingly) in economic theory under the heading of *externalities*—that is, interrelations whose connecting links are external to the economists' abstract world of commodities but very much internal to the world in which we live, move, and have our being. Perhaps "non-market interdependence" is a more descriptive term.

It would be easy to liken this concept to a *deus ex machina* lowered into the scene by our theoretical playwrights to save an awkward plot, but it is by no means easy to suggest a better treatment. A better treatment is called for, however, since externalities are spending more time on center stage and less time in the wings than previously. Or, changing the metaphor, to continue theoretical development via continued ad hoc introduction of externalities is reminiscent of adding epicycles and in the long run will lead only to Ptolemaic complications in economic theory. Our economic cosmos is not one of uniform circular motion of commodities among men but one of eliptical orbits through interdependent ecological sectors.

How does one integrate the world of commodities into the larger economy of nature? Perhaps this is a problem in which economics can provide a useful analogy. Leontief's input-output model has proved useful in dealing with phenomena of interdependence, and it may offer the most promising analytical framework within which to consider the above question.[5] Just as the annual flow of gross national product, or *final* commodities, requires a supporting matrix of flows of *intermediate* commodities, so does the annual flow of all economic commodities (final and intermediate) require a supporting matrix of flows of physical things which carry no price tag but nonetheless are necessary complements to the flows of those things which do carry price tags.

In its simplest input-output representation the total economy can be divided into its human and non-human sectors, as in Table 15.1.

Cell or quadrant (2) is the domain of traditional economics, that is, the study of inputs and outputs to and from various subsectors within the human-to-human box. Cell (4) represents the traditional area of concern of ecology, the inputs to and outputs from subsectors in the non-human–to–non-human box. Cells (1) and (3), respectively, contain the flows of inputs from human subsectors to non-human subsectors and from non-human subsectors to human subsectors. All of the items exchanged in (2) are *economic commodities,* by which we mean that they have positive prices. All items of exchange in cells (1), (3), and (4) may by contrast be labeled *ecological commodities,* which consist of free goods (zero price) and "bads" (negative price). The negative price on bads is not generally observed, since there usually exists the alternative of exporting the bad to the non-human economy, which cannot pay the negative price (that is, charge us a positive price for the service of taking the "bad" off our hands, as would be the case if it were transferred to another sector of the human economy). Ecological commodities that are bads are bad in relation to man, not necessarily to the non-human world. The difficulty, however, is that these more than gratuitous exports from the human economy in cell (1) are simultaneously inputs to the non-human economy and as such strongly influence the outputs from the non-human back to the human sector —that is, cell (1) is connected to cell (3) via cell (4), and cell (3) directly influences human welfare.[6] These relationships will perhaps be more evident in Table 15.2, which is an expansion of Table 15.1, with the four quadrants corresponding to the quadrants of Table 15.1. Note that in both tables the basic vision is still a "world of commodities," although a bigger world that now includes both economic commodities (the q_{ij} in quadrant (2)) and ecological commodities (the q_{ij} in quadrants (1), (3), and (4)). The q_{ij} in quadrants (1), (3), and (4) are the "biophysical foundations of economics."

In Table 15.2, quadrant (2) is the simplest form of the usual Leontief input-output table, with two transforming sectors (agriculture and industry) and one primary sector (households). Agriculture consists of living transform-

TABLE 15.1

	To	
From	Human	Non-human
Human	(2)	(1)
Non-human . . .	(3)	(4)

ers of matter-energy, and industry consists of non-living transformers of matter-energy. The non-human economy has likewise been divided into the "transforming sectors" of animal, plant, and bacteria (living sectors) and of atmosphere, hydrosphere, and lithosphere (non-living sectors). In addition, in row 10 we have a primary-service sector providing the ultimate source of low-entropy matter-energy, the sun, and, in column (10), the great thermodynamic sink into which finally consumed high-entropy matter-energy goes, forever degraded as devil's dust.[7] The annual flow of low entropy consists of direct solar energy currently received, plus a running down of the stock of low entropy that came from the sun in the distant past. The table records the passage of low-entropy matter-energy through its life-supporting input-output transformations into high-entropy waste. These transformations are not all known or understood, but certainly the scope they offer for non-market interdependence far exceeds the standard examples of externalities in the literature, "somewhat bucolic in nature, having to do with bees, orchards and woods" (Scitovsky, 1954).

Table 15.2 has thus far been considered only as a descriptive catalogue for economically filing vast amounts of information about the exchanges of economic and ecological commodities making up the total economy of life. Any realistic table would probably have to have at least one hundred sectors, and the resulting ten thousand cells would be pigeonholes for storing measured data about the ten thousand most important exchanges in the total economy of life. Would it be possible to convert the table from a descriptive and heuristic device to statistical tool, a matrix of technical coefficients useful for planning and prediction—that is, could one do with the whole table what Leontief has done with quadrant (2)?

Each row of Table 15.2 can be stated as a physical balance equation, thus:

$$\sum_{j=1}^{n} q_{ij} = Q_i; \quad i = 1, \ldots, n,$$

where i = row and j = column.

Technical coefficients could be defined as $a_{ij} = q_{ij}/Q_j$.

The a_{ij} in quadrant (2) are the usual technical coefficients of the Leontief system, and the a_{ij} in the remaining quadrants are natural technical coeffi-

TABLE 15.2

Output from	Input to										Total
	Agri-culture (1)	Industry (2)	Households (final consumption) (3)	Ani-mal (4)	Plant (5)	Bac-teria (6)	Atmosphere (7)	Hydro-sphere (8)	Litho-sphere (9)	Sink (final consumption) (10)	
	Quadrant (2)			*Quadrant (1)*							
1. Agriculture	...	q_{12}	...	...		...	q_{17}	...	...	...	Q_1
2. Industry	q_{21}	(q_{22})	q_{23}	...		...	q_{27}	...	...	...	Q_2
3. Households (primary services)	...	q_{32}	...	...		...	q_{37}	...	...	...	Q_3
	Quadrant (3)			*Quadrant (4)*							
4. Animal	...	...	...	...	...	...	q_{47}	...	...	...	
5. Plant	...	...	...	...	...	...	q_{57}	...	...	...	
6. Bacteria	...	...	...	...	...	...	q_{67}	...	...	...	
7. Atmosphere	q_{71}	q_{72}	q_{73}	q_{74}	q_{75}	q_{76}	(q_{77})	q_{78}	q_{79}	$q_{7,10}$	Q_7
8. Hydrosphere	...	...	...	...	...	...	q_{97}	...	...	...	
9. Lithosphere	...	...	...	...	...	...	...	...	...	...	
10. Sun (primary services)	...	...	...	...	...	...	$q_{10,7}$	...	...	...	

cients. For example, if i is water and j is alfalfa, then a_{ij} would be nine hundred, since it takes nine hundred pounds of water to produce one pound of dried alfalfa (Storer, 1954, p. 96). Assuming all a_{ij} are known, and noting that $q_{ij} = a_{ij}Q_j$, we have the following n equation in n unknowns:[8]

$$\sum_{j=1}^{n} a_{ij}Q_j = Q_i; \quad i = 1, \ldots, n.$$

These equations are formally identical to Leontief's quantity table, in which we can sum across rows but not down columns. The assumptions by which Leontief breathes usefulness into this formalism are discussed below and are shown to present no greater theoretical problems for the whole Table 15.2 than for quadrant (2). To begin, Leontief's basic assumption of constant (slowly changing) technology over time seems to be much closer to the facts for Table 15.2, since in the non-human economy technical change (evolution) is much slower than in the human economy. Linearity or constant-costs assumptions (a_{ij} constant with respect to Q_j) would seem to be at least equally appropriate as a first approximation. Perhaps this assumption, too, is closer to reality for Table 15.2, since biological populations grow by adding identical units—hence input-output relations of biological populations are more likely to be proportional to scale (linear) than are such relations for populations of firms (that is, industries) in which new members are never such close replicas of old members. The assumption of single production processes with no joint products appears, at first sight, to be less true for nature than for the human economy. However, this is not at all clear, especially if we include bads and free goods as outputs in our traditional production functions. In general, aggregation and classification criteria used in input-output models (similarity of input structure and fixity of proportions among outputs) would remain applicable in the larger table. Certainly no single classification would give a complete representation of the exquisitely tangled web of physical life relations—but then the usual input-output model is also a very incomplete picture of economic relations. Different classifications can be used to serve different limited purposes.

Although there appear to be no theoretical problems in extending the input-output model in this way, there is the obvious practical difficulty that most of the q_{ij} and a_{ij} in quadrants (1), (3), and (4) have never been measured. Nevertheless they all seem to be measurable or at least subject to indirect calculation. Probably the major reason this information has not been acquired is that we have not had many theoretical pigeonholes into which it would fit. Also, the model does not really require a Laplacian knowledge of the universe, as it may appear from the presentation. Application can be confined to a given spatial or conceptual region, with an export row and an import column summarizing relations with the "rest of the world." In any case, application appears rather less utopian than "cost-benefit analysis," which on the slender reed of exchange-value calculations attempts to "maximize the present value of all benefits less all costs, subject to specified restraints" (Prest and Turvey, 1965, p. 4). In fact, something like Table 15.2 would be necessary for identifying "all" costs and benefits in the organic sense of Hobson. The construction of such a table would require the co-operation of many disciplines—which may be a point in its favor.*

In conclusion, to summarize and support the point of view taken here, I can do no better than to remind the reader of the introductory aphorisms from Ruskin and Isaiah and to quote Lotka (1956, p. 183) one last time:

> For the drama of life is like a puppet show in which stage, scenery, actors and all are made of the same stuff. The players indeed, "have their exits and their entrances," but the exit is by way of translation into the substance of the stage; and each entrance is a transformation scene. So stage and players are bound together in the close partnership of an intimate comedy; and if we would catch the spirit of the piece our attention must not all be absorbed in the characters alone, but must be extended also to the scene, of which they are born, on which they play their part, and with which, in a little while, they merge again.

NOTES

1. Value is not permanently imputed to the (non-material) technology within which matter and energy are used, unless that technology is made artificially scarce by patents. Following Schumpeter we can say that a new technology, while it is temporarily scarce by virtue of its novelty, will earn a temporary profit but will not receive a permanent imputed share of total value produced.

2. To say that "total life value" is infinite is not to say that it is *ultimate*—"For whosoever will save his life shall lose it: and whosoever will lose his life for My sake shall find it. For what is a man profited, if he shall gain the whole world and lose his own soul? Or what shall a man give in exchange for his soul?" (Matt. 16:25, 26). On the commonsense infinitude of total utility, see Böhm-Bawerk (1891), Book III, pp. 147–53).

3. In which, using exchange-value calculations, Swift logically demonstrates the "economic desirability" of eating children!

4. And, Marx would argue, man even discovered that he could "cultivate and extract" an analogous surplus from other men in the factory "hothouse."

5. The Leontief input-output model derives from a line of thought beginning with Francois Quesnay's "tableau economique," which was described by Mirabeau as "the great discovery which glorifies our century and will yield posterity its fruits." (For an exposition see Leontief, 1966.) It is more than coincidental that we should find the input-output model relevant to economics considered as a life science, since Quesnay (a physician) and the physiocrats emphasized the supremacy of nature and the biological analogy.

---

*[Editor's note: For a critical review of this and other extensions of the input-output model to cover environmental sectors, see Peter A. Victor, *Pollution: Economy and Environment*, Toronto: University of Toronto Press, 1972.]

6. If the reader will pardon the liberties taken with Luke 11:24–26 we may say that sometimes a bad cast out of cell (2) wanders through the waterless places of cells (1) and (4) seeking rest. And finding none it gathers seven new bads, which then descend upon the well-garnished human household through the back door of cell (3). And the last state of that household is worse than the first.

7. Cf. Lotka's (1956, chap. xxiv) concept of the "world engine."

8. If we separate out household consumption as having no meaningful "technical" coefficients, then we would have n equations in $2n$ unknowns (n of the Q_j and n of the q_{ik}, where k is the household sector). Arbitrarily setting any n of these magnitudes determines the remaining n unknowns. This corresponds to the "open" Leontief model. The assumption of technical coefficients for the household sector would give the "closed" model.

REFERENCES

Bates, Marston, *The Forest and the Sea*. New York: Random House, 1960.

Böhm-Bawerk, E. *The Positive Theory of Capital*. Translated by William Smart. New York: Stechert, 1891.

Boulding, K. E. *A Reconstruction of Economics*. New York: Wiley, 1950.

Boulding, K. E., *The Skills of the Economist*. Toronto: Clarke, Irwin, 1958.

Boulding, K. E. "Economics and Ecology," in F. Frazer Darling and John P. Milton (eds.), *Future Environments of North America*. New York: Natural History Press, 1966.

Carson, Rachel. *Silent Spring*. Boston: Houghton Mifflin, 1962.

Georgescu-Roegen, Nicholas. *Analytical Economics*. Cambridge, Mass.: Harvard University Press, 1966.

Henderson, L. J. *The Fitness of the Environment*. Boston: Beacon, 1958. (Originally published 1913)

Hobson, J. A. *Economics and Ethics*. Boston: Heath, 1929.

Leontief, Wassily. *Input-Output Economics*. New York: Oxford University Press, 1966.

Lotka, A. J. *Elements of Mathematical Biology*. New York: Dover, 1956. Previously published under the title *Elements of Physical Biology*.

Marshall, Alfred. *Principles of Economics*. London: Macmillan, 1920.

Marshall, Afred. *Memorials of Alfred Marshall*. Edited by A. C. Pigou. London: Macmillan, 1925.

Marx, Karl. *Capital*. Edited by Friedrich Engels. New York: International Publishers, 1967. Reproduction of the English edition of 1887.

Prest, A. R., and Turvey, R. "Cost Benefit Analysis; A Survey," *Econ. J.* (December, 1965), pp. 1–49.

Robinson, Joan. *Economic Philosophy*. London: Watts, 1962.

Schroedinger, Erwin, *What Is Life?* New York: Macmillan, 1945.

Scitovsky, Tibor. "Two Concepts of External Economies," *J.P.E.* (April 1954).

Spengler, J. J. "The Economist and the Population Question," *A.E.R.* (March 1966).

Storer, John H. *The Web of Life.* New York: Devin-Adair, 1954.

Teilhard de Chardin, Pierre. *The Phenomenon of Man.* New York: Harper & Row, 1959.

Teller, Edward. Public address at Louisiana State University, Baton Rouge, 1965.

16

THE ECONOMICS OF THE
COMING SPACESHIP EARTH

Kenneth E. Boulding

We are now in the middle of a long process of transition in the nature of the image which man has of himself and his environment. Primitive men, and to a large extent also men of the early civilizations, imagined themselves to be living on a virtually illimitable plane. There was almost always somewhere beyond the known limits of human habitation, and over a very large part of the time that man has been on earth, there has been something like a frontier. That is, there was always some place else to go when things got too difficult, either by reason of the deterioration of the natural environment or a deterioration of the social structure in places where people happened to live. The image of the frontier is probably one of the oldest images of mankind, and it is not surprising that we find it hard to get rid of.

Gradually, however, man has been accustoming himself to the notion of the spherical earth and a closed sphere of human activity. A few unusual spirits among the ancient Greeks perceived that the earth was a sphere. It was only with the circumnavigations and the geographical explorations of the fifteenth and sixteenth centuries, however, that the fact that the earth was a sphere became at all widely known and accepted. Even in the nineteenth century, the commonest map was Mercator's projection, which visualizes the earth as an illimitable cylinder, essentially a plane wrapped around the globe, and it was not until the Second World War and the development of the air age that the global nature of the planet really entered the popular imagination. Even now we are very far from having made the moral, political, and psychological adjustments which are implied in this transition from the illimitable plane to the closed sphere.

Economists in particular, for the most part, have failed to come to grips with the ultimate consequences of the transition from the open to the closed earth. One hesitates to use the terms "open" and "closed" in this connection, as they have been used with so many different shades of meaning. Nevertheless, it is hard to find equivalents. The open system, indeed, has some similarities to the open system of von Bertalanffy,[1] in that it implies that some kind of structure is maintained in the midst of a throughput from inputs to outputs. In a closed system, the outputs of all parts of the system are linked to the inputs of other parts. There are no inputs from outside and no outputs to the outside; indeed, there is no outside at all. Closed systems, in fact, are very rare in human experience, in fact almost by definition unknowable, for if there are genuinely closed systems around us, we have no way of getting information into them or out of them; and hence if they are really closed, we would be quite unaware of their existence. We can only find out about a closed system if we participate in it. Some isolated primitive societies may have approximated to this, but even these had to take inputs from the environment and give outputs to it. All living organisms, including man himself, are open systems. They have to receive inputs in the shape of air, food, water, and give off outputs in the form of effluvia and excrement. Deprivation of input of air, even for a few minutes, is fatal. Deprivation of the ability to obtain any input or to dispose of any output is fatal in a relatively short time. All human societies have likewise been open systems. They receive inputs from the earth, the atmosphere, and the waters, and they give outputs into these reservoirs; they also produce inputs internally in the shape of babies and outputs in the shape of corpses. Given a capacity to draw upon inputs and to get rid of ouputs, an open system of this kind can persist indefinitely.

There are some systems—such as the biological phenotype, for instance the human body—which cannot maintain themselves indefinitely by inputs and outputs because of the phenomemon of aging. This process is very little understood. It occurs, evidently, because there are some outputs which cannot be replaced by any known input. There is not the same necessity for aging in organizations and in societies, although an analogous phenomenon may take place. The structure and composition of an organization or society, however, can be maintained by inputs of fresh personnel from birth and education as the existing personnel ages and eventually dies. Here we have an interesting example of a system which seems to maintain itself by the self-generation of inputs, and in this sense is moving toward closure. The input of people (that is, babies) is also an output of people (that is, parents).

Systems may be open or closed in respect to a number of classes of inputs and outputs. Three important classes are matter, energy, and information. The present world economy is open in regard to all three. We can think of the world economy or "econosphere" as a subset of the "world set," which is the set of all objects of possible discourse in the world. We then think of the state of the econosphere at any one moment as being the total capital stock, that is, the set of all objects, people, organizations, and so on, which are interesting from the point of view of the system of exchange. This total stock of capital is clearly an open system in the sense that it has inputs and outputs, inputs being production which adds to the capital stock, outputs being consumption which subtracts from it. From a material point of view, we see objects passing from the noneconomic into the economic set in the process of production, and we similarly see products passing out of the economic set as their value becomes zero. Thus we see the econosphere as a material process involving the discovery and mining of fossil fuels, ores, etc., and at the other end a process by which the effluents of the system are passed out into noneconomic reservoirs —for instance, the atmosphere and the oceans—which are not appropriated and do not enter into the exchange system.

From the point of view of the energy system, the econosphere, involves inputs of available energy in the form, say, of water power, fossil fuels, or sunlight, which are necessary in order to create the material throughput and to move matter from the noneconomic set into the economic set or even out of it again; and energy itself is given off by the system in a less available form, mostly in the form of heat. These inputs of available energy must come either from the sun (the energy supplied by other stars being assumed to be negligible) or it may come from the earth itself, either through its internal heat or through its energy of rotation or other motions, which generate, for instance, the energy of the tides. Agriculture, a few solar machines, and water power use the current available energy income. In advanced societies this is supplemented very extensively by the use of fossil fuels, which represent, as it were, a capital stock of stored-up sunshine. Because of this capital stock of energy, we have been able to maintain an energy input into the system, particularly over the last two centuries, much larger than we would have been able to do with existing techniques if we had had to rely on the current input of available energy from the sun or the earth itself. This supplementary input, however, is by its very nature exhaustible.

The inputs and outputs of information are more subtle and harder to trace, but also represent an open system, related to, but not wholly dependent on, the transformation of matter and energy. By far the larger amount of information and knowledge is self-generated by the human society, though a certain amount of information comes into the sociosphere in the form of light from the universe outside. The information that comes from the universe has certainly affected man's image of himself and of his environment, as we can easily visualize if we suppose that we lived on a planet with a total cloud-cover that kept out all information from the exterior universe. It is only in very recent times, of course, that the information coming in from the universe has been captured and coded in the form of a complex image of what the universe is like outside the earth; but even in primitive times, man's perception of the heavenly bodies has always profoundly affected his image of earth and of himself. It is the information generated within the planet, however, and particularly that generated by man himself, which forms by far the larger part of the information system. We can think of the stock of knowledge, or as Teilhard de Chardin called it, the "noosphere," and consider this as an open system, losing knowledge through aging and death and gaining it through birth and education and the ordinary experience of life.

From the human point of view, knowledge, or information, is by far the most important of the three systems. Matter only acquires significance and only enters the sociosphere or the econosphere insofar as it becomes an object of human knowledge. We can think of capital, indeed, as frozen knowledge or knowledge imposed on the material world in the form of improbable arrangements. A machine, for instance, originates in the mind of man, and both its construction and its use involve information processes imposed on the material world by man himself. The cumulation of knowledge, that is, the excess of its production over its consumption, is the key to human development of all kinds, especially to economic development. We can see this preeminence of knowledge very clearly in the experiences of countries where the material capital has been destroyed by a war, as in Japan and Germany. The knowledge of the people was not destroyed, and it did not take long, therefore, certainly not more than ten years, for most of the material capital to be reestablished again. In a country such as Indonesia, however, where the knowledge did not exist, the material capital did not come into being either. By "knowledge" here I mean, of course, the whole cognitive structure, which includes valuations and motivations as well as images of the factual world.

The concept of entropy, used in a somewhat loose sense, can be applied to all three of these open systems. In material systems, we can distinguish between entropic processes, which take concentrated materials and diffuse them through the oceans or over the earth's surface or into the atmosphere, and antientropic processes, which take diffuse materials and concentrate them. Material entropy can be taken as a measure of the uniformity of the distribution of elements and, more uncertainly, compounds and other structures on the earth's surface. There is, fortunately, no law of increasing material entropy, as there is in the corresponding case of energy, as it is quite possible to concentrate diffused materials if energy inputs are allowed. Thus the processes for fixation of nitrogen from the air, processes for the extraction of magnesium or other elements from the sea, and processes for the desalinization of sea water are antientropic in the material sense, though the reduction of material entropy has to be paid for by inputs of energy and also inputs of information, or at least a stock of information in the system. In regard to matter, therefore, a closed system is conceivable, that is, a system in which there is neither increase nor decrease in material entropy. In such a system all outputs from consumption would constantly be recycled to become inputs for production, as for instance, nitrogen in the nitrogen cycle of the natural ecosystem.

In the energy system there is, unfortunately, no escape from the grim second law of thermodynamics; and if there were no energy inputs into the earth, any evolutionary or developmental process would be impossible. The large energy inputs which we have obtained from fossil fuels are strictly temporary. Even the most optimistic predictions expect the easily available supply of fossil fuels to be exhausted in a mere matter of centuries at present rates of use. If the rest of the world were to rise to American standards of power consumption, and still more if world population continues to increase, the exhaustion of fossil fuels would be even more rapid. The development of nuclear energy has improved this picture, but not fundamentally altered it, at least in present technologies, for fissionable material is still relatively scarce. If we should achieve the economic use of energy through fusion, of course, a much larger source of energy materials would be available, which would expand the time horizons of supplementary energy input into an open social system by perhaps tens to hundreds of thousands of years. Failing this, however, the time is not very far distant, historically speaking, when man will once more have to retreat to his current energy input from the sun, even though with increased knowledge this could be used much more effectively than in the past. Up to now, certainly, we have not got very far with the technology of using current solar energy, but the possibility of substantial improvements in the future is certainly high. It may be, indeed, that the biological revolution which is just beginning will produce a solution to this problem, as we develop artificial organisms which are capable of much more efficient transformation of solar energy into easily available forms than any that we now have. As Richard Meier has suggested, we may run our machines in the future with methane-producing algae.[2]

The question of whether there is anything corresponding to entropy in the information system is a puzzling one, though of great interest. There are certainly many examples of social systems and cultures which have lost knowledge, especially in transition from one generation to the next, and in which the culture has therefore degenerated. One only has to look at the folk culture of Appalachian migrants to American cities to see a culture which started out as a fairly rich European folk culture in Elizabethan times and which seems to have lost skills, adaptability, folk tales, songs, and almost everything that goes up to make richness and complexity in a culture, in the course of about ten generations. The American Indians on reservations provide another example of such degradation of the information and knowledge system. On the other hand, over a great part of human history, the growth of knowledge in the earth as a whole seems to have been almost continuous, even though there have been times of relatively slow growth and times of rapid growth. As it is knowledge of certain kinds that produces the growth of knowledge in general, we have here a very subtle and complicated system, and it is hard to put one's finger on the particular elements in a culture which make knowledge grow more or less rapidly, or even which make it decline. One of the great puzzles in this connection, for instance, is why the takeoff into science, which represents an "acceleration," or an increase in the rate of growth of knowledge in European society in the sixteen century, did not take place in China, which at that time (about 1600) was unquestionably ahead of Europe, and one would think even more ready for the breakthrough. This is perhaps the most crucial question in the theory of social development, yet we must confess that it is very little understood. Perhaps the most significant factor in this connection is the existence of "slack" in the culture, which permits a divergence from established patterns and activity which is not merely devoted to reproducing the existing society but is devoted to changing it. China was perhaps too well organized and had too little slack in its society to produce the kind of acceleration which we find in the somewhat poorer and less well organized but more diverse societies of Europe.

The closed earth of the future requires economic principles which are somewhat different from those of the open earth of the past. For the sake of picturesqueness, I am tempted to call the open economy the "cowboy economy," the cowboy being symbolic of the illimitable plains and also associated with reckless, exploitative, romantic, and violent behavior, which is characteristic of open societies. The closed economy of the future might similarly be called the "spaceman" economy, in which the earth has become a single spaceship, without unlimited reservoirs of anything, either for extraction or for pollution, and in which, therefore, man must find his place in a cyclical ecological system which is capable of continuous reproduction of material form even though it cannot escape having inputs of energy. The difference between the two types of economy becomes most apparent in the attitude towards consumption. In the cowboy economy, consumption is regarded as a good thing and production likewise; and the success of the economy is measured by the amount of the throughput from the "factors of production," a part of which, at any rate, is extracted from the reservoirs of raw materials and noneconomic objects, and another part of which is output into the reservoirs of pollution. If there are infinite reservoirs from which material can be obtained and into which effluvia can be deposited, then the throughput is at least a plausible measure of the success of the economy. The Gross National Product is a rough measure of this total throughput. It should be possible, however, to distinguish that part of the GNP which is derived from exhaustible and that which is derived from reproducible resources, as well as that part of consumption which represents effluvia and that which represents input into the productive system again. Nobody, as far as I know, has ever attempted to break down the GNP in this way, although it would be an interesting and extremely important exercise, which is unfortunately beyond the scope of this paper.

By contrast, in the spaceman economy, throughput is by no means a desideratum, and is indeed to be regarded as something to be minimized rather than maximized. The essential measure of the success of the economy is not production and consumption at all, but the nature, extent, quality, and complexity of the total capital stock, including in this the state of the human bodies and minds included in the system. In the spaceman economy, what we are primarily concerned with is stock maintenance, and any technological change which results in the maintenance of a given total stock with a lessened throughout (that is, less production and consumption) is clearly a gain. This idea that both production and consumption are bad things rather than good things is very strange to economists, who have been obsessed with the income-flow concepts to the exclusion, almost, of capital-stock concepts.

There are actually some very tricky and unsolved problems involved in the questions as to whether human welfare or well-being is to be regarded as a stock or a flow. Something of both these elements seems actually to be involved in it, and as far as I know there have been practically no studies directed towards identifying these two dimensions of human satisfaction. Is it, for instance, eating that is a good thing, or is it being well fed? Does economic welfare involve having nice clothes, fine houses, good equipment, and so on, or is it to be measured by the depreciation and the wearing out of these things? I am inclined myself to regard the stock concept as most fundamental, that is, to think of being well fed as more important than eating, and to think even of so-called services as essentially involving the restoration of a depleting psychic capital. Thus I have argued that we go to a concert in order to restore a psychic condition which might be called "just having gone to a concert," which, once established, tends to depreciate. When it depreciates beyond a certain point, we go to another concert in order to restore it. If it depreciates rapidly, we go to a lot of concerts; if it depreciates slowly, we go to a few. On this view, similarly, we eat primarily to restore bodily homeostasis, that is, to maintain a condition of being well fed, and so on. On this view, there is nothing desirable in consumption at all. The less consumption we can maintain a given state with, the better off we are. If we had clothes that did not wear out, houses that did not depreciate, and even if we could maintain our bodily condition without eating, we would clearly be much better off.

It is this last consideration, perhaps, which makes one pause. Would we, for instance, really want an operation that would enable us to restore all our bodily tissues by intravenous feeding while we slept? Is there not, that is to say, a certain virtue in throughput itself, in activity itself, in production and consumption itself, in raising food and in eating it? It would certainly be rash to exclude this possibility. Further interesting problems are raised by the demand for variety. We certainly do not want a constant state to be maintained; we want fluctuations in the state. Otherwise there would be no demand for variety in food, for variety in scene, as in travel, for variety in social contact, and so on. The demand for variety can, of course, be costly, and sometimes it seems to be too costly to be tolerated or at least legitimated, as in the case of marital partners, where the maintenance of a homeostatic state in the family is usually regarded as much more desirable than the variety and excessive throughput of the libertine. There are problems here which the economics profession has neglected with astonishing singlemindedness. My own attempts to call attention to some of them, for instance, in two articles,[3] as far as I can judge, produced no response whatever; and economists continue to think and act as if production, consumption, throughput, and the GNP were the sufficient and adequate measure of economic success.

It may be said, of course, why worry about all this when the spaceman economy is still a good way off (at least beyond the lifetimes of any now living), so let us eat, drink, spend, extract and pollute, and be as merry as we can, and let posterity worry about the spaceship earth. It is always a little hard to find a convincing answer to the man who says, "What has posterity ever done for me?" and the conservationist has always had to fall back on rather vague ethical principles postulating identity of the individual with some human community or society which extends not only back into the past but forward into the future. Unless the individual identifies with some community of this kind, conservation is obviously "irrational." Why should we not maximize the welfare of this generation at the cost of posterity? "Après nous, le déluge" has been the motto of not insignificant numbers of human societies. The only answer to this, as far as I can see, is to point out that the welfare of the individual depends on the extent to which he can identify himself with others, and that the most satisfactory individual identity is that which identifies not only with a community in space but also with a community extending over time from the past into the future. If this kind of identity is recognized as desirable, then posterity has a voice, even if it does not have a vote; and in a sense, if its voice can influence votes, it has votes too. This whole problem is linked up with the much larger one of the determinants of the morale, legitimacy, and "nerve" of a society, and there is great deal of historical evidence to suggest that a society which loses its identity with posterity and which loses its positive image in the future loses also its capacity to deal with present problems, and soon falls apart.[4]

Even if we concede that posterity is relevant to our present problems, we still face the question of time-discounting and the closely related question of uncertainty-discounting. It is a well-known phenomenon that individuals discount the future, even in their own lives. The very existence of a positive rate of interest may be taken as at least strong supporting evidence of this hypothesis. If we discount our own future, it is certainly not unreasonable to discount posterity's future even more, even if we do give posterity a vote. If we discount this at five percent per annum, posterity's vote or dollar halves every fourteen years as we look into the future, and after even a mere hundred years it is pretty small—only about one-and-a-half cents on the dollar. If we add another five percent for uncertainly, even the vote of our grandchildren reduces almost to insignificance. We can argue, of course, that the ethical thing to do is not to discount the future at all, that time-discounting is mainly the result of myopia and perspective, and hence is an illusion which the moral man should not tolerate. It is a very popular illusion, however, and one that must certainly be taken into consideration in the formulation of policies. It explains, perhaps, why conservationist policies almost have to be sold under some other excuse which seems more urgent, and why, indeed, necessities which are visualized as urgent, such as defense, always seem to hold priority over those which involve the future.

All these considerations add some credence to the point of view which says that we should not worry about the spaceman economy at all, and that we should just go on increasing the GNP and indeed the Gross World Product, or GWP, in the expectation that the problems of the future can be left to the future, that when scarcities arise, whether this is of raw materials or of pollutable reservoirs, the needs of the then present will determine the solutions of the then present, and there is no use giving ourselves ulcers by worrying about problems that we really do not have to solve. There is even high ethical authority for this point of view in the New Testament, which advocates that we should take no thought for tomorrow and let the dead bury their dead. There has always been something rather refreshing in the view that we should live like the birds, and perhaps posterity is for the birds in more senses than one; so perhaps we should all call it a day and go out and pollute something cheerfully. As an old taker of thought for the morrow, however, I cannot quite accept this solution; and I would argue, furthermore, that tomorrow is not only very close, but in many respects it is already here. The shadow of the future spaceship, indeed, is already falling over our spendthrift merriment. Oddly enough, it seems to be in pollution rather than in exhaustion that the problem is first becoming salient. Los Angeles has run out of air, Lake Erie has become a cesspool, the oceans are getting full of lead and DDT, and the atmosphere may become man's major problem in another generation, at the rate at which we are filling it up with gunk. It is, of course, true that at least on a microscale, things have been worse at times in the past. The cities of today, with all their foul air and polluted waterways, are probably not as bad as the filthy cities of the pretechnical age. Nevertheless, that fouling of the nest which has been typical of man's activity in the past on a local scale now seems to be extending to the whole world society; and one certainly cannot view with equanimity the present rate of pollution of any of the natural reservoirs, whether the atmosphere, the lakes, or even the oceans.

I would argue strongly also that our obsession with production and consumption to the exclusion of the "state" aspects of human welfare distorts the process of technological change in a most undesirable way. We are all familiar, of course, with the wastes involved in planned obsolescence, in competitive advertising, and in poor quality of consumer goods. These problems may not be so important as the "view with alarm" school indicates, and indeed the evidence at many points is conflicting. New materials especially seem to edge towards the side of improved durability, such as, for instance, neolite soles for footwear, nylon socks, wash and wear shirts, and so on. The case of household equipment and automobiles is a little less clear. Housing and building construction generally almost certainly has declined in durability since the Middle Ages, but this decline also reflects a change in tastes towards flexibility and fashion and a need for novelty, so that it is not easy to assess. What is clear is that no serious attempt has been made to assess the impact over the whole of economic life of changes in durability, that is, in the ratio of capital in the widest possible sense to income. I suspect that we have underestimated, even in our spendthrift society, the gains from increased durability, and that this might very well be one of the places where the price system needs correction through government-sponsored research and development. The problems which the spaceship earth is going to present, therefore, are not all in the future by any means, and a strong case can be made for paying much more attention to them in the present than we now do.

It may be complained that the considerations I have been putting forth relate only to the very long run, and they do not much concern our immediate problems. There may be some justice in this criticism, and my main excuse is that other writers have dealt adequately with the more immediate problems of deterioration in the quality of the environment. It is true, for instance, that many of the immediate problems of pollution of the atmosphere or of bodies of water arise because of the failure of the price system, and many of them could be solved by corrective taxation. If people had to pay the losses due to the nuisances which they create, a good deal more resources would go into the prevention of nuisances. These arguments involving external economies and diseconomies are familiar to economists and there is no need to recapitulate them. The law of torts is quite inadequate to provide for the correction of the price system which is required, simply because where damages are widespread and their incidence on any particular person is small, the ordinary remedies of the civil law are quite inadequate and inappropriate. There needs, therefore, to be special legislation to cover these cases, and though such legislation seems hard to get in practice, mainly because of the widespread and small personal incidence of the injuries, the technical problems involved are not insuperable. If we were to adopt in principle a law for tax penalties for social damages, with an apparatus for making assessments under it, a very large proportion of current pollution and deterioration of the environment would be prevented. There are tricky problems of equity involved, particularly where old established nuisances create a kind of "right by purchase" to perpetuate themselves, but these are problems again which a few rather arbitrary decisions can bring to some kind of solution.

The problems which I have been raising in this paper are of larger scale and perhaps much harder to solve than the more practical and immediate problems of the above paragraph. Our success in dealing with the larger problems, however, is not unrelated to the development of skill in the solution of the more immediate and perhaps less difficult problems. One can hope, therefore, that as a succession of mounting crises, especially in pollution, arouse public opinion and mobilize support for the solution of the immediate problems, a learning process will be set in motion which will eventually lead to an appreciation of and perhaps solutions for the larger ones. My neglect of the immediate problems, therefore, is in no way intended to deny their importance, for unless we make at least a beginning on a process for solving the immediate problems we will not have much chance of solving the larger ones. On the other hand, it may also be true that a long-run vision, as it were, of the deep crisis which faces mankind may predispose people to taking more interest in the immediate problems and to devote more effort for their solution. This may sound like a rather modest optimism, but perhaps a modest optimism is better than no optimism at all.

NOTES

1. Ludwig von Bertalanffy, *Problems of Life* (New York: Wiley, 1952).

2. Richard L. Meier, *Science and Economic Development* (New York: Wiley, 1956).

3. Kenneth E. Boulding, "The Consumption Concept in Economic Theory," *American Economic Review*, 35:2 (May 1945), pp. 1–14; and "Income or Welfare?," *Review of Economic Studies*, 17 (1949–50), pp. 77–86.

4. Fred L. Polak, *The Image of the Future*, vols. I and II, translated by Elise Boulding (New York: Sythoff, Leyden and Oceana, 1961).

17

SPACESHIP EARTH REVISITED

Kenneth E. Boulding

I have no claims to priority in the use of the metaphor *spaceship earth*, though I think I did think it up independently, and it was a metaphor so appropriate to its time that it would have been very surprising if somebody had not thought it up. It is still a very good metaphor, but as with all metaphors, one has to be careful with it. When a metaphor parades as a model, it can sometimes be very dangerous and misleading, particularly as metaphors are so much more convincing than models and are much more apt to change people's images of the world. The spaceship metaphor stresses the earth's smallness, crowdedness, and limited resources; the need for avoiding destructive conflict; and the necessity for a sense of world community with a very heterogeneous crew. On these grounds the metaphor is certainly as good today as it was in the 1960s. One of the paradoxes, indeed, is that we seem to be more theoretically aware of the spaceship earth model than we were in the 1960s, with the Club of Rome reports, the energy crisis, and the United Nations population conference. But this theoretical awareness does not seem to have penetrated down to the level of political consciousness in the life and awareness of the ordinary human being. It seems to be very hard to organize a long-run crisis. Certainly the ordinary American today has very little sense of crisis. Every time he turns a switch, the lights go on; every time he pulls up to a gas station, there is gas for his car. The problems of the 1970s—inflation, the arms race, rising crime rates, battered children, tax revolts, and so on—are far more political and sociological than they are related to the long-run problems of a society nonsustainable in terms of energy, materials, and pollution.

Furthermore, something has happened in the 1970s which may have an enormous potential significance for the human race or may have none at all: the development of reasonably serious proposals for space colonies. This may sound like science fiction, and there may well be some unknown factor which would make them impossible. The idea is not, however, absurd, simply because of the low energy requirements of moving materials about in empty space. On earth we need energy mainly to overcome gravity and friction.

Solar energy, the great white hope of the virtuous, does not look very much better today than it did in the sixties, at least on the surface of the earth. It is fine for hot-water heating, moderately fine for space heating—but this is only 20 percent of our energy use. It still looks very expensive for electricity in spite of the tremendous advance in photovoltaic cells, and we are certainly no further along than we were in regard to solar developed fuel. The essential unpredictability of knowledge and technology, of course, means that in another ten years the whole situation may look very different. The probability of our failing to solve the problem of cheap solar energy in usable forms is at least high enough to be worrying. In outer space, on the other hand, the sun never sets. Solar energy is much more available. The possibility of capturing it to transport materials from the moons and asteroids is, at least on paper, not preposterous.

Going into space, however, would be a transition for the evolutionary process as great as that involved in going from sea to land. One of the group of Princeton scientists who have been spearheading the interest in space colonies, in a paper at the American Association for the Advancement of Science in 1978, proposed, perhaps a little tongue-in-cheek, that the carrying capacity of the solar system for human beings might be one sextillion—about a billion times the present population of the earth. This, one presumes, would involve filling a wide band on either side of the orbit of the earth with space colonies using solar energy and mining the asteroids for materials. This is outrageous, but it may be no more outrageous than the whole process of evolution. Perhaps the greatest case for space colonies is that they would reintroduce isolation and variety into the evolutionary process. The most worrying thing about the earth is that there seems to be no way of preventing it from becoming one world. If there is only one world, then if anything goes wrong, everything goes wrong. And by the generalized Murphy's Law, every system has some positive probability, however low, of irretrievable catastrophe. Evolution is able to persist on the earth because of the isolation and variety of its ecosystems. Thus a total catastrophe on Krakatoa was recoverable because it did not affect the more distant ecosystems, which then recolonized the destroyed island. Similarly, the total collapse of the Mayan Empire, an early example indeed of a Club of Rome report, affected Charlemagne or the Emperor of China not at all. They knew nothing of it.

Ultimately, of course, we must face the spaceship earth on earth. Uncertainty, however, is the principal property of the future, and time horizons themselves have an irreducible uncertainty about them. Perhaps the greatest weakness of the metaphor is that the spaceship presumably has a clear destination and a mission to accomplish. It is essentially a planned economy. The evolutionary process, however, is not a significant planned economy any more than an ecosystem. The biological ecosystem is not even a community, in spite of the fact that biologists sometimes call it that, it is the wildest example of free private enterprise and does not even have a mayor. I have argued that evolution is now moving out of the *biogenetic,* that is, DNA, genes and all that, into the *noogenetic,* which is the transmission of learned structures from one generation to the next by a teaching and learning process. This is a transition which begins with the human race. It may be as profound a transition as the development of DNA itself. I get the uneasy feeling sometimes that the human race is the link between the biogenetic and the noogenetic, and we may eventually produce a self-reproducing solid-state intelligence which would be our evolutionary successor. I won't like it, having great race prejudice in favor of the human race, but we have to admit that all species are endangered and that every species is a link, even biologically, between the biogenetic know-how of the gene that preceded it and those that will follow it. It would be presumptuous of us to think that the human race is any more than a link in the great evolutionary process of the universe that moves majestically from the unknown Alpha to the even more unknown Omega.

18

THE GROWTH OF AFFLUENCE AND THE DECLINE OF WELFARE

E. J. Mishan

In his endeavor to interpret the secular growth of per capita "real" income as a major component of a rising level of social welfare, the economist relies, *inter alia,* on two crucial premises: (1) that the individual is the best judge of his own interests, and (2) that over time tastes do not change—or, if they do, they change for the better as a result of better information.

In the absence of far-reaching spillovers, a consequence of new technologies and products, it seems to follow from these premises that more goods along with new goods widen the area of choice open to the citizen—which phrase may serve as a definition of an increase in welfare.

Although it is inconvenient to do so, a man of the world would not hesitate in rejecting both of these premises. First, although it is politically expedient to declare that each man is the best judge of his own interest, there can be few people so complacent as not to spend some of their idle time unwishing their

Published by permission of the author.

past follies. Again, the fact that a sizable proportion of the American population regularly subject themselves to psychoanalysis or other forms of therapy suggests that in respect of the larger questions that govern their lifestyles —which are the questions that matter—they are far from certain where their true interests lie.

Secondly, there cannot be the faintest doubt that a person's tastes do indeed change over time and, in a world of unprecedented change, they change rapidly also. After all, we have lived in this so-called permissive society for barely more than a decade. The only question is whether tastes are changing for the better. It would require a pretty licentious philosophy of life to assert that they do.

Changes in taste on the scale induced today by rapid technical change produce changes in the conventions of propriety and civility and, more important, changes also in the character and belief system of a people. Granted that a people's character and belief system are among the more potent ingredients of well-being, at least in any country where living standards are well above subsistence levels, there remains to consider the key issue in any debate about the merits of continued economic growth: whether the character and value system most conducive to a serene and enjoyable life are those being brought about largely as a by-product of, and as a response to, compulsive technological advance and unremitting expansionist pressure, commercial and bureaucratic.

If this much is conceded, it follows that the question of the relationship between economic growth and social welfare, within a particular historical context, cannot be settled by reference to economic analysis. The subject can be debated intelligently only as an exercise in speculation, drawing upon experience, imagination, intuition, and some familiarity with history. Disputants may agree about the facts and observe the same trends, yet their interpretation of them in connection with social welfare may be irreconcilable.

On the admittedly implausible assumption that the West, or the world as a whole, will survive the gauntlet of hazards I indicated recently,[1] we may now reflect on the likely course of human welfare.

Although economists currently absorbed in the task of producing measures of change in real income go to some trouble to prevent misinterpretation of the resulting magnitudes or indices, it is apparent that the public (including many economists) persist in the belief that there is a positive association between real per capita income and social welfare. After all, an increase in per capita real income—or, at least, in per capita real expenditure—entails an increase in the per capita consumption of goods. And, in enunciating allocative propositions, the economist builds on the basic psychological assumption that more goods raises individual welfare, *ceteris paribus*. In such a context, the *ceteris paribus* clause is apt to be treated as no more than a concession to the fastidious. Its restrictiveness has never prevented economists from throwing their weight about when advising governments or pontificating on the nation's economic problems.

Yet it is upon the realism and relevance of this *ceteris paribus* clause to the issues being broached that the controversy turns. Let me therefore measure my words carefully. For an individual at a given point of time, I do *not* challenge the proposition that he prefers more to less (I can recall to mind no instance of my ever having rejected an offer of additional pay that involved me in no additional effort). Nor do I deny the existence of initially perceived "good" uses of an innovation—the social value of which economists such as I affect to measure as a consumer surplus by reference, where possible, to market data. The fact that people freely choose to buy new gadgets is warrant enough for the proposition that they anticipate an immediate surplus, or net benefit, from their purchases of them. What I am also concerned with, however, are the spillover effects, falling on society at large, that are associated with the production and use of the increasing amounts and varieties of goods available to the citizens of the affluent society. These spillovers include not only the visible (and audible) effects on man's physical environment. They include the range of consequences on the character and capacity of men whenever they are regarded not only as consumers and producers, but also as citizens, companions, lovers, and as bemused and vulnerable human beings. By extension, they include as well the broad consequences upon the character and cohesion of society. For it is the sum of all these effects and consequences of economic growth that impart critical direction and shape to the complex, intangible, but quintessential entity commonly invoked by that somewhat hackneyed phrase, "the quality of life."

It should be manifest, therefore, that for an affluent society, continually in the throes of technological change—and, inevitably, in the throes of environmental, institutional, and social change as well—there can be no general presumption of a positive association between productivity, however measured, and social welfare.

The tenacious belief that, by and large, and in some significant sense, social welfare ought to be, and indeed has been, increasing within the advanced industrial nations, is partly a legacy of modern history. But it is also supported by current misinterpretations of the facts and figures. In ascending order of importance these include (1) a misinterpretation of the welfare significance of the real income figures, (2) a misinterpretation of the welfare impact of popular social goals, and (3) a misinterpretation of postwar permissiveness and its related movements. We take them up in that order.

First, the figures for real income and for changes in real income, as conventionally calculated by the economist, convey a misleading impression if only because a large and growing proportion of what passes for *finished* or *final* goods, or goods "wanted for their own sake," may more reasonably be classified as *intermediate* goods—as inputs rather than as final outputs.

Into this category should go substantial expenditures on those collective and private goods that are designed to reduce all those spillover effects accompanying the production and use of other goods, also the portion of expenditures on travel that is regarded simply as a means of reaching a destination. Again, much the larger proportion of the cost of education, particularly adult education (which is increasingly vocational) is a form of current expenditure that is analogous to replacement investment in physical capital. For this annual investment in education is incurred in order to replenish the stock of skilled human capital, without which capital the running of a modern industrialized economy is impossible. A large part of the expenditure on books, journals, and newspapers, even on television and radio, has become necessary for formal education and also for effective participation in the economic and political activities of a modern society. And in a civilization where stress and nervous diseases are increasingly common, a proportion of expenditures on vacations may appropriately be fitted into this category as conducive to the efficient functioning of the economy.

Finally, many of the services provided by banks, labor unions, employment agencies, stockbrokers, travel agents, marriage bureaus, and the like, are just not needed in a more traditional society of small towns and communities. They come into being as the economy becomes more complex and as urban areas take on metropolitan dimensions. The agencies that spring up in response to individual bewilderment and frustration in such a milieu may be regarded as "institutional lubricants" necessary for the more complex machinery of society which arises as a necessary by-product of economic growth.

One is tempted to go further. With the collapse of social life, once centered in town and village, the search for new forms of solace and diversion produced the music halls, carnivals, and brass bands of the Edwardian era, which would be followed in the interwar period by the cinema and the radio, and, in the postwar era, by television and stereophonics, supplemented by fantasy sex in magazines and porn shows. It is hard to call a halt to the train of instances of innovations that, looking like contributions to a higher *standard* of living on first blush, turn out, on further surmise, to look more like contributions to a higher *cost* of living. So much of the nation's effort and ingenuity is spent today in producing sophisticated products and specialized services that cater, ultimately, to those basic biological and psychological needs which were easily, and often more fully, met in preindustrial societies.

The view, then, that "economic progress over the last two centuries has succeeded only in making life increasingly complex, frantic, and wearing,"[2] is a pardonable exaggeration.

Second, the gist of the arguments of the more articulate growthmen reflect a persistent belief that a continuation of those developments most closely connected with economic growth must culminate in a better life for the citizen. These developments, the measures of which are then used as indicators of social welfare, include (1) more and better goods, (2) more mobility, (3) more income equality, and (4) more education. My brief comments on each of these four popular social goals are intended to suggest that if more time were available to us, a respectable case could be made for the contrary view: that continued attempts to realize each of them is more likely to reduce welfare than to augment it.

Since so much has already been written, pro and con, about the welfare value of yet more and better goods in already wealthy countries, I shall confine my remarks to little more than a summary of the more skeptical arguments. First, in an economy productive also of adverse spillovers, or of "bads" as well as goods, the operation of a market mechanism cannot ensure an excess of goods over bads—that is, a positive net social benefit—even under the restrictive *ceteris paribus* clause. In general, the greater the scale and the dispersion of these "bads" and, accordingly, the greater the transactions costs involved in any attempt to curb them, the less confidence can be reposed in a net social benefit of the resulting output pattern.

In addition, there are three more related reasons that tell against the presumed relation between goods and welfare. In order to ensure absorption of the products of modern industry, it is necessary to devote considerable resources to the creation of dissatisfaction with existing possessions. The intent and effect of the advertising industry as a whole is perpetually to renew the springs of discontent in economic man, often through invidious comparisons— which takes us to the next point. It is a common observation that perceived welfare is coming to depend, not on a family's absolute command over private goods, but increasingly on its command over private goods *relative* to others. The more this "Jones effect" comes to dominate, the more futile, as a method of raising social welfare, is the continued growth in the production of consumption goods. Finally, an affluent society can hardly avoid being also a "throw-away" society. This throw-away society is not to be understood merely as an instance of the operation of diminishing marginal utility, since from that reflection alone one might infer that the plethora of goods is acting to make people less materialistic over time. A decline in material greed, however, has not been one of the salient characteristics of Western man over the last century. We may acknowledge, then, that a man's growing desire to command more purchasing power—or more purchasing power relative to others —is entirely consistent with his attaching slight value to any item bought.

A mass consumption economy, one of rapid obsolescence and replacement, cannot but breed a throw-away attitude toward man-made goods irrespective of quality. There is no time to grow fond of any thing, no matter how well it serves. And in any case, it will soon be superseded by a new model. In consequence, everything bought comes to be regarded as "potential garbage," and treated as such.

Geographical mobility has long been linked with the idea of progress, sometimes in the innocent belief that travel broadens the mind. Whether in fact the packaged tour explosion of the postwar era has done much more for the affluent citizen than to narrow down the number of places worth traveling to is doubtful.

The motorized transport revolution has had other consequences. We think largely of the ambient environment, whether urban or suburban, largely in terms of traffic. We live, eat, work, sleep, in the midst of it all. Times and distances, road conditions, highway routes, peak hours, short cuts, traffic lights, freeways, road signs, parking spaces, auto repairs, car prices, car accidents, car gadgets, fuel bills—all these, along with the perpetual din, fumes, and danger, have become the everyday stuff of our hurried lives. New car-towers identify the modern city, which, since the war, has become more of a venue for arrivals and departures, a place of perpetual transit, one more node in an intricate network of roads and freeways, junctions and airways. In such an environment it is hardly surprising that over 40 million Americans change their "homes" each year[3]—the word *home* now being a shorthand for current residence, bungalow, apartment, hotel, motel, or caravan.

The belief that continuing economic growth is necessary for a more equitable distribution of incomes to be established is difficult to maintain. Despite extensive and determined government intervention, economic growth over the last two decades has not succeeded in making much impression on the distribution of real disposable income. What is more, while not denying the case for more discriminating methods of removing the remnants of hard-core poverty with the wealthier nations, the case in welfare and justice for spreading purchasing power within the nation more evenly is dubious. The measurement of "relative deprivation" may continue to provide occupational therapy for economists, but in countries where the overwhelming majority of families live well above destitution levels it is not a concept that can excite genuine compassion. Current preoccupation with it in the West springs largely from a growing impatience and resentment among the mass of people, who are active in any society whose economic life is shaped and powered by restlessness and discontent. Certainly the idea of equality of purchasing power as a component of the "just" society has no panoramic appeal. Its vindication rests ultimately on a belief in a deterministic universe, one in which each individual is wholly a captive of circumstances which he is powerless to influence.

The goal of increasing higher education serves, in the main, the needs of economic growth itself since, as indicated earlier, so much of it is vocational and technical. This sort of higher education is not education in the classical sense. It is not education in the humanities. It has no affinities with art or culture or civilized living. Indeed, the liberally educated man today is a figment. He may be literate and well-read in a popular book-review sense. But he can be learned only over a minute segment of the expanding spectrum of knowledge.

Thus the universities, the centers today of what cynics call the knowledge industry, are, in the nature of things, no longer able to produce educated men, men of cultivated intelligence. They are geared to produce specialists, in particular scientists and technicians. The hyperrefined specialization involved in postgraduate work, which cramps the spirit and warps the judgment, is the antithesis of the older ideas of education.

Even the spirit of humanity and toleration, wont to be associated with the university, has evaporated. Developments since the war have made it evident that in its new populist version the university can no longer be thought of as a sort of secular cathedral, conducive to detached reflection and uninhibited conjecture and debate. It is fast becoming a microcosm of the larger community. Into it are imported not only the political passions and prejudices but also the fashionable aberrations and trendy deviant movements of the world at large. It is sad to reflect that, on so many occasions over the last decade or so, the one place within the Western democracies where a controversial issue could *not* be publicly debated were the university precincts.

I mentioned earlier the legacy of the past as exerting an influence on our faith in economic growth. Arbitrarily perhaps (since it could be argued that the European Renaissance was the most significant development), we could take as our critical point of departure the Enlightenment of the second half of the eighteenth century—about which time begins the historic movement toward secularism, a movement away from a social order dominated by myth, folklore, and tradition, toward increasing reliance on reason and empiricism. The ideals of the age of Enlightenment are embodied in the notion of the "perfectibility of man," a notion still enshrined in the modern humanist movement. By the second half of the nineteenth century at the latest, the original conception of Enlightenment as a state or goal has changed to the conception of Enlightenment as a continuing process. Whereas Condorcet, writing under the shadow of the guillotine, reflected that "the perfectibility of man is truly infinite," Herbert Spencer, a century later, was expressing a law of progress when he proclaimed that "always toward perfection is the mighty movement."

The word *improvement* dominated the vocabulary of Victorian writers and reformers. The conviction grew that improvements in the morals, the character, and the culture of the mass of people were inextricbly linked with improvements in the material conditions of life, which later improvements— derving from the enterprise and ingenuity of man expressed in scientific knowledge and its applications to industry—were certain to continue. And although the dethronement of God as the arbiter of man's destiny (a destiny thenceforth to be controlled by man alone) is implicit in this conception of progress, much time had to pass before the implication was widely accepted and the transition to a Godless society effected.

Three nineteenth-century ideas are still powerful. Common to liberal, socialist, and Marxist doctrine is the unquestioned belief that improvement in the material basis of society and, as a corollary, the spread of education, are the preconditions of all social progress and individual fulfillment, however these are visualized. Yet it is a belief that has begun to be challenged. Although it will always be conceded that, beginning from levels close to subsistence, material improvement and education are likely to produce a better society, it is arguable whether the process can be continued indefinitely. To use the economist's jargon, at higher levels of real income and education returns to them diminish and, subsequently, may be negative. Certainly, the evidence of the postwar period suggests that in affluent societies continuing growth in real income and in education is not a sufficient condition, at any rate, for social betterment.

The most casual observer over the last two decades will have been aware of the growth in violence, delinquency, terrorism, and petty crime (shoplifting especially), and aware also of a growth in vulgarity and obscenity, along with a decline in individual liberty in consequence of the expansion of government intervention and control. Again, statistics over the last thirty years reveal a marked increase in crime in all Western countries, especially crimes of violence and especially among the young. There has also been a rising trend of homicide, suicide, divorce, and family breakdown.

Before attending to the crucial question of the relation between economic growth and the growth of the permissive society, it is worth making brief comments on some of the above trends, since the faithful liberal is prone to misconstrue their significance.

The marked rise in the divorce figures, for instance, may also be quoted with approval as signifying a growth in personal freedom or, more frequently, escape from the bondage of an unhappy marriage, rather than as signifying an increase in the number of unhappy marriages. It would require a highly sophisticated statistician to draw a balance sheet in this area of controversy, and a yet more gifted one to determine whether the gain in freedom from simpler divorce procedures more than compensates for the loneliness and the increase in distress of the children involved. If, however, one's concern extends also to the cohesion and stability of society, the unavoidable weakening of the institution of marriage is a significant agendum.

Concerning the alarming rise in crime statistics since World War II, it is common enough to draw comfort from the belief that it is the result chiefly of improvements in methods of gathering the statistics. For this belief there is little warrant. The contrary belief, that the crime statistics have tended to understate the rising trend, is more plausible. An increasing proportion of crimes go unreported because of the increasing permissiveness toward sexual crimes, petty theft, and vandalism; because, in a highly mobile society, in which time is increasingly scarce, citizens would rather not get "involved"; and because, in the cities, people have become increasingly apprehensive about possible retaliation if they report a crime.

What is more, the actual number of violent crimes perpetrated in an area is a very poor indicator of the danger to which a person, walking in that area, is exposed. In a limiting case, actual street crimes could approach zero simply because no sensible person would venture onto the streets during certain hours. The risk—as measured by the probability of being assailed, say, within the hour—could be so high as to deter anyone with his wits about him. The belief that this risk is high irrespective of the crime statistics goes some way to explain the almost frightening desolation at night of the streets of so many American cities.

As for the postwar decline in personal freedom, never has individual activity and enterprise in the Western democracies been so constrained by cumulative legislation and its enforcement by a diversity of government agencies manned by a growing army of government officials—in return for which the new "permissiveness" to stare at leisure at the manifestations of other people's erotic fantasies and to use four-letter words in public strikes me as being poor compensation. I do not touch here on the consequent frustrations of the citizen or the increasing temptations to evade taxes, to "milk" the welfare agencies, and wherever possible to slip through or circumvent constricting legislation—surrender to which temptations undermines his respect for the law and tends to corrupt his character. I wish only to point out that the rapid expansion of government activity is not just a wayward political development. It is an inevitable outcome of continuing economic growth, being society's response to a range of new spillovers that result from the direction taken by scientific and technological research and innovation.

I mentioned earlier those recent advances in small arms technology that have multiplied the power of the criminal and political fanatic to blackmail and terrorize the civilian population—in recognition of which greater police powers are more readily surrendered. At least as important in promoting an expansion of the powers of the state are those innovations having adverse social consequences, some of which I touched on earlier. There are innovations in industrial processes which also produce a variety of toxic wastes. Other innovations take the more familiar form of new gadgets that confer on the user a direct power to spoil the amenity of others or to endanger their health or their lives. The resulting conflicts of interest, and the dangers, favor ever more legislation and control.

Other innovations based on microfilm and computer technology have multiplied the capacity for the processing, storage, and retrieval of information. In consequence, the opportunities open to agencies, government and private, for accumulating information on activities and personal details of each citizen become more difficult to resist. Indeed, a system of detailed and up-to-date dossiers on each citizen can easily be rationalized both on humanitarian and medical grounds and on security grounds, especially in a high-technology society increasingly vulnerable to widespread disaster arising from human error, negligence, or sabotage.

Finally, the very pace of modern research and the haste to market its products are productive of grave dangers. One obvious example is the postwar nuclear energy industry, which can be regarded as safe only if the degree of the vigilance exercised is such as to entail further extensions of the existing internal and international security arrangements. Of course, the public's reaction may be thought to be unduly apprehensive. Nonetheless, its apprehensiveness issues in a demand for increased government control and regulation of the processes and products of modern industry.

It is far from impossible that the anxiety of the public will, over time, prompt it to cede to government powers of surveillance and control that are incompatible even with contemporary notions of personal freedom—a high price to pay for economic growth.

We come, at last, to the third point, at which my thesis requires that we look more seriously at one of the features that characaterize an era covering the last two decades—the growth of "permissiveness."

Lest the term be misunderstood, I should stress that this "permissiveness" is not simply characterized in a Western-type liberal democracy by permissiveness of debate and dissent. There has been debate and dissent in liberal democracies long before the permissive society of the last two decades or so. The permissive society of which I speak here is marked by three emerging and interrelated features: (1) most obviously, an apparent suspension of all norms of propriety and convention that is coming to make the question of what is decent or indecent (especially with respect to sexual behavior or entertainment), what is proper or improper, increasingly a matter of individual discretion; (2) an erosion of respect for traditional procedures upon which all forms of self-governing societies depend (as witnessed in the postwar period by a growth in open defiance of existing legislation and in obstruction of its implementation by direct action); and (3) a fragmenting, if not a crumbling, of the moral consensus of society. This last development is indeed portentous. For whatever our conflicts of interest, or our political differences about ideal or better arrangements for society, effective argument becomes impossible if there is no longer a common set of ultimate values or beliefs to which appeal can be made in the endeavor to persuade others.

The question of whether a liberal democratic society, which is a fragile growth, in which each individual is to be his own ultimate authority in all that touches on taste, convention, propriety, government legitimacy, and morality, can long endure will shortly be answered—in the negative. In the meantime, and before generalizing on the subject, let me speculate boldly on two movements associated with this era of permissiveness: homosexual liberation and women's liberation.

Of course, in the encompassing atmosphere of purposelessness any liberation movement offers relief and elation. The joy of snubbing conventional restraints, the sheer exhilaration of breaking through established barriers, should not be derided by those lacking the experience. Yet one cannot help wondering uneasily just what sort of society will remain once the barriers are irreparably breached.

Neither homosexuality nor militant feminism are new in history. What is new in the postwar movements are the scale and the nature of the phenomena, both of which today and for the first time in history threaten the institution of the family—that irreducible organic cell upon which, whatever its composition, all recorded civilizations have built. Each of these two popular movements may be attributed in part to economic growth.

Experiments with colonies of rodents have shown that when they are exposed to stress conditions, such as overcrowding, they invariably react by a rapid increase in the incidence of neglect (of themselves and their young), and of violence, cannibalism, and homosexuality. Perhaps I am stretching a point. But I ask you to consider seriously the possibility that the tensions induced by living in vast urban centers—tensions that arise from the excessive pace and movement, noise and overcrowding—issue in similar propensities among human populations. At all events, the emergence of a permissive ethic—itself an end-product of the secularism that is entailed by the idea of progress —weakens the traditional safeguards against mass surrender to fashionable indulgence.

Turning to the feminist movement, the lot of the housewife before the twentieth century appears a sad one only when seen through the eyes of people manifestly aspiring toward a push-button utopia. Yet it was the very absence of these modern domestic appliances that made the mother the central and indispensable figure in the home.[4] Nor is it historically justifiable to suppose that she took no pride in or derived no satisfaction from this role. For her senses were not, then, assailed daily by the ubiquitous media with their compelling visions of the joys of independence, travel, and sumptuous revelry.

With the introduction of domestic gadgetry, women were bound to become more nervous, restless, and, indeed, defensive. Too many found themselves cooped up in their apartments, fretting as the days slipped by, convinced they were being deprived of their share of "the good things of life." It is not surprising that, in increasing numbers, they wish to break out of this "woman's pen" into industry.

The vocation of housewife and home-building is, in effect, being rendered obsolete by the remorseless advance of technology. And with the decline of woman's role in the home, the institution of the family has begun to decline also. The consequences of this decline for the character and stability of society form an uneasy subject for conjecture.

I have argued elsewhere,[5] simply as a judgment of fact, that a moral consensus that is to be enduring and effective is the product only of a belief in its divine origin. A moral order, that is, can rest secure only on a religious foundation. It cannot, alas, be raised on humanistic principles—on enlightened sweet reason—at all events, not so long as society continues to remain in that imperfect state in which fools and knaves abound and sinners vastly outnumber saints. Especially in large communities in which the proportion of families known personally by an individual is negligible, the absence of a binding code of ethics or a strong sense of civic virtue or patriotism tends to resolve the inevitable conflicts between the individual's or family's perceived self-interest and the interests of the larger community in favor of the former.[6]

It is no exaggeration to assert that the triumph of secular progress, the child of the Enlightenment, is culminating today in an erosion throughout the West of that moral consensus which arose out of ecumenical Christendom. Today's generations, unpatriotic, impatient of authority and of any institution suspected of impeding their claims to gratification, may rightly claim to be forming a new amoral society. Increasingly they turn for guidance, not to precepts based on some transcendental ethic, but to what they choose to call an "own ethic." Increasingly they justify their conduct—whether inspired by impulse or by calculation—by reference to the depth and strength of their private convictions.

This amoral society that is coming into being is indeed that which is euphemistically referred to as a "permissive" or an "open," or yet more comprehensively, a "pluralist" society. The question of how it comes into being has been touched upon. Two other relevant questions invite conjecture: What purpose, if any, does it serve? And how, if at all, can it survive?

Economic determinism is, to some, a repulsive doctrine. Yet there is an undoubted connection, as suggested earlier, between today's feminist revolution and the rapid spread over the last fifty years or so of those domestic labor-saving innovations that have rendered women's traditional role in society increasingly expendable. What then of the permissive society which, beginning with the joyous rejection of "Victorian guilt," progresses to an abandonment of a vestigal sense of shame, moves on to a clamorous rejection of any restraint on appetite, and culminates in adopting the experience of pleasure as an infallible guide to the good life?

Why, it is surely a providential development by means of which the modern technically sophisticated economy, continuously under institutional compulsion to expand, can be kept going! For the continued expansion of modern industry as a whole depends directly on its success in whetting and enlarging the appetite of the consuming public so as to enable it to engorge the burgeoning variety and volume of goods. Clearly a discriminating public will not serve. Nor will a public whose demand for goods is restrained by consideration of propriety and good taste, or by accepted ideas of right and wrong. Promiscuity is the quality sought for, promiscuity coupled with insatiability.

In other words, the ideal public for the modern economy is one that is uprooted from all conventional constraints; one that is free-floating, volatile, plastic; one that can be molded and segmented and pulled hither and thither by the carefully planned campaigns of modern advertising agencies. This ideal public is, of course, that found in the permissive society. For a society in which "anything goes" is *ipso facto* a society in which anything sells.

But reflection has a little further to go. As Boulding and McKean have also perceived and as Fred Hirsch[7] has recently perceived and emphasized, the permissive society fosters attitudes that endanger the economic system it serves. For in the erosion of traditional moral values and of the pride taken in personal rectitude and personal responsibility, the efficient operation of both government and industry is placed under increasing strain. Yet this development is but a minor aspect of a more general problem emerging from the growth of permissiveness.

I argued above that economic growth in the West is producing innovations that create unprecedented social conflicts and ecological hazards, both of which lead to increasing government controls. This resulting trend toward more government and less personal freedom is reinforced by the perils of the permissive society. Not only does the permissive "own ethic" pose a threat to the bureaucracy and to the management of industry and commerce. More important yet, it poses a threat to civil law and order. In a society in which ideas of what is right and wrong become increasingly ephemeral, self-serving, and diverse—in a society, therefore, in which every person feels free to act on his own privately reconstituted conscience—the resulting atmosphere of unease and anxiety and the community's fear of anarchy will surely sanction surrender to the police, and to other internal security agencies, of increased powers of surveillance and control.

Thus as the moral order upon which any enduring civilization has to be founded is scrapped in the name of emancipation, so, in the name of security, does the state expand its powers. Repressive mechanisms internal to the individual are replaced by repressive mechanisms external to him. The permissive society, it transpires, is the precursor of the totalitarian state.[8]

Let me summarize my interpretation of events and conclude. How did we come to this sad impasse? The simple answer is man's *hubris*.

In his search for mastery over nature, and addressing his intelligence to specific and immediate ends, man has been all too successful. And his appetite has fed on his success. Today there are no bounds to his ambition, and no limits to his capacity. He has begun to wreck the social order as surely as he has begun to wreck the natural order.

Since the beginning of the nineteenth century, and far more rapidly since the end of World War II, industrial societies, in order to surge ahead economically, have thoughtlessly disencumbered themselves of myths and institutions that have spanned centuries and millennia. The great belief systems, the idea of a divine lawgiver, the sanctity of the family, the rich tapestry of custom and convention, the ceremonies and festivals, the rituals and benedictions—all that despite hardship, suffering, and occasional disaster gave purpose and ultimate dignity to the smaller communities of earlier ages—lie about us, discarded and in ruins. In our haste to throw off the burden of this heritage so as to give free rein to appetite and enterprise, we failed to recognize its providential character: Among other things, its creation of an intricate arterial system, along which the irrepressible currents of human love—parental love, filial love, romantic love, conjugal love, the love of loyal friends—can flow, freely and easily, through appointed channels fitting to the custom and occasion.

The unavoidable frustration resulting from this act of social vandalism has, alas, only aggravated man's lust for power and sparked his hopes with technological fantasies that can only remove him further from human fulfillment. The resulting despair has begot a craving to pierce more wantonly the seeming repressive integument of the social order, a craving expressed in the feverish search for novelty and excitement which, while admirably serving the forces of economic expansion, leads unerringly to the totalitarian state.

Again, then, it is not possible to end on an optimistic note. Yet if the outlook is grim indeed, it does not follow that we should feel depressed. The growth in our understanding of what is happening to our civilization does, of itself, provide some intellectual satisfaction. (I own to deriving no little pleasure from attacking the bearers of the blight of unwarranted optimism, and from habitually checking the spread of cheer and hope in order to give the gloom a chance to settle properly.)

Nor need our forebodings necessarily induce a spirit of resignation. For one cannot bring oneself entirely to abandon hope, if only because human beings are so obstinate as still to believe in miracles. But this slender filament of hope can be preserved only if public opinion in the West becomes rapidly and deeply perturbed by its daring to recognize the incredible dangers, physical and social, that today threaten our science-based civilization.

NOTES

1. See *Economic Growth Debate: An Assessment* (London: Allen and Unwin, 1977).

2. See my *Costs of Economic Growth* (London, 1967), p. x.

3. Vance Packard, *A Nation of Strangers* (New York: Pocket Books, 1972).

4. Omitting the period covering the traumatic experience of the first century or so of the Industrial Revolution in Britain (ending about the middle of the nineteenth century), the heyday of British capitalism vividly described by Marx, and the beginning of modern economic growth. In the early part of the nineteenth century, following the Enclosure Acts when dispossessed families flocked to the new industrial towns of the North, the bulk of working-class wives had no choice but to toil long hours in the mines and factories, along with children, simply in order to survive. The wife who had a husband able to keep her at home was then an object of envy to working wives.

   The Suffragette movement in Britain, inspired by Sylvia Pankhurst, which reached its peak just before the outbreak of World War I, had as its single objective the extension of the vote to women and of the right to take part in the political life of the country. (One of their compelling arguments, incidentally, was that if women entered freely into the political life of democratic nations, wars would never occur.)

5. *Economic Growth Debate.*

6. Belief in a diety, admittedly, is not sufficient to prevent men going to war. As I observed in *Costs of Economic Growth* any institution disposing of the enormous wealth, power, and patronage of the Church tempts corruption and fires worldly ambition. The spirit of good men could be inflamed to do battle under the banner of God when, in fact, the stakes were temporal and material.

   Who can say whether more crimes against humanity have been committed in the name of God, in the name of liberty, in the name of justice, or in the name of other slogans thrown up by all-sweeping ideologies? But a faith in a benevolent God is necessary for a good life inasmuch as such faith is the ultimate source of the morals and the traditional proprieties from which a society derives its identity and cohesion.

7. In *Social Limits to Growth* (Cambridge: Harvard University Press, 1976).

8. Such a totalitarian state, however, need have no compunction about promoting "permissiveness" and sexual circuses in order to divert the mind of the citizen from dangerous thoughts about the possibilities of retrieving political control of his destiny. In *Brave New World* Aldous Huxley admirably describes just such a totalitarian state.

19

ENERGY USE
AND MORAL RESTRAINT

Wherein are contrasted the views
of the economist and the engineer
on the use of finite resources

Bruce Hannon

14 November 1830

Professor Malthus:

Before this month began, I had only heard of your work through my friends and my professors. "The Summary View" makes it the clearest possible case for a policy of encouraging the restriction of the population before nature restricts its food supply. On the one hand, I am reassured by your data on the populations of England and Germany; on the other, I am disturbed by your finding that the French revolutions have increased the rate of growth in our population. The interplay is subtle indeed between your positive check of war and the fear that our population will be extinguished. Surely you are correct

Reprinted by permission of author and publisher from *Journal of Social and Biological Structures*, Vol. 1, 1978, pp. 357–375. Copyright © 1978 Academic Press Inc. (London) Limited.

that if our new population increases too quickly for the food supply, we shall be overrun with other troubles. A fear now exists in some parts of Paris that we are not careful enough with the cleanliness of our water. I am confident that our rapidly growing awareness of such things will lead to a means of conquering these problems.

Your connection of the population with the food supply brings to mind the argument of the Physiocrates—an idea which I must admit I have never been able to discard completely. From what does our wealth really derive? The soil? The labor of the people? Their tools? Perhaps all of these, but surely some are more important than others. If people prize their tools most highly, then what are these tools for? And if the answer is labor, for what do we strive? The soil is a vehicle for food. Yet, from whence does the soil derive our food? Clearly, the sunlight is the source of our food energy and consequently our labor.

Perhaps the energy of the sun is what we strive to capture, with our success determining the size of the population and how well it lives. This line of reasoning conforms to what I find in the beginning of "The Summary View," but I have tried to cast it in terms familiar to the engineer. I hope the slight transformation of your argument to a more physical line of thought does not do it an injustice.

With the hope that you shall find time to reply, I remain

Your most humble servant,
S. CARNOT

Professor T. R. Malthus
History and Political Economics
Haileybury College
Hertford, England

March 15, 1830
Dear Carnot,

I am most taken by your translation of my principles of population. Your mechanistic view is not unreasonable if you wish only to transform the concept of food into one based on the energy of the sun. Although I see nothing wrong with that, I do have difficulty in establishing the sun as the most important factor of those you mention. You seem to hold some particular theory of value about energy. However, I believe that the happiness and virtue of the people are supremely important and that all wealth, power, population and land should be devoted to those ends.

Surely we can only dimly perceive the manner in which to arrange the physical aspects of our economy. If we could find one or two sensitive issues by which to promote most easily the welfare of the population, I would consider my search as ended. As a mere shadow of that goal, I have enunciated what appears to be a limiting condition for the size of the population.

Also, I have attempted to demonstrate how best to use our wisdom and restraint in order to remain well clear of that limit, lest we be ploughed under by the positive checks into vice and misery.

Surely, the process of agriculture is the principal part of this limitation on the total population. We cannot expand the food supply to an excess for long. As I have stated, the population tends to expand and to press against any such increase. The best that agriculture can do is to exchange the various parts of the plant from an inedible stalk or root into a grain which can be consumed by man or by his animals. The total weight of the matter grown on a given acre is not changed by agriculture, but merely rearranged to suit our stomachs.

This is the basis of the real limit concerning the size of the population. Nature and man capture the same amount of sun into plants—those growing wild and those which man cultivates. The only way to overcome this limitation on the human population is to produce more of the same plant, either on each acre or by converting fallow ground to agricultural pursuits.

In like manner, the division or rearrangement of our labour can improve the rate of industrial production. But we made little progress in this endeavour for many years until machines appeared and made each worker more productive. As I look about Europe and especially England today, I realise how much more each person is working each day than they did in former, more agricultural times. This increased effort and its superior organization must surely be necessary for the industrial revolution.

Our agriculturalists indicate that domestic animals convert only about one part in ten of their food into their own weight. This, too, presents a limit. All of the plant which man cannot eat himself, can be converted but poorly into food for an animal for man to eat.

Let me say that I believe there is substance to your thought. I should be pleased greatly to hear from you again.

Truly yours,
T. R. MALTHUS

Sadi Carnot
Nr. 5bis rue de l'Est
Paris.

THE SETTING

Thomas Malthus (1766–1834), the English political economist, and Sadi Carnot (1796–1832), an engineer and the founder of thermodynamics, both lived at the beginning of the Industrial Revolution. Unfortunately, they never met. Yet their concepts of limits are the basis of much societal concern today.

An imaginary dialogue is fashioned between Malthus and Carnot— idealizing their thinking and extending their concepts of limits to illuminate a major current economic dilemma. Through such a fusion, an equitable condition is created for the surrender of human aspirations to physical limits.

Both men believed in physical limits: Malthus, on the size of the human population, Carnot, on our ability to extract work from energy. Neither man viewed energy as a social force nor understood its impact on population through food production and use. Had they exchanged views and blended their considerable talents, our perceptions of reality and consequently our ability to cope with contemporary problems could have been considerably improved. However, their concepts of absolute limits were lost in the economic and political struggles for equity in France and for development in England. Most economists and engineers since the early nineteenth century have been dealing with relative limits—the difficulties in expanding energy-using and labor-saving technology to increase productivity and personal income. The interplay between disciplines of economics and engineering has structured virtually every aspect of the Industrial Revolution. Yet only in recent times have engineers and economists begun to realize the narrowness of their views.

The dialogue presented here in letters between Carnot and Malthus reflects the author's own intellectual evolution, educated as an engineer, yet performing research in economic matters.

In 1306, Edward I of England issued a proclamation that the use of coal was punishable by death. At least one man so perished. The medieval English evidently believed that burning coal made the air unhealthy. Thus, home heating was accomplished by burning wood or charcoal. Although England possessed great coal deposits, the use of coal was limited to minor iron production. The wood supply was running low by the mid-1600s though, and coal mining had been considerably restrained by drainage problems.

The invention of the steam engine in the late seventeenth century and its early application to mine drainage freed England from its first recorded resource shortage. The well-timed appearance of the steam engine provided the first evidence to society that appropriate technology would come forth when the need arose. Increased coal production allowed the advantages of steam power to be applied rapidly. By 1830, steam cars were running in England, and steam ships were replacing sailing vessels at sea. International trade and communication were expanding. Urbanization and the specialization of labor were also well under way. The unhealthy air of London was now accepted.

The imaginary exchange of letters between Malthus and Carnot begins in 1830, when Carnot happens upon a copy of Malthus' recent summary of his work. The sequence ends with Carnot's tragic death in the cholera epidemic of 1832, snared by a Malthusian positive check.

The period is precariously balanced between a time when nations equated wealth with the size of the population and the time of rapid growth and dreadful collapse of the Irish population in 1845. Malthus speaks as a social scientist in the midst of a technological revolution; Carnot, as an engineer in the center of a social revolution. Malthus apparently heard the ominous drum beat of zealous overpopulation. Carnot seems to have had an idealistic vision of the technological future.

THE CHARACTERS

Thomas Robert Malthus entered Jesus College at Cambridge when he was 18, becoming proficient in many areas, including Latin, Greek, French, and especially mathematics; at the age of 27, he was ordained a minister in the Church of England.

His father had been executor for Rousseau, the refugee-writer who enunciated the case for the French Revolution in a series of novels. The elder Malthus was convinced that the French Revolution, seen by him as a movement toward complete interpersonal equity, was correct. Thomas Malthus, however, felt that such a goal was impossible to achieve. After several years of disagreement, the father persuaded his son Thomas to publish his views.

In 1798, at the age of 32, Thomas Malthus produced an anonymous essay on the principle of population, which sparked a great controversy. Over the next 32 years, Malthus refined and buttressed his arguments. In 1830, he published his final version, *The Summary Views*. By that time, Malthus was a highly regarded political economist. Among his many honors he had become a member of the Berlin Royal Academy and the French Institute, and he was a Fellow of the Royal Society in England. His ideas strongly influenced social decisions in England during the nineteenth century.

Malthus made a series argument: (1) the American population was apparently unfettered by food shortages of any kind; (2) the doubling time for the population was 25 years; (3) no other known human population was doubling at anywhere near that rate; therefore, (4) certain forces were constraining the reproduction rates of other populations. He classed these forces or "checks" on the growth rate as: preventive (moral restraint in the form of celibacy, delayed marriage and abstinence) or positive (war, pestilence, famine, disease, infanticide and exposure to the elements).

Malthus considered both contraception and abortion as positive checks, a penalty of the "vice" of overpopulation. When people failed to apply the preventive checks; then the "misery" of the positive checks would take over. If he had classed contraception and abortion as preventive and positive checks respectively, the preventive checks would have applied exclusively to the control of the birth rate, with the positive checks pertaining only to the death rate. His solution was the application of moral restraint, e.g. sexual abstinence or celibacy.

Malthus underestimated the power of technological progress and importation in terms of increasing the food supply. Neither set of checks needs to be applied as long as technological change allows the plentiful resources to be substituted for scarce ones. However, Malthus was quite correct when he said that the population will always tend to press against the food supply. Where the capacity to acquire food has increased, so has population.

Sadi Carnot[1] lived his entire life amid the turbulence of recurring revolutions in France. Although virtually unknown during his short lifetime, he is now regarded as one of the great scientists of the nineteenth century and as the founder of thermodynamics. His father, a major force in the revolutions ("the Organizer of Victory"), was alternately fleeing and returning to France with Napoleon. His mother, Sofi DuPont, was an accomplished musician. Sadi Carnot graduated from the Ecole Polytechnique in Paris and the military school at Metz. He then became an officer in the Corps of Engineers. The young Carnot spoke English, excelled at mathematics and was an expert violinist. He also kept notes on religion, natural history and political economics. At 23, Carnot published the now famous *Reflections on the Motive Power of Heat*. In this small book, his only publication, and in extensive notes which were preserved by his brother Henri, Carnot developed the laws of thermodynamics. Basically, these laws consist of the indestructibility of energy (conservation of energy), the degradation of energy (with use, energy always becomes less available to do mechanical work) and the transformability of energy (energy can be converted from heat to mechanical work and back).

Carnot's views were developed primarily around an idealized concept of steam engines and a theory of heat flow. Although his book contained a minor misconception about the nature of energy, his notes show that he actually understood the modern concept of thermodynamics. His classic maxim is still valid today: the greatest possible efficiency of a heat engine depends only on the absolute temperature of the heat source and the receiving environment. He understood the need to establish an absolute base of reference for the temperature in order to calculate these efficiencies. This need for an absolute rather than a relative frame of reference is an important concept, one not yet accepted in economics.

Malthus and Carnot were aristocrats, scholars, scientists and idealists. Both were deeply religious. Carnot believed in the existence of a "Supreme Being," Malthus believed in God but not in Hell. Both men were creative and intellectually courageous, yet very practical in assessing the utility of their work to mankind. This practical thread of inquiry was channeled by their certainty about the existence of limits. Malthus knew the ever-expanding population must eventually stop growing. Carnot demonstrated for the first time that perpetual motion is impossible.

Malthus, who was much older than Carnot, was an empiricist and a pessimist. Carnot, a theorist and a decided optimist, was incurably mechanistic and was a true believer in the Industrial Age. Malthus saw the wretched conditions of English factory life, the environment for children at work and cities already crowded and increasing in size. Malthus was consumption-oriented and believed in controlling demand to solve social problems. Carnot was production-oriented and believed that national problems could be solved by increasing the quantity and variety of supplies.

Malthus was married and had three children. Carnot never married. Malthus was a reformer, a sort of academic campaigner. Carnot, although skilled at athletics, was quiet to the point of shyness. He resigned from his army captaincy in 1828 and moved to Paris in order to pursue his thermodynamic studies without interruption.

14 August 1831

Professor Matlhus:

I believe you have correctly pointed out that man is like the other members of the living system. Each is competing for space and resources, apparently seeking to fill that space with its own kind. Man seeks nourishment and protection. He builds homes from the stones and trees in his space, clothes himself from the products of his agriculture, and, most importantly, derives his food from the sunlight that falls upon his territory. You have, I believe, also correctly identified the tendency of the population to increase so as to press against the available territory and supply of food.

As you have also indicated, food is a form of stored energy somehow derived from the sun. So the population tends to press against the available energy from the sun. Therefore, if man can increase the rate at which he captures the sun's energy, the population will also increase. It follows, then, that if by our cleverness we can induce the energy clearly contained in coal to augment that of the sun, the population would be able to increase still more.

Thus we would be able to say that the population will rise to press against the available supply of energy. We eat neither sunlight nor coal but both are forms of energy and, as such, contribute to expansion of the population. I have prepared a detailed discussion of this thesis for your comment.

Because the matter is so complex, future prescriptions are a mixture of improved insight, beliefs and closer observation. Generally, though, I find the prospect of achieving greater control of our destiny to be acceptable and even desirable.

Coal is the real wealth of England and its wealth increases at the rate at which coal is employed in useful enterprise. The use of coal and of the steam engine will grow, easing the life of a great many people. The poor will be freed from their drudgery. The way of life once available only to the upper class will be available to the whole nation. With coal we can free the farm laborers to pursue other needs. We can defend our soil with a smaller army. The coal and steam engine shall break forever that which revolution and aspiration seem unable to do, the bond between the servant and the master.

Your humble admirer,
SADI CARNOT

The following paper was enclosed with the letter from Carnot of 14 August 1831.

ON THE ABILITY OF COAL TO INCREASE THE POPULATION

S. Carnot, Paris, 1831

The modern view of the origin of coal is that it was probably derived from plants which grew from ancient sunlight on ancient land. Using coal is expanding the territory of a nation in time rather than in space. Properly used, the coal avoids the needs of military action to expand the present land available to feed a rising population.

It is my purpose to explain how the use of coal will cause an increase in food availability and a decrease in per capita *demand for food. I develop an equation which I claim can be used to predict the rate of growth of the population and its ultimate level.*

From Mr Griffith's book on population and from a set of available records, I have extracted data on the population of England and Wales since 1700. This country has kept superior records when compared to the continent. I then prepared a chart showing the variation of the whole population from 1700 to the present.

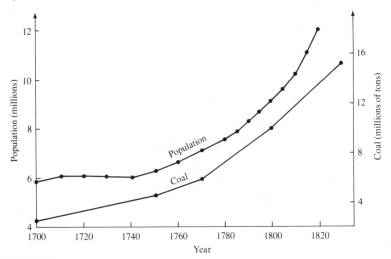

FIGURE 19.1

Population of England and Wales (Mr. Griffith's data). Coal consumed by Great Britain (British Coal Commission).

The population held steady as an agricultural society from 1710 to 1740. Then, a rapid rise began. From this first chart I have prepared a second: a plot of the relative rate of population growth (using the population of 1710 to 1740 as a reference) against the population (in excess of the reference level).

Along the curve, I have also noted the possible major technical changes in the economy of England and Wales.

When I say "relative rates of growth" I mean "the rate of change of the growth rate per unit of flow." The "relative rate of growth" of the population, in percentage terms, is the birth rate per 100 people less the death rate per 100 people.

This second type of graph has been deduced after much experimentation with information on growing species from the Belgian statistician, Quetelet. He has studied the growth of living things whose only resources are moisture, the soil in which they grow and the sun's energy. For example, the growth of plants increases more and more rapidly until a turning point is reached. After that, the growth rate slows more and more until a steady population level is reached. His data show that each human body also grows in this same manner. This type of growth I call "logistical." When the growth is increasing at a constant relative rate per year, it is generally referred to as "geometrical."

The results in the second chart are rather surprising. From 1740 until about 1775, the population grew in a logistical way. We know coal was being used in this time, a fact which I claim caused the departure from the steady population level (no growth) of 1710–1740. After 1775, the population grew geometrically, again I claim, primarily because of the rapidly rising use of coal. According to the data in the first chart, coal use in Great Britain was proceeding at nearly a geometric rate by 1780.

The Newcomen steam engine was certainly an advance over animal and wind power, but it was very difficult to cool after every stroke and required a considerable amount of coal to operate it. The Newcomen engine was used primarily to pump water out of the coal mines. Basically, this period allowed expanded iron production. The iron must have provided significant improvements in agricultural and in industrial production of England. This was also the period when vast improvements in agricultural practice were possible. The fallow land and commons were considerably reduced. Crop fertilization, rotation, drainage, and intensive cultivation were instituted.

Had Watt not developed the expansion steam engine, the earlier engine development and the subsequent improvements in agriculture would have run their course and the population would have probably risen another 1.4 million by the end of the century, to a total of about 7.4 million. I have shown this by the dashed line in the second chart. But the Watt engine was a most remarkable invention, efficiently producing rapid advances in transportation, steelmaking, weaving, grain milling and even engine-making. It has led, for example, to trade with other nations via steamship. Surely some day the food produced on other lands will be used by the British in a major way. Also, the engine directly replaces labor, in ways still being discovered. This engine is a major turning point in the history of the civilized world.

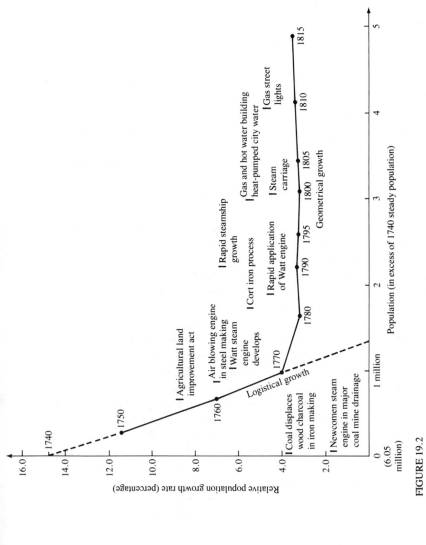

FIGURE 19.2

Population change for England and Wales (References to 1740 level).

Consider more closely the dashed-solid line in the second population chart. There appears to be a linear relation between the relative growth rate for the population and the population level. Quetelet's data showed the same simple phenomenon. I can thereby establish a type of demand-supply equation in which the relative population growth rate plus the population multiplied by a constant, B, are the demand factors, which are equal to a constant supply rate, A. Thus:

$$\frac{Population\ Growth\ Rate}{Population} + B{\cdot}Population = A.$$

A mathematical solution of the equation in general yields the "S" shaped or logistical growth curves of Quetelet. The equation shows that as the population begins to grow, based on the food energy supply rate, "A," countervailing forces, B·Population, which will eventually bring it to a stationary level, are set in motion.

I claim that logistical growth occurs when the rate of energy supply is constant, as in systems which depend only on the sun as an energy source. Growing plants and agrarian human populations are examples. When the energy supply suddenly increases relative to the demand rate, that is, when "A" grows rapidly compared to "B·Population," geometric growth occurs.

The leftmost term of the equation is a flow divided by a stock. As such it is similar to the interest rate on the investment in capital: the return on capital investment per year divided by the quantity of investment. A similar statement is true of the growth of a forest: the rate of increase of the wood in the forest divided by the total amount of wood in the forest. As the population approaches the steady state, this "interest" rate approaches zero.

Rather than study the solution to the equation, however, it is simpler to study the equation itself, to attempt to assign meaning to the values "A" and "B" and to interpret the meaning of changes in their value.

Suppose that a given piece of uniformly fertile land has no population. With the agricultural practices of the time, this land has a potential of capturing a fraction of the incoming sun's energy as food. This potential rate of capture is "A" per cent per year. The individual food energy demand rate, when compared to the potential supply, is "B" per cent per person per year. Thus "A" is the potential relative food energy supply rate and "B" is the relative per capita demand rate. In the second chart, the initial value of "A" is 14 per cent per year, and of "B" is calculated at 10 per cent per million persons per year. According to my equation, the total rate of food consumption will rise as the population increases. When the potential supply rate is realized and is equal to the total demand rate, the population will have reached the stationary level.

I examine the influence on "A" and "B" of a series of societal changes acting one at a time. Any changes which increase "A" or decrease "B" will increase the population growth rate and, if they persist, will increase the ultimate stationary population level. If the original agricultural practice had included the need for fallow land and now this fallow land is used to grow crops, then the potential capture rate "A" is unchanged and "B" is decreased in proportion to the ratio of the amount of presently used land to the former amount. If food is imported from another land, "A" is increased and "B" is decreased; the same for increases in soil fertility or the use of machines for agriculture; the same also for great road systems which connect productive but remote areas of land with other fertile areas and with the center of population. If coal can be traded for this imported food, then the original amount of land remains intact, for coal extraction does not interfere with agriculture. But if cotton had to be grown to be traded for food, the home production of food is decreased. If the cotton can be traded for more food than the cotton land could have produced, then "A" is increased and "B" is decreased; and conversely. If animals are raised for meat consumption, then "A" is decreased and "B" increased.

Now assume that the original land is not uniformly fertile and animals are raised on the poorest land. If this latter portion of the homeland can produce more food energy as meat than as grain, then "A" increases and "B" decreases; and conversely. If animals are used to displace the work of man, then human food demands are decreased because man will work less hard. But land used to raise animal food could have been used to raise food for humans. If this foregone human food production exceeds the decrease in human food demands allowed by use of work animals, then "A" is decreased and "B" is increased; and conversely.

If wood is burned to provide bodily warmth, this warmth decreases the food requirements which would have been needed to keep the body warm. The land which provided the wood can be used instead for food production. If this woodland were converted to food land and it could provide more food energy than the wood burning had displaced, then "A" would be increased and "B" decreased. The same argument is true for wool, leather, cotton and flax when used for clothing. If coal is used to provide bodily warmth or to power engines to do the work of man, and so in each case reduce his food demands, then "B" alone is decreased. If certain of these engines replace the food demands of work animals, then "A" is increased. If coal is used to heat our food to make its energy more available and its temperature more nearly that of the human body, then "B" alone is decreased. The use of coal is an unrestrained benefit to increasing the population when compared with the use of wood, animals or agricultural trade.

A society could make the transition to a condition of improved agriculture or to coal use either slowly or by a relatively sudden shift. In the third chart, I show how the transition is made by a geometric expansion (horizontal line) of the population to the improved agricultural state. Assuming a constant marriage age and family size, the improvements produce a geometrical growth rate (constant relative growth rate) if unfettered by any energy shortages. Since the demand rate is never negative, a geometrical growth rate is the

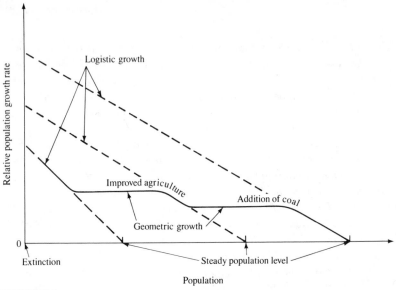

FIGURE 19.3

Showing the transition of an agrarian society to one of improved agriculture, and then to one using coal.

fastest possible one for the human population, excepting conditions of immigration. Eventually, the growth stimulating effects abate and geometrical growth gives way to logistical growth and the stationary state is approached. The addition of coal produces a similar effect as shown.

The use of coal increases the food supply. As Malthus has shown, the population tends to press against the food supply. Therefore, the use of coal operates to increase the population. Clearly, my thesis is that the population will expand to press against the available energy resources. If, for example, the agricultural society can double the rate at which useful solar energy is captured or halve the rate of energy demand per person, then it can reach a steady population level which is twice the original level, and is likely to do so. The value of coal energy in augmenting this process is difficult to underestimate.

There are two general ways, then, in which coal energy augments the population:

1. Increasing the food supply by:
    —Trading coal or coal products for food produced on foreign lands.
    —Using coal, directly and indirectly, to augment the capture of the sun's energy on the home soil.
    The first of these forces is limited only by the supply of coal; the second one is limited only by our ingenuity.

2. Decreasing the food demand per person by:
    —Providing bodily warmth.

—*Using coal fed engines to reduce physical labor.*
These decreases in the rate of demands are limited by our inability to
substitute coal for all subsistence needs of the body.

November 10, 1831
Dear Carnot:

I am most struck by your ability to translate the numbers of man to the plane of paper and pen. It is indeed an ingenious analogy. You must take care, however, to remember that one cannot even hope to enclose all the needs of man within an equation. He does not have us here merely to gather and group the economic and social mysteries of the day and fit them into an equation. We are here to intone a set of moral values as guiding principles for future societies. I can only suggest that you obtain more data on other countries and check your thesis further.

It seems to me that in your paper on the use of coal, you have proven my original thesis: regardless of our aspirations, the total level of population is limited by our sheer ability to produce enough food. I have argued for the last 34 years that for the working class to improve their well-being, they must control their numbers and reduce their population. Then their wage would naturally rise. But my opponents have argued that the Industrial Revolution will increase the production and therefore the wage of the common worker. Now, you have provided the basis for my counter-argument: that the essence of the industrial revolution—coal—will work to increase the food supply and also to reduce the need for food per capita. I shall henceforth argue that this coal energy will cause the population to rise coincident with the improvement in productivity and ultimately cancel these gains.

You can show by the same process of reasoning you have so ably developed for food use that the maximum coal usage is also geometric. Further, as the coal becomes more and more difficult to find, more and more of it will be used directly at the mine and indirectly to make the iron machinery for mining. Eventually, the net supply of coal must become steady at best, perhaps declining. In other words, will not the population of machines eventually rise to press against their coal supply? Will not the rising wage and cost of machines someday leave us unable to profitably mine a diminishing reserve of coal? Do we run the risk of overextending the population level such that when the coal supply fails, the population will fall back to the purely agricultural level? Although the machines today are wont to do our physical work, will they now someday try to do the work of the mind? I find these prospects much worse than proceeding to the agricultural steady population directly and with restricted use of coal. Note also that future wars will be over coal as well as land, adding a third dimension to the need for conquest.

Conversely, rather than a coal shortage, we could assume that the energy is infinitely available at a cheap rate. Then the population will expand at a rate limited only by our ability to produce more food. Eventually, the available land must experience diminishing returns from additions of energy. Also the crops, all being of the one or two most productive types, will periodically fail due to forces which we now only dimly understand. These failures will cause the population to be reduced drastically. Such people eventually learn to control their population at a low and steady level only after great and unnecessary misery.

The idea of a society of men free of hard work may be more of an illusion than you anticipate. In England, and in France to some extent, we can see the beginnings of a new enslavement. The spinning and weaving machines, for example, do not tire, nor do they possess a sympathy for the worker who attends them. The conditions of labour are crowded and generally unhealthy. Although the production of cloth by each worker is far greater, I notice no improvement in their general state of happiness.

In time, coal will become cheaper, and that will mean high wages. The workers then have the fruits of far more production per day than formerly. Where ten were employed making cloth before the coal engine, one can then provide the same cloth with the aid of the engine-loom. The one remaining worker could enjoy a higher wage rate than any of the former ten.

What of the other nine, though, the ones no longer employed? Shall these weavers become engine-makers? How are they to learn? Even if they were to learn the manner in which engines are made, might they not forego employment once again as the engine nearly learns to make itself? If such is to be the case, eventually men will be at ease, that is true, but how shall they feed themselves? And how shall they occupy themselves? They are too poor to own the engines. What will they exchange for food, and for coal?

There is no release from this pervasive change save one. We must become a society focused on growth in consumption of material things and must accept some small number of unemployed workers. Those who have work must sacrifice the dignity of knowing the true utility of their product for they will never know entirely how it is made nor who used it. The high rate of general consumption will become the benefit; loss of dignity by the worker, the cost. The quest for excellence which dwelt in every craftsman is today being abolished by the steam engine. This is the true and perhaps irrecoverable loss of the modern age. It is also possible that the working man could share his position in the workplace with others by working fewers hours. He will do this only if his income is not reduced. He will be able to share the workplace only if the increase in leisure time is committed to extending his material consumption.

The higher wages wrought by coal use will allow each labourer to bring more of his children to adulthood. This is the economic analogy to your explanation of how energy increased the population. It is the support of this growing population which gives rise to the needed growing consumption without causing great lack of employment. As we begin to use coal we become a society necessarily committed to economic growth. This growth has another feature not often recognized. The poorest of our people are appeased because each year they become richer. Yet our wealthy grow in richness faster than do the poor. I believe that the happiness of our people is lost when their attention is drawn to material goods which only wealthier people have—rather than letting us all be equally yoked together in a search for heaven.

We must be aware of other treacheries regarding economic growth. We should never forget the nature of the Corn Riots in England in 1789. Bad weather ruined our crops, and the freezing of the Thames blocked London's coal supply. Food prices rose very rapidly, leaving us with little to spend on other things. The result was that our industry was without work, particularly our iron millers and coal miners. So they banded together and carried their plight to the Parliament. There were riots throughout England.

We must recognize that all workers will eventually join together to claim the high wages wrought by coal use, to protect themselves from loss of jobs and to reduce the hazards in their place of work. These organizations must eventually adopt a policy of restricting entry to the work place in order to ensure that the members will actually capture the higher wages. This plan tends to slow the growth of the labour force to an arithmetical one, while coal use is pulling the population at a geometric rate. Eventually those not working will become an intolerable burden on the working population and on their employers.

Parliament will then debase our currency in order to expand the support of those not employed through an extension of our Poor Laws. This act will reduce the real wage of each worker and employer and as I stated in my "Summary View" will encourage higher birth rates among the poor. This increasing taxation to support the poor and unemployed plus the rising costs of everyday goods will keep higher wages as the principle goal of labour. The demands for higher wages, in turn, will increase the cost of everyday goods. More and more, labourers will seek to limit access to the place of work, without regard to the level of population.

The organizations of labour, as well as those of the owners of capital, will each strive for growth in material consumption. Such growth produces a fresh demand for the services of labour and capital. This rather artificial scarcity allows the workers to obtain higher wages and capital holders to receive greater returns. But the scarcity also requires a greater degree of labour and capital organization to prevent new individuals from entering the market at a lower rate of income.

The important distinction between the past and the future condition is that prior to the use of coal, man did not choose the ultimate level of his population. This level was set by the limit of food supply or, as you would say, the amount of the sun's energy. Now, we augment that energy with coal. Since man is able to control the rate at which he uses coal, he can also control the size of his own population. This appears to be a novel predicament for living beings.

Unfortunately, to restrict the demand for food or coal through voluntary efforts of the population seems at least arbitrary and absurd to most people. Coal is now thought to be essential. Yet, if it is truly limited in total supply, then why should not such essentials be at least partially reserved for future generations of man? Is it that we believe they would use them unwisely, or that they would act less wisely than we would? How can history ever know whether this is true or not if we consume our portion of the coal as well as that of the next generation? Being able, therefore, to control the level of our own population, might it not be prudent to restrain the population at a stationary level until we are sure growth is needed? I think so, I fear, however, that we will not restrain ourselves. We tend to think of ourselves as bees in an unending field of clover though in reality we are more like mice in a drawer of cheese.

The cost of coal is likely to rise as it becomes scarce. Yet, by then time and circumstances may have overcome us. The expansion of the population is not as easy to stop as the flow of coal. Some would no doubt argue that we should raise a tax on coal, or in some other way anticipate its limited supply and smooth the way to an energy-scarce economy. Perhaps a common ownership and rationing of the coal reserves would allow each individual the privilege of saving or using it. But what of the weavers and the millers? It would be difficult but possible to ration coal to them also. I believe that the owners of the coal are not always the best ones at sensing when the supplies are in jeopardy. Remember, the "Invisible Hand" of Adam Smith cannot create coal, only aid in its distribution.

I cannot find a reason for extensive optimism under the system which seems to be approaching. Its power is growing, but where will it lead us? I fear the motives of those who would control the population by limiting the flow of coal, and would much prefer that the sun, not the hand of government, control the population. Although it is unclear what we may lose by not growing, the consequences of overpopulation are quite apparent.

Incidentally, perhaps England should question its policy of exporting coal. For if you are right in that coal increases the population, we are making present Frenchmen out of what otherwise would have been future Englishmen. Would you agree?

My dear Carnot, through this letter I hope only to temper your enthusiasm, which is my intent, not to extinguish it. It is well to remember that the workings of the economy are exceedingly complex. Its driving force, the needs and wants of man, are unfathomable by the human mind. I may be asking too much of man by requiring a certain moral restraint regarding his reproduction and now, a kind of celibacy on the use of coal.

Truly yours,
T. R. MALTHUS

21 January 1832

Reverend Malthus:

Indeed economics is a most complex subject. No doubt its vexatious complexity derives from the apparent whimsy of the human spirit. Perhaps it will be this great complexity which will bring the population to a steady level, rather than a shortage of food or coal. Time itself may be the only scarce resource; a precarious balance between time for labor and time for consumption.

Your letter suggests that costs should operate as measures of need. Adam Smith has pointed out that relative costs are an accurate measure of the improved condition of man. In this sense I believe that the average wage in relation to the cost of coal provides an accurate measure of well-being in our Industrial Age. For example, average wages in Great Britain have increased in relation to the costs of coal more than 25 per cent since 1800. To me, this change indicates an improvement in the ability to buy coal as well as the fact that the use of coal is displacing workers. The rising use of coal per person makes each worker more productive and therefore allows him to support more non-workers. I believe your further arguments are correct if the real price of coal is rising faster than the real wage. This condition reflects that the scarcity of coal is greater than the scarcity of labor; labor will become relatively poor again and provide a force which will slow the population growth. But this price ratio only indicates the relative well-being of a population or an individual at a particular time period. How should we determine the absolute level of improvement?

I suggest another analogy from my studies of thermodynamics. In order to measure the heat content of a substance, we use an indicator called "temperature." This measure is useless, however, in determining efficiencies of heat engines unless it is referred to a point of absolute zero. At zero, all motion ceases. This absolute zero represents the total absence of energy. The temperature of the earth never even approaches absolute zero because of its continuous sources of energy. The variations about the average temperature of the earth are of vital interest to man because they strongly influence the physical conditions of life and thus of his economy.

We cannot expect all of the energy striking the earth to be captured and held for man's eventual use. Yet, we could classify the overall effects of man's activities on an absolute basis by examining the total population of a specific area of land and evaluating the efficiency of a proposed change in activity on the basis of how much of a population increase or decrease would be brought about only by the change. This efficiency could be taken as the change in the steady level population before and after a technical change is introduced into the society. By making population analogous to temperature, such measurements would clarify the real limits concerning improvement in economic activity.

In closing, there were two details of my previous letter which need an extension of thought.

To a great extent, we use coal and food energy to extend our span of life. The rate of deaths is only part, albeit an extremely important one, of how the population grows. The other part, of which you speak very little, is the rate of births. This is equally important. We act forcibly to prolong life, yet require the highest of human achievements, moral restraint by the individual, to reduce the rate of births proportionately. As surely as science has brought us the steam engines and a greater span of life, science will bring the means of controlling the rate of births. Therefore, it seems incumbent on a theologian to prepare the way for this change and perhaps even to find the means of bringing it into being.

As my last comment, it seems to me that the monopoly power and governmental control which you, Ricardo and Adam Smith have so brilliantly resisted is the secret to stopping the growth of the population in England. Monopolies will grow and merge into a few uncompetitive giants, which would control all of the flows, especially of food and coal. This view coincides with the cycle of nature on a parcel of land. The abandoned grain field turns to grass, then to many small trees, and in time to a few large trees that monopolize the sunlight, water and important compounds flowing from the soil. These giants are susceptible only to slow decay or to fire. The analogy with society at large is obvious to me, and I hope to you.

As before, I remain your humble servant.

S. CARNOT

May 15, 1832

Dear Carnot:

Seeking absolute or moral standards for behaviour has been my goal of longest standing. Mankind needs a clear procedure for declaring not only individual rights but also individual responsibilities. Unfortunately the Industrial Age is binding the entire population together so that increasingly, the excesses of one segment affect the whole. At the same time it becomes more and more difficult to define one's responsibilities. However, it is wrong to believe that any government can or should relieve the individual of the burden of his responsibilities. We must learn to separate the questions about equity from those of economic or material growth. We will not have the land and coal to grow forever. Mankind can survive well within physical limits but cannot survive at all without an equitable distribution of the available wealth.

I have often felt that the village life of England, in decline now for over fifty years, provides the basis for setting and enforcing these moral standards. The comparatively simple village society seems to have done better than the Kings or Parliaments. Indeed, even the police of London cannot always keep the peace these days. The closely knit village society provided personal discouragement for population growth and tended to encourage thrift.

The industrial development has required an increase in the movement of labour, to seek new jobs as the present jobs become obsolete. This mobility of labour has broken the bonds of the village community, leaving only the national community—one, I must add, more easily led to war. Ultimately such mobility and specialization of labour will destroy the family, as the most precious task of all—raising children—becomes simply another job.

I believe that we must never cease comparing our standards with those of the natural system, for nature is clearly the master in survival. But rather than learn from this truest of tutors, we seem to be destroying her. Living in large urban areas, we are disconnected from nature and her enterprise.

I cannot suggest that we intervene in a process so delicate as human birth. For to intervene is, inevitably, to mishandle. I maintain only that those who overpopulate must also suffer the consequences. Nature can be a harsh teacher, but a thorough one. Remember, there are no rights between man and nature. Rights are established between ourselves but nature owes us nothing. We engineers and economists must learn her rules, not try to force her to live by ours. I believe that nature provides us small discomfort now in exchange for less misery in the long run.

I often wonder if a universal catastrophe will always be necessary before man chooses to pursue the common good. I hope not. As man and nation, though, we probably shall continue to vacillate between seeking the identity of our higher selves as individuals and returning to the security of the community.

Your use of population as the absolute indicator of well-being shows the degree to which man has employed science to elevate himself. Why not be consistent with your closing biological analogy? Creation contains many others kinds of living things besides man, and their well-being is also important. If not important in and of themselves, would you not agree that their existence is important to man? If so, one could use as an absolute measure the total amount of life, human and otherwise, before and after a proposed change—a formal sharing of human rights with the rest of the natural system. No doubt man will be diminished as the coal unwinds, but life, the sum of all living things, may well be increased.

This equation containing both man and trees, as it were, may strike you as a modern form of pantheism. Yet I prefer it to the alternative: bowing before coal as a great power without God. I would rather the sun were God for by its relative uniformity and remoteness, it usurps all but very local forms of leadership, as long as we hold our population under control. The very concentrated location of coal produces an apparently irresistible force which organizes society about a small leadership that meters the coal mainly for their own gain. These leaders claim it is our duty and our destiny to use the coal but this spurs the population, as you have shown, to levels unsupportable by the sun alone. When the coal fails, the excessive population will allow, perhaps even demand, the most pervasive and rigid forms of leadership. It seems that we are doomed to create chaos in an orderly society, much like I presume, the steam engine creates chaos out of coal—scattering its heat about the air. If there be a general form of sin, it is surely our creation of disorder.

I would prefer to have a nation governed by a set of monopolies rather than by kings. It is unfortunately inevitable, I suppose, that a strong hierarchy of social class will develop under either form of government. I would most prefer an unrestricted freedom and a virtuous and happy population, which I believe can be realized through enlightened self restraint. This moral restraint is indeed the least price of freedom, for the individual or the nation.

Truly yours,
THOMAS MALTHUS

EPILOGUE

England, once coal and iron exporter to the world, now imports about 50 per cent of her food and energy resources. Her population, which has doubled three times since the Industrial Revolution began, is now 50 million and is still growing, yet the labor force is constant.

England has largely ignored the signs of her own disaster, including the starvation and collapse of the Irish population in 1846, a scant 12 years after the last warning from Malthus. America and most of the world's developed countries have used England as a model in developing their own economies, and they have seemed determined to follow England to her conclusion.

Neither Malthus nor Carnot understood the role of energy as the stimulant of social change and, consequently, of societal complexity. But in this text, Malthus and Carnot speak to us about ideas of limits which are merged to produce a picture of the single limit to man's numbers and his activity—the inevitably declining availability of the earth's energy resources. Since the time of Malthus and Carnot, individual moral restraint has not been able to control adequately the growth of population or the rate of energy use, particularly when many important resources seem to be abundant.

In a large, complex, urbanized society it seems to be nearly impossible for a majority of the population to perceive the connection between rising population and finite energy resources. The issue is not our ability to act in an altruistic manner or to discipline ourselves sufficiently, i.e. to restrain our aspirations within the absolute limits of our natural endowments; rather, it is one of perception. In other words, we have great difficulty in perceiving the appropriate course of action when an important resource becomes scarce. Lacking that ability, many people adopt an indifferent or conspirational view or, worse, a despairing one. However, if the importance of the energy shortage can be understood and appreciated fully, such solutions as energy taxing, rationing, or perhaps better ones, could be adopted with ease.

My solution to the perception problem is a particular type of education, one far from the standard sort. Each person, I believe, lacks perception of the finiteness of the energy resources because he fails to understand just how he is physically connected to the land, both from a resource-acquisition and waste-disposal point of view. In an agrarian society, formal education was not necessary to establish this connection. The lines to and from the earth in a farming community are short and simple. But the average person today lives in a city of about 350,000. He is not sure where meat, milk and electricity, for example, come from or where the things that go down the drain actually go. The average person is also unaware of the energy, labor and other resources required to provide for present-day consumption patterns. Likewise, people are generally unaware of the social and environmental consequences of their consumption, or even of those caused by the activities of their own profession.

An appropriate educational program is one that would begin with an identification of all the consumption items in the home, evolving into a quantification of these items and, ultimately, to their direct and indirect impacts. This process of education would clearly require the usual reading, writing and mathematical skills whose purpose for development now occurs to most students as irrelevant. As an adult, the process continues, but in a more complex fashion. The direct and indirect impacts of one's employment must be identified and quantified. Such a process prevents the individual from sliding into the belief that only positive benefits result from his labors. With such an education, I believe the web of imperception can be broken. Doing so is vital, because only then will we be able to convince ourselves about the value and necessity of equitable solutions to the problems of dwindling, non-renewable energy resources.

As a first step in this process, I propose a special role for government: collecting a tax on all raw forms of energy, a tax which would be returned to all consumers in proportion to their income, geared to rise with wages and interest rates. Such a tax would become an instrument of social and economic policy, reducing energy use in anticipation of a resource-short future. Since energy-lean activities are generally labor-rich, the energy tax would also increase employment. In the long term, the tax would probably give way to rationing and would produce smaller and more manageable cities, where individual perception and, thus, intelligent self-restraint become ever more possible.

NOTE

1. The name Sadi was from the Persian poet and moralist.

REFERENCES

Malthus and Carnot

Bonar, J. (1885). *Malthus and His Work*. New York: Harper & Bros.

Carnot, Sadi (1824). *Reflections on the Motive Power of Heat and on Machines Fitted to Develop that Power* (R. H. Thurston, Ed., London: Macmillan, 1890), and New York: American Society of Mechanical Engineers (1943). Contains memoir by Henri Carnot and some of the original notes of S. Carnot.

Flew, A. (1970). *Malthus, An Essay on the Principle of Population*. London: Pelican Classics. Contains the First Essay and the "Summary View" with an excellent discussion of each.

Malthus, T. R. (1798–1803). *Parallel Chapters from the 1st and 2nd Editions of an Essay on the Principle of Population*. New York: Macmillan (1916).

Meek. R. L. (1953). *Marx and Engels on Malthus*. London: Lawrence and Wishart. A series of statements on how scientific socialism and birth control will disprove the Malthusian dilemma.

Plank, M. (1932). *Theory of Heat*, vol. V of his *Introduction to Theoretical Physics*. London: Macmillan. Puts Carnot as the unquestionable father of thermodynamics.

Population and Labor

Griffith, G. T. (1925). *Population Problems of the Age of Malthus*. London: Cambridge University Press. An excellent text on the effect of employment, welfare, food, health, alcohol and medicine on the birth, marriage and death rates in England and Wales from 1700 to about 1850.

Hankins, F. H. (1908). Quetelet (Adolphe) as a Statistician. *Studies in History, Economics and Public Law*, Columbia University, New York 31 (4)

Her Majesty's Stationery Office. *Annual Abstracts of Statistics, 1975*, No. 112. London: Central Statistical Office. Recent population, p. 7; work force, p. 144; food use, p. 110.

Mitchell, B. R., and Deane, P. (1962). *Abstract of British Historical Statistics*. London: Cambridge University Press. Population data of England, Wales and Ireland, pp. 5 and 8; average wages in Great Britain p. 343; coal prices at Westminster School, pp. 480–481.

Smith, Adam (1776). *An Inquiry into the Nature and Causes of the Wealth of Nations*, in two volumes. London: Oxford University Press, (1928). See: vol. 1, p. 77, for the effect of income on population; vol. 1, pp. 275–276, for importance of relative prices of commodities as an indicator of economic well being; vol. 2, p. 533, for the effect of coal prices on wages.

Coal Supply and Use

Ashton, T. S., and Sykes, J. (1927). *The Coal Industry of the 18th Century*. University of Manchester Press. Coal use in London and the United Kingdom.

Darmstadter, J. (1971). *Energy in the World Economy*. Washington, D.C.: Resources for the Future Inc. Source of current British energy use and import condition, Table X.

Mitchell, B. R. (1975). *European Historical Statistics, 1750–1970*. Columbia University Press. Source of agricultural, coal and steel output and trade for England and Wales.

Nef, J. U. (1932). *The Rise of the British Coal Industry*. London: G. Routledge & Sons. Traces the roots of the industrial revolution from 1550 to 1770. Points out how lime was burned near coal mines to make a fertilizer (vol. 1, p. 237); coal used to provide salt (vol. 1, p. 325).

Report of the Commissioners appointed to Inquire into Several Matters Relating to Coal in United Kingdom, Vol. III, Statistics of Production and Consumption, and Export of Coal. Report to Parliament, London (1871).

Thomas, W. L. (ed.) (1970). *Man's Role in Changing the Face of the Earth*. University of Chicago Press, p. 367. Edward I of England banning coal use in 1306, especially in London when Parliament was in session.

Thurston, R. H. (1883). *History and Growth of the Steam Engine*. London: Kegan, Paul and Trench Publishing Co.

Agriculture

Davy, Sir Humphrey (1813). *Elements of Agricultural Chemistry*. London. Encouraged the use of potassium nitrate to restore soil fertility although first use was in the 1840s. Mineral fertilizers first used in England in 1670.

Landes, D. S. (1969). *The Unbound Prometheus*. Cambridge: Cambridge University Press, p. 72. Enclosure laws of early eighteenth-century England—elimination of fallow grounds, commons, selective livestock breeding, crop fertilization and rotation, more intensive cultivation, all fended off the "steady state economic condition."

Saussure, N. T. (1804). *Recherches Chemiques de la Vegetation*. Paris. Plants take carbon and oxygen from the air, nitrogen and minerals from soil; thus the need for chemical fertilizers in agriculture.

Epilogue

Hannon, B. (1975). Energy growth and altruism. Limits to Growth '75 Conference, Woodlands, Texas, 21 October. Mitchell First Prize Paper. Chapter 4 in *Alternatives to Growth—I* (Dennis Meadows, Ed.). Cambridge, Mass.: Ballinger Publishing Co., 1977.

Hardin, G. (1968). The Tragedy of the Commons. *Science* 162, No. 468, 1234–1248.

20

THE SEVERANCE TAX
AS AN INSTRUMENT
OF INTERTEMPORAL EQUITY

Talbot Page

It is possible to imagine a boundary between the economy and the environment. Crossing one way, materials are appropriated and extracted from the environment and put to use in the economy. In the course of processing and use, materials recross the boundary as wastes and pollutants. The management of pollution problems and the resolution of issues of depletion and intertemporal equity both occur at this boundary.[1] Economics has by and large confined its attention to the economy side of the boundary, while ecology has focused on the environment side. The role of the boundary and the flows across it, while recognized, has not yet been well-integrated in either discipline, which is not surprising since the boundary area overlaps the two domains. And, although there are increasing efforts to control pollution and rapidly increasing literature on the economics of pollution, the flow of mate-

---

Published by permission of the author.

rials across the boundary is, generally speaking, set by the rules of the market, largely unconstrained by considerations of ecology or intertemporal equity.[2] This article considers a policy instrument which operates directly at the boundary—the ad valorem severance tax.

A severance tax, which is a tax on material extracted from the environment valued at or near the point of extraction, has the incentive effects of increasing materials conservation, increasing recycling (by raising the price of virgin material relative to scrap material), and increasing product durability. The ad valorem version is essentially an excise tax (or a narrowly based sales tax) and is close to a mirror image of the percentage depletion allowance, which is also based on gross value of a material at or near the "mine mouth." But the depletion allowance is a "negative sales tax," representing a subsidy on a materials price instead of a tax on it.

When I began writing *Conservation and Economic Efficiency*, it occurred to me that a conventional neoclassical economic analysis would prescribe against both the severance tax and the depletion allowance equally, on the grounds that both lead to inefficiency. Yet it seemed to me that there might emerge a useful role for the severance tax if the neoclassical perspective were broadened to include the intertemporal equities involved in the long-run use of the resource base. In this chapter I will first sketch three of the ways this might be done and then discuss the role of the severance tax within this broader context. Reexamination of the present value criterion[3] by which the market sets the flow of materials reveals some inadequacies and unresolved issues of the usual interpretations of the criterion and suggests a rationale, based on equity considerations, for controlling the matter-energy flows across the boundary, while respecting market allocation of the limiited flow among alternative uses once within the economy.

THE PRESENT VALUE CRITERION

In resource economics one often finds a criterion of the form

$$\max_{(c_1, c_2, \ldots)} \sum_{t=1}^{\infty} \delta^{t-1} U(c_t) \tag{1}$$

such that $(c_1, c_2, \ldots) = c \ \varepsilon \ E$, where E is the intertemporal opportunity or feasibility set, and where c_t is consumption at time t, or more generally a description of this world at time or generation t, δ is the discount factor, and $U(\cdot)$ is a measure of social well-being or utility. For this criterion—the general form of the present value criterion—to have a claim for acceptability, it must rest on some normative base. However, the normative base is rarely discussed, and to make matters more difficult, the units of the variables are typically not defined so that the interpretation of the criterion is ambiguous.

There are two obvious interpretations of (1) and several justifications of its general form, none of which seems entirely satisfactory.

In the first interpretation (1) is a specialized form of the planner's criterion. In other words, we start by writing the planner's preference function:

$$U = U(c_1, c_2, \ldots, c_t, \ldots);$$

then it is assumed that U happens to be additively separable:

$$U = \sum_{t=1}^{\infty} U^t(c_t)$$

where $U^t(c_t)$ is utility experienced by the planner in contemplating consumption c_t by the future generation t. The planner is assumed to be altruistic toward the future, but not completely so. The planner values consumption in the present more than anticipated consumption in the future by another generation. As a particularly simple way of specifying his declining altruism over time, it is further assumed that

$$U^t(c_t) = \delta^{t-1} U(c_t),$$

which leads directly to (1).

To focus on the intertemporal problem, we assume here and below that each generation acts like a single unit, so that the planner speaks for the whole first generation. Hence under the first interpretation the units are:

$\delta^{t-1}U(c_t)$ = Utility enjoyed by the present generation in contemplating consumption c_t by generation t.

$U(c_t)$ = *Utility that the present generation would enjoy* if consumption c_t would be moved back in time to the present generation.

δ = The measure of the present generation's time preference or, in the intergenerational context, a measure of the present's altruism (its ability to feel utility from the contemplation of other generations' consumption).

Thus under the first interpretation (1) is the present generation's utility function. This interpretation is called *selfish altruism*—selfish because it is defined as the maximization of the present's utility; altruistic because the present experiences a contribution to its utility by contemplating consumption by other, later generations.

Under the second interpretation (1) is seen as the criterion of a neutral intertemporal observer, who is trying to be fair to all generations. In contrast, this interpretation is called *disinterested fairness,* because it results from an outside observer with no direct stake in the outcome, but with the desire to take the interests of all generations into account in some fair manner. The observer knows that if (1) is maximized with a zero discount rate ($\delta = 1$) and if there is productivity in the economy, satisfaction of the criterion with $\delta = 1$ requires that the earlier generations have lower levels of consumption than later generations.[4] This works as follows: Present consumption is curtailed to increase present investment in order to obtain an increment to future consumption that is greater than the reduction in present consumption. As long as the utility gained from greater future consumption is more than the utility lost from present consumption, the substitution will continue. But the law of diminishing marginal utility will eventually offset the force of productivity, halting the substitution where the sum of present and future utilities is a maximum.

The observer knows that in a baseline case with productivity—but no technical change, pollution, resource depletion, or uncertainty—discounting by the marginal productivity of capital will lead to a maximization of (1) with an intertemporally egalitarian consumption stream. For the second interpretation, motivated by a "baseline egalitarianism," we have

$$U(c_t) = \text{Utility } enjoyed\ by\ generation\ t \text{ in consuming } c_t.$$

$$\delta = \text{The marginal productivity of capital.}$$

Under the second interpretation (1) is a weighted average of utilities across time with the weights chosen to lead to egalitarian consumption under the baseline case. Of course, a criterion that leads to egalitarian consumption is not very interesting; if this were all that there is to the matter, it would be more direct to scrap (1) and state the criterion as simply requiring intertemporally egalitarian consumption. However, the situation offers richer possibilities when the second interpretation is preserved, but the criterion is applied to nonbaseline cases where there is uncertainly, technical change, pollution, and/or depletion.

These two interpretations are conceptually distinct and lead in different directions. The first interpretation has little ethical appeal for anyone who takes into account the interests of the future and the possibility that they may conflict with the interests of the present. The second interpretation has some appeal, although it is not clear what is the ethical strength of a criterion which is motivated by a baseline case and then applied to other, differing cases. Nonetheless, the second interpretation has normative aspects in the sense that it leads to comparisons of intertemporal Pareto improvements. In the interpretation of disinterested fairness the utilities of present and future generations are defined so that it is possible to consider actions which make some generations better off without hurting others. It is possible to consider discount rate calculations in terms of potential Pareto improvements, intergenerationally, as well.[5] But under the interpretation of selfish altruism only the first generation's interests or utility functions are defined so that it is not possible to talk about potential Pareto improvements intergenerationally.

FURTHER PROBLEMS
WITH THE PRESENT VALUE CRITERION

A. Consistency

Consistency is a desirable property, and the present value criterion is consistent, as long as δ is constant and each generation's resource endowment is treated as a sunk cost by that generation.[6] However, there are other criteria, such as the overtaking principle, which are fundamentally different from the present value criterion but which are also consistent. The overtaking principle says that if, after some point in time, all generations unanimously prefer x to y, then the intertemporal social choice should be x, y. Thus the desirable property of consistency does not single out the present value criterion. Moreover, consistency is a limited property, because it treats the resource endowment passed on from one generation to another as a sunk cost each time and consequently says nothing about the intertemporal equities involved. As an alternative, the intertemporal choice problem can be viewed in part as what opportunity set to pass on to the next generation. In this case the problem is not to choose an entire sequence of actions or states $(c_1, c_2, \ldots)$ but a pair (c_1, E_2) where E_2 is a "fair heritage" or opportunity set in the succeeding generation and c_1 and E_2 are compatible. In the next generation the task is to choose a compatible (c_2, E_3). As the decision sequences do not overlap, there is no consistency problem in its usual, formal sense, although there may be a need to look further ahead than one generation to specify a "fair" opportunity set for the next generation.

In any case, consistency is probably too narrow a condition. It does not allow, for example, the next generation to have a time preference (δ) different from our own. The desirability of the condition is further blurred by the observation that any criterion is consistent for choosing over the (smaller) set of paths which later planners would not modify.[7] Thus consistency is not an all-or-nothing property, but a more-or-less one.

B. Markets

It is sometimes suggested that (1) simply restates what markets tend to do by themselves. Unfortunately, it is still unclear just what are the normative properties of sequential market equilibria, even if there is perfect foresight, when resource inheritance and depletion are endogenous. Most of the work on sequential market equilibria has focused on efficiency aspects. It appears that the simplest thing that can be said is that markets tend to maximize the wealth position of the present generation. From the truism that generally only one thing can be maximized at a time, it is clear that the interests of the future can be in conflict with those of the present. Resolution of this potential conflict is precisely the problem of intertemporal equity. Thus to say that (1) is desirable as a criterion because it is in some way related to market behavior tells us little or nothing about the equities involved.

C. Paternalism

It is often argued that in an ultimate sense the present must be a dictator, because it is the only generation around to make choices. Thus an intertemporal criterion must necessarily be an expression only of the present's preferences, including its intentions and altruism toward the future and its estimates of conditions in the future. As a simple observation as to who is now living and who is yet unborn, this is true, but, as we shall see, this observation does not lead inexorably to the present value criterion.

THE AGGREGATION PROBLEM

The confining narrowness of the present value criterion can be seen when the choice problem is put in the more general framework of social choice. As before, to focus on the intertemporal problem we assume that each generation acts like a unit (or that the intratemporal problem of aggregation of preferences has been solved). Each generation has its own preference structure over feasible states of the world, where a state is a whole time path from generation one onward. As before, we can write a particular state or path

$$c = (c_1, c_2, \ldots, c_t, \ldots)$$

where c_t is a snapshot of the state at generation t.

If generation i considers path x to be at least as good as path y, we write

$$xR_iy.$$

Given that each generation has its own preference structure, and that these preferences are likely to differ because of different vantage points in time, among other things, the problem is to find some aggregation function F that takes us from the collection of all preference structures, one for each generation, to a single intertemporally social preference ordering:

$$F_i(R_1, R_2, \ldots, R_t, \ldots) \longrightarrow R.$$

With this small amount of notation, we can rewrite (1) in a social choice context. The intertemporal social preference ordering R corresponding to (1) is defined by:

$$xRy \overset{\text{def.}}{\Longleftrightarrow} \sum_{t=1}^{\infty} \delta^{t-1}U(x_t) \geq \sum_{t=1}^{\infty} \delta^{t-1}U(y_t); \qquad (2)$$

and the present value criterion directs us to find a maximal $x \epsilon E$ under the relation R.

Thus the present value approach is subsumed under the more general approach of intertemporal social choice, and (2) merely defines one aggregation rule among the infinite possibilities. Moreover, the two approaches are fundamentally different in spirit. Under the discount criterion the problem is one of *maximization*. Translated into a market setting, it is necessary to know or estimate future prices and other future conditions. Under the social choice approach the problem is first one of specifying a rule of *aggregation (F)*. As the interest of this paper is on intertemporal equity, the task is to specify a fair rule of aggregation. In doing so, it may actually be a hindrance to know either present or future interests (or preferences). Under a Kantian perspective one's only hope of describing a fair or just rule is to do so without calculating one's own or others' interests. For this reason the argument of paternalism (C) toward (1) is not forced. Lack of specific knowledge of the future's specific interests does not direct us to (1) with the first interpretation of the discount criterion; indeed, it favors the more general and abstract approach of looking for fair rules of aggregation.

We can rewrite the interpretation of selfish altruism with the aid of (2) as one particular choice of aggregation:

$$F:(R_1, R_2, \ldots, R_t, \ldots) \longrightarrow R = R_1.$$

This will be recognized as a dictatorship of the present. We can ask under what conditions is this interpretation forced. Since 1972 it has been known that in a setting of an infinite number of voters, the Arrow Impossibility Theorem does not hold.[8] In this setting, which is a natural one for the intertemporal choice problem where we do not want to have to specify the last generation, the Arrowian axioms of Pareto, irrelevant alternatives, and transitivity are consistent with an infinite number of aggregation rules that are nondictatorial. And quite to the contrary of the dictatorship of the present, which is highly present oriented, all the nondictatorial choice rules consistent with the Arrowian axioms satisfy the overtaking principle, which is highly future oriented—so future oriented that such rules are not appealing as they stand for practical decision making. Nonetheless, this class of nondictatorial choice rules illustrates an important observation. It is often thought that the alternative to discounting at a positive rate of interest is to discount at a zero rate of interest. The social choice formulation illustrates that there are an infinite number of choice rules beyond these two, narrow alternatives.

Nor is it necessary to view the choice problem as within the context of the Arrowian axioms. As a practical matter we may be willing to give up something in the way of narrowing the set of possible preference orderings, or the set of feasible alternatives, or transitivity, or irrelevant alternatives in order to define rules that are not "too" future oriented and do not depend on the number of generations being infinite. For example, as a practical matter we rely heavily, in the *intra*temporal setting, on majority rule voting, even though we know it can be intransitive. It happens that the overtaking principle, in the intertemporal context with an infinite number of generations, is very much like majority rule, favoring infinite majorities of future generations over finite minorities of generations near the present. Thus as a practical matter we may want to keep some idea of majority rule, in the intertemporal setting, even with a horizon of a finite number of generations.

For example, suppose that the next ten generations after us would prefer the resource base kept in some sense intact, but the present generation believes that it is intertemporally "fair" to follow (1) and exploit the resource base in a way that maximizes its present value but destroys its value for future use, providing in its stead many freeways and consumer durables. The most obvious interpretation of the posited situation is that the present has a naive idea of intertemporal fairness, which might change upon deeper reflection. Under the more general framework of social choice it is likely to seem unfair to choose an aggregation rule that ignores future interests except as reflected through selfish altruism. A ten-to-one majority is hard to ignore, and some form of intertemporal majority voting, with "constitutional" safeguards against the tyranny of the majority, is hard to dismiss altogether.

The approach of intertemporal social choice consists of two parts. First, the effort is to define "fair" conditions or axioms, which will specify a "fair" aggregation rule F. At this stage of consideration a Kantian would find it preferable not to know the actual preferences of the future (or the present either). The search is for certain symmetry properties. Second, after an intertemporal choice rule is defined, such as some modified intertemporal majority rule, one tries to satisfy the rule in actual situations. This requires estimating streams of costs and benefits into the future, just as in the case of (1). It may or may not require a process of maximization. For example, a modified majority rule would not require maximization.[9]

The Kantian perspective, which insists that just rules can only be defined independently from one's own and others' specific interests, underlies the intertemporal social choice approach sketched above. Moving toward this Kantian perspective is the first way in which the neoclassical approach, taken to be the satisfaction of (1), can be enlarged for a more fundamental discussion of intertemporal equities. This same Kantian base underlies the Rawlsian "original position" with its "veil of ignorance." In both cases the effort is to search for ethically attractive conditions of symmetry which will define decision rules that are thereby just. In both cases the future is considered on a symmetrical basis with the present, a condition notably absent in the neoclassical (1).

BASIC GOODS

I sketch here the second way in which the neoclassical perspective can be modified to provide a context for considering severance taxes and other instruments of intertemporal equity. It is convenient to introduce the need for a second change in perspective by considering Rawls's chapter on intergenerational justice.[10] His rule for intertemporal justice is a kind of golden rule of savings: One generation should make an effort of savings equal to what it would have liked the previous generation to have done for it. Capital is viewed in aggregate terms, with natural resources lumped together with finished capital, elevators lumped together with the energy to run them. Rawls is not alone in this view; the assumption that natural resources are just another kind of capital has been a very important one in natural resource economics in the last forty years. In this respect, in his aggregative approach to capital, Rawls appears to be following the neoclassical and utilitarian tradition, from which he distinguishes himself in the rest of his book.

In the neoclassical tradition the obvious instrument of intertemporal equity is the discount rate. The neoclassical tradition appears to be saying this: We do not believe that there is a problem of intertemporal equity in the sense of protecting the future, because we believe that the future is going to be better off than the present; however, *if* the present generation decides to (further) improve the lot of the future, it should subsidize the interest rate.[11] This is the most general, and hence the most efficient, way of transferring wealth from the present to the future. But this conclusion depends critically on the assumed homogeneity and aggregability of capital and other economic goods.

Many economic goods contribute to a sense of well-being without being essential to it. For such goods it is a simple matter, conceptually, to define an aggregate value in terms of a compensating variation (or a consumer surplus over compensated demand curves). It is quite possible to imagine, for example, that for an individual there is a certain sum of money for which the individual would be indifferent between having his camera and giving up his camera but gaining the sum instead.

In contrast to such "ordinary" economic goods, others have the property of sine qua non. They may trade at the margin, but a compensating variation becomes unbounded or indefinable for complete deprivation. For example, suppose the state erroneously imprisons an individual for a few hours, after which time the state realizes its mistake and attempts to make restitution. We can imagine that there could be a sum of money which would be just enough to make the individual indifferent between the state not making the mistake in the first place and the state making the mistake but also making the compensating restitution. But suppose the state had erroneously imprisoned the individual for forty years. Could we call the individual irrational if he states that he cannot define a compensating sum that would make him indifferent to so much lost life? Similarly, individuals are often willing to work at riskier jobs for additional compensation (risk premiums) in their wages, as long as the increased risk is in some sense marginal, perhaps an extra one out of a thousand chance of accidental death per year. But the risk premium becomes undefinable as the probability of hazard approaches certainty. In the same way it is possible to define a compensating variation, and hence a valuation, to a common cold but not to terminal cancer. For such goods, which are essential for a sense of well-being, there is no way of defining their aggregate value in terms of compensating variations; and in this way we can distinguish such goods, which can be called *basic*, from ordinary economic goods.

Basic goods tend to be the building blocks or requisites of other goods. As such they provide opportunities but not guarantees of the good life. In Rawls's inquiry into the nature of justice he focuses on the fair provision of certain basic goods, notably liberty, but also other opportunities. The fair provision from one generation to the next of the resource base, characterized in terms of materials, energy, and space per capita (population), can be looked upon in the same light.

Rawls identifies one of the characteristics of the utilitarian tradition as conflation,[12] which appears to mean a tendency toward uncritical aggregation, or "too early" aggregation. His example is the practice of early utilitarians to add utilities across people, as in the ambiguous statement of the greatest good for the greatest number. (Note that the second interpretation of (1) "conflates" utilities across time, but the first interpretation does not, as the only utility is for the planner). The suggestion here is that the neoclassical tradition conflates ordinary economic goods and basic goods. A more critical view of the assumptions under which ordinary goods and basic goods are aggregated provides a second path toward modification of the neoclassical perspective. It should be no surprise that questions of intertemporal justice often focus on the fair provision of certain basic goods and opportunities, and correspondingly in the intertemporal case of the provision of the resource base, with its implied opportunities.

THE FEASIBILITY SET

Just as the intertemporal state of the world c can be disaggregated into a sequence of generational snapshots $(c_1, c_2, \ldots)$, so too can the intertemporal feasibility set E be disaggregated into a sequence $(E_1, E_2, \ldots)$, where E_t describes the opportunities open to generation t. The intertemporal feasibility or opportunity set unfolds sequentially, and the opportunities available to generation t depend upon the specific actions taken by previous generations. Previous generations' depletion of materials tends to constrict future opportunities, but the use of materials in constructing capital instruments, along with advances in education and technology, may offset, at least in part, this tendency. Neoclassical economists have emphasized the substitutability of resources and the enormous growth in the power of technology, although other determining factors, such as population per unit of the resource base, limitations of institutional competence, and conditions of social and economic behavior, have also received some attention.[13]

Further, each generation's opportunity set is bounded by the set of physical laws, which do not change from generation to generation. There are limits to the efficiency which can be designed into an internal combustion engine. Try as we might, the performance of the car is not going to increase in an unbounded way, per unit input. For thousands of years, with increasing skill and knowledge of the underlying mechanics, boats have been designed to move through the water with less effort, but the bow wave is the same barrier now as it was for the pharoahs. Indeed, the less understood a physical phenomenon, the more scope for technological improvement. A physical phenomenon which is completely understood and exploited in an engineering sense offers no margin for further technological advance. When we are close to understanding, diminishing returns set in to further effort in technical design.

Often a situation is imperfectly understood, and it is hard to tell what constraints the laws of physics impose. Yet consideration of general principles often suggests a bound, though it may not be the lowest bound. A similar problem arises in statistics, where ever more efficient estimators are sought. In many cases, consideration of the information inequality provides a bound to the efficiency, even though this bound may not be the lowest bound and the most efficient estimator under this bound is entirely unspecified.[14]

In recent years more attention in neoclassical economics has been placed on the incorporation of general principles, greatly enriching the realism of the analysis. This represents a third broadening of the neoclassical perspective, which can be seen in the work by Kneese and his colleagues incorporating ideas of mass-balance into the analysis of pollution problems, and in the work by Georgescu-Roegen [see Reference 2] incorporating ideas of thermodynamics in the analysis of the evolution of economic systems.

THE STEADY STATE

One of the neglected questions in the neoclassical tradition is: What is the fair or proper inheritance, with respect to the resource base, for one generation to pass on to the next? We can go so far as to suggest that this question cannot even be posed in a substantive way under the interpretation of selfish altruism. For traditional societies which lived off renewable resources and left the resource base essentially the same from generation to generation, this is not a pressing question.[15] The normative question of the fair inheritance of the resource base is now more pressing, due to large-scale modification of the resource base resulting from our far greater numbers and greater power of technology.

As we become more cautious about aggregation and more willing to keep the difference between ordinary economic goods and basic goods in mind, we become less willing to accept uncritically the discount rate as the obvious instrument of intertemporal equity. Reflection suggests that subsidizing the interest rate can lead to a future with a smaller supply of basic goods (and larger supply of ordinary goods), beyond the level of sustainability. As aggregate investment is stimulated by a general subsidy of interest rates, so too are entropic processes, greater reliance on nonrenewable resources, more depletion, and more throughput. Thus it is entirely possible that discount rate subsidy would make the future worse off, providing it, figuratively speaking, with more elevators and less energy.

Greater attention to physical laws of nature, especially in terms of technical substitutability and entropic processes of depletion and pollution, gives a more realistic description of E, the intertemporal feasibility set. A close attention to physical, energy, and space constraints provides some understanding of the feasibility of sustainable states, at various levels of well-being and numbers of people. Given large-scale uncertainties, the normative problem can be restated as determining what is a fair distribution of risk burden to impose on the future, where part of the risk is that even the present level of well-being cannot be sustained.

The ethical attractiveness of the steady-state economy is that it provides an intertemporal world of equals in the basis goods of energy, materials, and space per capita. As such it provides one solution to the aggregation problem posed in the second section. If each generation is treated the same in terms of its basic opportunities, then, this may be fair enough from an intertemporal social choice perspective. A "steady state" is not forever, Georgescu-Roegen points out, but there is a normative difference in choosing a path which leads to severe dislocations in 200 years and another which holds a much greater possibility of tenure for the next 300 million years. It is easy to imagine a Rawlsian original position with representatives from all potential generations choosing a steady-state path over a nonsustainable laissez faire one.

THE SEVERANCE TAX

In a narrow neoclassical perspective it is possible to view the severance tax and the percentage depletion allowance as roughly equivalent distortions (though of opposite sign) of a neutral or intratemporally efficient tax structure. But with the three changes in perspective outlined above, the severance tax plays not a similar but an opposite role to the depletion allowance. The severance tax decreases the tax burden imposed on the future associated with waste generation and depletion and the uncertain search for substitutes by decreasing the rates of material and energy throughput; the depletion allowance increases the rate of depletion, decreases the lead time available for discovery and development of substitutes, and increases the risk burden associated with the uncertain search for substitutes. With the changes in perspective the severance tax is viewed primarily as an instrument of intertemporal equity, nudging the economy toward a sustainable path. It focuses on the basic goods of energy and materials, which are critical in terms of providing future opportunities. The severance tax is just one among many possible instruments leading toward a sustainable economy, and if a sustainable economy is to be achieved, many or at least several instruments will need to be applied simultaneously. Effective policies toward the stabilization of population are clearly necessary as well, and there should be little doubt that worldwide resource and political problems would be more tractable today if humane policies had been seriously applied fifty years ago.

In *Conservation and Economic Efficiency* I singled out the severance tax as the illustrative policy instrument of intertemporal equity for two reasons. First, in dealing with the long-term management of the material resource base, the severance tax appears to be the simplest pricing instrument which fits into a "minimally" modified neoclassical perspective. Besides this methodological reason there is a more skeptical and practical reason. As a society we do not deal well with long-term, latent problems. We tend to ignore them until they are thrust upon us. As long as there is some easy way to rationalize a laissez faire approach on the faith that the future will automatically be better off than we, we are likely to procrastinate. At the present moment we stand bemused in the face of massive energy depletion with no really satisfactory substitutes on the horizon; with unsupportable population growth and the dawning recognition that past token efforts have not been enough; with the world economy increasingly based upon pesticides and other synthetic chemicals, some of which the human species itself may not be able to live with for the long term.

In such a world of policy procrastination discussions of intertemporal equity may arouse a modicum of intellectual interest, but at the same time they seem abstract without the imminence to generate significant preventive action. We are in an interim period where energy, resource, and population problems have not landed on us with their full force. There is time to take action but not the urgency to take strong action. Much of what we do now is to provide flexibility and time so that when the blow falls it will be diffused rather than fatal. With this human constraint a useful policy instrument toward sustainability is one which is of little burden to the present but which accumulates its impact over time.

The severance tax has the virtue of low cost to the present with the potential of large leverage for the future. Consider the elimination of present depletion allowances and substitution of national severance taxes of the same percentage (roughly 15 to 20 percent) in their stead, phased in over a five-year period. From a neoclassical perspective, which focuses on intratemporal costs (especially under the interpretation of selfish altruism), there is little or no distortionary impact of trading the allowance for the tax, although there are different gainers and losers, *intra*temporally, and some adjustment costs in the transition. On the other hand, a permanent change in the price of virgin materials of 30 percent or so would have a strong impact on the use and conservation of materials over the long run of fifty years or more. As an added advantage the administrative cost of a national severance tax is no more than the present system, because the administrative apparatus for the depletion allowance can be directly transferred to the severance tax without additional cost, and the cutoff points have been precisely defined over the last fifty years.[16]

It may be noted in passing that marketable quota systems appear to have more political attractiveness when viewed as a pollution control. The California Air Resources Board, for example, has recently become interested in a marketable quota system to control sulfur pollution in the Los Angeles basin. In this case the rigidity of the number of quota permits is seen as a virtue, more nearly guaranteeing a prescribed standard of air quality than effluent taxes, which are uncertain in resultant air quality and often disparaged as mere "licenses to pollute" (whether the disparagement is just is another matter.) Further, preliminary investigation suggests that the most practical way of implementing a quota system on sulfur is to establish the quotas at the level of sulfur content of fossil fuels, including oil to be refined locally into gasoline consumed in the basin and sulfur in gasoline imported into the region, with provision for rebates in quota value for recovered sulfur in the basin, such as would be recovered from electric utility scrubbers or desulfurization of fuel oil. (In the control of pollution sometimes the gain in administrative feasibility in dealing with the smaller number of firms closer to the "mine's mouth" outweighs the potential loss of efficiency by not regulating at the point of release to the environment.) A quota system on sulfur entering the Los Angeles basin in fuels comes close to a quota system on the extraction of the virgin material.

We can compare the severance tax with its variant, a marketable quota system on the extraction of virgin materials. The principal difference between these two schemes is that the uncertainty associated with the tax is on the quantity of material extracted from the environment, while the uncertainty associated with the quota system is on the market price of the material extracted. With the quantity of material extracted rigidly fixed, the quota system is a stronger conservationist measure; but unfortunately the quota system involves more short-term dislocation and cost to the present. For this reason, in the present interim period it appears unlikely to be implemented.

The case of the severance tax is somewhat different, however. Because some of the potential gainers of the tax are in a position to implement it, the severance tax is a rapidly growing tax. The mundane reason for the tax's growing use has little do to with intertemporal equity. It has more to do with the ease with which the tax base can be "exported." For example, in Louisiana where oil and gas severance taxes have recently increased, much of the oil and gas is sold out of state so that people out of state bear much of the burden of the tax. It is little wonder that when Governor Edwards offered to the voters a choice between a property tax increase and an increase in oil and gas severance taxes, they chose the latter. Far from being a drawback of having the tax "accepted for the wrong reasons," the main route of success for long-term policy instruments is to find harmonies between the long-term goals and short-term interests.

The real mark of success of the severance tax depends on whether or not it is adopted in an internationally coordinated system of trade and economic assistance. It happens that many of the poor countries depend heavily on their resource extraction sector. They are not necessarily resource rich in an absolute sense, but their economies are relatively weighted toward the resource sector. At the same time many of the rich countries, which may be resource rich in an absolute sense, are still net resource importers. Since the Second World War the number of buyers has grown relative to the number of sellers, giving rise to concern of unstable markets and a "new mercantilism," replete with efforts for special commodity agreements and the resulting rivalries. Into this picture add the "North-South confrontation" and the demand for a "new economic order," and there arises the potential role of a system of internationally coordinated severance taxes, based on mutual interests, *intra*temporally. First of all, developing countries find severance taxes attractive, since they transfer wealth from the buyers to the sellers. Moreover, severance taxes tend to diversify the economies of the poor countries by making export materials more expensive relative to manufactured and other goods. At first glance it might seem that the buyers, the developed countries, would oppose a system of severance taxes as it involves transfers of wealth from the buyers to the sellers. Upon reflection, however, this might seem a relatively cheap and constructive way of providing economic assistance. The threat of a new mercantilism would be reduced by adjusting the present imbalance between buyers and sellers and by stimulating domestic production, conservation, and recycling in developed countries. Moreover, the North-South confrontation would be ameliorated by this system of assistance, which in the long run would tend to bring the poor countries out of their trap of raw material export dependence. And finally, a coordinated system of severance taxes may seem better to the developed countries than the present system, with its haphazard emergence of severance taxes and other export controls, including further attempts at cartelization, which are destabilizing even when they fail.

In this mundane discussion of present interests, nothing has been said about the future's interests or intertemporal equity. Discussion of the issues of intertemporal equity provides a new perspective for sustainable economies and a new role for severance taxes and other policy instruments toward this goal. But implementability of such measures depends on finding a harmony between long-term goals and short-term interests.

NOTES

1. This is not meant to suggest that all pollution control should be "at the end of the pipe" but that, in its essential nature, the pollution problem is a boundary problem.

2. Measures to control the costs of pollution focus on changing the form of the flow, not its volume, which is dictated by mass balance and the rates of extraction.

Transforming pollutants into less harmful forms is a worthy enterprise, but it is only part of the boundary problem.

3. The present value criterion is a more or less automatic expression of market forces, which lead firms to maximize the discounted, or present, value of their anticipated profit streams. Likewise, cost-benefit analysis generally dictates the maximization of the present value of the net benefit stream. For an elementary discussion of this criterion see [9], pp. 145–167.

4. Consumption of goods in the present is curtailed in favor of investment, in order to make a larger product in the future and hence a larger sum of present and future utility. But this process does not impoverish the present without limit if there is diminishing marginal utility for the future.

5. Elsewhere Mishan and I discuss some of the fundamental difficulties of the principle of potential Pareto improvement applied intergenerationally. The main difficulty is that a potential Pareto improvement becomes infeasible if not incorporated into actual Pareto improvement at the initial period. See [6].

6. For the seminal paper on consistency see the first half of [8]. *Consistency* is defined in the following way: Under some criterion a planner chooses, in period one, the best plan, which requires certain actions in the first period and other actions in succeeding periods. During the first period some actions are taken, and then at the beginning of the second period the planner, using the same criterion, but from the new vantage point in time and under the changed conditions brought about by the passage of time and the planner's first period actions, chooses a new best plan. If this new plan coincides with the continuation of the old plan, then the criterion is said to be consistent.

7. For example, suppose that this generation has a choice of two alternatives, *a* and *b*. If the first generation chooses *a*, the second generation can choose *c* or *d*, or one of the two paths *ac* or *ad*. If generation one chooses *b*, generation two can choose *e* or *f*, or one of the two paths *be* or *bf*. Generation one would like to plan for both periods, and its ranking of the two period paths is *ac* best, then *be*, *ad*, and last *bf*. However, generation two's ranking is *ad*, *ac*, *be*, and last *bf*. If generation one chooses *a*, desiring *ac*, generation two will modify the continuation of the plan to path *ad*. The smaller set of paths that generation two will not modify is {*ad*,*be*}. By construction, choice is consistent over this smaller set, and generation one is best off by choosing *be*, which will not later be modified.

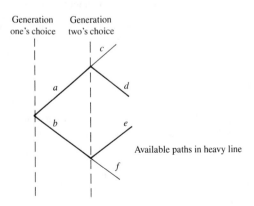

Generation one's choice   Generation two's choice

Available paths in heavy line

8. See [3].

9. Both the National Academy of Sciences and the Council on Wage and Price Stability recommended an overtaking approach in their analyses of the use of granular activated carbon filtration of carcinogens from drinking water. Construction of filtration plants would impose costs in the near term, while benefits would be delayed forty years and more due to cancer and mutagen latency. In order to avoid discounting the value of future life over long periods, it was recommended that the decision be based on current costs and benefits in the steady state after adjustment of cancer rates to the proposed action. In other words, the indefinitely long future should prevail over the transitory present, for this decision involving basic health. See [1], [5], and [10].

10. Chapter 44 of *A Theory of Justice* [11].

11. It is usually left unspecified how the interest rate could, or should, be adjusted. Business income taxes, dividend taxes, and changes in the supply of money affect interest rates, but these and other instruments also affect the rate of inflation, unemployment, and the tax base as well. Because the interest rate has several important macroeconomic effects, it is unclear how it could or should be used for the purpose of intertemporal equity and how the various effects should be traded off. In contrast, the severance tax has smaller and more localized "side effects." Krutilla traces back to Pigou the first suggestion to use the interest rate adjustment for controlling the use of natural resources by the government as "trustee for unborn generations." Besides suggesting the device of guaranteed interest, Pigou mentions taxes and State loans as other possibilities (conservation with Krutilla; see more generally [4]).

12. [11], p. 27.

13. For example, it is recognized that the difficulty of resolving simultaneous inflation and unemployment constitutes a real constraint on the opportunities available to society as a whole; moreover, simultaneous inflation and unemployment in part result from economic behavioral conditions of price and wage expectations.

14. See [4A] for a definition of the information inequality.

15. Such societies are a prototype of the steady-state or spaceship earth economy described by Daly and Boulding, but at a lower level of material well-being, and one of the present empirical questions is at how high a level of material well-being can a modern version of the steady-state economy be achieved.

16. A cutoff point is the stage of processing at which the market value of the material is taken as a base for the depletion allowance or for the severance tax.

REFERENCES

[1] Broder, I. "Analysis of Proposed EPA Drinking Water Regulations." Washington, D.C.: Council on Wage and Price Stability, September 1978.

[2] Georgescu-Roegen, N. (See Chapters 3 and 4 in this volume.)

[3] Hansson, Bengt. "The Existence of Group Preference Functions." *Public Choice,* 38 (Winter 1976):89–98. (Originally circulated as Working Paper No. 3, Mattias Fremling Society, 1972).

[4] Krutilla, John. "Conservation Reconsidered." *American Economic Review,* September 1967.

[4A] B. W. Lindgren, *Statistical Theory.* New York: Macmillan, 1968, pp. 272–275.

[5] National Academy of Sciences. *Nonfluorinated Halomethanes in the Environment.* Panel on Low Molecular Weight Halogenated Hydrocarbons of the Coordinating Committee for Scientific and Technical Assessments of Environmental Pollutants, Ch. 8. Washington, D.C., 1978.

[6] Mishan, E., and T. Page. "The Methodology of Cost-Benefit Analysis: With Particular Reference to the Ozone Problem." California Institute of Technology, Social Science Working Paper No. 249, 1979.

[7] Ferejohn, J., and T. Page. "On the Foundations of Intertemporal Choice." *American Journal of Agricultural Economics,* 60, 2 (1978).

[8] Strotz, Robert. "Myopia and Inconsistency in Dynamic Utility Maximization." *Review of Economic Studies,* 13 (1955–56): 105–180.

[9] Page, T. *Conservation and Economic Efficiency: An Approach to Materials Policy.* Baltimore: Johns Hopkins Press, 1977.

[10] Page T., R. Harris, and J. Bruser. "Removal of Carcinogens from Drinking Water: A Cost-Benefit Analysis." California Institute of Technology, Social Science Working Paper No. 230, 1978.

[11] Rawls, J. *A Theory of Justice.* Cambridge: Harvard University Press, 1971.

21

THE STEADY-STATE ECONOMY: TOWARD A POLITICAL ECONOMY OF BIOPHYSICAL EQUILIBRIUM AND MORAL GROWTH

Herman E. Daly

There is nothing in front but a flat wilderness of standardization either by Bolshevism or Big Business. But it is strange that some of us should have seen sanity, if only in a vision, while the rest go forward chained eternally to enlargement without liberty and progress without hope.
G. K. CHESTERTON

THE CONCEPT OF A STEADY-STATE ECONOMY

The steady-state economy (SSE) is defined by four characteristics:

1. A constant population of human bodies.

2. A constant population or stock of artifacts (exosomatic capital or extentions of human bodies).

3. The levels at which the two populations are held constant are sufficient for a good life and sustainable for a long future.

4. The rate of throughput of matter-energy by which the two stocks are maintained is reduced to the lowest feasible level. For the population this means that birth rates are equal to death rate at low levels so that life expectancy is high. For artifacts it means that production equals depreciation at low levels so that artifacts are long lasting, and depletion and pollution are kept low.

Only two things are held constant—the stock of human bodies and the total stock or inventory of artifacts. Technology, information, wisdom, goodness, genetic characteristics, distribution of wealth and income, product mix, and so on are *not* held constant. In the very long run, of course, nothing can remain constant, so our concept of a SSE must be a medium-run concept in which stocks are constant over decades or generations, not millenia or eons.

Three magnitudes are basic to the concept of a SSE:

1. *Stock* is the total inventory of producers' goods, consumers' goods, and human bodies. It corresponds to Irving Fisher's (1906) definition of capital and may be thought of as the set of all physical things capable of satisfying human wants and subject to ownership.

2. *Service* is the satisfaction experienced when wants are satisfied, or "psychic income" in Fisher's sense. Service is yielded by the stock. The quantity and quality of the stock determine the intensity of service. There is no unit for measuring service, so it may be stretching words a bit to call it a magnitude. Nevertheless, we all experience service or satisfaction and recognize differing intensities of the experience. Service is yielded over a period of time and thus appears to be a flow magnitude. But unlike flows, service cannot be accumulated. It is probably more accurate to think of service as a "psychic flux" (Georgescu-Roegen, 1966, 1971).

3. *Throughput* is the entropic physical flow of matter-energy from nature's sources, through the human economy and back to nature's sinks; it is necessary for maintenance and renewal of the constant stocks (Boulding, 1966; Daly, 1968; Georgescu-Roegen, 1971).

Reprinted in part from the University of Alabama *Distinguished Lecture Series, No. 2,* 1971, by permission of the University of Alabama, and in part from *Steady-State Economics: The Economics of Biophysical Equilibrium and Moral Growth,* © 1977, by permission of W. H. Freeman and Company, with revisions and additions by the author, 1979.

The relationship among these three magnitudes can best be understood in terms of the following simple identity (Daly, 1974):

$$\frac{service}{throughput} \equiv \frac{service}{stock} \times \frac{stock}{throughput}$$

The final benefit of all economic activity is service. The original useful stuff required for yielding service, which cannot be produced by man, but only used up, is low-entropy matter-energy—in other words, the throughput. But throughput is not itself capable of directly yielding service. It must first be accumulated into a stock of artifacts; it is the stock that directly yields service. We can ride to town only in a member of the existing stock of automobiles. We cannot ride to town on the annual flow of automotive maintenance expenditures, nor on the flow of newly mined iron ore destined to be embodied in a new chassis, nor on the flow of worn rusting hulks in junkyards. Stocks may be thought of as throughput that has been accumulated and "frozen" in structured forms capable of satisfying human wants. Eventually the frozen structures are "melted" by entropy, and what flowed into the accumulated stocks from nature then flows back to nature in equal quantity, but in entropically degraded quality. Stocks are intermediate magnitudes that belong at the center of analysis and provide a clean separation between the cost flow and the benefit flux. On the one hand, stocks yield service; on the other hand, stocks require throughput for maintenance. Service yielded is benefit; throughput required is cost.

The identification of cost with throughput should not be interpreted as implying a "throughput or entropy theory of value." There are other costs, notably the disutility of labor and the accumulation time required to build up stocks. In the steady state we can forget about accumulation time since stocks are only being maintained, not accumulated. The disutility of labor can be netted out against the services of the stock to obtain net psychic income or net service. In the steady state, then, the value of net service is imputed to the stocks that render the service, which is in turn imputed to the throughput that maintains the stocks. It is in this sense that throughput is identified with cost. The opportunity cost of the throughput that maintains artifact A is the service sacrificed by not using that throughput to maintain more of artifact B. The throughput is a physical cost which is evaluated according to opportunity cost principles. However, the opportunity cost of the throughput must be evaluated not only in terms of alternative artifact services forgone (which the market does), but also in terms of natural ecosystem services forgone as a result of the depletion and pollution caused by the throughput (which escapes market valuation). Depletion reduces the service of availability of the resource to future people who cannot bid in present markets, and pollution reduces the ability of the ecosystem to perform its life-support services. The true opportunity cost of an increment in throughput is the greater of the two classes: artifact service sacrificed and ecosystem services sacrificed. Thus throughput should be thought of as a cost-inducing physical flow, rather than identified with cost itself, which by definition must always be a sacrificed benefit, not a physical magnitude. In like manner the stock is a benefit-yielding physical magnitude and should not be identified with benefit or service itself. This is the case even for short-lived artifacts whose physical degradation is an immediate consequence of use, for instance, gasoline in the tank of a car.

We can arrive at the same basic result by following Irving Fisher's reasoning. Fisher (1906) argued that every intermediate transaction involves both a receipt and an expenditure of identical magnitude which cancel out in aggregation of the total income of the community. But once the final user has obtained the asset, there is no further exchange and cancelling of accounts among individuals. The service yielded by the asset to the final consumer is the "uncancelled fringe" of psychic income, the final uncancelled benefit left over after all intermediate transactions have cancelled out. Subtracting the psychic disservices of labor, Fisher arrived at *net psychic income,* the final net benefit of all economic activity. It is highly interesting that Fisher did not identify any original, uncancelled, real cost against which the final value of net psychic income should be balanced. Here we must supplement Fisher's vision with the more recent visions and analyses of Boulding (1966) and Georgescu-Roegen (1966; 1971) concerning the physical basis of cost. As everyone recognizes, the stock of capital wears out and has to be replaced. This continual maintenance and replacement is an unavoidable cost inflicted by entropy. Fisher treated it as cancelling out in the aggregate: House repair is income to the account of the carpenter and an identical outgo to the account of the house. But Fisher did not trace the chain all the way back to any uncancelled fringe at the beginning which would correspond to uncancelled final costs in the same way that net psychic income corresponds to uncancelled final benefits. If we do this, we come to the unpaid contribution from nature: the provision of useful low-entropy matter-energy inputs and the absorption of high-entropy waste matter-energy outputs. These contributions from nature have no costs of production, only a cost of extraction or disposal, which is paid and enters the cancelling stream of accounts. But we do not pump any money down into a well as we pump oil out, nor do we dump dollars into the sea along with our chemical and radioactive wastes. If service is an "uncancelled fringe," then so is throughput. In other words, if we consolidate the accounts of all firms and households, everything cancels out except service and throughput.

In the SSE a different behavior mode is adopted with respect to each of the three basic magnitudes. (1) *Stock* is to be *"satisficed"*—maintained at a level that is sufficient for an abundant life for the present generation and ecologically sustainable for a long (but not infinite) future.[1] (2) *Service* is to be *maximized,* given the constant stock. (3) *Throughput* is to be *minimized,* given the constant stock. In terms of the two ratios on the right hand side of the identity, this means that the ratio (service/stock) is to be maximized by maximizing the numerator with the denominator constant, while the ratio (stock/throughput) is maximized by minimizing the denominator with the numerator constant. These two ratios measure two kinds of efficiency: service efficency and maintenance efficiency.

Service efficiency (service/stock) depends on allocative efficiency (does the stock consist of artifacts that people most want and are they allocated to the most important uses), and on distributive efficiency (is the distribution of the stock among alternative people such that the trivial wants of some people do not take precedence over the basic needs of others). Standard economics has much of value to say about allocative efficiency, but it treats distribution under the heading of social justice rather than efficiency, thus putting it on the sidelines of disciplinary concern.Although neoclassical economists carefully distinguish allocation from distribution in static analysis, they seem not to insist on any analogous distinction between intertemporal allocation (one person allocating over different stages of his lifetime) and intertemporal distribution (distribution between different people, that is, present people and future people). Intertemporal distribution is a question of ethics, not a function of the interest rate. The notion of optimal allocation over time must be confined to a single lifetime unless we are willing to let ethics and distributional issues into the definition of optimum. Neoclassical economics seems inconsistent, or at least ambiguous, on this point.

Maintenance efficency (stock/throughput) depends on durability (how long an individual artifact lasts) and on replaceability (how easily the artifact can be replaced when it finally does wear out). Maintenace efficiency measures the number of units of time over which a population of artifacts yields its service, while service efficiency measures the intensity of that service per unit of time. Maintenance efficiency is limited by the entropy law (nothing lasts forever; everything wears out). Service efficiency may conceivably increase for a very long time, since the growing "magnitude," service, is nonphysical. There may, however, be physical limits to the capacity of human beings to experience service. But the definition of the SSE is in terms of physical stocks and throughput and is not affected by whether or not service could increase indefinitely.

Conceptually it is easier to think of stock as the operational policy variable to be directly controlled. Practically, however, as will be seen below, it would be easier to control or limit throughput directly and allow the stock to reach the maximum level sustainable by the fixed throughput. This presents no problems.

The above concepts allow us to make an important distinction between growth and development. *Growth* refers to an increase in service that results from an increase in stock and throughput, with the two efficiency ratios constant. *Development* refers to an increase in the efficiency ratios, with stock constant (or alternatively, an increase in service with throughput constant). Using these definitions, we may say that a SSE develops but does not grow, just as the planet earth, of which it is a subsystem, develops without growing.

How do these concepts relate to GNP, the more conventional index of "growth"? GNP makes no distinction among the three basic magnitudes. It simply adds up value estimates of some services (the service of those assets that are rented rather than purchased, including human bodies, and omitting the services of all owned assets not rented during the current year, with the exception of owner-occupied houses), plus the value of the throughput flow (maintenance and replacement expenditures required to maintain the total stock intact), plus the value of current additions to stock (net investment). What sense does it make to add up benefits, costs, and change in inventory? Services of the natural ecosystem are not counted, and, more important, services sacrificed are not subtracted. In fact, defensive attempts to repair the loss of ecosystem services are added to GNP. The concept of a SSE is independent of GNP, and what happens to GNP in the SSE simply does not matter. The best thing to do with GNP is to forget it. The next best thing is to try to replace it with two separate social accounts, one measuring the value of service (benefit) and the other measuring the value of throughput (cost). In this way costs and benefits could be compared, although this aggregate macro level comparison is not at all essential, since regardless of how it turns out the behavior modes remain the same with respect to each of the three basic magnitudes. If we really could get operational cost and benefit accounts, then we might optimize the level of stocks by letting it grow to the point where the marginal cost of an addition to stock just equals the marginal benefit. But that is so far beyond our ability to measure that satisficing will for a long time remain a better strategy than optimizing. Aggregate economic indices should be treated with caution, since there are always some kinds of stupid behavior that would raise the index and thus become "justified."

Neither the concept nor the reality of a SSE is new. John Stuart Mill (1881) discussed the concept in his famous chapter on the stationary state. Historically, people have lived for 99 percent of their tenure on earth in conditions very closely approximating a steady state. Economic growth is essentially a phenomenon of the last 200 years, and only in the last 50 years has it become the dominant goal of nations. Growth is an aberration, not the norm. Development can continue without growth and is, in fact, more likely under a SSE than under a growth economy.

Even "cornucopians" like Weinberg and Goeller (1976) evidently consider a SSE to be a precondition for achieving their Age of Substitutability, in which "society will settle into a steady state of substitution and recycling . . . assuming, of course, a stable population." But why postpone the SSE to some hypothetical future age? Why not seek to come to terms with the SSE now, before we use up the remaining easily available resources that could help in making the transition? Why continue to fan the fires of growth up to the point where the flame's appetite is so voracious that even to maintain it in a steady state would require technologies and social institutions that are so demanding and unforgiving as to reduce the quality of life to that of a regimented community of social insects? Freedom is in large measure a function of slack, of the distance between maximum carrying capacity and actual load. A system operating at its carrying capacity has no room for error or for the freedom that permits error.

SOCIAL INSTITUTIONS

The social institutions of control are of three kinds: those for maintaining a constant population, those for maintaining a constant stock of physical wealth, and those governing distribution. In all cases the guiding design principle for social institutions is to provide the necessary control with a minimum sacrifice of personal freedom, to provide macrostability while allowing for microvariability, to combine the macrostatic with the microdynamic.[2]

The Distribution Institution

The critical institution is likely to be the minimum and maximum limits on income and the maximum limit on wealth. Without some such limits private property and the whole market economy lose their moral basis, and there would be no strong case for extending the market to cover birth quotas and depletion quotas as a means of institutionalizing environmental limits. Exchange relations are mutually beneficial among relative equals. Exchange between the powerful and the powerless is often only nominally voluntary and can easily be a mask for exploitation, especially in the labor market, as Marx has shown.

There is considerable political support for a minimum income, financed by a negative income tax, as an alternative to bureaucratic welfare programs. There is no such support for maximum income or maximum wealth limits. In the growth paradigm there need be no upper limit. But in the steady-state paradigm there must be an upper limit to the total, and consequently an upper limit to per capita income as well. A minimum wealth limit is not feasible, since we can always spend our wealth and could hardly expect to have it restored year after year. The minimum income would be sufficient. But maximum limits on both wealth and income are necessary, since wealth and income are largely interchangeable, and since, beyond some point, the concentration of wealth becomes inconsistent with both a market economy and political democracy. John Stuart Mill put the issue very well:

> Private property, in every defense made of it, is supposed to mean the guarantee to individuals of the fruits of their own labor and abstinence. The guarantee to them of the fruits of the labor and abstinence of others, transmitted to them without any merit or exertion of their own, is not of the essence of the institution, but a mere incidental consequence, which, when it reaches a certain height, does not promote, but conflicts with, the ends which render private property legitimate. [Mill, 1881]

According to Mill, private property is legitimated as a bastion against exploitation. But this is true only if everyone owns some minimum amount. Otherwise, private property, when some own a great deal of it and others have very little, becomes the very *instrument* of exploitation rather than a guarantee against it. It is implicit in this view that private property is legitimate only if there is some distributist institution (as, for example, the Jubilee year of the Old Testament) that keeps inequality of wealth within justifiable limits. Such an institution is now lacking. The proposed institution of maximum wealth and income plus minimum income limits would remedy this severe defect and make private property legitimate again. It would also go a long way toward legitimating the free market, since most of our blundering interference with the price system (e.g., farm program, minimum wage, rent controls) has as its goal an equalizing alteration in the distribution of income and wealth. Thus such a distributist policy is based on impeccably respectable premises: private property, the free market, opposition to welfare bureaucracies and centralized control. It also heeds the radicals' call of "power to the people," since it puts the source of power, namely property, in the hands of the many people, rather than in the hands of the few capitalist plutocrats and socialist bureaucrats.

The concept of private property here adopted is the classical view of John Locke, Thomas Jefferson, and the Founding Fathers. It is emphatically not the apologetic doctrine of big business that the term *private property* evokes today. Limits are built into the very notion of property, according to Locke:

> Whatsoever, then, a man removes out of the state that nature hath provided and left it in, he hath mixed his labor with it, and joined to it something that is his own, and thereby makes it his property. But how far has God given property to us to enjoy? As much as anyone can make use of to any advantage of life before it spoils, so much may he by his labor fix his property in. Whatever is beyond this is more than his share, and belongs to others. [quoted in McClaughry, 1974, p. 31]

Clearly, Locke had in mind some maximum limit on property, even in the absence of general scarcity. Locke assumed, reasonably in his time, that resources were superabundant. Buth he insisted that the right to property was limited. Growing resource scarcity reinforces this necessity of limits. Some of the correlates of this view of private property are listed by McClaughry:

> Property should be acquired through *personal effort;* it is a reward for diligent industry and fair dealing. An inheritance or windfall may look and feel like property, and even be used as property, but it lacks this essence of reward for personal effort.
>
> Property implies *personal control* and individual responsibility. Where the putative owners are far removed from the men who make the decisions about the use of their wealth, this aspect of personal and individual responsibility is absent, and this wealth becomes something less than true property.
>
> Property is relative to *human need.* That which is accumulated beyond an amount necessary to suffice for the human needs of its owner and his family is no longer property, but surplus wealth.

> Although to own a home and a car is to own property, and although posses-
> sion of these consumer goods may have important effects upon the owner and
> his community, Locke and his successors thought of property as productive
> —yielding goods or services for exchange with others in the community—
> concentrated wealth means concentrated power—power to dominate other men,
> power to protect privilege, power to stifle the American Dream. [McClaughry,
> 1974, p. 32]

Maximum limits on income and wealth were an implicit part of the philosophy of all the prominent statesmen of early America except Alexander Ham-
ilton.

Maximum income and wealth would remove many of the incentives to
monopolistic practices. Why conspire to corner markets, fix prices, and so
forth, if you cannot keep the loot? As for labor, the minimum income would
enable the outlawing of strikes, which are rapidly becoming intolerably exploitative of the general public. Unions would not be needed as a means of
confronting the power of concentrated wealth, since wealth would no longer
be concentrated. Indeed, the workers would have a share of it and thus would
not be at the mercy of an employer. In addition, some limit on corporate size
would be needed, as well as a requirement that all corporate profits be distributed as dividends to stockholders.

With no large concentrations in wealth and income, savings would be
smaller and would truly represent abstinence from consumption rather than
surplus remaining after satiation. There would be less expansionary pressure
from large amounts of surplus funds seeking ever new ways to grow exponentially and leading to either physical growth, inflation, or both.

The minimum income could be financed out of general revenues, which, in
addition to a progressive income tax within the income limits, would also
include revenues from the depletion quota auction (to be discussed below),
and 100 percent marginal tax rates on wealth and income above the limits.
Upon reaching the maximum, most people would devote their further energies
to noneconomic pursuits, so that confiscatory revenues would be small. But
the opportunities thus forgone by the wealthy would be available to the not-so-
wealthy, who would still be paying taxes on their increased earnings. The
effect on incentive would be negative at the top but positive at lower levels,
leading to a broader participation in running the economy. If the maximum
and minimum were to move so close together that real differences in effort
could not be rewarded and incentives were insufficient to call forth the talent
and effort needed to sustain the system, then we should have to widen the
limits again or simply be content with the lower level of wealth that could be
maintained within the narrower distributive limits. Since we would no longer
be anxious to grow, the whole question of incentives would be less pressing.
There might also be an increase in public service by those who have hit the
maximum. As Jonathan Swift argued:

In all well-instituted commonwealths, care has been taken to limit men's possessions; which is done for many reasons, and, among the rest, for one which,
perhaps, is not often considered; that when bounds are set to men's desires after
they have acquired as much as the laws will permit them, their private interest is
at an end, and they have nothing to do but to take care of the public. [Swift,
1958, p. 1003]

Transferable Birth Licenses

This idea was first put forward in 1964 by Kenneth Boulding (1964, pp.
135–136). Hardly anyone has taken it seriously, as Boulding knew would be
the case. Nevertheless, it remains the best plan yet offered, if the goal is to
attain aggregate stability with a minimum sacrifice of individual freedom and
variability. It combines macrostability with microvariability. Since 1964 we
have experienced a great increase in public awareness of the population explosion and an energy crisis, and we are now experiencing the failures of the
great "technological fixes" (green revolution, nuclear power, and space). This
has led at least one respected demographer to take Boulding's plan seriously,
and more will probably follow (Heer, 1975).

So many people react so negatively to the birth license plan that I should
emphasize that the other two institutions (distributive limits and depletion
quotas) do not depend on it. The other two proposals could be accepted and
the reader can substitute his own favorite population control plan if he is
allergic to this one.

The plan is simply to issue equally to every person (or perhaps only to every
woman, since the female is the limitative factor in reproduction, and since
maternity is more demonstrable than paternity) an amount of reproduction
licenses that corresponds to replacement fertility. Thus each woman would
receive 2.1 licenses. The licenses would be divisible in units of one-tenth,
which Boulding playfully called the "deci-child." Possession of ten deci-child
units confers the legal right to one birth. The licenses are freely transferable by
sale or gift, so those who want more than two children and can afford to buy
the extra licenses, or can acquire them by gift, are free to do so. The original
distribution of the licenses is on the basis of strict equality, but exchange is
permitted, leading to a reallocation in conformity with differing preferences
and abilities to pay. Thus distributive equity is achieved in the original distribution, and allocative efficiency is achieved in the market redistribution.

A slight amendment to the plan might be to grant 1.0 certificates to each
individual (or 2.0 to each woman) and have these refer not to births but to
"survivals." If a female dies before having a child, then her certificate becomes
a part of her estate and is willed to someone else, for example, her parents,
who either use it to have another child or sell it to someone else. The advantage of this modification is that it offsets existing class differentials in infant

and child mortality. Without the modification, a poor family desiring two children could end up with two infant deaths and no certificates. The best plan, of course, is to eliminate class differences in mortality, but in the meantime this modification may make the plan initially easier to accept. Indeed, even in the absence of class mortality differentials the modification has the advantage of building in a "guarantee."

Let us dispose of two common objections to the plan. First, it is argued that it is unjust because the rich have an advantage. Of course, the rich *always* have an advantage, but is their advantage increased or decreased by this plan? Clearly it is decreased. The effect of the plan on income distribution is equalizing because (1) the new marketable asset is distributed equally; and (2) as the rich have more children, their family percapita incomes are lowered; as the poor have fewer children their family per-capita incomes increase. From the point of view of the children, there is something to be said for increasing the probability that they will be born richer rather than poorer. Whatever injustice there is in the plan stems from the prior existence of rich and poor not from Boulding's idea, which actually reduces the degree of injustice. Furthermore, income and wealth distribution are to be controlled by a separate institution, discussed above, so that in the overall system this objection is more fully and directly met.

A more reasonable objection concerns the problem of enforcement. What to do with law-breaking parents and their illegal children? What do we do with illegal children today? Often they are put up for adoption. Adoption could be encouraged by paying the adopting parents the market value, plus subsidy if need be, for their license, thus retiring a license from circulation to compensate for the child born without a license. Like any other law breakers, the offending parents would be subject to punishment. The punishment need not be drastic or unusual. Of course, if everyone breaks a law, no law can be enforced. The plan presupposes the acceptance by a large majority of the public of the morality and necessity of the law. It also presupposes widespread knowledge of contraceptive practices and perhaps legalized abortion as well. But these presuppositions would apply to any institution of population control except the most coercive.

Choice may be influenced in two ways: by acting on or "rigging" the *objective* conditions of choice (prices and incomes in a broad sense), or by manipulating the *subjective* conditions of choice (preferences). Boulding's plan imposes straightforward objective constraints and does not presumptuously attempt to manipulate people's preferences. Preference changes due to individual example and moral conversion are in no way ruled out. If preferences should change so that, on the average, the population desired replacement fertility, the price of a certificate would approach zero and the objective constraint would automatically vanish. The current decline in the birth rate has perhaps already led to such a state. Maybe this would be a good time to institute the plan, so that it would already be in place and functioning, should preferences change toward more children in the future. The moral basis of the plan is that everyone is treated equally, yet there is no insistence upon conformity of preferences, the latter being the great drawback of "voluntary" plans that rely on official moral suasion, Madison Avenue techniques, and even Skinnerian behavior control. Which is the greater affront to the individual—to be forbidden what he wants for objective reasons that he and everyone else ought to be able to understand, or to get what he "wants" but to be badgered and manipulated into "wanting" only what is collectively possible? Some people, God bless them, will never be brainwashed, and their individual nonconformity wrecks the moral basis (equal treatment) of "voluntary" programs.

Kingsley Davis points out that population control is not a technological problem.

> The solution is easy as long as one pays no attention to what must be given up. For instance a nation seeking ZPG could shut off immigration and permit each couple a maximum of two children, with possible state license for a third. Accidental pregnancies beyond the limit would be interrupted by abortion. If a third child were born without a license, or a fourth, the mother would be sterilized and the child given to a sterile couple. But anyone enticed into making such a suggestion risks being ostracized as a political or moral leper, a danger to society. He is accused of wanting to take people's freedom away from them and institute a Draconian dictatorship over private lives. Obviously then reproductive freedom still takes priority over population control. This makes a solution of the population problem impossible because, by definition, population control and reproductive freedom are incompatible. [Davis, 1973, p. 28]

The key to population control is simply to be willing to pay the cost. The cost of the plan here advocated seems to me less than the cost of Davis's hypothetical suggestion because it allows greater diversity—families need not be so homogeneous in size, and individual preferences are respected to a greater degree. Moreover, should it become necessary or desirable to have negative population growth (as I believe it will), the marketable license plan has a great advantage over those plans that put the limit on a flat child-per-family basis. This latter limit could be changed only by an integral number, and to go from two children to one child per family in order to reduce population is quite a drastic change. In the Boulding scheme of marketable licenses issued in deci-child units or one-tenth of a certificate, it would be possible gradually to reduce population by lowering the issue to 1.9 certificates per woman, to 1.8, and so on, the remaining 0.1 or 0.2 certificates being acquired by purchase or gift.

Part of our difficulty in accepting the transferable license plan is that it is so direct. It frankly recognizes that reproduction must henceforth be considered a scarce right and logically faces the issue of how best to distribute that right and whether and how to permit voluntary reallocation. But there is an amazing preference for indirect measures—find new roles for women, change the tax laws, restrict public housing to small families, encourage celibacy and late marriage, be more tolerant of homosexuality, convince people to spend their money on consumer durables rather than having children, make it popular to have children only between the ages of twenty and thirty, and so forth.

Whence this enormous preference for indirectness? It results partly from our unwillingness to really face the issue. Limiting reproduction is still a taboo subject that must be approached in contorted and roundabout ways rather than directly. Furthermore, roundaboutness and indirectness are the bread and butter of empirical social scientists, who get grants and make their reputations by measuring the responsiveness of the birth rate to all sorts of remote "policy variables." The direct approach makes estimation of all these social parameters governing tenuous chains of cause and effect quite unnecessary. If the right to reproduce were directly limited by the marketable license plan, then the indirect measures would become means of adjusting to the direct constraint. For example, with reduced childbearing, women would naturally find other activities. The advantage of the direct approach is that individuals would be free to make their own personal specific adjustments to the general objective constraint, rather than having a whole set of specific constraints imposed on them in the expectation that it would force them indirectly to decide to do what objectively must be done. The direct approach is more efficient and no more coercive. But the direct approach requires clarity of purpose and frank objectives, which are politically inconvenient when commitment to the objective is halfhearted to begin with.

There is an understandable reluctance to couple money and reproduction —somehow it seems to profane life. Yet life is physically coupled to increasingly scarce resources, and resources are coupled to money. If population growth and economic growth continue, then even free resources, such as breathable air, will become either coupled to money and subject to price or allocated by a harsher and less efficient means. Once we accept the fact that the price system is the most efficient mechanism for rationing the right to scarce life-sustaining and life-enhancing resources, then perhaps rather than "money profaning life" we will find that "life sanctifies money." We will then take the distribution of money and its wise use as serious matters. It is not the exchange relationship that debases life (indeed, the entire biosphere runs on a network of material and energy exchanges), it is the underlying inequity in wealth and income beyond any functional or ethical justification that loads the terms of free exchange against the poor. The same inequality also debases the "gift relationship," since it assigns the poor to the status of a perpetual dependent and the rich to the status of a weary and grumbling patron. Thus gift as well as exchange relationships require limits to the degree of inequality if they are not to subvert their legitimate ends. The sharing of resources in general is the job of the distributist institution. Allocation of particular resources and scarce rights is done by the market within the distribution limits imposed.

In view of the fact that so many liberals, not to mention the United Nations, have declared it to be a human right to have whatever number of children the parents desire, it is worthwhile to end this discussion with a statement from one of the greatest champions of liberty who ever lived, John Stuart Mill:

> The fact itself, of causing the existence of a human being, is one of the most responsible actions in the range of human life. To undertake this responsibility —to bestow a life which may be either a curse or a blessing—unless the being on whom it is to be bestowed will have at least the ordinary chances of a desirable existence, is a crime against that being. And in a country either over-peopled, or threatened with being so, to produce children, beyond a very small number, with the effect of reducing the reward of labor by their competition, is a serious offence against all who live by the remuneration of their labor. The laws which, in many countries on the Continent, forbid marriage unless the parties can show that they have the means of supporting a family, do not exceed the legitimate powers of the State: and whether such laws be expedient or not (a question mainly dependent on local circumstances and feelings), they are not objectionable as violations of liberty. Such laws are interferences of the State to prevent a mischievous act—an act injurious to others, which ought to be a subject of reprobation and social stigma, even where it is not deemed expedient to superadd legal punishment. Yet the current ideas of liberty, which bend so easily to real infringements of the freedom of the individual in things which concern only himself, would repel the attempt to put any restraint upon his inclinations when the consequence of their indulgence is a life or lives of wretchedness and depravity to the offspring, with manifold evils to those sufficiently within reach to be in any way affected by their actions. [Mill, 1952, p. 3191]

Depletion Quotas

The strategic point at which to impose control on the throughput flow seems to me to be the rate of depletion of resources. If we limit aggregate depletion, then, by the law of conservation of matter and energy, we will also indirectly limit aggregate pollution. If we limit throughput flow, then we also indirectly limit the size of the stocks maintained by that flow. Entropy is at its minimum at the input (depletion) end of the throughput pipeline and at its maximum at the output (pollution) end. Therefore, it is physically easier to monitor and control depletion than pollution—there are fewer mines, wells, and ports than there are smokestacks, garbage dumps, and drainpipes, not to mention such diffuse emission sources as runoff of insecticides and fertilizers from fields into rivers and lakes and auto exhausts. Land area devoted to mining is only 0.3 percent of total land area (National Commission on Materials Policy, 1973).

Given that there is more leverage in intervening at the input end, should we intervene by way of taxes or quotas? Quotas, if they are auctioned by the government rather than allocated on nonmarket criteria, have an important net advantage over taxes in that they definitely limit aggregate throughput, which is the quantity to be controlled. Taxes exert only an indirect and very uncertain limit. It is quite true that given a demand curve, a price plus a tax determines a quantity. But demand curves shift, and they are subject to great errors in estimation even if stable. Demand curves for resources could shift up as a result of population increase, change in tastes, increase in income, and so forth. Suppose the government seeks to limit throughput by taxing it. It then spends the tax. If government expenditures on each category of commodity were equal to the revenues received from taxing that same category, then the limit on throughput would be largely cancelled out, with the exact degree of cancelling depending on the elasticity of demand. If the government taxes resource-intensive items and spends on time-intensive items, there will be a one-shot reduction in aggregate physical throughput but not a limit to its future growth. A credit expansion by the banking sector, an increase in velocity of circulation of money, or deficit spending by the government for other purposes could easily offset even the one-shot reduction induced by taxes. Taxes can reduce the amount of depletion and pollution (throughput) per unit of GNP down to some irreducible minimum, but taxes provide no limit to the increase in the number of units of GNP (unless the government runs a growing surplus) and therefore no limit to aggregate throughput. The fact that a tax levied on a single resource could, by inducing substitution, usually reduce the throughput of that resource very substantially should not mislead us into thinking that a general tax on all or most resources will reduce aggregate throughput (fallacy of composition). Recall that there is no substitute for low-entropy matter-energy. Finally, it is *quantity* that affects the ecosystem, not price, and therefore it is ecologically safer to let errors and unexpected shifts in demand result in price fluctuations rather than in quantity fluctuations. Hence quotas.

An example will illustrate the reason for putting the control (whether tax or quota) on resources rather than on commodities. Suppose the government taxes automobiles heavily and that people take to riding bicycles instead of cars. They will save money as well as resources (Hannon, 1975). But what will the money saved now be spent on? If it is spent on airline tickets, resource consumption would increase above what it was then the money was spent on cars. If the money is spent on theater tickets, then perhaps resource consumption would decline. However, this is not certain, because the theater performance may entail the air transport of actors, stage sets, and so on, and thus indirectly be as resource consumptive as automobile expenditures. If people paid the high tax on cars and continued buying the same number of cars, then they would have to cut other items of consumption. The items cut may or may not be more resource intensive than the items for which the government spends the revenue. If the revenue is spent on B-1 bombers, there would surely be a net increase in resource consumption. The conclusion is that the tax or quota should be levied on the resource itself rather than on the commodity.

Pollution taxes would provide a much weaker inducement to resource-saving technological progress than would depletion quotas, since, in the former scheme, resource prices do not necessarily have to rise and may even fall. The inducement of pollution taxes is to "pollution avoidance," and thus to recycling. But increased competition from recycling industries, instead of reducing depletion, might spur the extractive industries to even greater competitive efforts. Intensified search and the development of technologies with still larger jaws could speed up the rate of depletion and thereby lower short-run resource prices. Thus new extraction might once again become competitive with recycling, leading to less recycling and more depletion and pollution —exactly what we wish to avoid. This perverse effect could not happen under a depletion quota system.

The usual recommendation of pollution taxes would seem, if the above is correct, to intervene at the wrong end with the wrong policy tool. Intervention by pollution taxes also tends to be microcontrol, rather than macro. There are, however, limits to the ability of depletion quotas to influence the qualitative nature and spatial location of pollution, and at this fine-tuning level pollution taxes would be a useful supplement, as would a bureau of technology assessment. Depletion quotas would induce resource-saving technological change, and the set of resource-saving technologies would probably overlap to a great degree with the set of socially benign technologies. But the coincidence is not complete, and there is still a need, though a diminished one, for technology assessment.

How would a depletion quota system function? The market for each resource would become two-tiered. To begin with, the government, as a monopolist, would auction the limited quota rights to many buyers. Resource buyers, having purchased their quota rights, would then have to confront many resource sellers in a competitive resource market. The competitive price in the resource market would tend to equal marginal cost. More efficient producers would earn differential rents, but the pure scarcity rent resulting from the quotas would have been captured in the depletion quota auction market by the government monopoly. The total price of the resource (quota price plus price to owner) would be raised as a result of the quotas. All products using these resources would become more expensive. Higher resource prices would compel more efficient and frugal use of resources by both producers and consumers. But the windfall rent from higher resource prices would be captured by the government and become public income—a partial realization of Henry George's ideal of a single tax on rent (George, 1951).

The major advantage is that higher resource prices would bring increased efficiency, while the quotas would directly limit depletion, thereby increasing conservation and indirectly limiting pollution. Pollution would be limited in two ways. First, since pollution is simply the other end of the throughput from depletion, limiting the input to the pipeline would naturally limit the output. Second, higher prices would induce more recycling, thereby further limiting materials pollution and depletion up to the limit set by the increased energy throughput required by recycling. The revenue from the depletion quota auction could help finance the minimum-income component of the distributist institution, offsetting the regressive effect of the higher resource prices on income distribution. Attempts to help the poor by underpricing resources are totally misguided, because the greatest benefit of subsidized prices for energy, for example, goes to those who consume the most energy—the rich not the poor. This is hardly progressive.

Higher prices on basic resources are absolutely necessary. Any plan that refuses to face up to this necessity is worthless. Back in 1925 economist John Ise made the point in these words:

> Preposterous as it may seem at first blush, it is probably true that, even if all the timber in the United States, or all the oil or gas or anthracite, were owned by an absolute monopoly, entirely free of public control, prices to consumers would be fixed lower than the long-run interests of the public would justify. Pragmatically this means that all efforts on the part of the government to keep down the prices of lumber, oil, gas, or anthracite are contrary to the public interest; that the government should be trying to keep prices up rather than down. [Ise, 1925, p. 284]

Ise went on to suggest a general principle of resource pricing: that nonrenewable resources be priced at the cost of the nearest renewable substitute. Therefore, virgin timber should cost at least as much per board foot as replanted timber; petroleum should be priced at its Btu equivalent of sugar or wood alcohol, assuming they are the closest renewable alternatives. In the absence of any renewable substitutes, the price would merely reflect the purely ethical judgment of how fast the resources should be used up—that is, the importance of the wants of future people relative to the wants of present people. Renewable resources are assumed to be exploited on a sustained-yield basis and to be priced accordingly.

The Ise principles could also be used in setting the aggregate quota amounts to auction. For renewables, the quota should be set at an amount equivalent to some reasonable calculation of maximum sustainable yield. For nonrenewables with renewable substitutes the quota should be set so that the resulting price of the nonrenewable resource is at least as high as the price of its nearest renewable substitute. For nonrenewables with no close renewable substitute, the quota would reflect a purely ethical judgment concerning the relative importance of present versus future wants. Should these resources be used up by us or by our descendants? The price system cannot decide this, because future generations cannot bid in present resource markets. The decision is ethical. We have found it too easy to assume that future generations will be better off due to inevitable "progress" and therefore not to worry about the unrepresented claims of the future on exhaustible resources.

In addition to the Ise principles, which deal only with depletion costs that fall on the future, the quotas must be low enough to prevent excessive pollution and ecological costs that fall on the present as well as on the future. Pragmatically, quotas would probably at first be set near existing extraction rates. The first task would be to stabilize, to get off the growth path. Later, we could try to reduce quotas to a more sustainable level, if present flows proved too high. Abundant resources causing little environmental disruption would be governed by generous quotas, and therefore relatively low prices, and a consequently strong incentive to technologies that make relatively intensive use of the abundant resource.

Depletion quotas would capture the increasing scarcity rents but would not require the expropriation of resource owners. Quotas are clearly against the interests of resource owners, but not unjustly so, since rent is by definition unearned income from a price in excess of the minimum supply price. The elimination of this unearned increment would no doubt reduce the incentive to exploration and new discovery. Geological exploration has many aspects of a natural monopoly and probably should, in any case, be carried on by a public corporation. As the largest resource owner by far, the government should not have to lease public lands to private companies who have more geological information than the government about the land. If private exploration is thought desirable, it could be encouraged by a government bounty paid for mineral discoveries. The current resource owners would suffer a one-time capital loss when depletion limits are imposed and, in fairness, should be compensated.

For many readers a graphical exposition of the depletion quota scheme will be helpful, as shown in Figure 21.1. DD' is the market demand curve for the resource in question. SS' is the supply curve of the industry. A depletion quota, in the aggregate amount Q, is imposed, shown by the vertical line QQ'. The total price paid per unit of the resource (price paid to resource owner plus price paid to government for the corresponding quota right) is OC. Of the total price OC, the amount OB is the price paid to the resource owner for one unit of the resource, and BC is the price paid to the government for a quota right to purchase one unit of the resource. Of the total amount paid, $OQAC$, the amount $OSEQ$ is cost, reflecting the necessary supply price. The remainder, $SEAC$, is surplus, or rent.

Rent is defined as payment in excess of necessary supply price. Of the total rent area, the amount BES is differential rent, or surplus that arises from the difference in the supply price of the marginal amount produced, which is QE, and all previous amounts produced. Price is determined at the margin, and is equal to QE, the marginal cost of production. Since the cost of production of all inframarginal units is less than QE, and since all units sell at the same price, equal to QE, a profit, or differential rent, is earned on all inframarginal units produced. The profit on the first unit is BS and declines slightly for each additional unit until it is zero for the last unit at Q. Thus BES is the sum of the diminishing series of inframarginal per-unit profits. It is called differential rent because its amount depends on the schedule of cost differences between the first and last units. The remainder of the surplus, the amount $CAEB$, is pure scarcity rent. It does not arise from cost differentials but simply from the excess of the market price above the marginal cost of production, by the amount AE. In effect, AE represents a kind of price per unit of resources in the

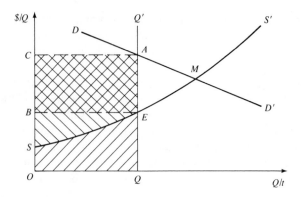

FIGURE 21.1

(From *Steady-State Economics* by Herman E. Daly. W. H. Freeman and Company. Copyright © 1977.)

ground that prior to the quota auction had implicitly been priced at zero. At the market equilbrium *M*, the entire surplus would be differential rent, and scarcity rent would be zero. Hence scarcity rent, as the name implies, emerges when the resource is made scarce relative to the quantity corresponding to market equilibrium, which, of course, is what happens when quotas are imposed.

The scarcity rent *CAEB* is captured by the government quota auction. The differential rent *BES* remains in the hands of the resource owners. The reason for this particular division of the surplus is that the resource market is assumed to be competitive (many sellers and buyers), while the quota auction market is monopolistic (many buyers, one seller). The government has monopoly power; the resource owners and buyers have none. The price in the resource market is set by competition at an amount equal to marginal cost, *QE*. The government, by charging what the market will bear with no fear of being undercut by competitors, is able to extract the remainder of the full demand price, or the amount *AE*. If the resource market were also monopolized, then the division of scarcity rent between the government and private monopolies would be indeterminate. Even in that case, however, the government would have an advantage in that the quota right has to be purchased *first*. Thus even if competition is less than perfect in the resource market, we would still expect the government to capture all monopoly profits (scarcity rents), because it constitutes the first tier of the market and controls the entry of buyers into the second tier.

Over time the supply curve for nonrenewable resources would shift upward as more accessible resources become depleted and previously submarginal mines and wells have to be used. In Figure 21.2 the higher supply curve is represented by *BS″*, which may be thought of as the "unused" segment of the original supply curve, *ES′*, shifted horizontally to the left until it touches the

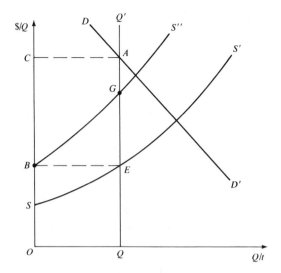

FIGURE 21.2

(From *Steady-State Economics* by Herman E. Daly. W. H. Freeman and Company. Copyright © 1977.)

vertical axis. Assuming an unchanged demand curve and quota, it is clear from Figure 21.2 that rising cost of production (now shown by the larger area, *OBGQ*) will eventually eliminate the pure scarcity rent, leaving only differential rent. Quotas will slow down the upward shift of the supply curve relative to what it would have been with faster depletion, but of course they cannot arrest the inevitable process. Probably the quota would have to be reduced as the supply curve shifted up in order to pass along the higher cost signals to users and to maintain some scarcity rent for public revenue.

For renewable resources, where the quota is set at maximum sustainable yield, there would be no upward shift of the supply curve. However, the demand curve for renewables would shift up as nonrenewable resource usage became more restricted and expensive and efforts were made to substitute renewables for nonrenewables. The quota on renewables would then protect those resources from being exploited beyond capacity in order to satisfy the rising demand while at the same time rationing access to the limited amount and diverting the windfall profits into the public treasury. In sum, the depletion quota auction is an instrument for helping us to make the transition from a nonrenewable to a renewable resource base in a gradual, efficient, and equitable manner.

The depletion quota scheme allows a reconciliation between the two conflicting goals of efficiency and equity. Efficiency requires high resource prices. However, equity is not served by high prices, because they have a regressive effect on income distribution in the same way that a sales tax does, and also because the windfall rents arising from the higher prices accrue to resource owners not to the poor. The latter effect can be reversed by capturing the scarcity rent through the depletion quota auction and using it to finance a minimum income, and/or to replace the most regressive taxes.

Two further efficiency increases could be expected. First, taxing rent causes no allocative distortions and is the most efficient way to raise government revenue. To the extent that a rent tax (or its equivalent in this case) replaces other taxes, then static allocative efficiency should be improved. Second, as conservatives and radicals alike have noted, the minimum income could substitute for a considerable number of bureaucratic welfare programs. Of course, the major increase in efficiency would result directly from higher resource prices, which would give incentives to develop resource-saving techniques of production and patterns of consumption. Equity is not served by low prices, which, in effect, give a larger subsidy to the rich than to the poor, since the rich consume more resources. Equity is served by higher incomes to the poor and by a maximum limit in the incomes of the rich.

A Coordinated Program

Let us now consider all three institutions as a unified program.

The allocation among firms of the limited aggregate of resources extracted during the given time period would be accomplished entirely by the market. The distribution of income within the maximum and minimum boundaries imposed would also be left to the market. The initial distribution of reproductive licenses is done outside the market on the basis of strict equity—one person, one license—but reallocation via market exchange is permitted in the interest of efficiency. The combination of the three institutions presents a nice reconciliation of efficiency and equity and provides the ecologically necessary macrocontrol of growth with the least sacrifice in terms of microlevel freedom and variability. The market is relied upon to allocate resources and distribute incomes within imposed ecological and ethical boundaries. The market is not allowed to set its own boundaries, but it is free within those boundaries. Setting boundaries is necessary. No one has ever claimed that market equilibria would automatically coincide with ecological equilibria or with a reasonably just distribution of wealth and income. Nor has anyone ever claimed that market equilibria would attain demographic balance. The very notions of "equilibrium" in economics and ecology are antithetical. In growth economics equilibrium refers not to physical magnitudes at all but to a balance of desires between savers and investors. As long as saving is greater than depreciation, then net investment must be positive. This implies a *growing* flow of physical inputs from and outputs to nature, that is, a biophysical *dis*equilibrium. Physical conditions of environmental equilibrium must be imposed on the market in aggregate quantitative physical terms. Subject to these quantitative constraints, the market and price system can, with the institutional changes just discussed, achieve an optimal allocation of resources and an optimal adjustment to its imposed physical system boundaries. The point is important because the belief is widespread among economists that internalization of externalities, or the incorporation of all environmental costs into market prices, is a sufficient environmental policy and that once this is accomplished the market will be able to set its own proper boundaries automatically. This is not so. Nor, as we have already seen, is it possible to incorporate all ecological costs in rigged money prices.

The internalization of externalities is a good strategy for fine-tuning the allocation of resources by making relative prices better measures of relative marginal social costs. But it does not enable the market to set its own absolute physical boundaries with the larger ecosystem. To give an analogy: Proper allocation arranges the weight in a boat optimally, so as to maximize the load that can be carried. But there is still an absolute limit to how much weight a boat can carry, even optimally arranged. The price system can spread the weight evenly, but unless it is supplemented by an external absolute limit, it will just keep on spreading the increasing weight evenly until the evenly loaded boat sinks. No doubt the boat would sink evenly, ceteris paribus, but that is less comforting to the average citizen than to the neoclassical economist.

Two distinct questions must be asked about these proposed institutions for achieving a steady state. First, would they work if people accepted the goal of a steady state and perhaps voted the institutions into effect? Second, would people ever accept either the steady-state idea or these particular institutions? I have tried to show that the answer to the first question is probably "yes." Let the critic find any remaining flaws; better yet, let him suggest improvements. The answer to the second question is clearly "no" in the short run. But several considerations make acceptance more plausible in the not-too-long run.

The minimum-income side of the distributist institution already has some political support in the United States; the maximum limits will at first be thought un-American. Yet, surely, beyond some figure any additions to personal income would represent greed rather than need, or even merit. Most people would be willing to believe that in most cases an income in excess of, let us say, $100,000 per year has no real functional justification, especially when the highly paid jobs are usually already the most interesting and pleasant.

In spite of their somewhat radical implications, the proposals presented in this chapter are, as we have seen, based on impeccably respectable conservative institutions: private property and the free market.

By fixing the rate of depletion we force technology to focus more on the flow sources of solar energy and renewable resources. The solar flux cannot be increased in the present at the expense of the future. Thus let technology devote itself to learning how to live off our solar income rather than our terrestrial capital. Such advances will benefit all generations, not just the present. Indeed, the main goal of the depletion quota plan is to turn technological change away from increasing dependence on the terrestrial stock and toward the more abundant flow of solar energy and renewable resources. As the stock becomes relatively more expensive, it will be used less in direct consumption and more for investment in "work gates" that increase our ability to tap the solar flow. Instead of taking long-run technical evolution as a parameter to which the short-run variables of price and quantity continually adjust, the idea is to take short-run quantities (and hence prices) as a social parameter to be set, so as to induce a direction of technological evolution more in harmony with mankind's long-run interests.

This new direction of technological change is likely also to be in mankind's short-run interests, if we accept the view that man's evolution in a solar-based and stable economy has programmed him for that kind of life rather than for the stresses of a growing industrial economy. The future steady state could be a good deal more comfortable than past ones and much more human than the overgrown, overcentralized, overextended, and overbearing economy into which growth has pushed us.

The depletion quota plan should appeal to both technological optimists and pessimists. The pessimist should be pleased by the conservation effect of the quotas; the optimist should be pleased by the price inducement to resource-saving technology. The optimist tells us not to worry about running out of resources because technology embodied in reproducible capital is a nearly perfect substitute for resources. As we run out of anything, prices will rise and substitute methods will be found. If we believe this, then how could we object to quotas, which simply increase the scarcity and prices of resources a bit ahead of schedule and more gradually? This plan simply requires the optimist to live up to his faith in technology.

Like the maximum limits on income and wealth, the depletion quotas could also have a trust-busting effect if accompanied by a limit—for example, no single entity can own more than x percent of the quota rights for a given resource or more than y percent of the resource owned by the industry of which it is a member. We could set x and y so as to allow legitimate economies of scale, while curtailing monopoly power.

The actual mechanics of quota auction markets for three or four hundred basic resources would present no great problems. The whole process could be computerized, since the function of an auctioneer is purely mechanical. It could be vastly simpler, faster, more decentralized, and less subject to fraud and manipulation than today's stock market. In addition, qualitative and locational variation among resources within each category, though ignored at the auction level, will be taken into account in price differentials paid to resource owners.

The depletion quota and birth quota systems bear an obvious analogy. The difference is that the birth quotas are privately held and equally distributed initially, and then redistributed among individuals through the market; the depletion quotas are collectively held initially and then distributed to individuals by way of an auction market. The revenue derived from birth quotas is private income; the revenue from depletion quotas is public income.

The scheme could, and probably must, be designed to include imported resources. The same depletion quota right could be required for importation of resources, and thus the market would determine the proportions in which our standard of living is sustained by depletion of national and foreign resources. Imported final goods would now be cheaper relative to national goods, assuming foreigners do not limit their depletion. Our export goods would now be more expensive relative to the domestic goods of foreign countries. Our terms of trade would improve, but we would tend to a balance of payments deficit. However, with a freely fluctuating exchange rate, a rise in the price of foreign currencies relative to the dollar would restore equilibrium. The balance of payments can take care of itself. If foreigners are willing to sell us goods priced below their true full costs of production, we should not complain.

It might be objected that limiting our imports of resources will work a hardship on the many underdeveloped countries that export raw materials. This is not clear, because such a policy will also force them to transform their own resources domestically rather than through international trade. Foreign suppliers of raw materials will be treated no differently than domestic suppliers. Finished goods would not be subject to quotas. In any case, it is clear that in the long run we are not doing the underdeveloped countries any favor by using up their resource endowment. Sooner or later (sooner, in the case of OPEC), they will begin to drive a hard bargain for their nonrenewable resources, and we had better not be too dependent on them. Probably they will limit their raw material exports, thus making unnecessary any limits that we might place on our raw material imports. Eventually, population control and environmental protection policies might become preconditions for membership in a new free-trade bloc or common market. Free trade would be the rule among all countries that limited their own populations and rates of domestic depletion, while controls could be put on trade with other countries whenever desirable.

All three of the institutions we have discussed are capable of gradual application during the transition to a steady state. The birth quota does not have to be immediately set at negative or zero growth, or even at replacement, but could begin at any currently prevailing level and gradually approach replacement or lower fertility. Initially the certificate price would be zero, and it would rise gradually as the number of certificates issued to each person was cut from, for instance, 1.1, to 1.0, to 0.9, or to whatever level is desired. The depletion quotas could likewise be set at present levels or even at levels corresponding to a slower rate of increase than in the recent past. They could be applied first to those materials in shortest supply and to those whose wastes are hardest to absorb. Initial prices on quota rights would be low but then would rise gradually as growth pressed against the fixed quotas or as quotas were reduced in the interest of conservation. In either case the increased scarcity rent would become revenue to the government. The distribution limits might begin near the present extremes and slowly close to a more desirable range. The three institutions are amenable to any degree of gradualism we may wish. However, the distribution limits must be tightened faster than the depletion limits if the burden on the poor is to be lightened. All three control points are price-system parameters, and altering them does not interfere with the static allocative efficiency of the market.

But it is also the case that these institutions could be totally ineffective. Depletion quotas could be endlessly raised on the grounds of national defense, balance of payments, and so forth. Real estate and construction interests, not to mention the baby food and toy lobbies and the military, might convince Congress to keep the supply of birth licenses well above replacement level. People at the maximum income and wealth limit may succeed in continually raising that limit by spending a great deal of their money on TV ads extolling the Unlimited Acquisition of Everything as the very foundation of the American Way of Life. Everything would be the same and all justified in the sacred name of growth. Nothing will work unless we break our idolatrous commitment to material growth.

A definite U.S. policy of population control at home would give us a much stronger base for preaching to the underdeveloped countries about their population problem. So would the reduction in U.S. resource consumption resulting from depletion quotas. Without such a base to preach from we will continue to waste our breath, as we did at the 1974 Population Conference in Bucharest.

Thus we are brought back to the all-important moral premises. A physical steady state, if it is to be worth living in, absolutely requires moral growth. Future progress simply must be made in terms of the things that really count rather than the things that are merely countable. Institutional changes are necessary but insufficient. Moral growth is also necessary but insufficient. Both together are necessary and sufficient, but the institutional changes are relatively minor compared to the required change in values.

ON MORAL GROWTH

Let us assume for a moment that the necessity of the steady state and the above outline of its appropriate technologies and social institutions are accepted. Logic and necessity are not sufficient to bring about social reform. The philosopher Leibnitz observed,

> If geometry conflicted with our passions and interests as much as do ethics, we
> would contest it and violate it as much as we do ethics now, in spite of all the
> demonstrations of Euclid and Archimedes, which would be labeled paralogisms
> and dreams.[3]

Leibnitz is surely correct. However logical and necessary the above outline
of the steady state, it is, on the assumption of static morality, nothing but a
dream. The physically steady economy absolutely requires moral growth
beyond the present level.

Economists and other social scientists of positivistic bias seem to consider
appeals to morality as cheating, as an admission of intellectual defeat, like
bending the pieces of a jigsaw puzzle. In economics there is a long and solid
tradition of regarding moral resources as static and too scarce to be relied
upon. In the words of the great British economist Alfred Marshall, "progress
chiefly depends on the extent to which the *strongest* and not merely the
highest forces of human nature can be utilized for the increase of social
good."[4]

Presumably self-interest is stronger and more abundant than brotherhood.
Presumably "progress" and "social good" can be defined independently of the
driving motive of society.

Another British economist, D. H. Robertson, once asked the illuminating
question: What is it that economists economize? His answer was "love, the
scarcest and most precious of all resources."[5] Paul Samuelson quotes Robertson approvingly in the latest edition of *Economics,* his influential textbook.
Nor are economists alone in ruling out reliance on moral resources. The reader
will recall that in his "Tragedy of the Commons" biologist Garrett Hardin
identifies a class of problems with no technical solution. He rules out moral
solutions as self-eliminating on a somewhat farfetched evolutionary analogy,
and advocates a polical solution: mutual coercion mutually agreed upon. This
is fine, but where is the mutual agreement to come from if not from shared
values, from a convincing morality? Political scientist Beryl Crowe, in revisit-
ing the tragedy of the commons, argues that the set of no-technical-solution
problems coincides with the set of no-political solution problems and that
Hardin's "mutual coercion mutually agreed upon" is politically impossible.[6]
Between them they present a convincing case that "commons problems" will
not be solved technically nor politically, assuming static morality. Mutual
coercion does not substitute for, but presupposes, moral growth.

Going back to Robertson's repulsive but correct idea that economists economize love, one may ask, "How?" Mainly by maximizing growth. Let there
be more for everyone year after year so that we need never face up to sharing a
fixed total. Unequal distribution can be justified as necessary for saving,
incentive, and hence growth. This must continue, otherwise the problem of
sharing a fixed total will place too heavy a strain on our precious resource of
love, which is so scarce that it must never be used. I am reminded of Lord
Thomas Balough's statement that one purpose of economic theory is to make
those who *are* comfortable *feel* comfortable.

To paraphrase the above, we are told "Don't worry about today's inequities, but anxiously fix your attention on tomorrow's larger total income." Compare that with the Sermon on the Mount: "Do not be anxious about tomorrow, for tomorrow will be anxious for itself. Let the day's own evil be sufficient for the day." The morality of the steady state is that of the Sermon on the Mount. Growthmania requires the negation of that morality. If we give out first attention to the evils of the day, we will have moral growth though not so much economic growth. If we anxiously give our first attention to tomorrow's larger income, we will have economic growth but little or no moral growth. Since economic growth is reaching physical limits anyway, we may now find the Sermon on the Mount more appealing and easier to accept.

The same idea is stated in Alexander Solzhenitsyn's *Cancer Ward,* in the chapter entitled "Idols of the Market Place," in which the position of "ethical socialism" is advocated. The main theme is "ethics first and economics afterwards"—a theme which finds as little accpetance in the Soviet Union as it does in the United States, perhaps even less. The following words are from the character Shulubin:

> Happiness is a mirage—as for the so-called "happiness of future generations" it is even more of a mirage. Who knows anything about it? Who has spoken with these future generations? Who knows what idols they will worship? Ideas of what happiness is have changed too much through the ages. No one should have the effontery to try to plan it in advance. When we have enough loaves of white bread to crush them under our heels, when we have enough milk to choke us, we still won't be in the least happy. But if we share the things we don't have enough of, we can be happy today! If we care only about "happiness" and about reproducing our species, we shall merely crowd the earth senselessly and create a terrifying society. . . .

There are other sources of moral support for the steady state besides the Sermon on the Mount. From the Old Testament we have two creation myths, the Priestly and the Yawistic, one which gives value to creation only with reference to man, and one which gives value to creation independently of man. In Western thought the first tradition has dominated, but the other is there waiting to receive its proper emphasis. Also, Aldo Leopold's "land ethic" is extremely appealing and would serve admirably as the moral foundation of the steady state. Finally Karl Marx's materialism and objection to the alienation of man from nature can be enlisted as a moral foundation of the steady state. Marx recognized that nature is the "inorganic body of man" and not just a pile of neutral stuff to be dominated.[7]

In writing this chapter, I've considered the steady state only at a national level. Clearly the world as a whole must eventually adjust to a steady state. Perhaps ultimately this recognition will promote unity among nations—or, conversely, the desire for unity may promote the recognition. However, when nations cannot even agree to limit the stock of "bads" through disarmament, it is hard to be optimistic about their limiting the stocks of "goods." There is no alternative except to try, but national efforts need not wait for international agreement.

Finally, one rather subtle, yet very powerful, moral force can be enlisted in support of the steady-state paradigm. That is wholeness. If the truth is the whole, as Hegel claimed, then our current splintered knowledge is so far from truth that it is hardly worth learning. I believe this is why many of our best university students do not work very hard at their studies. Why continue mining the deep, narrow, disciplinary shafts sunk into man's totality by the intellectual fragment makers? Why deepen the tombs in which we have buried the wholeness of knowledge? Why increase the separation of people by filling separate heads with separate fragments of knowledge? The malaise reflected in these questions is very grave, and is, in my view, a major reason for the new surge of interest in ecology. Ecology is whole. It brings together the broken, analyzed, alienated, fragmented pieces of man's image of the world. Ecology is also a fad, but when the fad passes, the movement toward wholeness must continue. Unless the physical, the social, and the moral dimensions of our knowledge are integrated in a unified paradigm offering a vision of wholeness, no solutions to our problems are likely. John Stuart Mill's idea of the stationary state seems to me to offer such a paradigm.

But there remains a deeper question. Is it realistic in our secular, "pluralistic" society to expect any kind of moral consensus? Where is this moral consensus to come from? Not from a spineless relativism or from the hallucinatory psychic epiphenomena that seem to haunt complex mechanisms. Let us state it directly in the strongest terms. Ultimately, the possibility of moral consensus presupposes a dogmatic belief in objective value. If values are subjective, or thought to be merely cultural artifacts, then there is nothing objective to which appeal can be made or around which a consensus might be formed. Consensus based upon what everyone recognizes to be a convenient cultural myth (like belief in Santa Claus) would not bear much stress. Only real objective values can command consensus in a sophisticated self-analytical society. We have no guarantee that objective value can be clarified, nor that, once clarified, it would be accorded the consensus it merits. But without faith in the existence of an objective hierarchy of value and in our ability at least vaguely to perceive it, we must resign ourselves to being driven by technological determinism into an unchosen, and perhaps unbearable, future. On what other grounds is technical determinism to be resisted? Just as physical research must be based on a dogmatic faith that nature is orderly, so research into policy questions must presuppose the reality of an ordered hierarchy of value. If *better* or *worse* are meaningless terms, then all policy is nonsense.

In C. S. Lewis's words, "A dogmatic belief in objective value is necessary to the very idea of a rule which is not tyranny or an obedience which is not slavery." The same insight underlies Edmund Burke's famous dictum that "society cannot exist unless a controlling power upon will and appetite be placed somewhere, and the less of it there is within, the more there must be without." Control from within can only result from obedience to objective value. If interior restraints on will and appetite diminish, then exterior restraints, coercive police powers, or Malthusian positive checks must increase. In Burke's words, "Men of intemperate minds cannot be free. Their passions forge their fetters."

A major reason for pessimism about the course of human affairs is that the very words "*dogmatic* belief in *objective* value" automatically shut the minds of most modern intellectuals. Why is this so? Probably because *dogmatic* has come to be almost synonymous with *egotistic,* and because the term *objective value* has connotations of absolutism and intolerance. The confusions underlying these two misinterpretations have been well stated by others whose words I will borrow.

G. K. Chesterton informs us,

> To be dogmatic and to be egotistic are not only not the same thing, they are opposite things. Suppose, for instance that a vague skeptic eventually joins the Catholic church. In that act he has at the same moment become less egotistic and more dogmatic. The dogmatist is by the nature of the case not egotistical, because he believes that there is some solid, obvious and objective truth outside him which he has perceived and which he invites all men to perceive. And the egotist is in the majority of cases not dogmatic, because he has no need to isolate one of his notions as being related to the truth; all his notions are equally interesting because they are related to him. The true egotist is as much interested in his own errors as in his own truth; the dogmatist is interested only in the truth, and only in the truth because it is true. At the most the dogmatist believes that he is in the truth; but the egotist believes that the truth, if there is such a thing, is in him.[8]

A related clarification was made by E. F. Schumacher:

> The result of the lopsided development of the last three hundred years is that Western man has become rich in means and poor in ends. The hierarchy of his knowledge has been decapitated; his will is paralyzed because he has lost any grounds on which to base a hierarchy of values. What are his highest values?
>
> A man's highest values are reached when he claims that something is good in itself, requiring no justification in terms of any higher good. Modern society prides itself on its pluralism, which means that a large number of things are admissable as "good in themselves," as ends rather than as means to an end. They are all of equal rank, all to be accorded *first priority.* If something that requires no justification may be called an "absolute," the modern world, which *claims* that everything is relative, does, in fact, worship a very large number of "absolutes." . . . Not only power and wealth are treated as goods in themselves —provided they are mine and not someone else's—but also knowledge for its own sake, speed of movement, size of market, rapidity of change, quantity of education, number of hospitals, etc., etc. In truth, none of these sacred cows is a genuine end; they are all means parading as ends.[9]

Science and technology, with their analytic-empirical mode of thinking, have led many into a kind of scientism which seeks to debunk all knowledge that does not have an analytic-empirical basis. Knowledge about ends—about objective value and right purpose—derives from an "illicit" source and is considered "forbidden knowledge" by the priests of the scientistic inquisition. Unless this error is recognized, unless we come around to a "dogmatic belief in objective value," or what Boris Pasternak called "the irresistible power of unarmed truth," then it makes no sense to concern ourselves with economics. Why strain our gnats of marginal inefficiency in the allocation of means to serve ends while swallowing camels of total incoherence in the ordering of those ends? Indeed, if our ends are perversely ordered, then it is better that we should be *inefficient* in allocating means to their service.

It is one thing to insist on the logical necessity of a dogmatic belief in objective value as a basis for resisting technical determinism, but it is something else to have clear and certain knowledge of what objective value is. We must be open-minded regarding differing understandings of the nature of objective value and corresponding principles of right action. But we must make an effort to state the general principles that should guide our decisions and apply them to economic questions.

Probably the rule of right action most accepted in practice is Jeremy Bentham's greatest good for the greatest number. Economists have avoided the difficult problem of defining *good* by substituting the word *goods,* in the sense of commodities. The principle thus became the greatest per capita product for the greatest number. More products per capita and more people to enjoy those products, lead, in this view, to the greater social good. Our commitment to growth is no doubt based in considerable degree on this principle, which implies that right action is that which leads to more goods for more people.

But there are two problems with the greatest per capita product for the greatest number. First, as others have pointed out, the dictum contains one too many "greatests." It is not possible to maximize more than one variable. It is clear that numbers of people could be increased by lowering per capita product, and per capita product could be increased by lowering numbers, since resources taken from one goal can be devoted to the other. Second, it makes a big difference whether "greatest number" refers to those simultaneously alive or to the greatest number ever to live *over time*.

To resolve the first of these difficulties, we must maximize one variable only and treat some chosen level of the other as a constraint on the maximization. For one of the "greatests" we must substitute *sufficient*. There are two possible substitutions: the greatest per capita product for a sufficient number, or a sufficient per capita product for the greatest number. Which is the better principle? I suggest that we adopt the latter, and that "greatest number" be understood as greatest number over time, which takes care of the second problem. The revised principle thus becomes *sufficient per capita product for the greatest number over time*.

It is hard to find any objection to maximizing the number of people who will ever live at a material level sufficient for a good life. However, this certainly does *not* mean maximizing the number alive at any one time. On the contrary, it means the avoidance of any destruction of the earth's capacity to support life, a destruction that results from overloading the life-support system by having too many people—especially high-consuming people—alive at once. The opportunity cost of those extra lives in the present is fewer people alive in all subsequent time periods, and consequently a reduction in total lives ever to be lived at the sufficient level. Increasing per capita product beyond the sufficient level (extravagant luxury) may also overburden life-support systems and have the same long-run life-reducing effect as excess population.

Maximizing number while satisficing per capita product does not imply that quantity of life is a higher value than quality. It does assume that beyond some level of sufficiency further increase in per capita goods does not increase quality of life and, in fact, may well diminish it. But sufficiency is the first consideration. To put it more concretely, the basic needs of all present people take priority over future numbers, but the existence of more future people takes priority over the trivial wants of the present. The impact of this revised utilitarian rule is to maximize life, or, what is the same thing, to economize the long-run capacity of the earth to support life at a sufficient level of individual wealth. The sufficient level may be thought of as a range of limited inequality rather than a single specific per capita income applicable to everyone. Some inequality is necessary for fairness.

This modified utilitarian principle certainly offers no magic philosopher's stone for making difficult choices easy. But it does seem superior to the old Benthamite rule in that it draws our attention to the concept of sufficiency, and it extends our time horizon. It forces us to face the question of purpose: sufficient *for what?* needed for what? It will be very difficult to define sufficiency and build the concept into economic theory and practice. But I think it will prove far more difficult to continue to operate on the principle that there is no such thing as enough.

NOTES

1. To *satisfice,* as used here, means to seek enough rather than the most. The concept of "enough" is difficult to define but even more difficult to deny.

2. See Daniel B. Luten, "Teleoeconomics: The Microdynamic, Macrostatic Economy," Department of Geography, University of California, Berkeley (mimeographed).

3. Leibnitz, quoted in A. Sauvy, *The General Theory of Population,* New York: Basic Books, 1970, p. 270.

4. Alfred Marshall, quoted in D. H. Robertson, *Economic Commentaries,* London: Staples Press, 1956, p. 148.

5. D. H. Robertson, *Economic Commentaries,* p. 154.

6. Beryl Crowe, "The Tragedy of the Commons Revisited," *Science,* November 28, 1969.

7. Karl Marx, *Karl Marx's Early Writings,* Translated and edited by T. B. Bottomore, New York: McGraw-Hill, 1963, p. 127.

8. G. K. Chesterson, Introduction to *Poems by John Ruskin,* London: George Routledge and Sons, no date given, pp. x–xi.

9. E. F. Schumacher, *A Guide for the Perplexed,* New York: Harper & Row, 1977, p. 58.

REFERENCES

Boulding, Kenneth E. *The Meaning of the Twentieth Century.* New York: Harper & Row, 1964.

Boulding, Kenneth E. "The Economics of the Coming Spaceship Earth," in Henry Jarrett, ed., *Environmental Quality in a Growing Economy.* Baltimore: Johns Hopkins University Press, 1966.

Daly, Herman E. "On Economics as a Life Science." *Journal of Political Economy,* May/June, 1968.

Daly, Herman E. "The Economics of the Steady State." *Amerian Economic Review,* May 1974.

Davis, Kingsley. "Zero Population Growth." *Daedalus,* Fall 1973: 15–30.

Energy Policy Project of the Ford Foundation. *A Time to Choose.* Cambridge, Mass.: Ballinger, 1974.

Fisher, Irving. *The Nature of Capital and Income.* London: Macmillan, 1906.

George, Henry. *Progress and Poverty.* New York: Robert Schalkenbach Foundation, 1951. (Originally published in 1879.)

Georgescu-Roegen, Nicholas. *Analytical Economics.* Cambridge: Harvard University Press, 1966.

Goldberg, Michael. "Less Is More." Unpublished manuscript, 1976.

Hannon, Bruce, "Energy, Growth, and Altruism." Urbana: University of Illinois, Center for Advanced Computation, 1975 (mimeographed).

Heer, David M. "Marketable Licenses for Babies: Boulding's Proposal Revisited," *Social Biology,* Spring 1975: 1–16.

Ise, John. "The Theory of Value as Applied to Natural Resources," *American Economic Review,* June 1925: 284.

McClaughry, John. "The Future of Private Property and Its Distribution," *Ripon Quarterly,* Fall 1974.

Mill, John Stuart. *On Liberty.* Chicago: Encyclopedia Brittanica Great Books, 1952 (originally published in 1859).

Mill, John Stuart. "Of Property." In *Principles of Political Economy.* Book II. New York: Appleton-Century-Crofts, 1881.

National Academy of Sciences. *Mineral Resources and the Environment.* Washington, D. C.: U. S. Government Printing Office, 1975.

National Commission on Materials Policy. *Material Needs and the Environment Today and Tomorrow*. Washington, D. C.: U. S. Government Printing Office, 1973.

Okun, Arthur. *Equality and Efficiency: The Big Tradeoff*. Washington, D. C.: Brookings Institution, 1975.

Ordway, Samuel H., Jr. *Resources and the American Dream*. New York: Ronald Press, 1953.

President's Commission on Population Growth and the American Future. *Final Report to President Nixon, Congress, and the American People*. Washington, D. C.: U. S. Government Printing Office, March 1972.

Swift, Jonathan. "Thoughts on Various Subjects." In G. B. Woods et al., eds., *The Literature of England*. Glenview, Ill.: Scott, Foresman, 1958.

Weinberg, Alvin M., and Geoller, H. E. "The Age of Substitutability." *Science,* 20 February 1976.

22

POSTSCRIPT: SOME COMMON MISUNDERSTANDINGS AND FURTHER ISSUES CONCERNING A STEADY-STATE ECONOMY

Herman E. Daly

In a survey article on recent contributions of economists to the study of scarcity and growth, Professor Richard B. Norgaard of the University of California at Berkeley commented:

> Daly and others argue that some sort of a steady state system relying largely on flow resources would both reduce many environmental and social problems and be viable over the long run. An invigorating, productive debate has not developed largely because economists have ignored or put down the challenge.[1]

Unfortunately, Professor Norgaard is correct both in his statement that the challenge has been largely ingored and in lamenting the absence of a productive debate. Such a debate is badly needed, since it is only through the critical interplay of many minds that errors can be uncovered and further implications discerned. Although such a debate has not yet emerged, there have been some scattered criticisms, objections, and comments which merit consideration. A productive debate will be facilitated by clearing the agenda of a number of nonissues.

PROBLEMS OF TERMINOLOGY

Previously, following J. S. Mill, I used the term *stationary state* in the same basic sense as the classical economists used it, to refer to an economy in which population and capital stock had ceased growing. This led to some confusion, because the neoclassical economists had redefined the term to refer to an economy in which tastes and technology were unchanging but in which population and capital stock could be growing. The classical sense referred to an actual physical state toward which the economy was presumably tending. The neoclassical meaning referred to a hypothetical concept or an ideal case, such as a frictionless machine or an ideal gas, which is a useful step in analysis but is not meant as a description of any real world state.

To avoid confusion, I adopted the term *steady state* from the physical and biological sciences. This seemed a happy choice, because I was arguing from biophysical first principles anyway and because the term *steady state* meant to physical scientists very nearly what the term *stationary state* had meant to the classical economists before the neoclassicals redefined it. The main difference and continuing problem is that in physical science a steady-state system implies both quantitatively and qualitatively identical replacement, whereas a SSE, as here defined, implies quantitatively identical replacement only, with quality free to change.

Unfortunately, that is not the end of the story. Some modern economists specializing in growth models have adopted the term *steady-state growth* to refer to models in which population and capital are growing absolutely but in which certain ratios between absolutely growing magnitudes remain constant. This case could more reasonably be referred to as *proportional growth*. The noun *state* literally means the standing or stability of a thing (from the Latin *stare*, to stand). The adjectives *stationary* and *steady* simply amplify this idea of standing as opposed to running, of constancy as opposed to increase or decrease. The term *steady-state growth* is therefore etymologically inept as well as contradictory to common usage in physics and biology.

The upshot is that, for orthodox modern economists, the terms *stationary state* and *steady state* now refer to special cases of growth rather than to the contrary of growth. One is almost led to suspect a conspiracy among growth economists to find every term in the English language that is in any way descriptive of nongrowth and redefine it to refer to some special case of growth. Thus robbed of any words with which to express an idea contrary to growth, all economists would have to become growth economists by preemption of vocabulary! The one word the growth economists have reserved for expressing nongrowth is, of course, *stagnation,* with its strong connotations of foulness, dullness, and putrefaction.

IS THE SSE A COUNSEL OF DESPAIR BASED ON A WILLINGNESS TO ACCEPT PRESENT EVILS AND A DESIRE TO STOP ECONOMIC EVOLUTION?

Professor William Nordhaus of Yale University, a recent member of the President's Council of Economic Advisors, noted that "the political and social impediments to metering or internalizing the undesirable consequences of our activities are becoming unmanageably high." He concluded that "it should not be surprising, then, that many responsible analysts simply throw up their hands in despair and opt for a steady-state society, accepting the familiar ills of today in preference to the unforseen consequences of continued economic evolution."[2]

Since these "responsible analysts" remain unnamed, no one can check a reference to test the possibility that Professor Nordhaus is setting up a straw man. As one who has identified himself with the advocacy of a SSE, I hope I may be forgiven the assumption that Professor Nordhaus had me in mind, among others. If so, I certainly appreciate being referred to as a "responsible analyst."

Be that as it may, however, I really am grateful to Professor Nordhaus for two things—first, for recognizing the existence of the problem to which the SSE is a response; and second, for making explicit three misunderstandings that result when critics make up rather than look up the position of those nameless advocates of the steady state whom they are criticizing. Let us consider each mistaken allegation in turn.

Does the SSE offer a counsel of despair?

On the contrary, from its first full expression at the hands of John Stuart Mill, it has been a counsel of hope. As Mill put it,

> I cannot . . . regard the stationary state of capital and wealth with the unaffected aversion so generally manifested towards it by political economists of the old school. I am inclined to believe that it would be, on the whole, a very considerable improvement on our present condition.
>   . . . It is scarcely necessary to remark that a stationary condition of capital and population implies no stationary state of human improvement. There would be as much scope as ever for all kinds of mental culture, and moral and social progress; as much room for improving the Art of Living and much more likeli-

hood of its being improved, when minds cease to be engrossed by the art of getting on.[3]

The truly despairing position, in my opinion, is that we are prisoners of economic growth and that when "impediments to metering or internalizing the undesirable consequences of our activities become unmanageably high," we are not allowed to follow the simple expedient of reducing the level of our activities until these undesirable consequences become manageable again.

Does the SSE accept the familiar ills of today?

Not at all. The position is that further growth is not the answer to present poverty, injustice, and alienation in developed countries. Rather, we must face up to the necessity of imposing limits to inequality, limits to population growth, and limits to the throughput of matter-energy. Smaller scale, more decentralized, less arcane and dangerous technologies are called for. A just, sustainable, and participatory economy requires a steady state rather than a growth mode of operation. The steady state is not an end in itself, but a means, a constraint imposed by the ends of justice, sustainability, and participation, as well as by the approximate steady-state nature of the total ecosystem of which the economy is a part.

The familiar evil of mass poverty in the Third World is by no means accepted. The SSE seeks to maintain levels "sufficient for a good life and sustainable for a long future." Rich countries have reached levels more than sufficient for a good life, though not on a sustainable basis. Poor countries have usually not reached a sufficient per capita level, but neither have they moved out quite so far on the limb of unsustainability. Present poverty makes further economic growth necessary in poor countries. But further population growth in poor countries, and further demographic and economic growth in rich countries, will make the attainment of a sufficient level in poor countries impossible. Furthermore, if the poor countries adopt the same pattern of large-scale capital- and resource-intensive growth characteristic of the rich countries, then they too will climb further out on the limb of unsustainability, adding the weight of their resource demands to the already excessive demands of the rich countries. Growth is not the cure for the familiar ills of today; in fact, it is the cause of many of them.

Does the SSE imply a halt to economic evolution?

The SSE imposes the condition that economic evolution (like the evolution of the planet earth) work itself out under the constraint of limited stocks and flows of matter and energy. Has the constant mass of the earth and the constant flux of solar energy halted terrestrial evolution? Certainly not. This limitation comes closer to being a precondition for evolution than an obstruction. Neither will the cessation of quantitative growth in the physical dimensions of the economy halt the qualitative evolution of wants, technologies, and institutions. Rather, such limits will channel economic evolution away from its current self-destructive path. Not all the consequences of continued economic evolution along the physical growth path are "unforeseen." Some consequences are quite foreseeable, and it is these discernible risks of catastrophe, not the unforeseeable novelty inherent in evolution, that the SSE seeks to avoid.

MISUNDERSTANDINGS OF THE "IMPOSSIBILITY THEOREM"

The "impossibility theorem" simply states that a U.S.-style high-resource consumption standard for a world of 4 billion people is impossible. Even if by some miracle it could be attained, it would be very short-lived. Even less is it possible to support an ever-growing standard of per capita consumption for an ever-growing population. Crises of depletion, pollution, and ecological breakdown would be the immediate consequences of generalizing U.S. resource consumption standards to the whole world. Development plans that take this generalization of the U.S. economy as their explicit or implicit goal, as most development plans do, are simply unrealistic.

I am aware of two attempts by economists to refute this "impossibility theorem." One, by Professor Lester Thurow, is an apparent refutation on logical grounds, but in fact it is a misunderstanding. The other, by Professor Wassily Leontief and his colleagues, is an empirical refutation or, rather, can easily be misinterpreted as such. Let us consider each in turn.

Thurow comments:

> In the context of zero economic growth and other countries, a fallacious "impossibility"argument is often made to demonstrate the need for zero economic growth. The argument starts with a question. How many tons of this or that non-renewable natural resource would the world need if everyone in the world now had the consumption standards enjoyed by those in the U.S.? The answer is designed to be a mind-boggling number in comparison with the current supplies of such resources. *The problem with both the question and the answer is that it assumes that the rest of the world is going to achieve the consumption standards of the average American without at the same time achieving the productivity standards of the average American.* This is, of course, algebraically impossible. The world can only consume what it can produce. When the rest of the world has consumption standards equal to those of the U.S., it will be producing at the same rate and providing as much of an increment to the world-wide supplies of goods and services as it does to the demands for goods and services [emphasis added].[4]

No one denies that consumption must be matched by production. But production of goods and services requires natural resources, and more production of goods and services does not provide more natural resources—it uses them up. It is the U.S. economy as a whole (resource productivity as well as resource use rates; production as well as consumption) that is generalized in the impossibility argument. The fact that consumption must be matched by production is an obvious truism having nothing to do with the adequacy of resources to the task of scaling up the U.S. economy to the whole world.

To be told in refutation of the impossibility argument that the world can consume only what it can produce is like refuting the statement that $2 + 2 < 5$ by demonstrating that $5^2 = 25$. It is a case of refutation by vigorous assertion of the irrelevant truism.

In fairness to Professor Thurow one should recognize that perhaps someone, somewhere, did actually commit the fallacy of generalizing U.S. consumption without generalizing U.S. production levels. Unfortunately, Professor Thurow gives no reference to any specific case of this unlikely fallacy, which he says is "often made." And even if someone did commit that fallacy, it hardly invalidates the correct version of the impossibility argument, which would seem to have a greater claim on the attention of scholars than does a fallacious substitute.

The 1977 United Nations study *The Future of the World Economy* (by Wassily Leontief and others) seems, on superficial reading, to offer an empirically based refutation of the impossibility argument.[5] Although the tone of the report is reassuring and optimistic, what it in fact says is more a confirmation than a refutation of the impossibility argument. The report says that if population grows only at the U.N. low-rate projection—if the developing countries' GNP can grow at 6.9 percent, while the developed countries lower their growth from the historic 4.5 percent to 3.6 percent—then, if we look ahead no further than the year 2000 (a mere twenty years, less than one generation), we can conclude that the average per capita income gap between rich and poor countries will be reduced from 12 to 1 down to 7 to 1, and that world resources will likely be adequate to the scenario.

What happens in the year 2025?[6] What happens if we reduce the gap from 12 to 1 all the way to 1 to 1? Are resources adequate to that task? The report does not ask questions of this sort. The impossibility theorem says, in effect, "this old car cannot make it from New York to San Francisco." The U.N. report says "this resilient previously owned automobile can very likely get you all the way to Cleveland." The report notes:

> In spite of the new more rational and economic ways of using mineral resources the world is expected to consume during the last 30 years of the twentieth century from 3 to 4 times the total volume of minerals that has been consumed throughout the whole previous history of civilization. Are the finite reserves of minerals in the earth's crust adequate to sustain this demand? [p. 5]

The report answers its own question in the affirmative for the next twenty years, but is silent about the future beyond that. History is somehow discontinuous, beginning anew on the year 2001. Even the adequacy of resources to the year 2000 is a matter of dispute, but it will not be pursued here.[7]

There is an exceedingly interesting asymmetry in the report's treatment of the growth rates of developed countries (DCs) and underdeveloped countries (UDCs). The UDCs' high growth rate is a policy goal to be brought about by planned action which is assumed to be successful. The lower growth rate of the DCs represents not a planned, conscious lowering of the GNP growth rate, but rather a failure to maintain past rates of growth. This is a curious mixture of planned conscious achievement and unplanned failure. The report does not advocate slower growth in DCs in order to allow UDCs to catch up. Rather, it just predicts that DC growth rates will, in fact, fall in spite of efforts to keep them at historic levels or even to raise them. No one is asked to change goals. Growth remains the goal in the DCs, and any reduction in the gap simply results from the fortuitous failure of DCs to grow as fast as UDCs.

It would seem that a careful justification of this crucial assumption is in order. All the report tells us is that "It was felt that an assumption of gradually declining growth rates in the developed countries would be more realistic than would a simple extrapolation of their past performance" (p. 3).

There may be good reasons for this assumption, and I do not want to make too much of the fact that the report does not mention any. But it is at least conceivable that the DCs could be successful in maintaining or increasing their historic rates of growth. They are certainly trying to. Would the success of the DCs in achieving higher growth make life easier or more difficult for the UDCs? Some economists argue that the best thing the DCs can do for the UDCs is to grow more rapidly. Others argue that rapid growth in the DCs preempts resources and makes growth more difficult for the UDCs, and of course also widens the gap. The U.N. report is silent on this critical issue—an issue that would become more obtrusive if DCs were assumed to be able to grow at historic rates.

A COROLLARY
TO THE IMPOSSIBILITY THEOREM

The demographic transition thesis has led many to advocate concentrating on economic growth in poor countries and trusting that population growth will take care of itself. "Development is the best contraceptive" was the slogan often quoted at the U.N. Population Conference in Bucharest. There are many objections to be raised against such a policy. It relies too mechanistically on an inverse correlation between development and fertility. There is probably an equally strong inverse correlation between development and illiteracy, yet no one invents a "literacy transition thesis" and argues that "development is the best teacher of reading and writing" and that when the stage of development reaches the point at which it is in people's interest to control their illiteracy they will do so, and not before. Of course, literacy programs and population control programs are not sufficient conditions for development, but they help.

The logical consequence of "development is the best contraceptive, teacher, political reformer, public health program, and so on" would be somehow to work for "development" directly without investing in any of the correlates of development, which would all presumably come about automatically. But what is "development" shorn of all its correlates? What is left to invest in?

But the impossibility theorem puts the demographic transition policy in an even worse position. The whole idea of such a policy is to buy a reduction in the rate of increase of human bodies by an increase in the rate of production of artifacts—in other words, to trade off an increase in consumption per capita in exchange for a reduction in "capitas." The total load on the ecosystem is the product of the number of people times per capita consumption. The demographic transition policy simply lowers one factor by increasing the other, with no guarantee that the product of the two factors will decrease. In fact, it is likely even to increase if we believe the oft-cited figure that one American child equals 50 Indian children in terms of lifetime demands on the ecosystem. Is the demographic transition's trade-off between production and reproduction 50 to 1? Will Indian per capita consumption have to reach U.S. levels before Indian reproduction falls to U.S. levels? Will that require an increase in Indian per capita consumption by a factor of 50? If not by 50, then by how much? Are world resources adequate to pay such a high price for population stability via the demographic transition policy? Certainly not, if the impossibility theorem is correct, and no proponent of the demographic transition policy has bothered to refute the impossibility theorem. The warranted conclusion is that direct population control measures cannot be avoided by appeals to economic growth and the "demographic transition." Indeed, if rich countries must lower their per capita consumption in the future, would we expect the demographic transition mechanistically to work in reverse, causing a rise in the birth rate? Probably not, but since all truly mechanical models work in reverse, maybe the demographic transition theorists would expect falling consumption to be accompanied by a rising birth rate. If so, all the more need for a direct policy of population control.

A STEADY-STATE ECONOMY
VERSUS A FAILED GROWTH ECONOMY

A situation of nongrowth can come about in two ways: as the failure of a growth economy to grow, or as the success of conscious policies aiming at a SSE. No one denies that when a growth economy fails to grow, the result is unemployment and suffering. The main reason for advocating a SSE is precisely to avoid the suffering of a failed growth economy, because we know that, sooner or later, the growth economy will not be able to continue growing —or rather that the marginal social cost of growth will be greater than the marginal social benefits, so that growth will cost more than it is worth, even if it is physically possible.

This simple distinction is often ignored, as when the editors of *Fortune* wrote, "the country has just gone through a real life tryout of zero growth [the period 1973–75, which is remembered not as an episode of zero growth but as the worst recession since the 1930's."[8] The distinction between a SSE and a failed growth economy is erased by referring to both cases as "zero growth." The failures of a growth economy really should not be used as arguments against a SSE! The fact that airplanes fall to the ground if they try to remain stationary in the air merely reflects the fact that airplanes are designed for forward motion. It does not constitute a proof that helicopters cannot remain stationary. A growth economy and a SSE are as different as an airplane and a helicopter. Needless to add, one would not attempt to attain a SSE by simply reversing current policies aimed at growth. Economies, like airplanes, do not fly in reverse, or neutral either.

PRICE-DETERMINED VERSUS PRICE-DETERMINING DECISIONS

There is a widespread belief among economists that market prices determine everything. It was recently claimed by three economists that

> Only if we eliminate the market incentives for innovation and investment, or reduce the scope of market forces through further attenuation of private property in resources, must we face a real long-term "resource crisis." The only non-renewable and nonsubstitutable resource is the set of institutions known as a market order, which eliminates crises with respect to physical resources.[9]

In other words, as long as we base all our decisions on free market prices, resource constraints disappear as a long-run concern. We do not, in this view, need any ecologically or ethically determined limits on the total flow of resources.

Prices are important but are not all-powerful. Market prices are relevant only to temporally and ecologically parochial decisions, whose major consequences lie wholly within the human economy of commodity exchange and within the present generation. Market prices are excellent means for efficiently allocating a given resource flow from nature among alternative uses in the service of a given population of already existing people with a given distribution of wealth and income. Market prices should not be allowed to decide the rates of flow of matter-energy across the economy-ecosystem boundary or to decide the distribution of resources among different people (or among different generations, which, of course, are different people). The first must be an ecological decision, the second an ethical decision. These decisions of course will and should influence market prices, but the whole point is that these ecological and ethical decisions are *price-determining,* not *price-determined.* Many economists simply fail to grasp this point.

ECONOMIC GROWTH REQUIRED TO MAINTAIN FULL EMPLOYMENT?

It is clear from the previous discussion that a SSE cannot be identified with a failed growth economy, and thus it does not imply unemployment. In fact, there are several reasons for believing that full employment will be easier to attain in a SSE than in our failing growth economies. One condition of a SSE is limits to inequality in the form of a minimum and a maximum income. The minimum income would substitute for the unemployment-causing minimum wage in providing a guaranteed subsistence. The maximum limit on income and wealth, and the more equal distribution generally, would reduce the aggregate saving rate, which would bolster aggregate demand and employment. Furthermore, the policy of limiting the matter-energy throughput would raise the price of energy and resources relative to the price of labor. This would lead to the substitution of labor for energy in production processes and consumption patterns, thus reversing the historical trend of replacing labor with machines and inanimate energy, whose relative prices have been declining. Another policy of the SSE, zero population growth, would also ease unemployment by lowering the number of job seekers, though only after a lag of about twenty years.

I do not claim that these considerations provide a sufficient answer to the question of how to provide full employment in a SSE. But I think they do demonstrate that this question is easier to answer than the analogous one faced by a growth economy—namely, how can full employment be maintained in an economy that becomes ever more capital- and energy-intensive in its technology while at the same time facing ever greater scarcity of the nonrenewable resources upon which its technology is based?

Occasionally the employment argument for growth becomes truly absurd, as in the case of the Concorde airplane. We are told that 40,000 British worker's jobs depend on the success of Concorde, and whoever opposes that technically overdeveloped white elephant must be a hard-hearted elitist with no feeling for working people. A moment's reflection will show that if the billions squandered on Concorde were spent on any of hundreds of less capital-intensive projects, employment would be *increased.* Also, working people would be much more likely to benefit from the services of their own product. With Concorde fares 20 percent above first-class fares, not many working people will be riding Concorde. They will remain on the ground to have their ears assaulted by the flatulent sonic booms of their jet-set betters, to have their skins absorb the extra cancer-inducing ultraviolet radiation resulting from ozone depletion, and to have their stomachs develop ulcers from worrying about how long their livelihoods can possibly derive from such an absurd product.

IS THE SSE CAPITALISTIC OR SOCIALISTIC?

The one thing that capitalism and socialism have agreed upon is the importance of economic growth. Both have accepted the criterion that whichever system can grow faster must be better, and each strives to win the growth race. The notion of a SSE is rejected by both. Both systems suffer from growth mania, and the SSE presents as much a challenge to Big Socialism as to Big Capitalism. But it also offers a point of reconciliation for the future. When old adversaries discover that they have made the same error, their brotherhood in humility should facilitate reconciliation.

The growth versus steady state debate really cuts across the old left-right rift, and we should resist any attempt to identify either growth or steady state with either left or right, for two reasons. First, it will impose a logical distortion on the issue. Second, it will obscure the emergence of a third way, which might form a future synthesis of socialism and capitalism into a SSE and eventually into a fully just and sustainable society. Neither capitalism nor socialism can make much of a claim to being just, sustainable, and participatory. Let us not insist on pouring new wine into old wineskins.

The difficulty of deciding whether the SSE is capitalistic can be seen from the following. Since the SSE would rely mainly on private property and decentralized market decision making, we might consider it ipso facto capitalist. But according to Karl Marx's definition of capitalism, the SSE would not be capitalistic, because with maximum and minimum income and wealth limits there would be no monopoly class ownership of the means of production and no correlative class of proletarians who must sell their labor power to the capitalist on his terms in order to survive. Nor with maximum wealth limits would there be the unrestrained drive to accumulate, which Marx said was "Moses and the Prophets" for the industrial capitalist and eventually would lead to collapse of the system. Whether the SSE is capitalistic or not depends on how one defines capitalism. I suggest that it is more profitable to work out the concept of steady state, of a just and sustainable society, as a third way—neither capitalistic nor socialistic but a way to which traditional capitalists and socialists are invited to contribute and within which they might find an embracing synthesis.

SPACE COLONIZATION
VERSUS THE STEADY STATE

One of the more interesting arguments against a steady state takes the form of the following syllogism:[10]

> *Premise 1:* Continuing growth is necessary for freedom. Only an iron-fisted worldwide dictatorship could control growth.
> *Premise II:* Continuing growth cannot occur on earth because earth really is finite.
> *Conclusion:* Space colonization is necessary to preserve freedom.

There is agreement between space colonizers and steady-state advocates regarding Premise II. The disagreement centers on Premise I. What evidence is there for such a statement? Have dictatorships come into being because nations were striving to become steady states or because they were dedicated to growth? Would a substitute for Premise I to the effect that only a dictatorship could provide the compulsion and discipline necessary to make space colonization work be any less plausible?

But there is yet a more basic problem with the argument. Even if the total number of space colonies can grow indefinitely, each individual colony must be managed in a steady-state mode. A single space colony cannot tolerate a population explosion either of human bodies or of artifacts. The aggregate of all individual habitats may grow and grow, but *each* habitat must be managed as a steady state with births plus immigration equal to deaths plus emigration, with an analogous materials balance for artifacts. The very discipline that is alleged to imply dictatorship on earth is encountered again on each and every space habitat. If a steady state requires a dictatorship on spaceship earth, then why not also on spaceship L–5X351? In as much as each space colony must be run as a steady state, does it not make sense, even if one favors space colonization, to learn to live in the steady-state mode on the large, resilient, forgiving, and relatively self-operating spaceship earth before attempting to manage an entire artificial ecosystem within a fragile, rotating torus protected from the cold vacuum of space by a few inches of aluminum and glass? I doubt that such an environment, vulnerable to sabotage in thousands of ways, would be able to tolerate much dissent. In all probability a military style of discipline and security, referred to no doubt as "rationality," would be necessary, and civil liberties would be deemed too dangerous to tolerate.

The space colonizers consider freedom to migrate as one of the most basic freedoms to be protected. But Garrett Hardin has raised a pertinent question. Suppose we have a new space habitat waiting for 50,000 inhabitants. Who gets to—or has to—go? Either way, people will have to be chosen. How? Perhaps by HEW guidelines requiring a fair share of blacks, whites, Chicanos, Indians, Catholics, Jews—not to mention Cajuns, Creoles, Mormons, and Unitarians? Or if that seems a recipe for tribal warfare, should we strive for "ethnic purity" and religious homogeneity on each habitat? What then happens to religious freedom and ethnic pluralism?

The alleged impossibility of a steady state on earth provides a poor intellectual launching pad for space colonies. A better (but still less than compelling) argument for space colonization might be made along the lines suggested by Kenneth Boulding ("Spaceship Earth Revisited") as a way to reintroduce isolation and variety into the evolutionary process. But even if space colonization were desirable, its feasibility presupposes the ability to live under steady-state rules of management.

DOES THE SSE IMPLY ECOLOGICAL SALVATION AND ETERNAL LIFE FOR THE SPECIES?[11]

The SSE cannot last forever because of the entropy law. In the very strict and inclusive sense, a steady-state economy is impossible. Indeed, any steady-state process is impossible. At some point in the past it had to have a beginning, and at some point in the future it will have to have an end. A steady-state economy cannot last forever, but neither can a growing economy, nor a declining economy.

Consider a candle. The flame is lit and grows to mature equilibrium size. It then burns in a steady state until the candle burns down; finally it flickers and dies. We must recognize that at some time in the past the candle had to be lit, and that it must go out sometime in the future. Therefore, if we draw temporal boundaries around the process so as to include the beginning and the end, we cannot call the process a steady state. But if we draw temporal boundaries after lighting and before going out, we can describe the greater part of the flame's life as a steady state, without implying that it will last forever or that it had no beginning.

The stocks of artifacts and people in the economy can exist in a quasi–steady state for as long as the resource "candle" lasts. We can turn our resource candle into a Roman candle and burn it rapidly and extravagantly, or we can seek to maintain a steady flame for a long time, or we can put out the flame before the candle has burned down. The steady-state view advocates the middle course. That any choice among the three alternatives represents a value judgment is quite evident.

The candle analogy, though useful, fails in two respects. First we have *two* candles—the sun, and the stock of terrestrial minerals. The sun cannot be burned up like a Roman candle. It burns with a steady flame as far as human time scales are concerned. But the terrestrial resource candle can be, and is being, used as a Roman candle. The second failing of the analogy is that, unlike the combustible material fed from the candle to the flame, the terrestrial resources fed to our economy do not remain constant in quality or accessibility as they are depleted. We first exploit the best and most accessible resources known to us. As depletion forces us to exploit progressively poorer-grade resources, the gross throughput of matter and energy will have to increase in order to yield the same net throughput of the minerals required to maintain stocks constant. Also, a larger fraction of the constant capital stock would have to be devoted to ever more capital-intensive means of winning mineral resources. At some point the extra minerals are not worth the extra sacrifice required to win them, and the remaining minerals cease to be "resources." The SSE seeks to guide the economy toward maximum feasible reliance on solar energy and renewable resources and away from the current unsustainable practice of living largely on accumulated geological capital.

In sum, the SSE does not proclaim "ecological salvation and eternal life for the species." Far from promising any future escape from the status of creature-hood and mortality, the SSE is based on the assumption that creation will have an end—that it is finite temporally as well as spatially. But creation is affirmed as good while it lasts, and its longevity is not a matter of indifference. Just as individuals strive to keep their bodies in a healthy steady state even while knowing that time and entropy are slowly but continuously defeating them, so we must strive to keep our collective exosomatic body, the economy, in a quasi–steady state as a strategy of good stewardship. Only God can raise any part of his creation out of time and into eternity. As mere stewards of creation, all we can do is to avoid wasting the limited capacity of creation to support present and future life. Indeed, if we thought that that capacity were infinite, we would not be concerned about wasting some of it. Conversely, those who are not concerned about the waste of life-support capacity are often those who believe that human beings can achieve an infinite life span for their species, thanks to the Faustian powers of technology. While recognizing the important, but limited, role that technology can play in increasing life-support capacity, and in "relieving man's estate," the SSE perspective rejects as idolatrous the widespread belief that technology can in any fundamental way raise humanity from the status of creature to that of creator.

It is curious that the traditional Christian view takes it for granted that creation will have an end and places its faith in immortality at the personal level and in the realm of the spirit. The modern world, having lost its faith in personal immortality and in the spirit as well, seeks to substitute a belief in species immortality which is in thorough contradiction to the most basic tenets of physical science, on which its idolized technology depends. A believer in personal immortality can at least claim to have some direct inner experience of his own immortal spiritual nature. But no one can claim to have any direct intimations of species immortality. And any reasoned argument for the possibility of species immortality must fly in the teeth of the entropy law and therefore forfeit any claim to scientific standing.

Far from having any truck with "eternal life for the species," the SSE is simply a strategy of good stewardship for taking care of God's creation for however long he wills it to last. In taking care of that creation, special, but not exclusive, attention must be given to humanity, including not only the present but also future generations and in a sense past generations as well. Just as our bequests to the future are meant for many future generations, not just the next one, so our inheritance from the past was meant for many generations, not just ours. To treat it as exclusively ours is to break faith with the past as well as with the future. Nor should our concern be exclusively with human beings, past, present, and future. If a man is worth many sparrows, then a sparrow cannot be worthless. Stewardship requires an extension of brotherhood first to all presently existing people but also to future and past people, and to sub-human life, all in some appropriate degrees.

Of course, these issues of the just and sustainable society far transcend the notion of a SSE, which is advocated not as a solution to the problems of justice and sustainability, but as a framework of economic life that at least allows these problems to be taken seriously.

NOTES

1. "Scarcity and Growth: How Does It Look Today?" *American Journal of Agricultural Economics*, December 1975: 811.

2. "Metering Economic Growth," in Kenneth D. Wilson (ed.), *Prospects of Growth*, New York: Praeger, 1977, p. 208.

3. J. S. Mill, *Principles of Political Economy*, vol. II, London: John W. Parker and Son, 1857, pp. 320–326.

4. Lester Thurow, "The Implications of Zero Economic Growth," in *U. S. Prospects for Growth: Prospects, Problems, and Patterns*, vol. 5, *The Steady-State Economy*, Joint Economic Committee of Congress, Washington, D.C.: U.S. Government Printing Office, December 2, 1976, p. 46.

5. Leontief, Wassily W., and others, *The Future of the World Economy*, New York: Oxford University Press, 1977.

6. It is worth remembering that the year 2025 is well within the expected lifetime of the average reader of this book.

7. One of the co-authors of this study, Professor Anne Carter, at a World Council of Churches Conference in Zurich (June 1978) vigorously disassociated herself from the conclusion that growth as usual is feasible, which was drawn from the report by many, including, it would appear, Leontief himself. In Professor Carter's view the model has very little of value to say on the subject of environmental and resource constraints on growth.

8. "Well, How Do You Like Zero Growth," *Fortune*, November 1976, p. 116.

9. G. Anders, W. Gramm, and S. Maurice, *Does Resource Conservation Pay?* International Institute for Economic Research, Original Paper 14, July 1978, p. 42.

10. This is essentially the position taken by Princeton physicist Gerard K. O'Neill in his opening statement at the Edison Electric Institute's Symposium on Prospects for Growth (Washington, D.C., June 1978), and later confirmed in private correspondence.

11. This section deals with some of the criticisms of the SSE raised by N. Georgescu-Roegen (see pp. 66–68 of this volume).

DA